EMIL BRUNNER

THE LIBRARY OF LIVING THEOLOGY

Edited by

CHARLES W. KEGLEY and ROBERT W. BRETALL

VOLUME III

THE THEOLOGY OF
Emil Brunner

THE LIBRARY OF LIVING THEOLOGY

VOLUME III

THE THEOLOGY
OF
Emil Brunner

Edited by

CHARLES W. KEGLEY

New York

THE MACMILLAN COMPANY

Macmillan New York, London

45450   Aug. '63

Grateful acknowledgment is hereby made for permission to quote from the
published works of Emil Brunner:

To Charles Scribner's Sons, New York, N. Y., for permission to quote from
Philosophy of Religion by Emil Brunner, in the International Library of Christian Knowledge, edited by William Adams Brown, copyright, 1937, by Charles
Scribner's Sons; and from *Christianity and Civilization* by Emil Brunner, copyright, 1948, by Charles Scribner's Sons.

To John Nisbet and Company, Ltd., London, England, for permission to
quote from *Christianity and Civilization* by Emil Brunner, Part I, copyright,
1947, and Part II, copyright, 1948, by John Nisbet and Company, Ltd.

To Lutterworth Press, London, England, for permission to quote from *The
Christian Doctrine of God* by Emil Brunner, published, 1949, by Lutterworth
Press; *The Christian Doctrine of Creation and Redemption and Eternal Hope*
by Emil Brunner, copyright, 1954, by Lutterworth Press; and *The Great Invitation* by Emil Brunner, copyright, 1955, by Lutterworth Press.

To The Westminster Press, Philadelphia, Pennsylvania, for permission to
quote from *The Christian Doctrine of God* by Emil Brunner, translated by
Olive Wyon, copyright, 1950, W. L. Jenkens, by The Westminster Press; *Revelation and Reason* by Emil Brunner, translated by Olive Wyon, copyright, 1946,
W. L. Jenkens, by The Westminster Press; *Eternal Hope* by Emil Brunner,
translated by Harold Knight, published 1954, by The Westminster Press; *The
Great Invitation* by Emil Brunner, translated by Harold Knight, published
1955, by The Westminster Press.

To Zwingli Verlag, Zürich, Switzerland, for permission to quote from the
Bibliography of the writings of Emil Brunner in the *Festschrift zum 70 Geburtstag*, copyright 1959, by Zwingli Verlag, and passages from various books and
essays of Emil Brunner published by Zwingli Verlag.

And, to the editors and publishers of the many periodicals and journals from
which the contributors have gathered additional insights into the thought and
writings of Emil Brunner.

First Printing

The Macmillan Company, New York
Collier-Macmillan Canada, Ltd., Galt, Ontario
Divisions of The Crowell-Collier Publishing Company

PRINTED IN THE UNITED STATES OF AMERICA

Library of Congress catalog card number: 62-16886

CONTENTS

GENERAL INTRODUCTION
TO
THE LIBRARY OF LIVING THEOLOGY

As we enter the second half of the twentieth century, religion and theology are less likely to be neglected by thinking men. Whatever may be the causes of the present-day return to religion, the fact remains that religious thinking has again become intellectually respectable. As against the climate of a generation and more ago—when the notion of a "Christian intellectual" was almost a contradiction in terms—we now see religiously minded men—motivated in their thinking by basic religious and theological assumptions—taking a more and more prominent and commanding place in the world of thought.

The Library of Living Theology is dedicated to the furthering and the clarification of this phenomenon of our times. Granted that religion and theology are again in the forefront of thought and life, and that they are once more "respectable," *which* religion is best, *which* theology is the most valid? There is much vigorous discussion, but little general agreement. Certain trends may be seen—for example, the swing away from humanism and liberalism—but these are only straws in the wind, and in any case prove nothing about *validity.* Neither the good nor the true can be derived from the "is."

In 1939 Professor Paul Arthur Schilpp, of Northwestern University, set out to clarify the issues in contemporary philosophy through a series of books entitled *The Library of Living Philosophers.* His idea was original and unique: to devote each volume in the series to the thinking of a single living philosopher, and to include in each (1) an intellectual autobiography; (2) essays on different aspects of the man's work, written by leading scholars; (3) a "reply to his critics" by the philosopher himself; and (4) a complete bibliography of his writings to date. This philosophical series has met with universal acclaim. The editors of the present series gladly acknowledge their debt to Professor Schilpp, not only for the general plan of the volumes but also for valuable criticism and friendly advice in planning this series. Our aim, quite simply, is to do for present-day theology what he has done and is continuing to do so well for philosophy.

A note on the use of the word "theology" is in order. In the Christian tradition "theology" has usually meant *dogmatic* theology, that is, a systematic account of God, man, immortality, and the like, based either on the Bible (Biblical theology) or on the creedal standards of a given church (Confessional theology). Within the last fifty or seventy-five years, however, the term has been extended to include the rather different theologies constructed by the liberal theologians in the tradition of Schleiermacher and Ritschl—theologies based not on authoritative revelations or Church councils, and thus "once for all delivered," but on changing human experience and even on empirical, scientific knowledge. In America the leading representative of this empirical theology was probably the late Douglas Clyde Macintosh; today it is being carried on in a somewhat different way by Henry Nelson Wieman. For this liberal "theology" is not clearly distinguishable from "philosophy of religion."

The Library of Living Theology will remain neutral on this issue of terminology. For us "theology" will include theologies of both types: subjects and essayists will be selected from representatives of both schools of thought, as well as from points of view which cannot properly be ranged under one banner or the other. Paul Tillich, the subject of our first volume, is probably a good example of the last-mentioned type of "subject."

At this point the question may be asked, whether we intend to confine ourselves to *Christian* theology, or perhaps to theology within the Western Judaeo-Christian tradition. The answer to this question is No. We begin with writers who stand firmly within this tradition simply because they represent the most vigorous theological thinking that is being done today. Quite apart from any natural prejudices we Westerners may have, it is simply the case that outside the Western framework theology is almost dormant today, or

at least quiescent,* whereas within that framework it is very much
alive. The choosing of subjects for the various volumes of the Library will be governed as far as possible by this criterion of "alive-
ness," creativity and individuality of thought. If these qualities
should appear in a Buddhist or Mohammedan philosopher, for example, we shall gladly consider him as a possible "subject" of a
future volume.

The Library of Living Theology will thus be catholic in character, that is, in the correct sense of the word: universal. It might
be called religious and theological in its subject matter, philosophical in its method and basic approach. Its editors happen to represent just this union of religious and philosophical interests; they are
at home in the "borderland" between philosophy and religion, and
they feel the desirability of promoting clarification and mutual understanding in this embattled region. The odium theologicum is
well known, and asserts itself today as in the past. Perhaps a certain
amount of "fighting spirit" is essential to a good discussion, and in
this sense our aim is to provide a real battleground for some of the
keenest intellects of our day. It is only through unlimited freedom
of discussion that clarification can result. With clarification should
come sympathetic understanding of positions other than one's own.
At the very least it should call for a refusal to dismiss these positions and those who uphold them with the conveniently opprobri-
ous tags of "liberal," "modernist," "fundamentalist," "neo-orthodox,"
and the like. These labels may be useful in a rough way, but
as applied to almost every great thinker of our time—and certainly
to those who are to be subjects of this series—they will, upon examination, reveal their inadequacy to convey the true "inwardness" of
the man's thought. In view of these considerations, The Library of
Living Theology may serve as an agency not only of enlightenment
but also of mutual understanding and good will.

CHARLES W. KEGLEY
ROBERT W. BRETALL
Editors, The Library of Living Theology

* An exception to this statement might be found in the work of the Indian
philosopher-mystic Sarvepalli Radhakrishnan, who was the subject of a volume
in Professor Schilpp's series (New York: Tudor Publishing Company, 1952).

SPECIAL INTRODUCTION
TO
THE THEOLOGY OF EMIL BRUNNER
Vol. III in The Library of Living Theology

It is appropriate that this, the same year which witnesses the completion of Emil Brunner's three-volume dogmatics, should also be the occasion for the completion of a major critical analysis of Brunner's thought. Both have been several years in the making. The time is acceptable because Brunner's span of increasingly influential writing, over more than thirty-five years, has come to a climax and completion though not, it is hoped, to a close. Clearly, we are now in a position to examine, and with Professor Brunner's own participation, to clarify and assess one of the two or three finest comprehensive theological efforts of our century.

In the broad field of theology and philosophy of religion it is a commonplace observation today that "the age of the giants is over." To change the figure of speech, whereas the towering figures of a Brunner and a Barth, a Dewey and a Whitehead, like the Jungfrau and the Matterhorn, are objects of contemplation and admiration for the entire world, the academic world scarcely expects any similar new creations or creators. One reason for this is plain: ours is surely, among other things, the age of analysis and specialization and not of comprehensive syntheses. Indeed, the latter probably are and will, for an unpredictable future, be impossible. It behooves students of the best thought of our age, therefore, to take a long look—at once critical and appreciative—at this synthesis of Brunner's.

There are, moreover, two special reasons for engaging in such a study, reasons which are seemingly contradictory but actually complimentary. One is that Brunner's total work is characterized by a balance and judiciousness which, if the phrase did not now have undesirable connotations, could best be described as "the middle way." Thus, Brunner's interpretation of Christianity is free from the extremes of the right, the early neo-orthodox and supernaturalist's denial of natural theology and the like, and of the left, the radical empiricist denial that we may achieve anything knowledgeable and/or significant unless it grows out of and can be tested and confirmed by experience. The question here is not whether either of these perspectives is "right" or "wrong"; it is that Brunner, writing in the heat of this twentieth century battle, is perhaps the leading exponent of the balanced or middle way. I do not say "mediating," for, as the reader will discover, Brunner explicitly rejects this estimate of his theology. This same capacity for assessing the merits and dangers inherent in extreme positions is evidenced in the way in which Brunner, over three decades, has drawn together with increasing effectiveness the central Calvinistic and Reformed emphasis on the sovereignty of God, on the one hand, and the Lutheran emphasis on a loving God's will to create eternal fellowship, on the other. This stance is seen similarly in his discriminating assessment of the role of nature and grace, and of rational and experimental criticism vis-à-vis the biblical revelation and the attitude of faith. Precisely that stance, however, together with some of the more extreme judgments expressed, for instance, in his early *Philosophy of Religion*, have elicited probing questions from his interpreters and critics in at least three of the studies in this volume. However one assesses Brunner's Reply, most readers are likely to conclude that, in an overall record of our age, it is in his theology that one finds a saner balance and a wiser moderation than in most other major parallel efforts. Far from constituting a mere eclecticism, Brunner's thought appears to embody the better insights of certain extremes in present-day theology and philosophy of religion. Here, then, we may have a theology which is more sound and fruitful, more nearly an authentic interpretation of the full Gospel message, than almost any other parallel efforts.

In seeming contradiction with the above, another compelling reason for pondering Brunner's thought is the almost unique way in which it absorbs and reassesses the important issues of the turn of the century expressed in part and always unsatisfactorily by the terms "fundamentalism," "liberalism," and "neo-orthodoxy," at the same time as it points to the largest and most vital movements in the second half of the twentieth century. By the latter, or forward-pointing reference, we refer chiefly, of course, to the increasing emphasis on the existentialist approach. This characteristically contemporary outlook, arousing at once great enthusiasm among some and deep suspicion among others, has a longer record in Brunner's thought than is usually realized. As such, it is far from being the recent fad or sideline enthusiasm exhibited in many contemporary writers. It is worth noting that there is a steady development in Brunner's writing from the earliest appearance of the existentialist's theme of truth-as-encounter to the pivotal role which the existentialist outlook plays in the third and concluding volume of his dogmatics. So, in Brunner's thought, and in philosophy of religion generally, the second half of the twentieth century is forced to make a careful assessment of the merit or demerit of the existentialist outlook.

Two personal comments have a proper place in this context. First, living as we do in a "one world" situation in which the leaders in political, economic, and cultural life are literally recognized as citizens of the world, Emil Brunner has anticipated and in fact personally played this role of world leadership for decades. Thus he, as a theologian, early extended his personal influence beyond that of a writer to that of a commanding figure on lecture platforms, in pulpits, and at conference tables beyond Europe to North America, and more recently to Japan and the Far East. What is equally characteristic of the major theologians and philosophers of our time, and is to many nonacademic minds exceedingly interesting, is the fact that Brunner has consistently exhibited a lively and ᵗᵇˡᵉ concern to see the insights of his field applied to the ᵘᵣ day. Note, accordingly, that his title, from ᵉˢˢorship, is that of systematic and practical the appropriate stress placed by his inter-ᵑ this feature of his vocation, namely, con-ᵗᵉʳ of serious professional discussion groups ᵈ civil administrators, doctors, and business-ᵃture and aim of their work in the light of their ˢ and the peculiar problems of contemporary ᵇᵒ speak of "ivory tower" theologians and phi-ᵉ Brunner—or Reinhold Niebuhr, Henry Nelson ᵇᵇ, or most of the creative minds of this century. ᵇᵉ documented by striking evidence. It is in the address delivered by the President of the German Bundesrepublik, Eugen Gerstenmaier, when he presented Professor Brunner with the Grosse Verdienstkreuz (the Great Cross of the Order of Merit). (The manuscript of that address, although not containing extended interpretation and criticism of Brunner's thought, and therefore not included in Part II of this volume, dare not be ignored here.) For President Gerstenmaier makes the point that his former teacher not only has had universally recognized influence upon Anglo-Saxon and Far Eastern as well as American and European thought generally, but that "In Germany . . . he has reached an importance which is unknown to very many people and of which he himself is perhaps only partially aware, . . . in Germany we faced the serious problem of letting the foundations of our belief be reduced illicitly or be 'dissolved in the fog of a state-mythology.' Then you [Brunner] came and presented the book on Justice. I can remember the day when I took your manuscript . . . to read it during one evening . . . The morning appeared when I had finished it, and I knew that I had read about the basis for rebuilding Germany. . . ." (Manuscript of the Address of Eugen Gerstenmaier at the German General Consulate, Zurich, 14th May, 1960, on the occasion of the seventieth birthday of Emil Brunner.) Nor was Brunner's theology for jurisprudence the only contribution, for also, according to President Gerstenmaier, he helped indispensably to clarify the nature and the limits of possible cooperation between Protestant and Catholic work.

The second and concluding personal statement for the record is that during the past two decades I have come to know Emil Brunner as a wise and good man and as a friend. There is, after all, a meaningful relation between one's public address and writing, on the one hand, and the quality of one's personality—what one is and does—on the other hand. As with the preceding subjects of volumes in this Library, so also of the subject of this volume, one can say: here is a warm and wonderful person of the sort the world surely needs in its intellectual leadership and each one of us cherishes in personal friendships.

CHARLES W. KEGLEY

WAGNER COLLEGE
NEW YORK CITY, NEW YORK

I

INTELLECTUAL AUTOBIOGRAPHY
OF
EMIL BRUNNER

1

INTELLECTUAL AUTOBIOGRAPHY
OF
EMIL BRUNNER

INTELLECTUAL AUTOBIOGRAPHY *

To write about his own life is for the theologian a meditation on that divine providence which takes its course through human failure and success. Right at this point our knowledge is especially piecemeal but, nevertheless, the following lines are written in a spirit of deepest thanksgiving for God's wonderous guidance which I have learned to recognize as basic reality in my life and work.

The leading ideas of my work are rooted in my early life. My ancestors were farmers who for centuries had tilled the soil of this wonderful land and citizens of this state which, from the viewpoint of world history, confronts us with something unique. Nowhere else in the world is there such a small country which can look back on almost four hundred years of uninterrupted peaceful and independent existence. Among the presently existing states, Switzerland is the world's oldest republic, dating from 1291. Her roots extend deeply into the Middle Ages, in contrast to all other modern republics, and have left their distinctive stamp on her. The Swiss Confederation forms a happy synthesis between the federal principle of the rural confederation and the majority rule of a modern parliamentary democracy. This connection makes possible a fruitful relationship between authority and freedom, thereby providing a harmonious compromise between group interests and the freedom of the individual. Within this structure Switzerland has been able to contain four different cultures and languages (German, French, Italian, and Romanish) with fully equal rights for each of them. Equally important is the fact that, in spite of modern industrialization, the opposing interests of capital and labor did not produce a real class struggle. The result was, on the contrary, a type of legislation and social order which were at the same time conservative

* Translated by Keith Chamberlain.

and progressive, assuring our people of a peaceful existence based on mutual cooperation. In Switzerland we have a European microcosm in which Protestants and Catholics, rural and urban populations, Latin and German cultures exist side by side. Here the solution of the problems of European history in the sociopolitical realm has proved itself as good in an unusual measure and it could well be regarded as exemplary in some respects. I hope that this observation will not be considered presumptuous. It is apparent that I am here showing my colors as a Swiss citizen.

I became aware of these things rather late, only after coming to grips with the sociopolitical currents of the present. I am not unaware of the fact that we are "strangers" in this world, nor do I say that the best of all solutions for our social problems is that same goal which is the center of the Gospel of the Kingdom of God. It is one of the basic errors of our time, a superstition of the whole of modern history, that a just and free order of society somehow comes closer to the message of the Kingdom of God than the decisions in the individual, personal realm. The New Testament leaves us with no doubt on this point. It is, indeed, our duty to try to make the power of Christ operative in the sociopolitical realm as well as in others. However, in this particular area the love commandment will, at best, find expression in a very indirect sense. This can take place much more immediately on the level of direct, interpersonal relationships.

This insight has become decisive for my whole thinking. Here the value of personal life stands above all other values. Similarly, in society, the personal orders of marriage and family take precedence over all others. Long before I learned to think in terms of social ethics the family was for me the very center of concrete, visible life. From my father I learned in expressive and convincing fashion that the father is intended to be the "priest" in this "temple." He was a schoolteacher who understood his work as a calling and a service to God. From my mother, who stood at his side in this service, I learned to pray. Using an old picture Bible, she introduced me to biblical history and thereby laid the foundation on which my theology was later to be built. Through her influence, my father, descended from a family of nonbelievers, came into contact with Christoph Blumhardt. Through Blumhardt and his two important pupils, Hermann Kutter and Leonhard Ragaz, our family was drawn into the Religious Socialist Movement. The church in Europe had just begun to take note of the Industrial Revolution and to understand its meaning. "Religious Socialism" was the *avantgarde* of this church which was just becoming sensitive to the appalling plight of the industrial laborer. Hermann Kutter's book, *Sie müssen* (They Must, 1904), which appeared in numerous editions and languages, proved to be a rude awakening for the church in that it portrayed the Social Democrats, in spite of their atheistic leanings, as true bearers of the message of the Kingdom of God in our time. Leonhard Ragaz and a number of Swiss pastors then joined the Social Democratic party in order to demonstrate their solidarity with the workers, whose predominant concern was the struggle for social justice. To be sure, this Religious Socialism differed decisively from Marxist "Scientific Socialism," as well as from the American "Social Gospel," in that faith in Jesus Christ always stood at its center. The propelling force of this movement was the hope of the approaching Kingdom of God. During my years of study, this movement drew me into its orbit much more strongly than the theological liberalism that then dominated the scene. As young theologians at the University of Zurich we received solid, scientific tools for our later work. Such prominent scholars as P. W. Schmiedel, a proponent of rationalistic biblical criticism, and Walter Köhler, a pupil and follower of Ernst Troeltsch, were among our professors. We made good use of this historical and critical training. The ideology connected with the Religious Socialist Movement was, nevertheless, unable to shake the sound Christological foundation which Blumhardt had given it.

In contrast to the spirit of this movement, I began at an early stage to search for a scientifically satisfying formulation of my faith. There probably are not many theologians who began their studies with such concern for scientific logic. The epistomological works of Kant and the newest philosophy of the time, the Phenomenology of Husserl, kindled real enthusiasm in me. A thorough understanding of Husserl is evident in my first writing, *Das Symbolische in der Religiösen Erkenntnis* (The Symbolic Element in Religious Knowledge, 1914). I am still a little proud of the fact that Husserl then wrote to me, saying that I had understood him better than most of his contemporaries. But in spite of this relationship to Husserl, I have generally held to the critical standards of Kant up to this day. In this I was repeatedly encouraged by my friend in Basel, the prominent Christian philosopher Heinrich Barth, with whom I have always had more intimate contact than with his more famous brother, Karl.

Along with my philosophical studies I began quite early to study social economy, which was almost a prerequisite for those involved in the Religious Socialist Movement. *Die Arbeiterfrage* (The Question of Labor) by H. Herknew, Sombart's standard work *Der Kapitalismus* (Capitalism), as well as the lectures of the famous "Kathedersozialist" (conservative socialist) in Berlin, Adolf Wagner, captured my imagination. This work was extremely helpful to me when I myself later lectured on social ethics in Zurich.

But my deepest concern was not so much with the problems of social ethics as with the more fundamental question about God. Since becoming acquainted with Kutter, the certainty of the Living God was always a firm reality for me. There was a time when the currently reigning agnostic humanism and the materialism, which was identified with Darwinism, occasioned doubts in me. The critical idealism of F. A. Lange, *Geschichte des Materialismus* (History of Materialism) strengthened me against these temptations, but in a very different way the biblical realism and prophetism of my teachers Kutter and the one even greater than he who stood in back of him, Christoph Blumhardt, kept my faith alive.

Kutter's favorite writer was Scotus Erigena *(De Divisione Naturae)*. I always found an open copy of Plato in Greek lying on his desk. There was in him an unusual union of biblical realism and neo-Platonic idealism. These two elements were so combined in his thinking that he felt at home with the Greek fathers as well as with Augustine. (He had read all their complete works in the Greek and Latin original.) But the more I reflected on this synthesis, the more questionable it became to me. As a result of being immersed in the thought of Martin Luther and becoming intimately acquainted with the works of Søren Kierkegaard, this synthesis was slowly but decisively dissolved.

After having completed my studies with a doctorate in theology —something rather unusual in Switzerland in those days—I ventured forth into the world. I had already studied for a semester in 1911 at the University of Berlin. However, neither the theology of Harnack nor the atmosphere of the great metropolis nor the state of Wilhelm II had made much of an impression on me. In 1913-1914 I was drawn to England, the traditional land of freedom and progress. During my stay in England, I became acquainted with the

Christian Labor Movement and its distinguished leaders, Ramsay MacDonald, Philip Snowden, and others. These men whose roots were in Carlyle, Morrison, Ruskin, and Kingsley, had close ties with the Fabian Socialists. I translated into German the speeches held at the yearly "Christian Labour Week" in the Browning Settlement and was, on this occasion, particularly impressed by the "Guild Socialism" of H. Cole. At that time the "Brotherhood Movement" was thriving in England. In connection with this movement I first got to know the subsequent Archbishop of York and Canterbury, William Temple, who later became a personal friend. I also soon felt at home in the Christian Adult School Movement, followed its development with lively interest, and took part in numerous conferences and work groups. In the course of this work my opposition to the atheistic, pseudoscientific Marxism was intensified rather than abated.

My sojourn in England came to an abrupt end with the outbreak of the First World War in 1914. I spent the first year of the war in the Swiss border defense as Soldier Brunner. For me, as well as for most of my educated comrades, the catastrophe of war in our time was at first something inconceivable. With this event my faith in progress was shattered and my Religious Socialism began to look suspiciously like a beautiful illusion. But my Christian faith itself was not thereby shaken. I came to see that the catastrophe resulting from those conditions in Europe which had led to this collapse was a divine judgment upon the godlessness of the Christian peoples.

After serving the church for six months as a vicar in Hermann Kutter's congregation, I was called in 1916 to be pastor of a small congregation in the mountains, called Obstalden in the Canton of Glarus. I was a pastor with my whole heart and am still that today, although I have had no congregation of my own since 1924. In 1917 I married Margrit Lauterburg who came from Bern and who was a niece of Hermann Kutter. Shortly after the end of the war my work in the rural pastorate was interrupted by a visit to the United States. This was made possible by Professor Adolf Keller who arranged a fellowship for me at Union Theological Seminary in New York. My invitation was apparently the result of my early theological publications and my experience in England. I was able to accept this invitation because my wife, who had already borne our first son and was expecting a second child, selflessly encouraged me to go. In the autumn of 1919 I sailed from Le Havre for the first time to the New World. At this point in my life history I cannot avoid pointing to the way God's hand led me. For this year in America provided the foundation for my particularly fruitful contacts with the English-speaking world for the rest of my life. At the hospitable Union Seminary I was not so much intrigued by the reigning theology (McGiffert's Ritschlianism and W. A. Brown's Mediation Theology), but rather by my encounter with the American people. I was impressed by the particular character of their democratic institutions (to which, when viewed historically, we owe as much as they to ours). Harry Ward, one-sided though he was, ably introduced us to America's social problems with which he was so intimately acquainted.

Deeply filled with impressions, new insights, and questions, I returned to Europe and to my Glaronese congregation in the summer of 1920. I devoted myself primarily to preaching, pastoral work, and religious instruction. Scholarly work in theological and philosopical areas was and still is strictly subordinated to the proclamation of the Gospel. I see in it the possibility better to understand and express the Divine Word, so that it may be relevant and understandable for the more demanding and intellectually inclined people of our time. The question of the relation of faith to philosophy was and still is a fascinating question for me but, nevertheless, basically a secondary problem. I was and am above all a preacher of the Good News.

The catastrophe of the First World War indicated clearly that the foundation and aims of Religious Socialism were due for a thorough reappraisal. In these years it became clear to me that this examination would have to begin at the roots, namely, the message of Christ itself. This insight came simultaneously with my first encounter with Karl Barth, who also was then a pastor in a Swiss village congregation. His *Römerbrief* (Epistle to the Romans), written in 1918, I hailed as a forceful confirmation of my own thoughts. If I am not mistaken, I was the first one, who in reviewing this book (in the *Kirchenblatt für die Reformierte Schweiz*), emphatically pointed to its epoch-making character. My enthusiasm was all the more understandable because Barth, as well as our mutual friend Eduard Thurneysen, came from that circle in the center of which Hermann Kutter and Christoph Blumhardt had been. While I was trying to state the case for this new theology at

Union Seminary, Barth was breaking into the camp of German theology with his famous lecture, "Der Christ in der Gesellschaft" (The Christian in Society). Shortly thereafter, the periodical *Zwischen den Zeiten* (Between the Times) was founded, in the columns of which the theological revolution was largely to take place. The result of my absence in America was that I never became an intimate member of the circle publishing this magazine. From the very beginning I had taken a position independent of that of Karl Barth, which in the course of the ensuing years was to receive a more pronounced character. In the solitude of my mountain parsonage I worked on my inauguratory thesis "Erlebnis, Erkenntnis und Glaube" (Experience, Knowledge and Faith, 1921), and then my first more extensive work *Die Mystik und das Wort* (The Mysticism and the Word, 1924). This book, which was a critical assessment of Schleiermacher, "the church father of the nineteenth century," proved to be an effective weapon for the new theology in the sharpening conflict with Liberalism. These publications then led to my appointment to the Chair of Systematic and Practical Theology at the University of Zurich, which I occupied from 1924 until 1955. During the first years of teaching in my home town, *Der Mittler* (The Mediator) was written, which was the first presentation of the doctrine of Christ in terms of the dialectical theology. Barth's *Christliche Dogmatik* (Christian Dogmatics) appeared a little later.

In the meantime, in the political realm, an event of world-historical importance had taken place—the emergence of the totalitarian state. In its Communistic and later Fascist and National Socialistic forms the totalitarian state is more than merely a political or economic phenomenon. It is an intellectual-spiritual power, based on atheistic principles. Its concept of man is determined by its atheistic basis. Man is not understood as a person, responsible to God, but rather as a mere functionary of the state. In this sense it is to be clearly differentiated from the dictatorships of earlier times. It is a child of the twentieth century, that age that had provided the scientific and technical means for its realization. Toward the end of the twenties I began to follow up the implications of this new phenomenon and to work them into my lectures on Christian ethics. At the same time it became clear to me that the totalitarian state is understandable for us only when considered from the viewpoint of the *ekklesía*, that is, the brotherhood of men based upon the communion with Jesus Christ as we see it in the New Testament. It is comprehensible as the antithesis to the *ekklesía*. During these years, the unity of faith and community, as I understood it from the biblical witness, was impressively illustrated by an example of the time. In 1932 I met for the first time Frank Buchman and became acquainted with the "Oxford group" which he had founded. As a result of my participation in the so-called "group movement," which had initiated a remarkable religious revival in Switzerland in the thirties, I learned a number of lessons which were not only important for my practical work in the church but which also were fruitful for my theology. It was no accident that my small popular compendium of theology appeared during this period (1935), which under the title *Unser Glaube* (Our Faith, translated into nineteen languages) is one of the dearest fruits of my lifework. A systematic presentation of biblical personalism in the realm of social ethics and a comparison and contrast of the Christian and non-Christian doctrines of society were given in my comprehensive ethics, which first appeared in 1932 with the title *Das Gebot und die Ordnungen*. (Unfortunately the English title, The Divine Imperative, fails to express the double aspect of "command" and "orders" which was so important for me.) This work, which was published in Germany shortly before Hitler came into power, was soon recognized by the National Socialists as being basically antitotalitarian and was accordingly confiscated and destroyed. So it remained unknown in Germany, where it could have done its best service, until it was republished with ecumenical funds toward the end of the war and then enjoyed a wide, if late, circulation in postwar Germany.

This is perhaps the best place to say a few words about my activities in the world church. Very early, in 1923, my first lecture tour brought me to Holland. Then in 1928 I traveled through the United States, where I was invited to deliver lectures at numerous theological seminaries. These were followed in 1931 by lectures in London, Glasgow, and Edinburgh and in the following years I was invited to lecture in Hungary, Denmark, Finland, and Sweden. However, my activities were not restricted to lecturing and teaching. From 1930 on, I worked intensively with a number of study groups in the framework of the Ecumenical Movement as a member of the study commissions on "Life and Work" and "Faith and Order." The opportunity for an exchange of ideas and sharing of experiences in the Ecumenical Movement, rather than an interest in organizational unity, moved me to accept J. H. Oldham's invitation to take part in the preparations for the World Church Conference in Oxford in 1937. In the course of these preparations I attended numerous study conferences, thereby receiving as well as contributing. These meetings with Christian theologians, church leaders, and laymen from varying walks of life and from all lands are among my most pleasant and fruitful experiences. I devoted a great deal of time and energy to the theological preparation for and to participating in numerous meetings and conferences. However, I was somewhat skeptical about the organizational structure of the World Council of Churches. I still feel that the World Church Conference in Oxford in 1937 was somehow the point of culmination in the Ecumenical Movement which has yet to be surpassed. It stood under the influence of that great Christian layman, J. H. Oldham, who kept reminding us theologians that the Church of Jesus Christ is founded on the priesthood of all believers and must beware of becoming a clerical institution.

In coming to grips with the decisive practical questions which the events of the time had thrust into the foreground (church and state, proclamation of the Gospel in a secularized society and to the peoples of the world), I came to the conclusion that the root of the whole problem was the question of anthropology. Every political and social system grows out of a particular concept of man, out of an anthropological foundation. In the realm of sociology my thinking was stimulated by Max Weber and, above all, in the sphere of philosophy, by Ferdinand Ebner and Martin Buber. Here I saw the rationalistic thought-scheme of object and subject overcome by understanding the human person as basically related to the divine Thou and by the distinction between the I-Thou world and the I-it world. Through this I came to see what was the heart of the biblical concept of man. Neither Ferdinand Ebner nor Martin Buber made a secret of the fact that they owed this most important insight to the Bible and the Christian philosopher, Søren Kierkegaard. Today I, in contrast to Karl Barth, still profess allegiance to this great Christian thinker to whom present-day theology, Catholic no less than Protestant, owes more to than anyone since Martin Luther. Armed with this biblical insight, I then wrote my outline of a Christian doctrine of man, which appeared in 1935 under the title *Der Mensch im Widerspruch* (Man in Revolt), which suffered the same fate as the *Gebot und die Ordnungen*, that is, it was suppressed by the Hitlerite censorship. This anthropology was the first attempt

to deal comprehensively with this subject since the theological reorientation at the end of World War I. Reinhold Niebuhr's *Nature
and Destiny of Man* came eight years later and Karl Barth's treatment of the problem *(Church Dogmatics III)* only in 1944/1948.
As I had anticipated, the treatment by my great colleague in Basel
of this complex of questions led to a turning point which made almost meaningless our disagreement during the thirties concerning
the "point of contact." Barth, however, never explicitly retracted
the anathemas, which he had pronounced in his *No!* (1934).

My anthropological studies then led me to an even more fundamental question, namely to a reformulation of the biblical concept
of truth. A series of lectures held in Upsala in 1936 were devoted
to this attempt and were printed in the following year under the
title *Wahrheit als Begegnung.* Unfortunately, the English title, *The
Divine-Human Encounter,* doesn't succeed in expressing the fundamental thought of the book, namely, that which is specific about
the Christian understanding of truth. Here I placed the biblical
understanding of truth over and against the Greek understanding
which is the foundation of our Western philosophy and science.
Since then, all of my work in dogmatics has been done in the light
of this aspect: the God who communicates himself. As a result of
this, the old concept of revelation was freed of its intellectual misunderstanding and the basic connection between knowledge and
communion came to have its rightful place. In this I see my most
important contribution to the theological concept of knowledge.

Although this is, in accordance with the general plan of these
books, supposed to be an intellectual biography, a completely false
picture of the person standing behind this theology would arise if
the human climate in which this work took place were left unmen-
tioned. Just as the family of my parents had much to do with my
theology, so has my own family certainly influenced my activity in
the church. This is true in a very immediate sense when I think of
my wife who has accompanied me with lively interest and feminine
intuition through my theological career. Moreover, she provided invaluable assistance by assuming the tiresome, thankless task of
proofreading for my publications. Even more important was her
service as the first reviewer of my works. She helped me with loving
but penetrating criticism better to understand the questions of my
nontheological readers as well as to tone down my polemics where
that was necessary. Our four sons provided the basis for my lively

contacts with the younger generation. Our hikes, our music-making, discussions on literature and history, our games and vacations were all parts of this common life. As my sons grew up, went to school and to the university, our dinner table became a forum in which I was confronted not only with the problems of other faculties, but also with the current political trends. It was a real joy for me when our oldest son told me of his intention to study theology. The effects of World War II were felt in our family when my three older sons were called to active service in the Swiss army. During the following years two of our sons were taken from us by illness and accident. Their deaths made their impact upon my theological work, as can be seen in my treatment of the problem of eschatology, especially in *Das Ewige als Zukunft und Gegenwart* (Eternal Hope, 1953).

The threat to our country in those years brought out some of the best in our people. As a teacher in a Swiss university and a responsible member of the church, I also felt the need to contribute. Our period of isolation from the rest of the world was not lost time. It gave me the opportunity to rethink the tasks of a Christian community and to explore new ways of reaching those for whom traditional forms of witness were meaningless. My monthly sermon in the Fraumünster, which more and more took on the nature of a discussion with the congregation, remained the very center of my activity. At the university we found a rewarding form of activity by organizing informal study groups with students from the various disciplines. They were similar to the "open evenings" which I had held for my students since the beginning of my academic career and were among the best and most fruitful aspects of my university work. In the shadow of that horrible war, the questions of the reconstruction of Europe and the basis for a peaceful and just order between the nations assumed top priority in our thinking and discussions. When the honor and office of rector of the university was given to me in those decisive years (1942-1944), I had the opportunity to reconsider the Christian foundations of European culture and to appeal to the Christian responsibility of our people for those in the countries devastated by war. Our declaration of solidarity with the students in the University of Oslo, who were then under severe oppression by the Nazis, did not remain without effect. Immediately after the end of the war, practical measures were undertaken for assisting members of the academic communities in emergency areas. A product of the awakening by these wartime problems was my book *Gerechtigkeit* (Justice and the Social Order), which appeared in 1943.

Faced with the breakdown of law and order by the Nazi regime in almost all the countries of Europe, I tried to formulate the Christian foundation of society based on the Divine Law. This book was received by jurists, politicians, and economists with much greater interest than by (Protestant) theologians who, preoccupied by their primary task of preaching the gospel of reconciliation and justification, were not used to think in terms of law and order, while the Roman Catholic theologians recognized in it a conception parallel to their own tradition of "natural law" in a Christian, not in the rationalist modern sense. The practical proof of this was the later cooperation of the Protestants and Catholics in postwar Germany. The main thesis of the book is this alternative: either society is grounded on the Divine Law or it has to submit to the compulsion of totalitarism, be it of the Communist or Fascist variety. Since my struggle against totalitarism is not taken up in any of the following essays, I may be allowed a brief excursion into the problem here.

The position and task of the church in the present age can be understood only against the background of the general cultural and, especially, political situations (see Pauck's article). The apocalyptic nature of the situation becomes increasingly evident and can be recognized at two points. On the one hand, the present age is characterized by the appearance of the atheistic totalitarian state, which puts the state in the place of God and necessarily is hostile to Christianity. It is the task of theology and the church to recognize the true character of this totalitarism. For the first time in history, a large portion of the human race, perhaps more than half of the world's population, is ruled by a political system which has not only made the denial of God's existence part of its program, but openly proclaims the liquidation of religion as one of its goals. This was already the case in Hitler's totalitarian state, even if not so obviously, but it lacked the systematic unity and thoroughness that the Marxist-Leninist social philosophy gives to the Communist totalitarian state. Therefore, "Communism" is essentially an anti-religion without God. There appear to be no grounds for denying that all the elements of the antichrist are present in this godless machinery of dehumanization. It is the exact antithesis of the *ekklesía* in the New Testament. Christianity has never been threatened by a more dangerous enemy in its nineteen hundred years of history. It is a frightening sign of blindness that many theologians, pastors, and church leaders today do not recognize this as anti-Christianity but see in Communism a very unpleasant but nevertheless discussible phenomenon. Here the word of our Lord to the Pharisees applies: "You know how to interpret the appearance of the sky, but you cannot interpret the signs of the times" (Matt. 16:3).

The second symptom of the apocalyptic character of our time I see in the fact that mankind now possesses the means to annihilate itself and all life on earth, whether by atomic war or by atomic contamination of which the effects are, as is well known, irreversible. Above all the situation of the church must be considered as apocalyptic in that she faces a ghastly alternative. Never and under no condition can the Christian approve of atomic war which would most probably imply the total extinction of the human race. On the other hand it is the ethical task of the ecclesia to oppose to the utmost a diabolical system of essential godlessness and inhumanity, which by its basic principles as well as by its practice transforms man into a mere functionary of a soulless state machinery and must end in a complete dehumanization. An unconditional surrender of the atomic weapon, that is, a *unilateral* nuclear disarmament would, with certainty, lead to the Communist world dominion, to the extermination of all religion, and the complete functionalization of mankind, namely, dehumanization of life. In this terrific situation our only hope is the universal conversion of mankind to a new recognition of God's law as the basis of all life which would transcend the ideological conflict. For such a miracle we can only pray and work as individual members of the *ekklesía*. While my judgment of the totalitarian state was formed during many years of study, the apocalyptic perspectives of current history have become visible to me only in recent years.

In spite of all of this, or rather because of these ominous perspectives, the main task of theology is not in the area of social ethics but rather in the area of kerygma and dogmatics. The struggle for the right understanding of faith in Christ must be its primary concern. So, my theological efforts in the last fifteen years have been devoted primarily to this end. It has always been my conviction that the community of Christ lives not on the basis of theology but by the word of God, the understanding of which is a gift of the

Holy Spirit. But it is just as evident that we cannot do without theological reflection of the church about the Gospel entrusted to her, especially during a period dominated by the superstition that science has made faith superfluous. In this situation of Christianity within a world which predominantly understands truth as "scientific, objective truth," the Christian conception of truth which I had set forth in *The Divine Human Encounter* proved to be of great help setting personal truth over against scientific, impersonal truth. The task of making clear to the man of our age this fundamental distinction as well as the abyss which separates men's origins was tackled in my book *Revelation and Reason* (*Offenbarung und Vernunft*, 1941), a new kind of so-called apologetics. As a matter of fact these two tasks, apologetics and dogmatics, cannot be separated from each other. Every dogmatic statement is at the same time an apologetic-polemic statement and vice versa. These were the new insights that necessitated the completion of my theological works which so far had been monographies on special topics of the Christian faith, by a comprehensive presentation of the whole Christian doctrine. This *Dogmatik*, consisting of three volumes, differs from Karl Barth's monumental *Kirchliche Dogmatik* (Ecclesiastical Dogmatics) not only by its far more modest proportions but above all by the fact that the Christian conception of truth, truth as encounter, revelation conceived as God's self-communication, dominates and permeates the treatment of every single theological topic. In this writing I became aware of the fact that a dual concept of faith is characteristic of all post-Reformation theology: faith in Christ and belief in the Bible as the infallible word of God. This dualism was blurred by the distinction of a material and formal principle of the Christian faith, namely, justification or reconciliation by Jesus Christ and the Scriptures as the all-comprehensive object of faith. By the consistent identification of revelation with God's self-communication, thereby overcoming the fatal distinction of object and subject, I hope to have made a decisive contribution to removing this dual conception of faith. With this new concept of faith, which is essentially the biblical one, I also hope to have made a useful clarification for ecclesiology and eschatology. This was presented in detail in two publications during the early fifties. In *Das Missverständnis der Kirche* (The Misunderstanding of the Church), which first appeared in 1951, I attempted to show that the church, in theology as well as in the world, can be properly understood only if we recognize the unique character of the *ekklesía* of the New Testament, over and against all institutions which call themselves "churches." We must regard them as necessary but questionable auxiliary structures. Our task is to work for recapturing the spirit of Christ whereby the true *ekklesía* can become operative within and transcend these institutions. The resulting controversy, mainly with the representatives of traditionalism, is still in its early stages. Two years later *Das Ewige als Zukunft und Gegenwart* (The Eternal as Future and Present), translated under the title *Eternal Hope*, was published. Concentrating on Christ-faith, interpretated by the newly discovered conception of encounter, I attempted to work out the main lines of New Testament eschatology. It should thereby be freed from the inadequate temporal conceptions of traditional theology (as we still have them today in fundamentalism and in the writings of Oscar Cullmann). At the same time it was my intention to distinguish sharply between this understanding of Christian hope and the reduction of biblical eschatalogy to the mathematical point of "existential encounter," as we see it in the Bultmann school. Here also, the discussion is still going on.

Yet, in this last stage of my life as a theologian, I have not retreated into a more exclusively scholarly climate, as is often considered appropriate for those of advancing age. These last years have not been devoted to the *vita contemplativa*. It is frequently the case that the young theologian goes forth as an active missionary and then retreats to a quieter, more contemplative position in his later years. In my case the opposite is true. The missionary concern, which was always central in my theology, has found its most concrete expression in the last twelve years. This took place in three stages, all of which are accidentally connected with the year 1948.

In 1947-1948 I accepted an invitation to deliver the famous Gifford Lectures in Scotland. I took this opportunity to survey in its various aspects the relationship between Christianity and civilization. In retrospect, however, I recognize that these lectures (which appeared in two volumes under the title *Christianity and Civilization*) did not measure up to the task. In the first series I examined the foundations and in the second the various areas of civilization. But to deal with such colossal problems as freedom, truth, and justice, each in a forty-five-minute lecture, was possible only by adjusting my treatment to the demands of my audience, the college students of St. Andrews. Specialists in these areas could hardly be satisfied with such cursory treatment. Nevertheless, the attempt to present the Christian faith as the foundation of our culture and as the most important and indispensable bulwark against the destructive forces of our time remains essential.

In that same year the *Reformierte Heimstätte* (Reformed Homestead), in Boldern on the Lake of Zurich, was opened. It represented the first Swiss venture into a new area of church work which attempts to provide a forum for a conversation between the church and the world. Since the end of the war the *Evangelische Akademien* (Protestant academies) in Germany have been pioneers in this area. Together with a number of like-minded friends I participated intensively and enthusiastically in the development of this place of encounter. I saw in it the fulfillment of one of the most important prerequisites for the mission of the church in a secular world. Here, without the barriers of a traditional ecclesiastical setup, the church had the opportunity to find new ways of confronting the world with the Gospel. This was a good chance to speak relevantly to the thinking and feeling of modern man, to experiment in the field of human relations with people from widely differing intellectual and social groups, to replace the solo performance of lecturing theologian with the teamwork of theologians and laymen. In such a way it is possible to overcome the usual monologue typical of our continental churches by conversation which is more appropriate to the essential nature of the Gospel as encounter. Boldern is one of the enduring fruits of my theological efforts and is especially close to my heart.

Finally, I received the call from John Mott to participate in the worldwide work of the YMCA as a theological adviser. The task of helping in the Christian training of the YMCA secretaries in important lands overseas appealed to me very strongly, since this was an opportunity to do missionary work in the full sense of the word. For the first time (1949) I traveled to the Far East where for several months I was intensively involved in lecturing and running training courses in Japan, Korea, India, and Pakistan. My stay in Japan resulted in a new and even more rewarding venture. I was asked to help in building up the new International Christian University in Tokyo, which had been founded after the war. In spite of some natural hesitations I felt myself irresistibly led to accept. My experience during those two years in Japan (1953-1955) confirmed my conviction that this had been a call of God. The chance to assist in the Christian training of young Japanese laymen (future doctors, lawyers, teachers, and so forth) not only was a tremendously important challenge in itself, but it was also the joyous and fitting culmination of my career as a missionary theologian and churchman. The orientation of my lectures toward the students at ICU and to students in many other Japanese universities, who were for the most part non-Christians, made necessary a clear recognition of what I had long ago postulated and called the "point of contact." Now in this strictly missionary situation where I had to teach students who had not the slightest knowledge of the Christian faith, it became of primary importance to find "the point of contact." That very concept, which in the early days of dialectical theology had caused so much controversy, and which I had defended so steadfastly against a doctrinaire theological opposition, proved to be that thing that decided success or failure of Christian teaching. Also I came to realize that it was exactly that aspect of theology which I had called "the other task," and which traditionally is known under the name of apologetics, which was of greater importance than the mere exposition of the Christian or biblical doctrine and which the interest of my non-Christian students was primarily focused upon. In fact, it was the problem of man, *der Mensch in Widerspruch,* (Man in Contradiction), where the decision for or against the biblical message took place. The presentation of the impact which Christianity had made upon the basic problems of life and civilization proved to be a good approach to the center—as far as teaching was concerned. The most important way leading to Christ is, of course, the transparency of Christ's spirit in the character, in the life, and in the face of the one who presents the Christian doctrine. My new acquaintance with the civilization of the Far East, my encounter with the Japanese people, and the necessary practical cooperation on the missionary front taught me to see in a new different light some of the problems at home and in the church in general. Above all, I received an inkling of the upheaval presently taking place in East-West relations, the depth of which we are only dimly beginning to perceive. In the process of wrestling with the many problems of the church, side by side with Japanese, American, and European Christians, under completely different conditions, I gained a considerably clearer view of the obstacles standing in the way of the missionary church. Perhaps the most important insight is that the main difficulties lie within the church itself and not outside of it.

A final word must be devoted to my connections with America. Ever since my first trip across the Atlantic as the first Swiss fellow of Union Seminary, New York, my personal and theological life has been very closely linked to all that goes on in the Christian church in America. Shortly before the outbreak of World War II, I was on the verge of emigrating to the United States to accept the tempting offer of a combined professorship at the university and the theological seminary in Princeton. But my love and responsibility for our homeland and for our church made it impossible for me to leave at a time when my country was so threatened. So I remained only one year as a guest professor at that venerable institution and immediately after the war the old contacts were renewed. As early as 1946 I made another lecture tour, this time through the eastern states and the Middle West and a few years later I interrupted my stay in Japan long enough to spend a few weeks in California in order to deliver the Earl Lectures, *Faith, Hope, and Love*. Although these manifold and intensive activities of the last few years took their toll on my general health, I have never for one moment regretted this service. I am inexpressibly grateful that the Lord of my life has granted to me in such abundance these opportunities to take part in the life of his *ekklesía* and to bear witness to the Living Christ in so many places and in so many ways.

EMIL BRUNNER

ZÜRICH, SWITZERLAND

II

ESSAYS OF INTERPRETATION
AND CRITICISM OF
THE WORK OF EMIL BRUNNER

1

Wilhelm Pauck

THE CHURCH-HISTORICAL
SETTING OF BRUNNER'S THEOLOGY

THE CHURCH-HISTORICAL SETTING
OF
BRUNNER'S THEOLOGY

E mil Brunner's theological thought has always been awake to the actual conditions of Christian life in the world of today. In saying this, I do not mean to suggest that he has let himself be guided in his interpretation of the Christian gospel by the needs and desires of man. What I mean to affirm is that his theology is a modern theology in the sense that it interprets the gospel in such a way that men of today can feel themselves addressed thereby in their particular conditions.

We shall try to substantiate this thesis by attempting answers to the following three questions:

1) At what points does the modern world situation impinge most decisively upon the life of the church?

2) What are the unique developments in the life of the churches which distinguish them in their present situation from the churches of the past?

3) What, in the light of the developments in world and church, are the major themes and concerns of the contemporary theological interpreters of Christianity?

I.

The Christian churches now occupy the position of a minority in Western civilization and generally in the world. This was not always so. Insofar as we still tend to identify our civilization with Christianity, we give expression to the historical judgment that, once upon a time, the Christian institutions exercised an influence upon the cultural life which shaped its very character. To be sure, one can rightly raise the question: How Christian, in the full sense of the word, the civilization of the Middle Ages, of that world which is called *corpus Christianum*, really was? or whether the Christian nations of post-Reformation Europe ever deserved to be called "Christian." Indeed, one may go so far as to consider this so-called Christianity of former societies in the West fictitious, as Emil Brunner has done.

Nevertheless, the churches, if not the Christian faith itself, then determined the whole of the common life and they could rely upon the support of all the people. The church could claim their allegiance, because every man was born into church membership just as he was born into the collective body of the political community.

Nominally, this situation still prevails in most European countries, where, as statistics show, ninety-five out of every one hundred persons are church members. They have been baptized and confirmed and pay their church taxes and they are therefore entitled to all the rights and privileges of church membership. Actually only ten among every one hundred persons practice responsible churchmanship. In certain countries, the situation is even worse than that. Recent reports show, for instance, that in Lutheran Sweden, where practically every citizen is a baptized Christian, only a little more than 2 per cent of the population attend the services of the church with any degree of regularity.

This means that in most European countries the churches are still endowed with the privileges they had acquired when they were supported by the entire population but that they are actually important for only a small number of people. Still surrounded with the prestige of their former position in society, they have been pushed from the center of the common life to its fringes.

At present, there is no sign that this trend toward a reduction of active church membership has been halted, although everywhere in Europe, in both Protestant and Catholic countries, the minorities that rally around the churches are witnessing boldly and sometimes heroically to their faith.

In the United States, the churches have never held a majority position in public life, except for a period of time, during the Colonial era in certain regions, particularly New England. Today, they can point to a steady growth in membership and, instead of losing popular support, they appear to gain it. In America, the churches are, therefore, more actively supported than they are in traditionally Christian Europe, but this should not be interpreted as if it indicated that American civilization were not also marked by the trend toward the emancipation of the common life from the Christian religion.

One of the most important points of difference between America and Europe is this: whereas, in the United States the separation between church and state and the establishment of religious liberty became two of the pillars on which the American people built their new nation, the Christians among them striving to make it a Christian nation, in Europe the introduction of the freedom of religion marked the end of the Christian phase of civilization. One can rightly assert that the coordination of religion and politics which had determined the life of Christendom since the days of the Emperor Constantine had never been anything else than a mixture of good and evil, and that their separation effected under the influence of the American and French revolutions produced much good both for politics and religion, because both were now brought under the sway of liberty while the church was rebuked for having usurped worldly power and the political governments for having used religion as a mere instrument for the maintenance of social unity. Nevertheless, the establishment of religious freedom disclosed also the estrangement that had come to prevail between the states and the churches and between the cultural forces and the religious ones.

We are here face to face with the paradoxical historical fact that the Enlightenment, which Americans are rightly wont to praise as the spiritual-intellectual movement that liberated Western civilization from heteronomous authoritarianism and particularly from the dogmatic authoritarianism of the churches and the institutions of power by which both the states and the churches tried to maintain their alliance with one another, thus inaugurated the emancipation of the peoples of the West not only from the churches but also from the practice of the Christian religion.

In the course of the nineteenth century, a withdrawal from organized religion took place, which was unique in Western history. Many members of the educated classes severed all spiritual connection with the churches and interpreted the character and purpose of civilization by way of a criticism of Christianity. These cultural despisers of religion were not greatly impressed by the efforts of enlightened churchmen and theologians who attempted to show that they shared many of the criticisms which were being pointed at the churches, but that religion could be interpreted in such a way that its outlived doctrinal and social forms could be replaced by new ones. At the same time, these so-called theological liberals never succeeded in gaining the support of a majority of the churches and their people. Indeed, the churches tended to assume a reactionary attitude toward themselves and the world. The result was that they thereby caused their critics to feel justified in their opposition to them. For they appeared to prove themselves incapable of coming to terms with the social environment which the industrialization of Western man produced. Indeed, when they failed to recognize the fact that modern science and technology were bringing about a social revolution, they lost the support of all who sensed that great historical changes were in the making. Thus it was not surprising that, during the second part of the nineteenth century, the industrial workers, particularly of the European continent, who were led by leaders highly sensitive to the major trends in civilization, followed the example of many intellectuals and proceeded to forsake or ignore all traditional religious and ecclesiastical teachings and traditions.

Under the auspices of growing religious freedom, a criticism of religion and its historical institutions thus became possible which had not been known before in Western civilization. The churches were not able to cope with it, largely because they refused to criticize themselves. This attitude of theirs only increased the hostility that was being displayed toward them.

Now it is a noteworthy fact that this open or hidden desertion of Christianity by so many people of the Western nations did not bring about the rise of a new religion which conceivably might, some day, become an actual rival of Christianity. What did happen was that some of the world views and cultural and social-political programs, which came into being in connection with the profound cultural changes of the world, were imbued by some of their adherents with a religiousness that sometimes rivaled the faith of Christians, especially in the case where the forms of these movements were patterned after the orders, procedures, and even the rituals of the churches. We can say that Communism, socialism, scientific humanism, nationalism, and even the so-called democratic faith have been or are being embraced in some parts of the Western world by some people as if they were secular gospels destined to take the place of the gospel of Christ. But we can hardly maintain that this tendency is characteristic of modern man and his attitude toward religion. What is characteristic of him is that he has become profoundly critical of and uneasy with historic Christianity.

The emergence of this negative mood in respect to Christianity must be seen as one of the most important features of modern civilization. We cannot properly assess the prospect of religion unless we recognize the unique significance of this fact in the whole context of Western cultural history.

We can perhaps understand more readily what has been happening when we consider who are today regarded as the most competent interpreters of basic human attitudes toward the cosmos, man, and God. They are thinkers of the nineteenth century who coupled the advocacy of their own programs and philosophy with sharp criticisms of traditional religion. Søren Kierkegaard undertook an attack upon Christendom, because he believed that its conventionalism and institutionalism made it impossible for a churchman really to become a Christian. He has become the fountainhead of a criticism of the churches which constitutes an attack upon their institutionalism in the name of existential truth, informed, to be sure, by the gospel, but tending to avoid or bypass or even oppose the practice of real churchmanship. Karl Marx taught his followers to regard religion as the opium of the people. He thereby directed his criticism against the churches' tendency of allying themselves with the ruling or dominating classes of society, thus making religion appear subservient to the interests of those who wield political and economic power. Friedrich Nietzsche proclaimed that God is dead. He was the profoundest of the prophets who are wont to proclaim the message that a renewal of human culture cannot be realized except against the background of a consciously cultivated hostility against the spirit of the Christian religion because it is felt that it tends to enslave men. Sigmund Freud considered religion an illusion. Because he has so profoundly shaped the outlook upon life of contemporary novelists, poets, and artists generally, he is chiefly responsible for the fact that most of those who see life about them through the eyes of artist-interpreters tend to regard religion and its cultural forms as some kind of a cloak under which men struggle for self-identity and an authentic existence.

All these attitudes are marked by the spirit of a sharp criticism of religion, particularly if they are brought to bear on the historic

Christian churches and institutions. This must be kept in mind when one tries to evaluate the widespread indifference toward religion. It is now customary to describe this indifference as secularism. But this term is an inadequate description of the spiritual situation of modern man, because it does not suggest with sufficient clarity that the neglect of religion and the emancipation from its rituals and mores are inspired by a profound hostility toward Christianity and by a conscious denial of its truth. This means that, as Hendrik Kraemer has shown in his lectures on "The Communication of the Christian Faith," that communication has broken down in the Christian world, because communication can take place only if there prevails some community among men, indeed, "if there is a common universe of discourse among them which is based on the same fundamental assumptions and on the same imponderable reactions to the totality of life."

This observation should cause us to understand that the partly open and partly secret persecutions to which first the Bolshevists and then the Nazis subjected the Christian churches were expressions of an extremistic possibility that inheres in the present mood of Western civilization. In this connection, we must also recognize the tragic fact that both German National Socialism and Russian Communism were and are products of Western civilization itself, though they represent the declared enemies of Western Christian civilization. Indeed, they constitute the proof of the fact that modern Western civilization has brought forth spiritual forces which design its destruction. This means that the so-called East-West conflict is not properly understood if it is not seen as a conflict within the realm of Western civilization itself. Its outcome will be decided by the respective strength of the forces of true Christianity and antireligion.

It is one of the most distinctive features of the work of Emil Brunner that he has attempted to take into account this condition of Christianity in the life of modern civilization. He has directed his attention not only to the problems of the relation between Christianity and civilization and repeatedly so and on several levels of depth, but also to the question of the proper understanding of the church. In this connection, he has endeavored to show how a true Christian life and a true Christian church must and can be realized in Christendom. What is particularly interesting is that, in these latter years, he has raised his warning voice against the threat of totalitarianism of any form but especially of Russian Communism that hangs over Western civilization. Assuming that in the following chapters the implications of all this will be dealt with in detail, I content myself here with this general statement.

II.

Turning to the churches themselves and to the new developments in their history, we are bound to say, first of all, that at the same time that modern totalitarian regimes strove to suppress the free functioning of the Christian religion, the churches expanded to the ends of the world. Making use of the modern means of communication, they succeeded in extending the tremendous missionary effort of the nineteenth century by filling Christians everywhere with the sense of membership in one world-church. This development is characteristic of Roman Catholicism and Protestantism alike and it runs parallel in their recent history, but it has failed to bring about a rapprochment between them.

The most remarkable aspect of this manifestation of a world-church-consciousness is not the fact that by it international Christian bodies like the International Missionary Council or the World's Student Christian Federation have become perfected, but that the younger churches, the product of Western missionary enterprise, have come to participate actively and creatively in the affairs of world Christendom. And nothing has been more impressive in this participation than the ever new insistence of the spokesmen of the younger churches of Asia and Africa that the churches of the West should learn to overcome their divisions, that they should learn to distinguish the gospel from the historical forms which were created to serve it, and that new forms should be fashioned for the gospel now freshly understood in its universal character.

The actual realization of the world-church and the formation of new bodies exhibiting it will be brought about, if at all, through the services and by the activities of the World Council of Churches. This ecumenical organization represents the most important and effective countermove of non-Roman Christianity against those forces which erode the churches from within and undermine them from without. To be sure, the ecumenical movement did not come into being by way of a conscious defense of organized Christendom against its opponents, but it must be regarded as the result of a conscious effort of Christians to correct those weaknesses of the churches from which their critics derive justified support.

In the work of foresighted, bold Christian men like Brent, Mott, Söderblom, Temple, and Visser 't Hooft, to mention only a few of the outstanding leaders, the ecumenical movement fulfills and serves certain basic Christian needs: 1) it demonstrates that the gospel in the name of which worldwide missions were and are being undertaken is one, even in a divided Christendom; 2) it seeks to bring about a fellowship of the churches through mutual recognition and to cause them to break their tendency of staying bound to the exclusivistic isolationism of their denominational particularisms in spite of their own profession of faith in the unity and catholicity of the church; 3) it lets Christians everywhere act as agents of reconciliation in a divided world and give evidence of repentance for the fact that the churches had proved themselves unable to prevent two world wars on the soil of so-called Christian civilization; 4) it organizes worldwide services of mutual assistance, interchurch aid, and relief of suffering in order that the healing power of Christian love may overcome some of the evil produced by the hatred of some men for their fellow men.

Until now, these purposes have just begun to be realized. It is therefore impossible to say how much has been definitely achieved by the ecumenical enterprise. But there can be no doubt that the formation of its several organizations, and especially of the World Council of Churches, represents a very great accomplishment. In fact, it represents the most important event in the history of Christianity since the beginning of this century. Despite the fact that the World Council is still small in size and power and that next to the numerous historical and conventional Christian undertakings it constitutes but a little effort on the part of the churches, its function and its activities far exceed in importance any other enterprise in recent Christian history.

The work of Emil Brunner fully reflects this important event. Just as he himself, throughout his career as a professor of theology, has been active in the different phases of the ecumenical movement, so he has given his theological work a character and form appropriate to the spirit of ecumenicity. Brunner himself has carried the responsibility of a preacher, teacher, and spiritual leader in his own Reformed Church of Zurich; indeed he has practiced churchmanship in an exemplary way, but he never permitted himself to observe or display denominationalist partisanship or provincialism. He has always been an ecumenically-minded theologian. He will be remembered with special respect and affection for the fact that as he brought his work in his own church and university to a close, he chose to serve for a time as a professor in the International Christian University in Japan. Thus he demonstrated even more effectively than he had done before, through lectures and many other contacts in the countries of Europe and North America and through the following that he had acquired then by his books, that he had always understood himself as a worker in the world church. Very few Christian theologians, especially among the Protestants, have conceived their work on such a broad catholic basis as he has done and achieved a truly ecumenical theological stature similar to his.

III.

Brunner's theological writings show very fully what doctrines and themes those theologians found it necessary to stress who understood themselves to be the interpreters of the gospel in a world determined by forces and movements of the kind we have described. The Protestant thinkers who are commonly regarded as the theological leaders of the present age, that is, as those who set the tone, are, to name only the most prominent ones, Karl Barth, Emil Brunner, Rudolf Bultmann, Anders Nygren, Paul Tillich, Reinhold Niebuhr. They all belong to the same generation. All were born in the late eighties of the last century and are now in the eighth decade of their lives. They all were brought up and educated in a world which, as we now know, was headed toward the cataclysm and debacle of the world wars but, before the actual outbreak of the conflict, was held to be the scene of certain human progress and achievement. They all had just begun their careers at the time when the First World War broke out and they had to make a new beginning of sorts when the war was over. In some way, every one of them became, sooner or later, conscious of the fact that the phase of Western civilization which had begun in the Enlightenment had come to an end and that a new era was beginning, a cultural era whose character they were destined to shape.

As Protestant theologians, they all had been trained in the methods and traditions of theological liberalism. Their thinking was determined by concerns of which Schleiermacher had been the first and principal spokesman. But when, after 1918, they formulated the plans and programs for their theological careers, they found themselves driven to break with the tradition that had formed their thinking. They all became "neo-orthodox" or were so labeled by their critics. Most of these belonged to the older generation who thought that the affirmation or reaffirmation of any kind of orthodoxy constituted a betrayal of the hard-won achievements of liberal theology. Harnack, the most representative man of this generation of scholars, professed, with special respect to the thought of Karl Barth who, from the beginning, was the most prominent of the neo-orthodox theologians, that he would never have thought it possible that during his own lifetime a way of thinking would emerge which he would be unable to receive and comprehend for lack of an "aerial."

There was no unanimity among the neo-orthodox—neither at the beginning nor at any later time. To be sure, Barth, Brunner, and Gogarten were united, for several years, as editors of the journal, *Zwischen den Zeiten,* and Bultmann too belonged to this circle. There developed profound differences between Barth and Brunner, and, indeed, in the course of the years, Barth was criticized by every one of these neo-orthodox theologians and he in turn attacked them in some connection or other. Some of these thinkers should never have been called neo-orthodox, Tillich and Bultmann, for example. Others were in fact never neo-orthodox, theologically speaking: Reinhold Niebuhr, for instance. He was called by this name chiefly by the social and political liberals among the American Protestants whose easy optimism and amelioristic utopianism he had subjected to scathing attacks. And there are deep differences between Tillich and Niebuhr, and between Tillich and Bultmann— but then there is the very interesting fact that despite many points of divergence which set his theology apart from the teaching of the others, Brunner's thought is closely related to or can at least readily be connected with that of all the others. This means that his theology is linked by the most lines of contact to that of others. In this sense, he can be regarded as the most representative of those theologians who shaped the thought of the last generation of Protestants.

There are five large themes with which these theologians have been preoccupied. These themes indicate on which foundations the Christian churches stand today as they occupy a minority position in society, at the same time having become spiritually more powerful through the ecumenical movement.

There is, first of all, the emphasis upon the word of God, the interpretation of the Christian faith in terms of what God says to man rather than on what from his own "religious resources" man finds himself able to say to himself about God. This emphasis has brought about a theology of revelation, that is, an interest in the knowledge of God which is guided by the acknowledgment of God's disclosure of himself in Christ and not by a preoccupation with the epistemological resources of the human mind—all this is in radical opposition to the line of thought of modern Protestant theology since Schleiermacher who, in his *Glaubenslehre,* had chosen to say that the term "revelation" is better applied only to the region of the higher self-consciousness. The consequence of this reorientation was that first the theological and then also the ecclesiastical leaders turned away from so-called "cultural Protestantism" and from all attempts "to make the gospel intellectually respectable" (as a telling phrase ran that was current among American ministers a generation ago). Instead of asking: What has modern man to say about the gospel? the theologians now concerned themselves with the question: What does the gospel say to modern man?

Closely connected with this predominating theme is a new Biblicism. It must be called "new" in contrast to the traditionalist and the modernist views of the Bible. It is a view of the Bible which is different from that which can be obtained by the use of the historical method for the interpretation of historical texts and documents, because it takes the books of the Bible as the bearers of a kerygma, a message of salvation that must be believed. On the other hand, it has nothing in common with the view of the fundamentalists, who stress the literal inerrancy of the Bible as if this were the foremost article of the Christian faith. The new Biblicism is oriented to the message of the Bible, the gospel of Christ, insofar as it is to be conveyed to the men of today. It is preoccupied with the concern: how to communicate the gospel. It is marked by the deep awareness of the fact that most men of today find the gospel to be a scandal and a provocation to them. But it knows that deep down this provocation is not caused by the form in which the gospel is expressed in the Bible, say in connection with the Ptolomaic world view but that it is because of the fact that the gospel promises healing and salvation to man by calling him to the obedience of God and by offering him renewal through the forgiveness of sins. This view is basically that of all the theologians we have named, but they present it in different ways. Its most radical and incisive spokesman is Rudolf Bultmann who, unfortunately, was misunderstood by many when he introduced the term "demythologizing" in order to make plain in what way the Bible must be translated both as to form and content in order that it can be understood by the man of today. Bultmann does not discard what he considers the archaic mythological world view of the Bible. He stresses again and again that the men of the Bible presuppose this world view. Yet he says that because we no longer think in the same mythical terms as the men of the Bible, we must demythologize the Bible, that is, speak of the message the Bible presents in ways that translate it so that it can be comprehended.

Throughout his career, Brunner has been a powerful defender of this new Biblicism. It is characteristic of him that, although he too finds something to criticize in Bultmann's view (Cf. *Dogmatics*, Vol. II, pp. 262-270), he is on the whole more sympathetic to it than, say, Barth on the one hand and Tillich on the other.

He is sharply critical of liberal theology and he rejects Schleiermacher and Harnack much more severely than even Barth does, but at the same time he freely acknowledges his indebtedness to the accomplishments of this theology, especially in the field of the history of doctrine. This is the third important trait of the work of contemporary theology: the liberal theology, which it censures so strictly in many parts, nevertheless is allowed to live on in its connection with the historical interpretation of Christianity—to the point that it is recognized on principle that because everything human is subject to change, also Christianity and particularly Christian theology, are not exempt from it. Though their accomplishments as historical interpreters differ, and though they assess the importance of the historical method in different ways, the influential contemporary theologians have given evidence of the importance they attach to historical work. Barth has published a very competent series of lectures in the history of modern theology, and the volumes of his *Church Dogmatics* are filled with large and small historical analyses of all sorts of Christian ideas. Nygren's fame as a theologian rests upon his historical-theological analysis of the idea of love. Niebuhr's chief work, *The Nature and Destiny of Man,* is basically a historical analysis of the Christian doctrine of man. Bultmann is a specialist of Biblical exegesis and as such a master of the historical method. Tillich thinks basically in historical terms and so also does Brunner.

The liberal theology in which they were trained has left them a powerful legacy. This is as it ought to be—for it is impossible for any modern interpreter of Christianity to think in any other historical terms. Here much still remains to be done.

In this connection, we must, fourthly, note the indebtedness of contemporary theology to Reformation research. What would neo-orthodoxy in all its shades and shadings be without the Luther-and-Calvin Renaissance which has been going on now for more than a generation and which has made it possible for the great Protestant Reformers to speak in their own name as they have not been able to do in any previous period of Protestant history! And to what a remarkable extent are all the leading contemporary theologians under the sway of Luther and Calvin, even if each of them, here too, is not uncritical. There are large passages in Barth's *Dogmatics* which are nothing other than reverberations of Luther's faith. Brunner calls upon Luther again and again as his chief ally, especially insofar as he understands the Christian faith and life as a personal encounter with the gospel of the forgiveness of faith. Bultmann's existentialism is Lutheran through and through. Niebuhr's basic teaching is nothing but a modern version of Luther's view of men as *simul iustus ac peccator*. And it is characteristic even of Tillich that the most powerful and persuasive passages of his book *The Courage to Be* are directly inspired by Martin Luther.

We should recognize that this remarkably influential revival of the teaching of the Reformers has been brought about chiefly not by their denominational followers, that is, those who would cultivate a study of their thought because of denominational loyalties and interests, but by a historical-scientific investigation and interpretation of the teachings of the Reformers undertaken in connection with work on the critical edition of their writings. Also this contemporary interest in the Reformation is the result of the historical labors which the liberal theologians introduced into the life of Protestantism.

Finally, we must call attention to the fact, especially in connection with the work of Emil Brunner, that present-day theology is ecumenical in character and outlook. This is so, not only because all the leading and representative contemporary theologians, and especially those with whom we deal here, have been active participants in ecumenical work, but especially because the very nature and character of their theological thinking is ecumenical. None of them think and speak on behalf of the particular denomination to which he happens to belong and none chooses to deny his denominational home in any way (for the simple reason, in the last resort, that no man can jump out of his skin!), but every one of them addresses himself as a theological interpreter of Christianity to Christians everywhere and to all sorts and conditions of men. This may not be the expression of an ecumenical theology in the strict sense of the term but it is certainly a fine display of ecumenicity: the interpretation of the Christian gospel on the basis of the recognition of the fact that Jesus Christ is believed in and worshiped as the revealer of God in many ways and forms and that these ways and forms must be respected, listened to, and understood. Indeed they must become the subject of conversation and communal thinking, a thinking that includes both a sharing and a readiness to bestow and to accept criticism and therefore leads to rethinking.

As we have already indicated in connection with our discussion of the ecumenical movement, it is our conviction that Brunner has proved himself to be throughout the years an ecumenical theologian *par excellence.*

WILHELM PAUCK

DEPARTMENT OF HISTORICAL THEOLOGY
UNION THEOLOGICAL SEMINARY
NEW YORK, N.Y.

2

Eberhard Müller

THE CHURCH IN ACTION

THE CHURCH IN ACTION

E mil Brunner is a strange phenomenon for many present-day theologians and churchmen. The reason is that in the rather unusual situation in which we now find ourselves, Brunner is at one and the same time a church activist and a learned professor. This combination was still quite customary in the days of Martin Luther, but today many European theologians feel that it is detrimental to the seriousness of scholarly work and to its prestige for the scholar at the same time to get involved in church activities. If someone says of the professor that he is a church activist many people raise the question whether this does not in itself reveal a theologically dubious tendency toward Americanism.

The reason why Emil Brunner combines scholarship and activity within the church is not because he wants to keep his finger in the pie, so to speak, of church activities—a desire which among good Christians even occurs among professors—it is rather a question of principle and is connected with his theology. It was his theology that caused Brunner to get involved in the Oxford Movement and to make his house available for the planning of missionary campaigns in Switzerland. It was also his theology that caused him to abandon his library (just imagine a professor doing that!) and go to Tokyo for two years. The reason for Brunner's church activism lies especially in his anthropology and in his concept of the church. Both of these prevent him from being satisfied with systematic theology alone. Brunner cannot work theologically without having participated intensively in the life of those who are to be the final consumers of his theology, that is, the Christian community, or even the communities of people who are distant from Christianity. Brunner feels that it is impossible for a theologian to do his work well if he is turned only toward those things which come to him from

41

the past, that is, the Holy Scripture and the confessions of the church. The theologian must know what he is doing if he wants his theology to "get across." Correct interpretation alone does not fulfill the demand of the church for true doctrine. Only that doctrine can be understood which in addition to right interpretation also has the right point of contact (*Anknüpfung*) with that which the listener already knows and understands. Otherwise the interpretation is nothing but the fruitless monologue of the interpreter. For this reason Brunner is interested not only in theology and the doctrine of the church, but equally in modern man and the service of proclaiming the gospel to him.

In Brunner's theology one may observe, then, the constant movement from exegetical and systematic theology toward practical theology. It is of prime importance to him that his message is communicated. He feels responsible for this as a theologian. One almost gets the impression that he would like to be promoted from professor of systematic theology to professor of practical theology. This too has its theological reasons. If the church is mainly interested in the intended content of its proclamation, that is, in pure doctrine, and no longer in the means of proclamation (as we constantly hear from the Barthian school of theology), then the professors of practical theology are indeed only a kind of *clarus menar* of their exegetical and systematic colleagues.

Concern for the missionary and pastoral tasks of the church is for Brunner a theological necessity. Dialectical theology for Brunner is always a dialogue, not only one between theologians or, even less, between antagonistic theological concepts. An essential part of theological dialectics is the tension between the church and the world, between the proclaimer of the gospel and the unbelieving listener. For Brunner man is not simply a phonograph record passively receiving the word of God. Before the gospel reaches him, even the most Godless man is not just a *trunkus et lapis,* a clod or stone, as the old Protestant orthodox theologians, Amsdorf and Flacius, taught,[1] presumably following some of Luther's extreme remarks on the subject. Man, even fallen man, is not simply nothing vis-à-vis God. It is worthwhile to speak with even the most Godless man and to listen to him because even this man already knows

---

[1] Brunner, *Der Mensch im Widerspruch* (Berlin: Furche Verlag, 1937), pp. 550 ff. See: "Die andere Aufgabe der Theologie"; *Zwischen den Zeiten,* III, 1929, p. 264.

something which has to be taken seriously, to be taken into consideration, and which, under certain circumstances, may even have to be included in the act of proclamation. "The gospel does not turn to a man who knows nothing about God." [2]

There exists, then, for Brunner "another task of theology." In addition to the systematic, exegetical discipline of the theologian there is another one which is turned toward the world and which Brunner calls eristic theology (from the Greek word *aredzene*, "to debate"). This word does not imply that Brunner is a special friend of theological quarrels which usually are simply quarrels among theologians. Rather, it is his intention that theology should be in a constant state of communication with the actual present world, with its thoughts, its needs, and its temptations. A theology degenerates if it retreats to the area of "right" interpretation and conceptualization. Hence the demand for an eristic theology. Brunner does not call this theological task apologetics, as had been previously the custom, because his eristic is not concerned at all with the defense of Christian faith, but rather with its attack. Also, he does not call his theological task a polemic one because he is not engaged in polemic against something, but in battle for something.

It seems to be that in his dialectical theology Brunner is concerned with something which has been clearly defined by the Americans. The Americans distinguish between discussion and debate. Both are forms of human dialectic. The two forms are differentiated by the attitude one takes toward the person with whom one is engaged in this dialectical process. In a debate both sides start with the assumption that the partner knows nothing of the truth. The debate is supposed to convince him of the worthlessness of his opinions or even of his person. As early as Greek philosophy, Protagoras wrote the first textbook on debating, and gave it the title *The Conquering Speech*. In theology, which is of the opinion that Godless man finds himself in complete benightedness and that there is no point of contact *(Anknüpfung)* with which it would be worthwhile to discuss with him questions of faith, one seems compelled to regard the debate as consisting of conquering speech, the only form of spiritual communication possible with such a person. Some modern evangelists, indeed, are of the opinion that missionary proclamation consists of the administration of a kind of spiritual electro-

[2] Brunner, "Die andere Aufgabe der Theologie," *loc. cit.*, p. 262.

shock with the purpose of total conversion. Proclamation has, for them, only one purpose: that the listener should be brought to silence so that the word of God alone should speak.

The situation is completely different if I am engaged in a discussion in which I assume that the other person, even if he is a Godless, unbelieving man, already knows something. Then it becomes worthwhile to discuss matters with him, to take seriously his knowledge and his good intentions, even if both are far removed from that which is said by God's Word. Because even in this knowledge and in these good intentions there is still something of the gift of true human dignity and of the image of God which is given to every man by the spirit of God.

It is this respect for the other person, this taking seriously even of his unclear thoughts, which Brunner would like to defend in his "contact theology." It is as if with every one of his theological propositions Brunner calls to his opponents in the words of Isaiah: "do not destroy it, for there is a blessing in it." (Isa. 65:8). This blessing is the secret of personality in every man, even the one who is farthest from God. Theology is to address this personality, and to address that which it already knows, and it is for this reason that Christ's command is to go out into the world and make all peoples disciples. (Matt. 28:19).

The command to make disciples of all peoples includes the task of going to the physical and spiritual place in which people are located in order to find out what they are in this place. The Christian preacher must regard man as a person who can be addressed as the possessor of a conscience, as a man "in contradiction with himself." It is the task of theology to enter this contradiction of man with himself through the proclamation of God's message. Theology and proclamation, despite the fact that they bring God's message, cannot simply place themselves against man or over man. They must place themselves at the side of man. Christian proclamation must take the side of Godless man who has been called into existence by the love of God. The Christian proclamation must struggle with this person against his own contradiction. Brunner is convinced that in every man there is a will and a knowledge at the side of which the proclaimer can place himself, where he can find his "point of contact."

According to Brunner, then, dialectical theology is to use the method of discussion, not of debate. If, indeed, man who has not yet heard the gospel finds himself in total night, if in him there is

no knowledge, no will, and no being with which it would be worthwhile to enter into communication before the face of God, then of
course discussion with him would be useless. Then there is no point
in discussing anything with him. Then one can only try to annihilate
his resistance spiritually. He should be brought not to speak, but
to be silent, because hearing then no longer means the association
of one's own with other thoughts, but it becomes the receptivity of
a phonograph record in which everything must be cleared that has
previously been written on it.

Probably Brunner is not without justification in fearing that the
thoughts of his theological opponents have these consequences with
regard to the conception of man and his relationship to God. Ed-
mund Schlinck, for instance, states that the church should indeed
attempt to understand the special circumstances of a man's existence
and position. The place must be discovered "where he may be taken
so that he should realize that he is intended in the message." [3] However, Schlinck feels that in the last resort this attempt will be fruitless. He even sharpens his thesis in the proposition: "the commandment to make disciples cannot be carried out." In a certain sense
Schlinck's understanding of theology would also include a process
of communication between church and world, between the proclaimer and he who is supposed to listen to the proclamation. But
this process simply has the didactic role which the Americans would
express by the words "to debate." It is to wake men up and interest
them in a question so that they may be ready to listen. After this
interest has been aroused, however, it would be quite fruitless to
enter into discussion with the other man because he who is caught
in sin lives in total night. He knows nothing about God and about
the good which would be of any use. It is senseless to assume that
fallen man possesses an element where something is dawning, where
one could attempt to "get across" with a proclamation of the gospel.
Such human speculations and attempts are senseless. It is the task
of the divine radar station by remote control to see to it that the
airplane of proclamation gets to its destination. It would seem that
the proclaimer himself can in the meantime go ahead and sleep in
the pilot's seat. At the most he should see to it that his "airplane"
should be theologically and exegetically in good condition. Naturally none of Brunner's theological opponents would put it this

[3] Schlinck, *Der Mensch in der Verkuendigung der Kirche*, p. 249.

way. But is this not the consequence of a theology that denies any point of contact in man for the proclamation of the gospel?

Brunner passionately opposes such views. If the word can reach its destination only through a divine miracle, and without human means, then, indeed, the theologian has no other task than to proclaim pure doctrine. Then theology can only debate with men in order to bring them to a silent listening of the Word of God. Brunner maintains, however, that the church should enter into a genuine discussion with man. It should take seriously the fact that every man already has something which may contribute to true insight, that he is capable of responding to the address of God so that the continuing discussion may lead to increasing insight.[4]

Brunner, of course, recognizes that without the action of the divine spirit all our actions, including those of the proclaimer and the listener, are senseless. Luther is right when he says, "all our actions are in vain, even those of the best light." It is true that everything depends upon God's blessing.[5]

Without the sovereignly free action of the divine spirit, even the most skillful *Anknüpfung* and condescension, the most convincing discussion, will not make disciples. But was it not Christ himself who commanded his followers to make disciples? Did not Paul even describe himself as God's collaborator?[6]

Has Christ not ordered the task of making disciples in the same way in which he has ordered the listening to the Word and the proclamation of the preacher? It is for this reason that Brunner says: "God builds his church, but he makes disciples only through human actions, taking those as his tools, and it is for this reason that the concern for man is on principle the same as the concern for the Word of God. . . . If all human actions are senseless, then certainly theology is senseless too."[7]

---

[4] "The relationship between God and man can never be described in terms of the sole efficacy of God, because God's creation of man posits from the beginning a relationship of mutality. This means, and it is God's will, that the divine actions with regard to man always respect man's subjectivity. Also God's acts of grace are not a manipulation of man, but an intercourse with him. This intercourse is the opposite of manipulation, because through it God's Word of love changes man's defiance into voluntary obedience. . . . God is always concerned that man, even as a sinner, be not overwhelmed, but addressed as a subject. The decisive fact behind the concept of *Anknüpfung* is that God always approaches man by addressing him" (Brunner, *Der Mensch im Widerspruch*, p. 553).

[5] *Ibid.*, p. 547.

[6] 1. Cor. 3:9. Brunner, *Der Mensch im Widerspruch*, p. 548.

[7] *Ibid.*, p. 548.

This leads to the following consequence: If practical theology cannot hope to receive any enlightenment as to where and how men are to be met with the word of God, as to how man can be addressed, and as to what way he may listen (because supposedly God has reserved this prerogative to himself), with what right then, does exegetical and systematic theology hope to be enlightened about the right content of the Word of God? Perhaps God has also reserved that prerogative to Himself. Perhaps He gives this kind of illumination without any theological work, and without any human attempt, if He so desires.

No, says Brunner. God directs man to activity, not to passivity. "Human reason and divine revelation stand not only in a negative, but in a positive relationship to each other." "The secret of faith which becomes effective in love is the union of both the divine and the human word." [8]

"The Bible never understands man, least of all in matters of faith, as a *trunkus et lapis,* as an object. It always considers him as a responsible subject. This responsible subject is not created by the proclamation, but it is presupposed in the act of proclamation. The subject, Paul, is not created anew by the Word of God; it is rather presupposed to exist by the Word of God." [9]

There can be disagreement as to whether Brunner is entirely right in this conception. It is quite possible that the condition, being a person, does indeed only emerge as that person is addressed, as he becomes responsible. Luther once put it this way: "if God talks to anyone, be it in anger or in grace, then this one is truly immortal." Indeed, being a person, a subject, is not something given in itself, but something which only emerges in the polarity with the vow (compare the psychological concept of individuation). It is even possible that the *thou* of my fellow men only becomes a thou for me after my eye has been redeemed from its loneliness by God's address, so that I can become a partner for the other man, indeed, become an I. But even if this would be the case, the proclamation of the gospel would still be faced with the theological and pastoral task of looking for the point of contact at which unbelieving man may be found, at which his insight is beginning to dawn, at which a responsible subjectivity has awakened in him. For God has already spoken before the proclaimer begins to speak. Man already possesses the consciousness of responsibility and contradiction

[8] Brunner, *Der Mensch im Widerspruch,* p. 549. See Gal. 5:6.
[9] *Ibid.,* p. 550.

which may be addressed by God's Word even before he meets the bearer of the proclamation. Unless this faith exists, there is no sense at all for the church to enter into action.

Also, the commandment to make disciples of all peoples can be carried out only in this confidence. God Himself gives Moses the assurance that He, God Himself, will go in advance of Moses and proclaim His name.[10]

Before God's people come to a strange place, before God's messengers speak to men there, God has *already* spoken to them. Only there, where the rain of divine blessing is already come down, is there any sense to sow the Word. Should it not be a task of theology to search for those places where God has already awakened in man something of true knowledge and true subjectivity, and to take these places seriously and to use them as points of departure?

No one should say that it is impossible for the proclaimer to recognize that condition in man wherein God has already spoken to him and wherein he may be addressed, wherein he *is* a responsible subject. Otherwise how would it be possible for the theologian to recognize the Word of God in the Bible, even to translate it into our language, if he were not in a position to recognize this word of God also in his human brother?

For Emil Brunner, then, church-in-action is nothing else but the task of translation, of building of bridges between two shores. It appears senseless to him if the messenger of the gospel only walks up and down proclaiming on one shore in order to go back and forth between the two. This going back and forth is part of dialectical theology.

Brunner has seen more clearly than other theologians what the significance for theology is of the various attempts of the church to understand the place of the temptations and decisions of men in their everyday life. Both the journeys of the theologians into history and his journeys into the world of present-day reality appear for Brunner to be indispensable for the translation of the Christian message which is the task of theology.

This theological position links Brunner with our evangelical academies in Germany and made him the founder of the Institution of the Church of Zurich where in constantly changing groups men from different occupational areas enter into communication with

[10] Exod. 33:19.

the church. Theology has the task of making available the work of Scripture and of purifying the proclamation of the church. This task can be fulfilled only in action and the constant meeting with men as they live today and so with their questions: "Brethren, what shall we do?" [11]

This question was a burning concern to us in Germany when in the year 1945, we asked ourselves what we as Christians could do for the inner regeneration of our people. Most of us agreed about the spiritual developments that brought about the moral catastrophe of the Hitler regime. We ascribed this to the philosophy of positivism for which there is no reality and no binding orders unless they be objectively knowable. Our judges and government officials had concluded that there was nothing but the "positive law," that is, the law as proclaimed by the state, and brought together in statutes. Everything else they had been taught was subjective, relative, and uncertain. The moral task of the judge consisted exclusively in interpreting correctly and honestly the existing statutes. Unfortunately this philosophy simply could not imagine the case of the state itself incorporating positive injustice in law.

During the Nazi period we had learned that there had to be a higher justice, unless the law of the state were not to be simply based upon sheer power. In 1945 the question was this: How can this higher power be used as a criterion for legal order and legal practice in society? During the first conference of the newly founded Evangelical Academy of Bad Boll some higher judges passionately posed this question. These judges had been removed from their positions by the American military government despite the fact that "they had always carefully observed the laws." During this conference one of the participants made the remark that Professor Brunner in Zurich under the impact of the Nazi experience had written a book entitled *Justice*. Supposedly this book would contain some answers for the German question of 1945 and in such a way that not only theologians but also jurists could find in it some guidance for the exercise of their profession. It is for this reason that Brunner's *Justice* was one of the first theological books printed in Germany after the war (and printed on paper that had been donated by Americans). To many people this book was more important than calories.

[11] Acts 2:37.

So—Brunner wishes to interpret God's orders for the real world, for the generation living today, in such a way that people may use its standards for shaping the society, the economy of the twentieth century, and the patterns of a just order. It is this task which Brunner also attempted to meet in his other great work, *Das Gebort und Teordsungen*. Both works are in fact a practical application of his theology of dialogue. It is a theology which has listened to the world because it speaks to it, which has taken seriously the good which is to be found in the law, the order, and in the conscience of men in the world, before it demands that men should take seriously the revelation of God.

Church-in-action is precisely that church which goes into all the social, political, scientific, and cultural situations of the modern world, which goes wherever man is concerned, where his responsibility is awakened or is being silenced, where humanity is being protested, where attempts are being made to bring about a better human existence. For it is in all these places, in the structure of modern society where modern man is concerned with man in the best sense of the word, that God somehow has already spoken to men before we appear as the proclaimers of the gospel.

Brunner's bitterest enemy is the false sense of security of the church and theology. We live in a time in which all sciences are attempting to solve cooperatively the problems posed by cooperative society. A theology remaining in splendid isolation, not concerning itself with its possible points of contacts with the conditions of this world, can thus become itself one of the great dangers of the church.

This brings us to the second basic concern of Brunner's theology and of his church activity, namely, his conception of the church. At first, Brunner's doctrine of the church seems to have a disintegrating tendency, "the ecclesia of the New Testament, the community of Jesus Christ is a pure community of persons and has nothing in it of the character of an institution. For this reason it is misleading to identify with the community of Christ any of the historically developed churches which all have the character of institutions." [12]

With this proposition Brunner challenges two millenia of church history. The reader might ask himself whether Brunner with such a thesis does not himself forsake the practice of Anknüpfung and

---

[12] Brunner, *Das Missverstaendnis der Kirche* (Zurich: Zwingli Verlag, 1951), p. 21.

whether he does not attempt to build a church in thin air under wings of New Testament exegesis. It would not be the first time that such a thing has been attempted. We would do well first to investigate what Brunner's practical aims are in proposing this conception of the church in the present world. After that we might be in a better position to decide whether his conception of the church is adequate to grasp either the church or the world.

EBERHARD MÜLLER

PASTOR AND DIRECTOR
EVANGELICAL ACADEMY
BAD BOLL, GERMANY

3

Hugh Vernon White

BRUNNER'S MISSIONARY THEOLOGY

BRUNNER'S MISSIONARY THEOLOGY

Emil Brunner contributed an article to *The Christian Century* in 1949 in which he declared that first among new understandings in his thinking was "that of the 'missionary situation' of the church." He writes:

This is probably a matter that distinguishes my thinking from Karl Barth's. Barth thinks as a churchman for the church; I think rather as a missionary . . . this is the problem of my *Man in Revolt,* and especially of the two books that followed it, *The Divine Human Encounter* and *Revelation and Reason.* But I am aware that I have only begun this task. . . . I shall have to entrust its continuation to the younger generation. The word I leave with them is, 'Missionary Theology.' [1]

In the Foreword to his *Dogmatik,* published three years earlier, Brunner had said that the church has always had a twofold teaching function, one directed inward to the church itself and one outward to the unbelieving and doubting world. Of these two the first is the most fundamental but the latter, in our time, is the most urgent. "Hence dogmatics serves first of all those who themselves exercise a teaching office in the Church, as clergy and missionaries, evangelists, pastors, and catechists." [2]

The same missionary and pastoral interest is expressed in the Foreword of the second volume of the *Dogmatik* where fruitfulness of the idea of revelation as the truth of a divine-human encounter is counted on to "awaken in the Church a missionary and pastoral spirit." [3]

Consistently with these statements Emil Brunner has been a

[1] *The Christian Century,* Vol. 66, 1949, p. 817.

[2] Brunner, *The Christian Doctrine of God,* Eng. trans. (London: Lutterworth Press, 1949), p. v.

[3] Brunner, *The Christian Doctrine of Creation and Redemption,* Eng. trans. (London: Lutterworth Press, 1952), p. vi.

preacher and missionary. The two years he spent teaching in the Japan International Christian University represent a natural and logical result of his theology as well as of his personal dedication. In more general terms he may be characterized as an *evangelical* theologian. Thus he embodies the basic emphasis of the Reformation and indeed of Western Christianity upon Redemption. He sees that theology is not just a discussion within the church, as to how we are saved by the gracious revelation of God in Christ, but that it is also a declaration to the world of its need of salvation and a setting forth of the Way in the common language of mankind. This means that the missionary task of the church is not an afterthought or a peripheral interest for the theologian but a primary responsibility. Here Brunner follows St. Paul whose great theological work, the letter to the Romans, is a basic exposition of the nature and necessity of the world mission of the Church, and also Thomas Aquinas, who wrote his *Contra Gentiles* as a help toward the conversion of the Moslem invaders of Europe.

While we find explicit statements by Brunner of missionary concern such as those quoted above, the basis of a missionary theology is to be discovered in the underlying conceptions and principles of his systematic theology. Here, at vital points, is rooted the *necessity* of the missionary task of Christianity as historic revelation and in the nature of man as both *imago dei* and *im Widerspruch*. Paralleling the relation of revelation and reason as one of mutual involvement yet also of tension and even conflict, is the fact that the Christian faith is intimately involved with culture, yet never to be identified with it. I shall undertake in this chapter to show the significance of these doctrines and ideas for a developed missionary theology. Since I find myself in substantial agreement with Brunner's basic ideas, I shall simply try to outline briefly such application of them as he has left to the "younger generation," even though I cannot claim to be in that category. It will remain to be seen to what extent Brunner himself accepts as valid this application of his doctrine to missionary theology.

The Doctrine of Man

The doctrine of man developed most fully in *Man in Revolt* is the most important contribution of Emil Brunner to theology.[4]

[4] Brunner, *Man in Revolt* (New York: Charles Scribner's Sons, 1939), pp. 57-167.

The special importance of this doctrine for missionary theology lies in the fact that it demonstrates both the need of all men for salvation, and the possibility of man as man being made aware of his need and receiving the gift of salvation in Christ. The first presents the universal character of man's lostness as *sin;* the second deals with one of the primary problems of missions—that of *communication.* Together they reaffirm in our time and in terms of present-day thought the original Christian conviction that all men have sinned, and also give a theological basis for the confidence that all men can hear and receive the gospel. Both this fact and this possibility have been called in question in recent years.

The doctrine of man as created "in the Word" and as "responsible" determines for Christian faith the fundamental nature of man. It means that the *humanum* consists in a relation to God, a relation that is established by the address of God to each individual. Whatever man's organic origins may be, the emergence of the human *person* is his individual response to God. The universal response of men, however, is one of self-assertion, and of denial and disobedience toward God, despite the fact that the nature of His address is love. This means that the nature but not the original reality of man is that of a sinner, a person whose actual existence is egoistic opposition to his Creator—even while engaged in the religious quest. It also means that while the actual relation of man to God is that of "contradiction," it is still his nature to be related to God; this is his *imago dei.* There is no such thing as a man apart from God, and without some form of consciousness of God. Therefore all men have a knowledge of God even though it be a consciousness of judgment, of wrath, and of separation.

The sin of man, this universal lostness, however understood in the religions of the world or even in secular thought, is really a personal alienation from and enmity against God. It is, therefore, not a predicament with which man himself can cope, because it involves the other Person. The attainment of spiritual enlightenment or of moral perfection or of inner peace cannot effect salvation because these ends are subjective states of the individual; only one person is affected thereby, whereas man's real problem is his relation to the divine Person. Salvation is found in reconciliation. But man cannot reconcile himself with One against whom he has rebelled; God himself must act both to make man aware of his true conditions and to deliver him from the perversion of his nature and the futility of his efforts toward self-salvation. God acts to this end in Christ who is the Mediator, the Word made flesh. The possibility of salvation lies in the fact that man can, through hearing the gospel, recognize and receive this Word as the real Word by which God originally addressed the creature and called him into existence as man, a human person. Here the two parties involved in the act of redemption are both fully involved in their proper and characteristic roles; God the party of the first acting in grace and forgiveness, and man the party of the second part acting in faith and obedience. Thus the necessity of the Mediator, the historic appearance of Jesus Christ, and the witness to this saving act of God by those who have been reconciled.

This doctrine describes the fundamental predicament from which man needs to be saved. It is always a problem for the missionary to awaken men to their sin and the realization of their personal alienation from God. Strangely enough, almost the last thing that man can know is himself, and particularly his relation of personal responsibility to God. Men are always aware of their ignorance, their weaknesses, and their moral defects and in religion seek help from their gods to overcome these evils. But the basic personal relationship, in which responsibility to the holy and loving God constitutes the very nature of man's existence, comes to light only in the self-revelation of God through the prophets and His incarnation in Christ. The first knowledge of this relationship came through the Law but the first effect of Law was to produce a consciousness of sin; the Law made men aware of their responsibility to God but it also condemned them for their disobedience. This in the life of Israel prepared the way for salvation in Christ. But no such revelation of the personal relationship appeared in any other religious tradition. Therefore the Christian missionary faces a fundamental problem, that of awakening men to a true consciousness of sin, not that there is any virtue in having a sense of sin, but that the recognition of a really personal relationship to God must begin with the realization that that personal relationship is wrong and that the wrongness is sin, which is the root of man's predicament and determines his need of salvation.

It is because of this that, as Brunner points out,[5] the scriptures of the world's religions cannot be an "Old Testament" for the gospel.

[5] Brunner, *Revelation and Reason* (Philadelphia: Westminster Press, 1946), pp. 218-236.

For none of them sets man in his true relation to God nor makes him aware of his real need. None has a true anthropology. None formulates aright the problem of man. The quest for salvation, even when it is most intense, is frustrated by man's lack of a true knowledge of himself, through knowledge of God as Creator and Redeemer. Such knowledge cannot be arrived at without revelation. The natural knowledge of God that man has does produce a bad conscience as Paul points out in the first chapter of the Roman letter, but beyond that it cannot go. And the saving knowledge of God's personal relationship to his human creature is not an indirect revelation through nature; it is not information about God and His demands upon man, or the way to gain His favor. It is the direct manifestation of God in His personal presence and acts in Jesus Christ in whom men are both called to repentance and freely forgiven. This, however, is not an achievement of man but the act of God.[6]

Now, there are two dimensions to this historic act. There is the preparation in the prophetic word and in the conscience created by the Law; this is the historic movement, forming in the mind of Israel of a knowledge of God as One who is Himself faithful and who demands responsible conduct—obedience—of man. When this was in some measure accomplished the "time was fulfilled and God sent forth His Son." The Son was known not only in terms of a historic expectation, but also in terms of a relationship made intelligible by the spiritual history of Israel. Still, he was not known by reflection upon history nor by identification of his person with an idea historically formed. He was known as the Son of God by faith; this is revelation. Accordingly the saving knowledge of God which the missionary seeks to communicate requires both the Old Testament and the New. The work accomplished in Israel through its own history must be patiently done by the missionary to prepare the way for a full acceptance of the revelation in Christ, a revelation that itself is received by faith as indeed it was by the first disciples and by all subsequent believers.

Thus Brunner has laid the foundations for a missionary theology that will cope concretely with this problem. In the discussion which follows I shall try to bring to light his contributions to such a theology especially in the doctrine of revelation, in the treatment of the

---

[6] *Ibid.*, pp. 220, 221.

problem of communication, and finally in the relationship of the Christian faith to the non-Christian religions and to culture.

The Doctrine of Revelation

The doctrine of revelation is set forth systematically in *Revelation and Reason* [7] and *The Divine-Human Encounter* [8] and is briefly and cogently stated in Chapter 4 of *The Christian Doctrine of God.* [9] This is not the place for a full discussion of the doctrine, but rather to call attention to certain aspects of Brunner's development of it that have direct significance for missionary theory. And, first, is his affirmation of general revelation. He points out the common assumption in the Bible that the creation reveals the Creator, His power, His wisdom, His majesty, His divinity. Accordingly Brunner holds that all men have an objective knowledge of God. Through his essential nature as a being-in-relation to God man also has what might be called a subjective awareness of the divine. This is the original "preparation" for the gospel; the missionary goes to men who are religious, who are consciously in relation to deity, who know themselves dependent upon God.

But these two sources of the knowledge of God are also obstacles to true knowledge. The world not only reveals God, but also stands between man and God obscuring and distorting the divine. The first result of this distortion is idolatry, the understanding of God in terms of the objects and forces man finds in the world. Brunner reflects Ritschl's judgment of any rational conception of God derived from man's total knowledge of the world. "Reason is not given us to know God, but to know the world. Where reason pretends to know God, it creates a reason-God, and that is always an idol." [10]

Similarly man's awareness of God, the religious consciousness, subjectively perverts the truth of God. Brunner's continuous battle

[7] Brunner, *Revelation and Reason* (Philadelphia: The Westminster Press, 1946).

[8] Brunner, *The Divine-Human Encounter* (Philadelphia: The Westminster Press, 1943). German title, *Wahrheit als Begegnung.*

[9] Brunner, *The Christian Doctrine of God* (London: Lutterworth Press, 1949).

[10] Brunner, *The Word and the World* (London: The Student Christian Movement, 2nd ed. 1932), p. 33. Cf. Albrecht Ritschl, *Theologie und Metaphysik* (Bonn: Adolph Marcus, 1881), p. 9, "The all-embracing, eternal Being which excludes from itself all determination, and which being conceived of as beyond the order of extension and opposition is posited as its Ground, is yet only the idea of the world and nothing more" (translation mine, H. V. W.).

against rationalism, idealism, and mysticism can be summed up in his assertion that all this is a monologue, man talking to himself. This subjective religiousness represents a preoccupation of man with his own thought and feeling and the identification of God with the structure and process of consciousness, just as idolatry is the identification of God with the structure and process of the world.

This account of the state of "natural" man which recognizes both a knowledge of God through creation and an awareness of God in the religious consciousness reveals the necessity both from the objective and the subjective point of view for the preaching of the Gospel. The "distortion" of revelation in nature makes urgent the full and true personal revelation in Christ. Here God stands forth in His true character and in person, and reveals His love in the act of redemption. The saving knowledge of God is found in His unique, personal, redemptive revelation in Christ, where God is known not in terms of the world process, but in the act of personal spirit, not in the form of the religious consciousness but in the historical person of Jesus Christ.

Accordingly the Christian missionary goes always to men prepared for and in desperate need of the Gospel. He shares with them a general revelation and a common religious consciousness. But he has received the direct and personal self-revelation of God in Christ which has completed and corrected the general revelation. This knowledge of God in Christ is not mere understanding; more fundamentally it is transformation, redemption. It is the true answer to man's basic need for salvation. In Christ, God comes to man not through a *medium,* the world, nor even through an *intermediary,* the prophet who speaks for Him, but in a *Mediator,* one who is both God and man, the Word made flesh. This is an act of God in history, therefore open to all men, but it is not a development of history.

In this brief but I hope not inaccurate summary of Brunner's doctrine of revelation can be seen the necessity for the missionary witness of the Church. The saving revelation of God in Christ being a historic act, knowledge of it starts from a point in time and in space. That knowledge comes through the witness (preaching) of the disciples "beginning at Jerusalem" and extending to the whole world. It is not a knowledge that can be arrived at by religious devotion or rational reflection. It is not a universal quality of the world or a truth of reason that can be discovered at any time and in any place by the earnest spirit. It must be carried to the world by those who have received it. This is the logic developed by Paul in the tenth chapter of Romans. But how are men to call upon him in whom they have not believed? And how are they to hear without a preacher? And how can men preach unless they are sent?" [11]

Thus the revelation of God in Christ, just because its fullness and power lie in the concrete reality of a historic person, imposes the obligation of being carried, declared, and witnessed to by the living Church. Here is the primary missionary character and responsibility of the Church.

The Problem of Communication

The communication of the Gospel involves two questions, (1) the nature of the historic process and (2) the "point of contact," *(anknüpfungspunkt)*. Brunner has dealt with both of these questions; indeed they are involved in his doctrines of general revelation and the nature of man. In *Die Mystik und das Wort* [12] he contrasts the historicism of Schleiermacher and Ritschl and the nineteenth century generally with the New Testament teaching of judgment. The whole book is a basic criticism of Schleiermacher and his doctrine of continuity *(Stetigkeit)*. The particular issue in this section is that of historic continuity, and optimism about the development in time of the God-consciousness. Brunner does not relate this discussion to the missionary expansion of the faith, but his treatment furnishes a negative background to the affirmation made above of the necessity for active effort on the part of the Church to make the Gospel known.

Schleiermacher conceives of the growth of the God-consciousness within the individual and in the Church and even in the world as a natural process which will eventually include the whole of humanity.[13] It operates in history as the constant and increasingly effective pressure of the power of the God-consciousness which originates with Jesus and works naturally through history. This is essentially a psychological and cultural power and process. The Church and Christian individuals are indeed the medium of its operation, but the real power is the irresistible influence in history of the person of the Redeemer. Moreover the state of every man,

[11] Rom. 10:14,15.
[12] Brunner, *Die Mystik und das Wort* (Tübingen: J. C. B. Mohr [Paul Siebeck], 1928), pp. 276-300.
[13] Friedrich Schleiermacher, *The Christian Faith* (Edinburgh: T. & T. Clark, 1928).

Christian or heathen, represents a stage of progress toward the triumph of the God-consciousness over the sense-consciousness which is redemption. In the saint within the Church it is at a maximum though never perfect; in the heathen it is at a minimum though never completely absent. But the increase of the God-consciousness is assured; once inaugurated by the person of Christ it is automatic in operation and certain of triumph in humanity at large, although we cannot conceive of the complete suppression of the sense-consciousness in history. Much of this comfortable assurance of the spread of Christianity and of the gradual Christianizing of the world prevailed before the First World War. It has become apparent since that time that to witness to the Christian gospel in any land at any time may call upon the Church and Christian individuals to be real "martyrs," and that the spread of the Gospel is not the irresistible natural expansion of the power of the divine (a contradiction in terms) but a divine-human enterprise in which the cross must not only be preached but also borne. Brunner's doctrine of revelation sustains this conviction.

Over against the naturalistic optimism of the nineteenth century Brunner asserts:

The New Testament understanding of history which is in all essential respects that of the Reformers, is most concisely indicated by the parable of the tares and the wheat. . . . Who would be certain here as to what is to be counted good and what evil? In other words: it is impossible for us men to determine simply the things of history, to say nothing of a single course of history. The two courses, the way that leads to eternal life and the way that leads to damnation are always for our eyes together and interwoven. Therefore judge not! But fear! [14]

Thus the Christian faith derives from the revelation at a particular time and place in history; it must be preached to all men, a historic activity. And yet no natural historic movement can be recognized by which this spread of the faith can be assured. This would seem to invalidate the attempt to represent the progress of the faith by any kind of graph, and even to render suspect the idea of successive advance and retrogression with an overall certainty of forward movement, such as constitutes the pattern in Latourette's *History of the Expansion of Christianity*.[15] The gospel must be

[14] *Ibid.*, p. 296 (Translation mine).
[15] K. S. Latourette, *A History of the Expansion of Christianity* (New York: Harper & Brothers, 1937-1945. 7 vols.).

preached but no calculation should or can properly be made as to its "success." That all lies in the wisdom and power of God. There is varying progress in history, "I planted, Apollos watered; but God gave the increase." [16] Tares and wheat grow together but their ultimate separation is not an outcome of history but the judgment of God. For a theology of mission this means that at all times and in all places the Church must make its witness but that it must never put its faith in any of the movements of history, either to be too much encouraged by their development or discouraged by their decay. The Christian mission is an activity within history but it is not a product or a result of history.

But this still leaves open the question of communication which may be simply stated thus: Is it possible and how is it possible to communicate the gospel to men generally? This is the question of the *point of contact,* the *"anknüpfungspunkt."* How can the word of faith be spoken to and heard by the natural man? Brunner addressed himself directly and critically to this question in an article entitled "Die Frage nach dem 'Anknüpfungspunkt' als Problem der Theologie." [17] "The question of the 'point of contact' is fully understood and urgent only for those who have part in the work of the church as preachers, missionaries, and pastors" (p. 529).

In this article Brunner points out that the first preaching of the gospel and the translation of the New Testament have already assumed a common speech of mankind and the possibility of communication. The gospel is the "news" of God's gracious act of redemption in Jesus Christ. The communication of the good news assumes the rational capacity and nature of man.

Reason is the prerequisite of faith. Of course we cannot say that we believe through the reason or with the reason; in a certain sense we must say the opposite, that we believe against the reason. The *humanum,* that which distinguishes us from the beast, is necessary in order that faith may occur. The Word of God, although it distinguishes itself as God's Word from everything that man knows of himself, can only be spoken to one who has the general capacity of speech. This capacity for speech or power of using words, of speaking and being spoken to, precisely this formal personality *(persona quod)* is the *conditio sine qua non* of faith, it is that also which is not destroyed but preserved in faith (p. 514).

---

[16] I Cor. 3:6.

[17] *Zwischen den Zeiten,* 10 Jahrgang, 1932, Heft 9, pp. 505-532 (translation mine).

The change that takes place in the one who receives the gospel in faith requires not a change in the rational meaning of words but a change in the man himself. The radical character of this change is indicated by the assertion that it involves the death of the "old man" and the birth of the "new man." But in this drastic change the same man or subject persists. This is the continuity of reason in the discontinuity of faith (pp. 510, 511).

The point at which the Word of God touches the natural self-consciousness of man is the conscience.[18] The preaching of the Word both makes the conscience aware of its bondage to sin and frees it from that bondage by the gift of forgiveness. Thus the point of contact is the sense of guilt and lostness that all men have even though not recognized as such (p. 517). "This 'point' is the common point of contact, just as it is the common imminent possibility" (p. 518).

Preaching must be not merely teaching but the direct address of the evangelist to the latent sense of lostness; even then its effectiveness depends on the action of the Holy Spirit. This awakening of the conscience, "This is the contact upon whose success, humanly speaking, the issue of preaching is just as dependent as it is upon 'pure doctrine'" (p. 530).

According to this exposition the communication of the Christian faith whether in the preaching of the gospel in a "Christian" community or in the midst of a non-Christian people has two aspects or dimensions. There is, first, the intelligible use of the common language of the moral and spiritual life and the direct address to the rational mind. Men of all faiths can understand one another to a large extent in this discourse because they are all basically the same in formal personality. But this form of communication does not of itself make converts. It can only give theoretical knowledge about Christ. "Accepting Christ" or becoming a Christian lies in another dimension, namely, that of personal confession of sin and acceptance of forgiveness in and through Christ. No one can ques-

---

[18] Cf. Brunner, *Man in Revolt* (New York, Charles Scribner's Sons), pp. 62, 63. "The perception of the Divine law as law, that is, the *cogitio legalis,* also belongs in principle, according to the most strict Reformation view, to the realm of 'natural' knowledge. No one is without some sense of responsibility, and there is no Christian missionary or spiritual adviser who does not make this sense of responsibility his point of contact. According to Kierkegaard, the sense of 'guilt' belongs in contradistinction to the sense of sin, to the sphere of immanence."

tion the necessity of personal response and the fact that it goes beyond the theoretical knowledge of Christ; nor that the real point of effective contact for the preacher or missionary is this inner awakening and conviction. But missionary theology is indebted to Emil Brunner for so clearly showing the relation of reason to faith, and the continuity of the *humanum* as subject, for this really constitutes a basis for the preaching of the gospel to the non-Christian world. It shows that Christianity does not constitute the fulfillment of the religions of mankind by bringing to completion the spiritual quest as it has already been carried on. It means that Christianity is not just the final point on a straight line of development, or the ultimate point of a curve generally established. Christian faith is not primarily a theological point at all. It is the personal meeting of God in Christ and the response of repentance and faith. It is for the non-Christian ultimately exactly what it is for the "Christian." This means that the non-Christian faith cannot grow or develop into Christianity without a little help and encouragement from the missionary.

But for the missionary himself, granted this basic possibility of communication, the problem remains of the "veil" of a sincere and intelligently held understanding of man, God, and salvation that makes the Gospel unintelligible or repugnant to the non-Christian. Brunner has given us a critique of some of the major world religions in *Revelation and Reason*.[19] He has here drawn the distinction between such claims to revelation as they make and God's self-revelation in Christ, the Word made flesh. It is necessary that this be done to clarify for the Church itself the nature and necessity of its missionary task. The problem of the missionary, however, lies precisely in the fact that the Muslim and the Jew, to say nothing of the Buddhist who does not even claim revelation, have fundamental understandings of God and of man that make the Christian gospel a stumbling block and foolishness. The structure of their thought (the proper realm of reason) is such that the Christian gospel is either unintelligible or in conflict with their religious ideas. The barrier between Christianity and the Muslim world, aside from political and military considerations, is theological. So with the Jewish world. We may be grateful that no political obstacles enhance the problem with the Buddhist, only here a far more profound issue

---

[19] Brunner, *Revelation and Reason* (Philadelphia: The Westminster Press, 1946), pp. 218-236.

arises: the Buddhist conception of personality and of salvation either obscures the very meaning of the Christian gospel or dissolves it into psychology.

The theological task that confronts the Church in its world mission theoretically remains in the work of the mission itself practically. It is only through patient, sustained intercourse with the mind of the non-Christian that an understanding can be created of God as truly Person whose law is love and whose act of salvation is neither justice nor caprice but grace. A corresponding doctrine of man must be patiently taught. The Buddhist, for example, must learn to think of himself and be aware of himself not as a temporary collection of "skandhas" but as a responsible person created in the image of God and made for fellowship with God. This is precisely the theme of an article which Brunner contributed in 1930 to the *International Review of Missions*.[20] It was written at a time when secularism seemed to many within the Church to be a more formidable rival to the gospel than the non-Christian religions. In this article Brunner equates preaching to the modern secularized man with the work of the missionary:

Missionary preaching is and must be different from preaching in a congregation composed of believers; and just in the same way, in a world which has virtually lost all knowledge of the revelation of God in Christ, theology has a different task from that incumbent on her in quieter times of assured "churchliness." In her theological work the Church must seek for the point where the modern man can be got at. And that is his interpretation of himself which is the root of modern secularism. Hence theology must take shape as a perpetual discussion and debate with this "personal" conception of the world and culture in which the secret of the present dissolution lies (p. 508).

He brackets the world's religions with secularism under the designation of "sacralism":

Every other faith is itself secularism though perhaps concealed under sacralism. Christian faith alone stands above the antithesis of secularism and sacralism, for it is not "religion"; it does not have its basis in religious thought, feeling or action, but in the divine action and the divine word.

And the attack upon secularism "is just theology, theology as a struggle for the truth of the Word of God, for the true self-interpretation of man which is given in revelation" (p. 507).

[20] Vol. 19, 1930, pp. 495-511.

This recognition of a common problem confronting the preacher in a secularized "Christian" society, and the missionary among a non-Christian people is certainly valid. It means that in both cases there must be a teaching ministry accompanying the evangelistic appeal, a cooperation of reason and faith. It means that the non-Christian world must be reeducated not before but while it is being evangelized. Communication of the Word of God must take place in and with the slow and patient process of teaching men to understand themselves in the light of that Word. This is possible because of the *Wortfähigkeit*, the natural capacity of man to speak and be spoken to. Faith as response to the personal encounter with God in Christ is not the highest act of this natural reason but, as seen above, reason is the formal presupposition of that response which is itself an act of faith. Accordingly Brunner declares that we need a Christian philosophy, a Christian psychology, a Christian sociology, a Christian type of history, and even a Christian natural science (p. 510). The great place education has had in modern missions is justified by this principle, but it is a constant problem for the missionary educator to escape the secularism of this very program of education. Education in a truly Christian understanding of man is too easily lost and even denied by the "content" of the various disciplines. Such education is basically theological.

Christianity and Culture

The Christian missionary is constantly confronted with the problem of the relationship of religion and culture. In any society, to convert an individual or to win a family to the Christian faith raises this question in particular, personal, and often painful form. This is due to the fact that religion is a part of culture. Brunner's remark quoted above that "Christian faith . . . is not 'religion'" represents his basic approach to the problem. It is fully developed in *Revelation and Reason*. Briefly stated, it distinguishes between Christian faith as response to the revealing act of God in Christ, and religion as a development of man's natural and rational consciousness, that is, as a phase of culture. This is what religion has been generally in the history of the race. It is indeed man's response to revelation but it is essentially a product of the human spirit and therefore not merely culturally conditioned but itself a form of culture. This is true both of primitive religions and of highly advanced, philosophical religion.

But the Christian faith itself cannot recognize this general conception, without losing its own identity. It cannot admit that its faith is one species of the genus "religion," or if it does so, only in the sense in which it regards itself as the true religion in contrast to the other false religions.[21]

The object of Christian faith is not religion but God's self-revelation in Christ. "But this revelation ought not to be called 'religion,' nor should faith in it bear this name. For in Jesus Christ 'the Christian religion' is judged as much as the other religions." [22]

This distinction between the Christian faith as response to revelation, and "religion" as a product of the human spirit does not confer absoluteness or infallibility on any actual historic form of the Christian religion. Neither does it deny dignity and importance to man's religious quest. What it does is to acknowledge (confess) a divine absolute in the historic incarnation of God in Christ. Brunner points out that no other religion has or even claims any such historic revelation. This claim seems to the non-Christian arrogant and intolerant. But Brunner rightly meets this natural and understandable objection by appeal to the simple standard of truth.[23] Truth is always intolerant. It is at this point of truth that the Christian faith declares its independence of culture. So long as the Church truly believes that God, the one sovereign God, has spoken to *man* in Jesus Christ; so long as it believes its gospel to be *true,* it must humbly but faithfully preach that gospel to all men so far as opportunity offers. Cultures are relative; truth is absolute. Cultures, moreover are plural and represent the rich diversity of the creative genius of man; but God is one and His Word is the same Word to all men.

---

[21] Brunner, *Revelation and Reason* (Philadelphia: The Westminster Press, 1946), p. 258.

[22] *Ibid.* p. 272.

[23] For example, in a sermon preached in the Fraumünster Kirche, Zurich, on the text, "And in none other is there salvation: for neither is there any other name under heaven, that is given among men, wherein we must be saved" (Acts 4:12). ". . . this is so in all matters where it is a question of truth. The recognition of one truth excludes the possibility of recognizing its opposite to be true as well. Truth itself is intolerant. . . . Truth is always single and exclusive. If there is only one God then there is not more than one. The spiritually tolerant attitude of Indian religion implies secretly in fact the idea that none of the various religions is true in the full, serious, unconditional sense. Naturally we can admit very well alongside of each other any number of partial truths, so that we may say: That is true, partially, and the opposite is also true partially or up to a certain point. But if something is wholly and not merely partially, or to a limited extent, true, then this simultaneous recognition of something other as true is no longer possible; then we have an Either-Or." *The Great Invitation* (Philadelphia: The Westminster Press, 1955), p. 107.

In this sense Brunner completely rejects the identification of Christianity with culture. But he is equally positive about the inner relation of religion to culture.

> All reason and all culture arise from religion, and without it are bound to become sterile. Without it, fully freed from it, they dwindle into mere civilization with an *art pour l'art* and a *science pour la science*.[24]

> The reason why the history of religion is the inner shrine of history, why religions are the soul of all culture, is that in religion there dawns upon us something of the meaning and yet the absurdity of life as a whole and of historical existence. . . . In history, therefore, religion is the human element which stands in the nearest relation with revelation.[25]

Religion, therefore, has a primary role in culture. There are three basic factors that enter into the formation of a culture; natural factors like climate, the physical and spiritual equipment of men within a given area, and

> the spiritual presuppositions of a religious and ethical nature which, not in themselves cultural, we might call the culture-transcendent presuppositions of every culture. This third factor lies within the sphere of historical freedom, within that area which is open to the free self-decision of man. Assuming equal natural data and equal physical and spiritual forces, two cultures will develop differently if this third factor, the culture-transcending presuppositions, is different. It is this third factor which affords the possibility for a spiritual force like Christianity to enter the field of culture and give it a certain direction and character. Once more assuming the natural data and the physical and spiritual forces of two nations to be equal, the culture and civilization within them will greatly differ, if the one is dominated by the Christian religion and the other has another religion or an irreligious conception of life, forming its culture-transcending factor. This third factor then is the one within which the Christian faith, as distinguished from its alternatives, becomes relevant.[26]

Against this general background of the dependence of culture upon religion and the difference in cultures as determined by the kind of religion that prevails within them, we place Brunner's specific assertion that the truly human character of life in any culture can be created only by Christian faith.[27]

[24] Brunner, *The Philosophy of Religion* (New York: Charles Scribner's Sons, 1937), p. 146.

[25] *Ibid.* p. 127.

[26] Brunner, *Christianity and Civilization* (London: Nisbet & Co., 1948), Vol. I, p. 11.

[27] Brunner, *Christianity and Civilization* (London: Nisbet & Co., 1949), Vol. II, p. 129.

The following statement completes the form of his argument for the necessity of a Christian center for civilization; "In this book I seek to formulate and to justify my conviction that only Christianity is capable of furnishing the basis of a civilization which can rightly be described as human." [28]

These assertions set forth the substance of the conception developed widely in Brunner's writings regarding the importance to human history and culture of the Christian faith. They link with the Christian doctrine of revelation as God's historic self-disclosure in Jesus Christ, the doctrine of man as created in the Word and as responsible. The true nature of man is revealed in Christ who re-establishes through faith the original relation to God which is that nature, the *imago dei*. Since God is always the same and since man is man always and everywhere, all the works of man, his culture as well as his religious life, come into proper focus in a personal and social existence determined by this revelation and the faith that it creates. This is the *truth* about God and man; it is not a special variation of human thought or culture. It is as exclusive as truth is in any sphere, and it is as necessary to the spiritual life of man as the truth of science is to his technical manipulations of nature, and infinitely more necessary as the issue itself is immeasurably greater.

HUGH VERNON WHITE

PACIFIC SCHOOL OF RELIGION
BERKELEY, CALIFORNIA

[28] *Christianity and Civilization,* Vol. I, p. v.

4

David Cairns

BRUNNER'S CONCEPTION OF MAN AS RESPONSIVE, RESPONSIBLE BEING

BRUNNER'S CONCEPTION OF MAN
AS RESPONSIVE, RESPONSIBLE BEING

I. *The Question and Its Setting*

(a) The Great Question

For Emil Brunner there is no more important question in the whole universe than the question, "What is man?" It is, accordingly, no accident that his greatest book should be a study in the doctrine of man. And there is something of the passion of Pascal in these words from its first chapter:

. . . But the riddle of man cannot be shelved; it does not wait on our opinions. It lives by virtue of its own necessity as the special, the incomparable question. For whatever other problems seem to us greater or more important, they are still *our* problems. It is we who plumb the infinities of the world, it is for us that the thousand phenomena of the universe become questions. All problems, as it were, focus themselves into the one question, "Who is the questioner behind all questions, who is this being that knows the infinities of the world, that feels all its daunting problems, both those concerned with human existence, and those beyond it; who is this that sees himself as an insignificant atom in the universe, and in so doing measures this boundless universe with his thoughts? [1]

The aim of this essay will be to record, explain, criticize, and defend Brunner's own answer to this tremendous question—"Man's being is essentially responsible being."

Brunner would probably wish above all to be judged as a thinker on behalf of the Gospel, a Christian maintaining continual contact

[1] Brunner, *Der Mensch im Widerspruch* (Berlin: Furche Verlag, 1937), p. 4. English translation, London, Lutterworth Press: pp. 17-18. (While admiring Dr. Wyon's excellent translation, I have throughout ventured on my own versions. In subsequent notes, the original German reference is first given, and the second reference is to the English translation.)

with the doubting and unbelieving world. And for a man who gives himself to this task there is no more important field than anthropology. "The knowledge of man," he writes, "is the common theme and the common interest of secular and Christian theological inquiry. It is possible, at least in appearance, to assert that one is not interested in God; it is not possible to deny an interest in man. . . . Accordingly, man is the favourite theme of all philosophy, at least since the days of Socrates, as he is the favourite theme of psychology and the wisdom of the poets. But it was not for nothing that the inscription at Delphi, where men sought and received instruction in abstruse matters, was "γνῶθι σεαυτὸν" [know thyself]. For up to the present day there is hardly another subject in the world of our experience, about which there are so many contradictory views and teachings, as about this theme, which lies nearest to us, and is seemingly the most familiar." [2]

Seeing then that the various views on man's nature are so diverse, are the prospects hopeless for a profitable discussion on our theme between the Christian theologian and the secular thinker? Brunner does not believe so, and refers to St. Paul's belief that the natural man has a good deal of knowledge about his own nature. Further, such a knowledge is a precondition of the success of every evangelistic preacher, and of every pastoral or missionary conversation. Brunner's hopes for the outcome of such a conversation obviously imply that if there are differences between Christian and secular thought about man's nature, the gulf is not so wide as to make the disputants unintelligible to each other. Here the governing principle of his thought is the "law of contiguity," which Brunner has himself described as "My guiding principle in all problems which concern the relation of the Christian to the world." [3]

(b) The Law of Contiguity

The old theologians, including the Reformers, expressed the relation of faith to reason by means of the simple formula, "In things of this world, in matters of science, as in practical affairs, reason is competent; in spiritual things, faith." [4] Brunner argues that this was an oversimplification, for there are certain fields where both

[2] Brunner, *Dogmatik II* (Zürich, Zwingli Verlag, 1950), p. 53. (London: Lutterworth), p. 46.

[3] Brunner, *Offenbarung und Vernunft* (Zurich, Zwingli Verlag, 1941), p. 379. (London: Student Christian Movement Press), p. 383.

[4] *Mensch im Widerspruch*, p. 50. (London: Lutterworth), p. 61.

reason and faith can legitimately claim a competence. So we cannot just draw a clear line of demarcation; only a proportional proposition will do justice to the facts. This proposition is the "law of closeness of relation," which Brunner expresses thus:

The nearer anything lies to that centre of existence where we are concerned with the whole—i.e. man's relation to God and his personal being, the greater is the dislocation of rational knowledge through sin. The further anything lies from this centre, the less this factor makes itself felt, and the smaller, accordingly, is the difference between the knowledge of the believer and the unbeliever.[5]

Thus no one will maintain that there is a Christian logic, mathematics, or physics, but the irrelevance of Christian belief to psychology can be maintained only by restricting the latter discipline to a study of elementary processes and sensations. We cannot speak of a Christian science of law as we can of Christian theology, but there is an important, though indirect, relevance of Christian belief to our doctrine of law, since our view of justice will be influenced by our view of divine justice.

One thing should already be clear, that if the principle of closeness of relationship holds, Christian belief will not be able to base itself upon any neutral or professedly neutral philosophical anthropology, in stating its doctrine of man. There will, in fact, be no such neutral discipline, since man's nature lies at the very center of his existence, and can be regarded as one of the main fields of theology itself.

As we have said, Brunner holds that, in spite of the divergence of the various doctrines of man, the task of Christian eristic in this field is not hopeless. We shall later have to see on what grounds he hopes to make good to his secular partners in the discussion his claim that "Man can only understand himself truly, realistically, without doing violence to the reality, when he understands himself from the standpoint of faith in the Creator revealed in Christ." [6]

(c) Assured Scientific Truth and Speculative Anthropologies

Naturally, Brunner is very ready to accept the assured results of the various special sciences as data which the Christian doctrine of man must take into account. Man is indeed a piece of the physico-chemical world, and, accordingly, can be described in terms of

[5] *Offenbarung und Vernunft*, p. 378. (London: Lutterworth), p. 383.
[6] *Dogmatik II*, p. 87. (London: Lutterworth), p. 72.

physicochemical processes. He is also a living being, and as such is describable in biological terms. As a piece of matter, and as a living being, he is an object among objects. But man is also a subject, the possessor of reason, culture, and art. Accordingly, his life is lived in relation to the absolute norms—in short, he is not only matter, but also spirit. All these things must be taken into account in the Christian doctrine of man. It is, however, a most frequent tendency for thinkers not to rest content with the claim to such partial truths about man as can be tested by experiment or common experience. Thus conflicting theories about human nature, which may be called speculative, have been built up. It may be claimed that in essence man is matter, or a biological being, or a spark of the Eternal Mind, or the product of economic forces, or an expression of the sex- or power-instinct, or of some more vaguely defined collective libido.

Brunner is accustomed to classify here the constitutive elements of the various secular anthropologies according as they spring from the consideration of man's nature as an object or his nature as a subject. From the first aspect of man arise the various naturalistic anthropologies or components of anthropologies; while from the second arise the various idealistic anthropologies or components of anthropologies. Sometimes he adds to these two types a third type of speculative doctrine of man, corresponding to the identity of subject and object in immediate feeling, or the identity of soul and body in the unconscious, which he claims to be the source of the romantic anthropologies.[7]

However important this classification may be, it does not cloud his vision of the varied and complex character of the elements which enter into the doctrines of man that took their rise from the thought of four of the most influential thinkers of the last hundred years, Marx, Darwin, Nietzsche, and Freud. It is not the scientific investigations of men like Darwin and Marx that have made history so much as the views of man's nature which have developed out of their work, often at the hands of much inferior thinkers. The popularizers have sometimes drawn conclusions that the savants for example, (for example, Darwin) have not drawn themselves, or have expressed themselves with a crudeness that would have made the savants (for example, Nietzsche) indignant. These views have become creative

[7] As in *Gott und Mensch* (Tübingen: J. C. B. Mohr, 1930), p. 75. (London: Student Christian Movement Press), p. 143.

factors in history only by receiving a religious or quasi-religious pathos. For if man does not worship God, he will inevitably worship some other absolute—an idol.

(d) An Anthropology Without Presuppositions?

The men of the Renaissance had every confidence that they would discover the nature of the physical world and the nature of man. They congratulated themselves that they had an approach that was entirely without presuppositions. This general viewpoint prevailed widely till toward the close of the nineteenth century. And what was its success in the advancement of knowledge? In the physical sciences the progress made was astonishing; in anthropology the results were on the whole meager and disappointing. What was the reason for this great discrepancy in results? The reason was that the prevailing empiricism was not nearly so free from presuppositions as men had believed. It rested upon one very important presupposition, namely, that man, like nature, is accessible to the methods of causal investigation. In the case of nature, this presupposition happened to be true. But only with very great reservations could it be said to be true of man. Insofar as man is "a piece of nature" these methods were, indeed, successful. But man, as we have seen, is much more.

Brunner's conclusions are that there is no science without presuppositions, and that emphatically no anthropology can exist without such. "The question is not whether man, to be intelligible, must be understood in the light of presuppositions beyond his empirical givenness, but as to what these presuppositions must be. The understanding of man's nature leads us always—and we may choose which alternative we like—either into the region of metaphysics, or into that of religious faith, whether the metaphysic be a materialistic, or an idealistic, or a mystical-pantheist one, and whether the faith be the Christian one or another." [8]

II. The Christian Doctrine of Man

(a) The Word of God as the Source of Our Doctrine of Man

Over against the speculative doctrines of man, Brunner places the Christian doctrine, contrasting it with them. When he asserts

[8] *Mensch im Widerspruch*, p. 48. (London: Lutterworth), p. 60.

that the Word of God is the source of that doctrine, he makes it clear that he is not committing himself to a Biblicism which tries to achieve a harmony among the different scriptural statements about man. "We shall, rather, start from the centre, from the revelation of God in Jesus Christ, and ask ourselves in what light man is there revealed. Only then shall we take the various anthropological utterances of the Old and New Testaments, interpreting them in the light of this central knowledge, and adducing them to complete and confirm our conclusions." [9]

This doctrine, he continues, is not a doctrine about the humanity of Christ, but rather the expression in words of an insight into man's nature in the light of Jesus Christ. "Jesus Christ as the Incarnate Son of God is not the object, but the source and norm of our knowledge." [10]

When Brunner talks of the Word of God being the source of our knowledge, we should note that the kind of knowledge to which he refers is not theoretic, but existential. It is not a "knowledge that," but a "knowledge of." We know God thus by being confronted by Him in His Son, the Word, in an act of revelation. This is a knowledge mediated through the historical record of certain events. Accordingly, it does not arise without the words of Scripture, which constitute the biblical record. But it is a personal knowledge of faith, created in us by the Holy Spirit bearing witness to God in Christ. It is, therefore, at the same time an act of love, trust, and obedience.

How is this knowledge the source of our Christian doctrine of man? Because, Brunner says, to know God as one's Creator is also to know oneself as a created being. And this knowledge, too, is existential; it is the other side of our knowledge of God. "When God the Lord meets me in Jesus Christ, I know that He is the Creator, and that I am His creature, and conversely, only in this encounter do I know that I am His creature." [11]

The Christian doctrine of man is a part of theology, the attempt to express in propositional form the content of this existential knowledge. Without the revelation in Jesus Christ we would not know what man really is.

---

[9] *Dogmatik II*, pp. 61-62. (London: Lutterworth), p. 53.
[10] *Ibid.*
[11] *Dogmatik II*, p. 62. (London: Lutterworth), p. 53.

(b) The Content of the Christian Doctrine of Man

i. *Correlation of knowledge of the Word and knowledge of myself*

Developing the point we have just made, Brunner writes:

> In Jesus Christ, God meets me as the One who gives Himself freely to me, and at the same time claims me entirely for Himself, as holy Love. As such He reveals Himself to me. But in so doing, He reveals me at the same time to myself in the original nature He has given me. . . . Once more, both are linked in correlation; it is one and the same thing to know of the holy, loving God, and of this human nature of mine as it springs from the Creator's hand.[12]

ii. *A living, free response*

In so doing:

> God wills to have a creature which does not reflect to Him His glory as the other created beings do, as the mere object of His will, like a mere mirror of His glory as Creator. He desires an active and spontaneous "reflection." He, who creates through the Word, who creates as Spirit, creates in freedom, looks for a reflection that is more than a reflex, an answer to His Word, which is a free act of spirit. . . . Only thus can His love really impart itself as love. For love can only impart itself when it is received in love. That is why the creaturely existence of man is in essence freedom, selfhood.[13]

iii. *A conditioned, answering freedom*

This freedom is not unlimited, self-positing, as is the self of idealism; it is posited, not by itself, but by God. God wills my freedom as the possibility of this answer; my freedom is thus from the first a responsible freedom. Responsibility is a dependent freedom and a free dependence. The beasts and God have no responsibility, the beasts because they have no freedom, God because He has unconditioned freedom.

Man has conditioned freedom. It is precisely this which is the essence of his humanity, and the condition under which he has his freedom is the same as the purpose for which he has his freedom;—to respond in such a manner to God that God glorifies Himself and imparts Himself in this answer.[14]

---

[12] *Dogmatik II*, p. 65. (London: Lutterworth), p. 55.
[13] *Dogmatik II*, p. 65. (London: Lutterworth), p. 55.
[14] *Ibid.*, p. 66. (London: Lutterworth), p. 56.

iv. *Formal and material Image—an open question*

But now it belongs to the essence of this responsible freedom that it can fulfil its purpose or not fulfil it. This open question is the consequence of freedom. Thus it belongs to the divinely created being of man that it has a formal and a material side. The fact that man must answer, that he is responsible, is unalterably fixed; and no use of freedom, or sinful misuse of it can alter this. . . . Responsibility is the unalterably given structure of man's being. The being of man,—not of the believer, but of every man,— is responsible being-in-act. Whatever man may answer to the call of the Creator, even if his answer be, "I know no Creator, and will acknowledge no God over me," this answer too is an answer, and fulfils the structural law of responsibility. This formal structure of man's being . . . is identical with his humanity, and only disappears at the frontiers of idiocy or insanity.[15]

v. *Old Testament and New Testament Image*

This formal side of human nature is described in the Old Testament as the Image of God. How can this purely formal element be considered a likeness to God? The similar thing is man's being as subject, his personal being, his freedom, which distinguishes him from the lower creatures.

The New Testament simply takes this structural existence in God's Image for granted, and does not concern itself further with it. The apostles are interested only in the material content given to this structure; that man should really give to God the answer God intends, an answer of reverent and thankful love, not given in words alone, but with the whole life of man. The New Testament says that this answer is not given, that man gives honor, not to God, but to His creatures. And further, it tells what God has done to change this wrong answer to the right one.

In this sense the Bible speaks of the Image as lost, and not merely partially, but totally lost. Man has no longer this Image of God, but it is restored to him in Jesus Christ. The new creation of the original image of God is identical with the gift of God to man received by faith in Jesus Christ.

vi. *Man's true being is in God*

The Image of God in the New Testament, material sense of the word, is identical with existence in the Word of God. This means that man has

[15] *Ibid.*, pp. 66-67. (London: Lutterworth), pp. 56-57.

his true being, not in himself, but in God. . . . The Image . . . is not the self of idealistic philosophy, but it is a self received from the Thou. . . . To be a true man a man must not, as is commonly thought, "be himself," and in order to understand his true being, he must do the reverse of keeping his eyes on himself. Man is truly human when he is in God. Precisely then, and only then, is he truly 'himself.' [16]

From the standpoint of sinful man, the Image of God is existence in Jesus Christ, the Incarnate Word. He is the true Image of God, and faith in Him is the restoration of the Image, because He restores to us that life in the Word of God which we have lost in sin.

vii. *Confusions due to failure to distinguish the Images*

It is clear, Brunner continues, that a failure to make the distinction between the formal and the material Image will lead to grave confusion. We have seen that the formal Image is to be equated with man's universal humanity, while the material Image is to be equated with the true life of man by faith. If we deny this distinction, then we are left with three disastrous alternatives. Since there will now be only one concept, "Image of God," which must be used for the description of the Christian believer, we must either deny that the Image has anything to do with man's universal humanity, or else, since "the Image" and "humanity" are now terms applied to the believer only, we shall be forced to deny that the sinner is human. Or we shall have to falsify the facts in a third way by saying that the man of faith is only in degree different from the sinner, the former possessing the whole Image, and the latter only a relic of it.

viii. *The Image in both cases is relational*

The problem of the Image is made more difficult by the fact that it is a concept describing two relationships, and not substances. Roman Catholic teaching has erred in this respect when it described the Image as man's reason, or his creative freedom. If this be true, then man has the Image of God in himself, a door is opened to the pantheistic or idealistic error, whereby man is affirmed to have an element of the Divine in himself. It *is* hard, Brunner concedes, to equate structure and relationship, but this is the singular thing about our existence as man, that the structure

[16] *Dogmatik II*, p. 69. (London: Lutterworth), p. 58.

of our being is a relationship-responsive actuality. The loss of the Image in the material sense presupposes the existence of the Image in the formal sense. The man who has lost the material Image does not cease to be responsible.

ix. *The distinction between "material" and "formal" due to sin*

And yet, continues Brunner, however important the distinction between the formal and material images may be from our standpoint, we must urge that

from the point of view of the divine Creation it does not exist . . . God calls man into existence in order that he may respond to Him aright, not in order that he may respond to Him wrongly or rightly. God does not destine man to choose between faith and unbelief, obedience and disobedience, but to answer Him "in correspondence" with His Word. A freedom of choice to be distinguished from the right act of response is itself a possibility which only appears once the wrong act has been committed. Formal freedom, severed from material freedom, from existence in the Word of God, is already a result of sin. Man ought to know of his freedom only in the form of his free choice of the love of God.[17]

(c) The Word of God as Source of Man's Being

We spoke above of the Word of God in Christ as the source of our knowledge of man's nature. Now we must expand Brunner's teaching on the Word of God as the source of man's being itself. Here, for clarity's sake, it is well to set down a recent explicit statement of Brunner's, which gives his answer to a question and criticism of Karl Barth's.

Brunner writes:

There is complete agreement between us on the point that the Word of God, that is, Jesus Christ as the perfect Word of God, is the *ratio cognoscendi* of the creaturely nature of man. Difference of opinion begins only when Barth asks me if for me Jesus Christ is only the *ratio cognoscendi,* and not as for him the *ratio essendi,* the ground of the creaturely being of man. Let me first confess my incapacity to understand what is meant by saying that every man, including also such as lived a thousand years before Christ, has his being in the history of Jesus.[18]

I can only understand this by substituting for what is said, an-

---

[17] *Dogmatik II,* p. 71. (London: Lutterworth), pp. 60-61.
[18] Barth, *Kirchliche Dogmatik III,* 2, p. 194.

other thought that also appears in Barth, that man is created in the Pre-temporal Logos, the eternal Word and Purpose of God, which was revealed and became historic reality in Jesus." [19] Not only is Brunner able to understand this position—it is his own. For him, man is not only related to God through the incarnate Christ and the historical revelation, but also through what he calls the revelation in creation. It is this which constitutes man's humanity and responsibility, otherwise we would have the very strange result that moral responsibility did not exist B.C. The only other alternative to Brunner's view would be to take moral responsibility right out of relation to God, a position which in one passage Barth appears inclined to adopt.[20] To return to the exposition. In the fourth chapter of *Mensch im Widerspruch*, Brunner has a paragraph on the Word of God as the *ratio essendi* of man's nature, the salient points of which are as follows:

There is a distinctively Christian ontology; all being is either God's being, or created being. The Bible tells us that God created all things by His Word, and sustains them also by His Word. But God's Word is the ontological source of man's being in a special sense.

It is not a mere phrase or figure of speech to say that man lives by the Word of God. So also the original man in the divine original act of creation is begotten by the Word of God. And just as the begetting in the Word of God includes in itself the hearing and believing of the Word . . . so also the original creation of man in the Word is one which makes him not only product but recipient of the Word of God.[21]

The argument, abbreviated, runs on as follows: This actual sinful man (that is, ourselves as we are), is to be understood in God and in God alone. This actual man has his continued existence and the source of his being in the Word of God. There is thus a special relationship of all men to the Word, sinners and saints, a relationship which we describe as responsibility. And all men have some inkling of the fact; the why and the wherefore of it they would also know if it were not for sin. Were there not responsibility, man could

[19] Brunner, "The New Barth," *Scottish Journal of Theology* (Edinburgh, Oliver & Boyd, June, 1951), p. 132.
[20] Karl Barth. *Kirchliche Dogmatik II*, 1 (Zurich, Verlag der Evangelischen Buchhandlung, 1940), pp. 99-100.
[21] *Mensch im Widerspruch*, p. 61. (London: Lutterworth), pp. 71-72.

not be a sinner. Even the responsibility of the godless man can be understood only as a result of his special relation to God.

We shall understand this connexion more clearly if, instead of the formal conception of responsibility, we use the pregnant idea of love. The meaning of all responsibility is love, for love is the fulfilling of all law. Hence man can only be understood as issuing from love and made for love. Here too is something that everyone understands, even if dimly. But what he does not, and cannot, know of himself, is, why this is the case, and what the true content and meaning of love is. That is the content of the revelation of God in Jesus Christ. Only in this revelation . . . is this love revealed as ground and goal of our life. In this revelation we know why we are responsible, and to whom, and for what end.[22]

In the Christian doctrine of the Trinity, Brunner continues, we have revealed to us the love of the Triune God, a love which is eternal in God, a mutual love of the Father and Son through the Holy Spirit—a love which imparts itself freely to us as the Father is revealed in the Son, and the Holy Spirit bears witness in our hearts. And, as God is thus revealed to us as love, we see that our true nature is answering love. Thus the Christian revelation places this one fact which so many living beyond its limits are willing to acknowledge, in a powerful and closely integrated context of meaning, throwing new light upon it, and deepening our understanding of it.

(d) Man's Personal Being as Response to His Neighbor

It would be a grave omission in our account of Brunner's teaching on man as responsive, responsible being, if we were to omit the whole extremely important "dimension" of man's relation to his human neighbor. Nothing could be further from Brunner's thought than the conception of man's humanity being exclusively grounded in a one-to-one relationship to God.

To the one great commandment of love to God there is added the second that is "like unto it"—a second command, and yet not a second one,—the command of love to men. But here too the command is not the first thing, but the gift; with the divine "Thou" man receives also the human "thou" as the possibility of his selfhood.[23]

On this vast theme I shall not say more here; this doctrine of

[22] *Ibid.*, p. 63.
[23] *Mensch im Widerspruch*, pp. 96-97. (London: Lutterworth), p. 106.

our relationship to the human "thou" is the nerve of Brunner's opposition to rationalism, mysticism, and idealism; its importance in his thought is far greater than the length of this short paragraph would indicate. His large book on Christian ethics *(Das Gebot und die Ordnungen)* and his book on the Church *(Das Missverständnis der Kirche)*, deal in detail with important aspects of it, and the concept of the human "thou" is so central to him that in the recent article mentioned above he could speak of his surprise and delight at finding Barth agreeing so closely with "one of the central thoughts of my anthropology." [24]

As, however, the Church and ethics are being dealt with in separate chapters in this book, I shall leave this subject, indicating in closing that as there is a formal Image and a material Image in relation to God, so there would appear to be in relation to men. The material Image in relation to men is that responsibility which expresses itself in true care and love for one's neighbor; the formal Image is that relationship to our neighbor which cannot be lost even in sin. Even in sin man receives his being not only through his I-Thou relationship to God, but also through his I-thou relationship to his neighbor. Even though he may attempt to escape from this confrontation, he cannot do so without crossing the borders of idiocy or insanity.

III. *Appreciation and Questions*

(a) Appreciation

It will already be apparent that the writer of this essay takes Brunner's side in general as against Barth in the question of an original or general revelation, or revelation in creation, to which the revelation in Jesus Christ serves to open our eyes, as well as giving its own special light. Not only does this view seem undoubtedly to be supported by both Testaments, but it also gives us a doctrine of responsibility which is distinctively Christian, and which the Christian thinker can maintain over against naturalist and idealist alternatives. It will be objected that the meaning of "responsibility" here given is much wider than that of "moral accountability" which is the usual sense of the word in ethics. But there is justification in the law of closeness of relation for such a divergence of interpretation,

[24] Brunner, "The New Barth," *Scottish Journal of Theology*, June, 1951, p. 127.

so long as the Christian can feel that his special use of the term does not falsify his own experience of responsibility, but rather throws light upon it.

Here we see an interesting example of the eristic method at work. And it may be possible now to suggest why Brunner was able to make the claim that the eristic discussion was possible, and offered some hopes of success, on the grounds that "Man can only understand himself truthfully, realistically, without doing violence to the reality, when he understands himself from the standpoint of faith in the Creator revealed in Christ." [25]

Brunner not only makes this claim, but points to other writers who have had striking success in this field, citing the names of Pascal and Kierkegaard, and describing their Christian psychology as "a kind of 'proof of Christian truth' and therefore the most important means of Christian apologetic." [26]

He has himself shown the method in action, notably in the description he gives of the way in which the Christian doctrine of creation enables man to interpret rightly his dual nature as body and spirit, avoiding on the one hand the intellectual bankruptcy of naturalism, which can give no account of its own claims to truth, and on the other hand the idealistic tendency to identify the self with the Divine Reason. [27]

Again, as we have seen, in his discussion on responsibility, Brunner shows how the insights given by the revelation in Christ clarify some of the half-perceptions that all men have about moral responsibility, and throw a bright light upon the widely held belief that the true nature of man is love, giving to it an added depth and content, and explaining why things should be thus.

How can we account for such success? Surely, if, with Brunner, we believe in a revelation in creation, then we will believe that this action of God is continually impinging on the minds of the friends with whom we are discussing. While maintaining a sober estimate of our own powers, may we not expect that on occasion our reasoning may be able to appeal past them, as it were, to this revelation which has been soliciting their attention, and which, it may be, they have been partly misinterpreting, or only apprehending in fitful and isolated gleams of light? May the Spirit of God not be

---

[25] *Dogmatik II*, p. 87. (London: Lutterworth), p. 72.
[26] *Dogmatik II*, p. 146. (London: Lutterworth), p. 126.
[27] *Dogmatik II*, pp. 73-74. (London: Lutterworth), p. 62.

the cause of such illumination as comes to them and to us, as together we try to open our eyes to the mysterious realities before us? Why should we readily admit that His help is needed for the preacher, but regard apologetics as below His dignity? Is He hostile, then, to reason: has He not the power to clarify the understanding?

(b) Two Questions to Brunner

i. I have here two questions for Dr. Brunner. The first is this: What does he mean, when, in the following passage, he speaks of "Man's original existence in the Word of God."

In God's creation, man is not only created for the love, but in the love, of God, and lives from it. The original existence in the love of God, and the existence-unto-eternal-life which is its counterpart, is not a mere ideal or imperative law, it is the divinely created being of man.[28]

Here Brunner seems to speak of this existence in God's love as if it were the actual responsive existence of a man who loves God, for it is spoken of as "existence-unto-eternal-life." But, we would rejoin, it can hardly be this, for, until the Word of salvation is believed, all that man actually has, is an existence in disobedience to the Word in which he has been created, which is described as the possession of the formal image.

Brunner cannot be referring to the integrity of Adam in Paradise, for, rightly, I think, he rejects the literal interpretation of that story as a myth.

He clearly cannot mean the existence of the believer, to whom the Word of salvation has been preached. Nor does he merely refer to "man in the divine purpose," for he explicitly says:

The original existence in the love of God, and the existence unto eternal life which is its counterpart, is not a mere ideal or imperative, it is the divinely created being of man. Where man decides against this destiny, he is in opposition not only to the divine destiny, but to his own nature, and this contradiction is now within himself. . . . Even in sin, he has within him the original divine creation, which he contradicts by his wrong choice, but which is also always in contradiction to his wrong choices.[29]

There is indeed profound truth in this if we take "man's nature" to refer to man's actual endowments, environmental, physical, emo-

[28] *Dogmatik II*, p. 88. (London: Lutterworth), p. 73.
[29] *Ibid.*

tional, mental, and spiritual, which are made for existence in the Word, and which fall into conflict and disharmony when man tries to use them for another end. This disintegration Brunner has beautifully described in *Mensch im Widerspruch*.[30]

But this endowment has a different status from an "original existence in the love of God" or an "existence-unto-eternal-life." At the most it is a means to that existence.

Man's original existence in the Word of God is never directly accessible to our experience by itself, but is always known only in the experience of faith. Does an analysis of this experience enable us to say more than that we are aware that we belong to God, and have always belonged to Him, even in our disobedience, and that all that we have comes from Him, including our special relationship to the Word, which hitherto we have only known in the form perverted by our sin? Now we know that even the law was "a schoolmaster unto Christ."

It does seem to me that we are faced by a clear alternative. Either we regard our original existence as a divine intention for us, not canceled by sin, but temporarily balked by it. So doing we would equate it with the material image. Or else, if we insist on regarding it as an actual gift, we think of it as consisting in our endowments, still possessed under sin, and in particular that existence in personal relation with God which even God continues to give us under sin.

Brunner claims that his view preserves the essential truth that "is hidden under the mythical conception of a primitive state of integrity in Paradise."[31] If, however, the content be reduced to the material contained under the above alternatives, it may well be asked whether the truth stated here could not be expressed without using the concepts of "integrity" or "original humanity" at all.

ii. My second problem concerns Brunner's teaching on human freedom. He writes:

Now it belongs to the essence of this responsible freedom that it can neither fulfil or not fulfil its purpose. This open question is the consequence of freedom. Thus it is part of the divinely created nature of man, that it has a formal and a material aspect.[32]

---

[30] *Mensch im Widerspruch*, Ch. 9., "The Unity of the Person, and Its Disintegration."
[31] *Dogmatik II*, p. 89. (London: Lutterworth), p. 74.
[32] *Ibid.*

This looks as if Dr. Brunner were saying that man's freedom is what the Greeks called a "power of opposites," and that this is what it essentially is, in God's original purpose. Yet we are told, a few pages further on:

Formal freedom, severed from material freedom, from existence in the love of God, is already a result of sin. Man ought to know nothing of this freedom save in the form of the generous love of God. The fact that he is aware of this freedom of choice is already the effect of sin, and of separation from his connection with God. . . . From the side of God, therefore, this distinction between the "formal" and the "material" does not exist; it is not legally valid. But it does exist, wrongly.[33]

What does Dr. Brunner mean by saying that "From the side of God this distinction does not exist?" He certainly appears to mean more than that God wishes man to turn his back resolutely on the possibility of sin, when it appears to him. But if man's freedom of choice is the effect of sin, and, it appears, of his own sin, must we not go on to say that to be tempted is itself sinful? For only he can be tempted who realizes the wrong course of action as a live possibility. How then can we account for the temptations of Christ, who quite clearly was faced by the possibility of His own will differing from the Father's, and was really tempted, yet prayed "Nevertheless, not what I will, but what thou wilt"?[34]

And if the distinction between formal and material freedom from the standpoint of God does not exist, how can God, as Dr. Brunner suggests, have so seriously taken into account the possibility of man's sin that He actually created His world "With such a character as would correspond to a sinful humanity"?[35]

The position which I hold involves agreement with Dr. Brunner's general position that the Christian conception of freedom will vary from the views of various secular or non-Christian thinkers but I am not satisfied that he has here rightly defined that difference.

IV. Vindication of Brunner's Doctrine Against a Rival Interpretation of Man

In closing I would like to indicate briefly one other view of man at present fashionable, with which the view here expounded

[33] *Dogmatik II*, p. 72. (London: Lutterworth), p. 61.
[34] Mark 14:36.
[35] *Dogmatik II*, p. 153. (London: Lutterworth), p. 131.

is in conflict, and to indicate reasons why Brunner's view is to be preferred to it. This is the doctrine of Rudolf Bultmann, which has been developed in dependence on the studies of Martin Heidegger.

Heidegger's great work *Sein und Zeit* is an attempt to analyze the fundamental ontological structures which underlie personal being *(Dasein),* and to define the horizons of possibility within which personal being is free to act, and able to think validly of itself.[36] This existential analysis has for its particular realm the ontological; the scientific disciplines are all concerned with the realm of the ontic, the realm of the particular, of our experience. Among these sciences (in the wide sense of the word) theology takes its place. Thus Heidegger claims that he has written an ontological preface to all theology. He writes:

Faith and *Weltanschauung* . . . if they are speaking about personal being as being-in-the-world, will have to have recourse to the existential structures here laid bare, if they wish their statements to make a claim to *conceptual* understanding.[37]

Here brevity of space compels me to restrict myself to two comments. First, the phenomenological method of Heidegger, is, he asserts, able, by careful consideration of the ontic, to disclose the underlying ontological structures. But where the theme, as here, is human nature, even in his hands the method is unable to justify the high claims which he makes for it. Heidegger himself admits that his views will be resisted, and asserts that this resistance is the result of a tendency native in personal being to run away from the truth about itself. But his attempts to verify his theory by references to new phenomena amount in the end to little more than repetitions of his witness that "So it seems to me." Only this time the confirmatory "evidence" results from the discussion of a field (that of conscience), which many will find, for all its insights, one of the least convincing parts of the whole book. It is true that neither party in the debate can demonstrate its views to be right, but it is enough for Heidegger's critics to have shown that his claim to command the assent of the careful observer is unfounded. To say this is not to deny the profundity and acute observation of much of his writing. Secondly, so little are the ontological structures here "disclosed" neutral, that a very definite heroic and pes-

[36] Martin Heidegger, *Sein und Zeit* (Tübingen: Max Niemeyer Verlag, 1927).

[37] *Ibid.,* p. 180.

simistic ethic clearly arises from them, though Heidegger's reserve and obscurity partly conceal this fact.

But only if the phenomenological method could establish itself in philosophical anthropology, and only if it were truly formal, and did not contain in itself a definite outlook on the universe other than the Christian one, would the Christian theologian be able to accept Heidegger's work as a prolegomenon to theology.

Bultmann's relation to Heidegger, when examined, is seen not to be altogether clear. The careful reader of his works may distinguish as many as four contrasting positions:

(1) There is the suggestion, not perhaps to be taken altogether seriously, that the existential philosophy has been able by its own efforts to reach the same doctrine of man as that which is grounded in the Christian revelation.

Bultmann writes:

Heidegger's existentialism is a secular philosophical presentation of the New Testament view of human existence. . . . Is not man thus understood also in the New Testament? We should be concerned about the fact that philosophy . . . sees the truth of what the New Testament is saying.[38]

Here there is no avoidance of conflict by neat apportioning of different levels to philosophy and theology. The context shows that the truth that philosophy sees is believed to be the same as that expressed by the New Testament, presumably in both cases ontic truth.

(2) Then there is what we may, perhaps, call Bultmann's official position, where the ontological field is sharply distinguished from the ontic, the former being handed over to Heidegger and the latter to the Christian theologian. By exposing the ontological structures of personal being, the existential analyst is able to define the limits within which the statements of faith must fall, to be intelligible. This will enable the true offense and challenge of the gospel to come home to the hearer, for no confusing intellectual hurdles which are really irrelevant to his decision of faith will be put before him.

Such would appear to be the position entailed by the following quotation from Bultmann:

The God of the Christian revelation is the answer to the questions which

[38] Kerygma und Mythos, I, p. 36. (G.M.B.H. Hamburg-Volksdorf: Evangelisher Verlag, 1951). English translation by R. Fuller, Kerygma and Myth (London: Student Christian Movement Press), pp. 24-25.

concern our existence as *existential,* but He is not the answer to the questions of the philosophical *existential* analysis, so that, in my opinion, it is senseless to call the latter "atheist" when it does not reckon with God in its work—as if it ought to have done this.[39]

This is an intellectually serious and respectable position; the facts of the case, however, turn out to be against it, for Bultmann's description of man's being is by no means the ontic particularization of a formal ontological account by Heidegger, as we shall see; while Heidegger's account of man's being does not remain on the ontological level.

(3) We have the very strange position adopted in *Glauben und Verstehen,* I, pp. 305-312, which dates from as early as 1931.[40] Here is discussed the relation of Christian theology to the existential analytic (described as "philosophy"). In the earlier parts of the concluding section of this essay, Bultmann believes himself to have demonstrated that theology adopts, with unchanged meaning, many concepts whose content is determined by philosophy. All that he has in fact established, however, is that there is sufficient common content in these concepts as used by the disputants, for the debate between philosophy and theology to be possible, a result most natural, if Brunner's law of contiguity be valid.

Bultmann suggests, however, toward the end of the essay, that a threatening fact appears, which would appear to veto discussion on the anthropological theme between philosophy and theology. Does not Christian theology claim that the essential character of fallen personal being is unbelief? And philosophy does not see this at all! But philosophy, he continues, *does* see it, only "for it, this phenomenon is freedom, the original freedom, in which personal existence constitutes itself." [41] And the phenomenon of faith is seen by philosophy on its side, but only as a "lost, senseless possibility." [42]

Here, with a vengeance, is a reversal of the position maintained earlier in the essay. In this fundamental point the existential analysis is apparently so opposed to Christian faith, that the two are held to be in almost complete contradiction.

Here we must pose a question of method. What has happened

[39] *Ibid.,* p. 126. English translation, p. 108. Note: "existential" questions are questions relating to matters in the realm of the ontic.

[40] *Glauben und Verstehen,* Vol. I. "The Problem of Natural Theology," Section III (Tübingen: J. C. B. Mohr Verlag).

[41] *Ibid.,* I. p. 310.

[42] *Ibid.*

to the neutral ontology on which we were so recently building? On what grounds has confidence, then apparently so complete, now all at once been withdrawn? Would Heidegger agree to this last-moment indictment of his method and results? Would he not retort, "Take me not at all, or all in all"?

Lastly, when Bultmann comes to give us his own sketch, in exist-tential terms, of man's existence in unfaith and in faith,[43] we are hardly surprised to find that his relation to Heidegger does not con-form to any of the patterns above suggested. Bultmann's picture seems to be a mixture of Christian-Pauline, idealist, and Heideg-gerian motifs. For Heidegger "authenticity" is the resolute accept-ance of our own existence as a "being unto death." In Bultmann's account, this is replaced by a willingness to give up all attempts at finding our security by reliance on the visible, and by surrender to the invisible, a category unknown to Heidegger. Thus "authenticity" is given here a quite different content from what it has for Heideg-ger. This position is at this point in agreement with the third of Bultmann's positions outlined above, but in conflict with the first and second. In Bultmann's account, the Christian contrast between God and His creature is replaced by the idealistic contrast between the visible and the invisible, and the Bultmannian concept of "the flesh" would seem to be partly Christian, but also distorted by assimilation to the Heideggerian concept of the inauthentic mode of personal being, *das man.*

Here, in fact, we have a picture of man, predominantly Chris-tian, yet influenced by Heidegger's conception, and in conflict with it at the same time.

Breaking away from these obscure and not very consistent rea-sonings of Bultmann's, we may indeed affirm our general acceptance of Brunner's doctrine of man, and welcome the guidance given by his "law of closeness of relationship." True, there are dangers here, which Dr. Brunner himself sees.[44] There is the danger that theology, or Christian eristic, may encroach on other territories where it has no right. There are dangers of slovenly thought on the boundaries of theology and other disciplines, where the theologian may seek to claim immunity from attack by virtue of his possessing insights of faith not available to his interlocutor. But these are dangers which

---

[43] *Kerygma und Mythos,* Vol. I, pp. 27-31. English translation, pp. 16-22.
[44] *Mensch im Widerspruch,* p. 556. (London: Lutterworth), p. 544.

can be guarded against, and in the other camp there is the danger of theologians swallowing whole the unfounded pretensions of each passing non-Christian metaphysic, and building upon the unstable and impossible foundations of a rival *Weltanschauung*.

DAVID CAIRNS

CHRIST COLLEGE,
ABERDEEN, SCOTLAND

5

Paul Tillich

SOME QUESTIONS ON BRUNNER'S EPISTEMOLOGY

SOME QUESTIONS ON BRUNNER'S
EPISTEMOLOGY

One day several years ago, Emil Brunner was sitting in my apartment in New York and agreed happily and gratefully when I said, "It seems to me that in spite of the many divergences which exist between you and Barth and Bultmann and Niebuhr and myself, a kind of common ground in theology has developed in our generation." I still believe that this is a correct statement and I feel confirmed in it, for instance, by the latest developments of Barth and Bultmann. Any comparison with the preceding period which ended in Europe with the death of Troeltsch and Harnack, and in America with the approach of the Second World War, would provide additional confirmation; and so would a comparison of the theology of those mentioned above with the newly strengthened Confessional and Orthodox theology in Europe and America.

The part of Emil Brunner's thinking to which I shall address myself is a point in case. In perhaps his most suggestive book, *The Divine-Human Encounter*, Brunner develops a theological epistemology which seems to me both Biblical and existentialist and, most important, adequate to the subject matter with which theology has to deal. The concept of "encounter" is highly useful in a situation where the word "experience" has lost any definite meaning. It helps greatly to overcome the enslavement to the subject-object structure of knowing that dominates most of our ordinary and scientific thought. In a genuine encounter, subject and object are taken into something third in which they cease to be mere subject or mere object.

This principle has a wide application to the different realms of knowledge. Brunner refers to the person-to-person encounter between human beings as analogy to the person-to-person encounter between God and man. But one can speak of "cognitive encounter" with many realities that have no personal character but which are not mere things either and where the radical application of the subject-object scheme falsifies the subject matter, for example, in historical, psychological, and even biological knowledge. Life in all its dimensions cannot be grasped without an encounter of the knowing and the known beyond the subject-object scheme. If this is the case, the question may arise whether the person-to-person encounter is the only valid analogy to the Divine-human encounter and whether, therefore, in the description of the way of knowing God, the personalistic categories should be used exclusively. They are conspicuously predominant in all of Brunner's writings and can be partly explained in terms of his nominalistic-Reformed tradition.

Inherent in this attitude is Brunner's profound dislike of Schleiermacher whose transpersonal-mystical categories, applied to our knowledge of God, contradict the personalistic emphasis of Brunner. One must ask, however, whether it is possible to establish the divinity of the divine in merely personalistic terms, and whether classical medieval as well as classical German philosophy of religion were not right in combining Biblical personalism (which is excellently interpreted by Brunner) with the basic ontological categories like being, life, spirit, and so on. I think they *were* right.

One of the great achievements of Brunner's theological epistemology is his discussion of the concept of faith. He puts into the sharpest contrast to the orthodox understanding of faith as the acceptance of a doctrine about God, an understanding which presupposes the identification of "Word of God" with doctrine, and in some cases, as in American Fundamentalism, identification of the Word of God with the inspired letters of the Bible. All this is in Brunner's terminology wrong objectivism, missing the existential character of the Divine-human encounter. It is gratifying to note that Brunner, although rather cautiously, criticizes the orthodox-hierarchical development which grew out of the German Church struggle and out of the victory of the so-called "dialectical" theology to which he himself contributed so much. Of course, this theology was never "dialectical," but it was paradoxical and had an almost prophetic impact when it arose. However, the "pupils of the prophets" became "priests," priests of a new kind of pure doctrine and a new form of ecclesiastical authoritarianism. They fell into what Brunner calls "objectivism."

If faith is not the acceptance of doctrinal statements, it must be defined in an existentialist way. Brunner does this by calling faith the "obedience-in-trust" toward the Word of God, identifying the Word with the Biblical message, but not with the letters of the Bible. The Word calls for and creates the acknowledgment of the Lordship of God and it gives the assurance of God that he is seeking fellowship with man. The right relation to God, therefore, is obedience and personal communication. Brunner has powerfully removed the intellectualization of faith by his fight against "objectivism." But has he removed the voluntarization of faith? It was easier for him, on the basis of his tradition, to do the former, but is it not equally necessary to do the latter?

What does the concept of obedience as an element of faith mean? It can mean obedience to a heteronomous command to believe; this certainly would be rejected by Brunner. It can mean the "will to believe" in the way William James has used the concept. This pragmatic-experimental way would not be accepted by Brunner either. It can mean the Thomistic doctrine of the will supplementing the shortcomings of evidence which belong to the Thomistic concept of faith. But this very concept has been attacked consistently by Brunner. Obedience of faith then can only mean obedience to the demands implied in the content of faith. But then the act of faith must already have happened when the "obedience of faith," takes place. Faith cannot be defined by obedience, not even partially.

The image of God as Lord is one of the contents of faith, but it cannot produce faith, because it does not exist, except in the act of faith. But it is not only the concept of Lordship, it is also that of fellowship, which produces epistemological difficulties. One must ask (as in the case of Lordship), what does it mean that God wants to enter into fellowship with man? There can be no doubt that this is highly symbolic, for God is not a "fellow" to man (although many improvised prayers treat him just as that). "Fellowship" between God and man is a symbolic kind of speaking. It presupposes a concept of the Divine-human encounter which transcends the category of fellowship, a concept which points to God as being the subject and the object of all fellowship, who therefore is unable to be only the one side of that relationship. But if God is more than one side of a fellowship, the category of "fellowship" loses its ultimacy (as does the category Lordship) and the question of transpersonal categories arises.

Every existentialist epistemology faces the problem of how the knowledge by encounter and the knowledge by objectifying detachment are related to each other. Brunner is fully aware that "the word of God contains doctrine in some way and the faith . . . entails knowledge" (p. 22). Even the first commandment "conceals doctrine" (p. 110) and Brunner says in the same context that God "instructs us authentically" about Himself. Doctrine is not the Word of God, but it is the "token and framework" within which we have the Word, and the one cannot be separated from the other. Metaphoric terms like these are not very illuminating, but they reveal sharply the difficulty of the problem.

First of all, one must acknowledge that Brunner shows a great consistency in his discussion of the traditional *loci dogmatic:* He always tries to elaborate the existential meaning of a doctrine and to distinguish from it the doctrinal formulation. In many cases this leads to a rather sharp criticism even of very important tenets of classical theology, Catholic as well as Protestant, as, for example, the Trinity and predestination. In his own solution he always refers to the Biblical intention, which has been distorted in the objectifying reflection of theology. This method seems to me fruitful and adequate to the theological task.

One may ask, however, whether the concepts used by Brunner in formulating the dogmatic assertions are sufficiently subjected to the same criticism. I am referring to concepts like substance (which is rejected in relation to God) and subject (which is applied to God), or concepts like person (which is the central category of Brunner's whole theology) and the impersonal (into which everything not personal is thrown without distinction), or concepts like history, nature, and world which are taken from the history of metaphysical thought and remain philosophical problems even if used in everyday language.

Brunner often speaks of the invasion of speculative or metaphysical concepts into the biblical forms of language. If the terms "metaphysical" or "speculative" are used, connotations of such depreciative character are provoked that the question of the truth or untruth of such a concept is not even asked. The mere terms "speculative" or "metaphysical" condemn them a priori. Brunner, who has broken in so many other respects with the Kant-Ritschlian line of thought, is still under the influence of its antiontological skepticism. But this is not justified within the context of his thinking. His own existentialist reinterpretation of many traditional terms is also "metaphysical" and based on the observation of reality as a whole (the original meaning of *speculari*). He could have asked the question for instance, how much and what kind of encounter, even Divine-human encounter, underlies the concepts of the great philosophical systems. The question, it seems to me, is not the distortion of revelatory truth by speculative truth, but the question is the conflict between revelatory experiences of a preparatory character, symbolized in myths and conceptualized in metaphysics, and the revelatory event, on which Christianity is based. The existentialist approach implied in the metaphor encounter must be applied to all of them.

This leads to the problem of religious language generally, the problem of symbol and myth. Perhaps it is because of my own preoccupation with this issue, as well as the discussion provoked by Bultmann's program of demythologization, that I am surprised to find little reference to it in Brunner's constructive writings. The semantic problem does not play a significant role in his thought. He refers to it passingly when he defends the so-called anthropomorphisms of the Old Testament—rightly so, for instance, in connection with the idea of the unchangeability of God. God "repents"— this is a true statement according to Brunner, for it expresses the freedom of the creature in the frame of God's providential acting. I agree, but I ask in what sense can the human experience of repentence be applied to God? It is symbolic language, however, which makes it not less, but more adequate than even the most precise nonsymbolic language, could. And this refers to every utterance about God.

For instance, if Brunner compares the meaning of "person" applied to man with the meaning of "person" applied to God, he sees the difference only in the removal of the human limitations with respect to being a person. But he does not point to the qualitative transformation the concept of person undergoes if the limitations of temporal and spatial existence are removed. If this happens—and it certainly must happen—the term "person" becomes symbolic, a consequence which cannot be prevented by the correct assertion that the full meaning of person can be known only on the basis of the person-to-person encounter between God and man. It seems to be impossible to avoid the semantic problem in systematic theology in our time—or in any time.

The form in which semantics was formerly discussed by theologians was an essay under the title, "De Nominibus." In this and several other contexts the doctrine of *analogia entis* was developed. Brunner affirms its significance; but he seems to be reluctant to discuss it fully and to compare it with the present discussions concerning symbol and myth. One of the reasons for this omission is that this would bring him dangerously close to natural theology, which used the *analogia entis* as its main tool. He would be right if theological semantics necessarily had this consequence. If *analogia entis* (or any theory of religious symbols) meant the epistemological foundation of a natural theology which leads with rational conclusions from man to God, the radical rejection of this concept and all its implications would be mandatory.

But the three main concepts used in the preceding sentence, *analogia entis,* natural theology, and reason, are not as unambiguous as such a rejection would imply. *Analogia entis* can simply mean the semantic fact that in order to speak of that which transcends finite being, we must use a language which is produced by the encounter with finite being. Such language, if applied to God, is used analogically or—a term I would prefer for semantic reasons—"symbolically." The symbols are born, according to an existentialist approach like that of Brunner, out of the Divine-human encounter. This is not *analogia entis* in the mode of traditional natural theology, but it is semantic analysis of the relation of the religious language to other types of language, a task required of both analytic philosophers and systematic theologians.

This leads to the question of natural theology as such. It is one of the important things our generation has learned from people like Brunner and Barth that any attempt to reach God conceptually by logical conclusions is as contrary to the Protestant principle as the attempt to reach God morally by fulfilling the commandments of the law or ritually by fulfilling the sacramental prescriptions. Against this stands the uncompromising Protestant principle. It is in this point above all that I see the basic agreement among the theologians mentioned in the introductory remarks. However, I do not believe that the concern of natural theology must or even can be dismissed on this basis.

Although Brunner, in opposition to Barth, enlarges the concept

SOME QUESTIONS ON BRUNNER'S EPISTEMOLOGY   105

of revelation so that it includes revelation through nature, through the Holy Spirit, through ultimate fulfillment, he does not apply it to the history of religion and culture. I suspect that his not very sympathetic treatment of the non-Christian religions is rooted in this omission. I do not think that it follows necessarily from the structure of Brunner's theology, but it probably follows from his fear of natural theology.

We certainly cannot say that any religion *qua* religion is revelation and this refers to Christianity as a religion as much as to any other religion. This earliest teaching of the so-called dialectical theology remains valid because it is an application of the Protestant principle and a necessary expression of the relationship of God and man. But as the Christian religion is based on revelatory events and, above all, on the appearance of Jesus as the Christ, so other religions may be the reception and distortion of a preceding revelation which is more than the nonhistorical revelation through nature defended by Brunner. In these original revelatory experiences the presence of a divine ground in everything may have become manifest—not in terms of a logical conclusion, but in terms of an ecstatic awareness. The actual state of the non-Christian religions, as well as the attitude toward them in Bible and Church show that God has never left mankind to itself. If there is any genuine—however distorted—piety other than the revelation on which Christianity is based, then this piety must be a result of a divine self-manifestation. (This statement is in line with the Protestant principle as restated by Brunner himself.)

It is at such points as these that I feel that "dialectical" theology, including that of Brunner could make an important step beyond the self-limitations of its beginnings. And sometimes—while writing this—I have had the feeling that Brunner himself would be ready to transcend some of his statements on which this discussion is based. This, however, is an anticipation of the answer he will give in the present book.

Besides *analogia entis* and natural theology, I have referred to reason as an ambiguous and intricate concept. Brunner's important book, *Reason and Revelation,* deals with it. Brunner acknowledges in principle that the term "reason" is more embracing than cognitive reasoning. He knows that there is a logos-reason which embraces all functions of human culture, the aesthetic and moral, as well as the cognitive. And he knows that there are many realms of cognitive reason which are not neutral with respect to the principles of revelatory truth. This elevates the discussion immediately to a higher level than is possible if reason is restricted to analysis, calculation, and management.

The logos type of reason embraces more than the inductive-deductive method of scientific research. But if this is accepted, one must ask, as does Brunner, how are the logos of revelation and the logos of reason related to each other? It certainly is not enough to say that revelation cannot reject reason because it must express itself in a structured language, that is, in the rational terms. This is obvious and must be emphasized against the theological and, even more, popular-religious despisers of reason. But it does not solve the problem. This can be done only if we reach a sharply defined concept of reason. Brunner comes near to it when he uses the word "meaning" as a possible translation of "logos." But he does not pursue this line sufficiently.

It seems to me that the Stoic doctrine in which the logos embraces the structure both of mind and reality is nearer to the early Christian and even Johannine logos doctrine than Brunner admits. Certainly, the logos of the stoics is not with God in the way in which the logos of the Fourth Gospel is. But if he is the mediator of the creation this symbol can only mean that the structure of reality is *logikon,* logos-determined, meaningful. However, this would remove the radical Ritschlian gap between cosmological and soteriological concepts (a gap which is unfair to Greek thinking and impoverishing to Christian thinking). The cosmological potentialities are eternally present in the logos, the divine principle of self-manifestation. On this basis the relation of the logos-concept of reason (universal structure of meaning in world and mind) and Christian revelation looks different. In revelation that transcends reason is the paradox of the self-manifestation of God in a personal life under the conditions of existence, establishing in him the ultimate power and the ultimate criterion of the new being in which the estrangement of God and his world is conquered. This is not implied in logos-structure or reality (as estrangement is not implied in the logos-structure of reality), but it is the same logos, the divine self-manifestation through whom the world has received its structure of meaning and through whom the estranged world is reunited with God.

What I have tried to do in this article constitutes neither a report about Brunner's theology, nor a critical rejection of it. But it is the continuation and formalization of a conversation which has been going on between us for many years—sometimes directly—and which I hope will continue, at least indirectly, for many more years.

PAUL TILLICH

UNIVERSITY PROFESSOR
HARVARD UNIVERSITY
CAMBRIDGE, MASS.

6

George A. Schrader

BRUNNER'S CONCEPTION OF PHILOSOPHY

BRUNNER'S CONCEPTION OF PHILOSOPHY

K ierkegaard, the religious thinker who has been of such decisive importance for Protestant theology in the twentieth century, cannot be accused of having been anti-intellectual. No writer ever pushed his own intellect to the limit in the analysis of ultimate questions more than Søren Kierkegaard. He was not opposed to the exercise of the intellect but only to its *secular* or *objective* employment. The proper use of the mind in the quest for truth is within the bounds of Christian faith. Reason as it attempts to operate apart from the commitment of faith is doomed to become *fantastic* and to issue in despair. Whereas faith begins with existence and reasons from it, reason transforms existence into possibility. The way of faith is the way and the only way of *truth;* the way of knowledge is the way of *possibility*. Faith and knowledge, then, move in different and opposite directions, the one toward and the other away from existence. To apprehend truth means to live in the truth, to exist in one's thought. And this is possible only through the commitment of faith.

On Kierkegaard's view, then, philosophy cannot apprehend the truth of existence because the priority it assigns to the intellect requires it to transform existence into possibility. Philosophy cannot apprehend the truth of the self, of the world, or of God, but can only construct various possible views of them. Objective metaphysics cannot apprehend ultimate truth nor can it be really *serious*. In the last analysis, objective thought can be nothing more than a *game* in which one plays with possibilities. If Kierkegaard is not anti-intellectual he is surely antiphilosophical, for only the most radical skeptic would admit that the whole movement of philosophical thought is away from existence. This view of philosophy has the effect of reducing it to an abstract logic which can make no claims to truth at all. Some contemporary philosophers would not be unwilling to accept such a characterization of philosophy. They would have no difficulty in admitting that the philosopher begins with abstract conceptual schemes from which he selects some combination to conjoin with existence by pragmatic rules. It might appear, in fact, that this positivistic conception of philosophy is perfectly consonant with a Kierkegaardian view of reason and faith. And at least some disciples of Kierkegaard have so declared themselves. Since positivistic philosophy has surrendered any and all claims to even the possibility of truth about ultimate reality, it has granted Kierkegaard's entire indictment of philosophic reason. It is no accident that neo-reformation theology and positivistic philosophy have flourished on a common soil.

But tempting as this resolution of the conflict between faith and reason may appear, the matter is by no means so simple as this. Positivistic philosophy effects a retrenchment not only of philosophy and its speculative ventures but, also, of theology. If metaphysical assertions are "meaningless" and hopelessly subjective, the same is true, from their point of view, of theological assertions.[1] If it is meaningless to think or talk of a being who transcends the world, it makes no better sense to speak of the self-disclosure of such a pure transcendent subject or of a *personal encounter* with such a subject. The annihilation of philosophy as a speculative venture, an organon of truth, carries with it, and necessarily, the annihilation of theology. Or, to put the same thing in different terms, the reduction of metaphysics to a kind of poetry reduces theology, also, to poetic utterance.

If it sees clearly what it is really about and is serious, theology cannot allow such a reduction. Even if objective ontology be disavowed, theology cannot surrender its own claims to encounter with transcendent being. It is one thing for theology to insist that God is not an *object* in the world and that He cannot be treated as a being alongside other beings. But a negative theology which goes so far as to deny all positive references to God, to deny that He may be even symbolically designated as "the ground of all being," becomes tantamount to a sophisticated atheism. Unless theology itself is willing to embrace an equivalent positivism which limits

[1] Brunner, *Revelation and Reason* (Philadelphia: The Westminster Press, 1946) pp. 5-6: "The Christian claim to revelation stands in sharpest possible opposition to this conception of truth."

the meaning of religious language to human history, it must reject the positivistic reduction. But, and this is the important point, to do this it must reconsider the original Kierkegaardian repudiation of metaphysical inquiry.

If philosophy is not allowed even to know the name of God, it cannot be expected to take seriously the claim that He has disclosed Himself uniquely to man in human history. For theology to emasculate reason in this fashion is, inevitably, to deprive itself of the support it requires for its own declarations. Even Karl Barth admits the necessity of employing reason and philosophical categories in the explication of revealed truth. But what he does not recognize is that such an employment of philosophical concepts would not be possible if philosophy were to be deprived of its *autonomy*. Greek metaphysics was available for the use of the Church Fathers in the formulation of the early creeds. This indebtedness, which some Protestant theologians have deplored, was essential if Christian doctrine were to receive intelligible structure. It is inconceivable that Augustine, for example, could have developed his own theology without reference to Plato and Plotinus. If Greek philosophy did not provide a ready-made theoretical vessel for the receipt of Christian revelation, it surely provided a metaphysical concern and well developed theoretical tools.

As Cornford has shown, Greek philosophy was not so unqualifiedly secular as has generally been maintained. The philosophy of Plato and Aristotle, and even of the pre-Socratics, was infused with religious and theological concern. The usual contrast between Hebraic-Christian religious thought and Greek speculation ignores the philosophical element in Hebraic thought and the theological concern among the Greeks. But we need not appeal to the facts of history to make the point that Christian theology requires the secular office of philosophy. Questions concerning the nature of knowledge, its origin and its limits, the nature of truth, the structure of existence, and so on, are essentially *philosophical* questions that must be posed and answered by reason. Any theology which has not itself reflected on these questions is in so far *naïve* and runs the risk that it may make unwarranted claims that confuse knowledge with faith.[2] The purity of theology requires *philosophical sophistication* fully as much as the purity of philosophy requires

---

[2] Brunner, *Philosophie und Offenbarung*, (Tübingen: J. C. B. Mohr [Paul Siebeck], 1925), p. 10.

theological sophistication. The history of the interpretation of the Bible within Protestant thought provides abundant illustration of this point. Fundamentalism, for example, commits theology to defend claims about man and the world which cannot survive the criticism of science and philosophy. If no secular science and no secular philosophy had existed to perform this function, it would have been necessary for theology itself to develop such disciplines. Where no *secular* office of philosophy exists, theology has no alternative but to remain naïve and mute. And, we should add, the situation is in no wise altered if the secular function of reason is exercised within the domain of theology itself. Where the distinctive though related functions of reason, namely as a relatively autonomous mode of inquiry and as the instrument for the expression of revealed truth, are not explicitly recognized, confusion is inevitable. The philosopher is bound to think that he has proved more than he can prove and the theologian to conclude that his own philosophical assertions require no validation.

In spite of his great indebtedness to Kierkegaard, it is one of the great merits of Emil Brunner that he fully appreciates the importance of the secular function of reason. Faith not only recognizes the function of philosophy, but presupposes it. There can be no "double truth," a truth of reason and a truth of faith.[3] "Revelation and reason possess one common element: they both claim truth." It is precisely for this reason that the two can converse with each other, be mutually relevant, and disagree. Since Brunner recognizes that there is only one truth, even though it may be apprehended and conveyed in radically different ways, the relationship between rationally attested truth and revealed truth is especially acute. If there is only *one truth* and if both reason and faith are at least relatively independent modes of apprehending truth, the possibility that they may conflict is by no means precluded. But, we must ask, is it possible to acknowledge the full *autonomy* of reason and faith while avoiding, if not a double standard of truth, *antinomy* and *paradox*? Is philosophy to be appraised from the standpoint of faith or faith from the standpoint of philosophy? Or is there, possibly, a *transcendental* perspective from the vantage point of which it is possible judiciously to assess the status of both and to determine

---

[3] Brunner, *Revelation and Reason, op. cit.,* p. 205; cf. *The Philosophy of Religion* (N.Y.: Charles Scribner's Sons, 1937), p. 55: ". . . for dual truth means no truth at all."

their limits? If, in case of dispute, faith is assigned the supremacy, with what *right* is this decision made? Can only a faith informed by reason or a reason with the commitment of faith resolve such disputes? And is this, in fact, what Brunner himself has in mind in speaking of a *Christian philosophy?* If a Christian philosophy is possible, why not a philosophical Christianity? These are some of the questions which need to be clarified and, if possible, answered in an examination of Emil Brunner's conception of the status and function of philosophy.

Philosophy, Brunner states, is "both possible and necessary, because as Christians we neither can nor should cease to think. It is not reason but rationalism that makes Christian philosophy appear impossible." [4] It is, of course, to *Christian* philosophy that he is referring here. But, in this context, the qualification *Christian* does not appear to be necessary. It is "possible and necessary" for the Christian to engage in philosophy and, we might add, on Brunner's analysis perfectly legitimate for him to do so. Philosophy as Brunner conceives of it is the quest for knowledge about man, the world, and the ultimate ground of both. To leave philosophy aside would be to surrender one's intellect. And there is nothing in the Christian faith that militates against the free use of the mind either in science or philosophy. "Faith does not stand in opposition to knowledge, as little as to ethical will. Rather, it presupposes both." [5] The better the science, the deeper the philosophy, the greater the advantage for faith. Only as man engages in the quest for knowledge does he arrive at an absolute limit. This "An-die-Grenze-Kommen" is an essential condition for the possibility of faith. The threat to faith is not reason but a sinfully employed reason which will produce everything from itself. "All conflicts between faith and reason are sham conflicts." [6] It is only insofar as reason fails to recognize its own proper limits and pretends to a *false autonomy* that it can conflict with the disclosures of faith. Theology honors critical philosophy.[7] Not only is a conflict between reason and faith unnecessary, but, Brunner affirms, Christian faith *cannot* conflict with critical idealism.[8]

[4] Brunner, *Revelation and Reason, op. cit.,* p. 392.
[5] Brunner, *Philosophie und Offenbarung, op. cit.,* p. 39.
[6] Brunner, *Revelation and Reason, op. cit.,* p. 217; cf. *Philosophie und Offenbarung, op. cit.,* pp. 95 ff.
[7] Brunner, *Philosophie und Offenbarung, op. cit.,* p. 9; cf. *The Philosophy of Religion, op. cit.,* pp. 95 ff.
[8] Brunner, *Revelation and Reason, op. cit.,* p. 352.

I suggested above that the qualification "Christian" is not necessary because, presumably, it is equally necessary and legitimate for the non-Christian to exercise his mind and to know all that it is possible for him to know. Brunner's point was to affirm the legitimacy for a *Christian* believer to engage in the secular discipline of philosophy. But, obviously, the justification holds for all human beings and not for Christians alone. It is not the fact that he is a *Christian* believer that keeps his pursuit of philosophy from conflicting with his faith, but rather that he has a proper conception of the nature of philosophical endeavor. If there is no double truth, there cannot be one *true* conception of science and philosophy for the Christian thinker and another for the non-Christian.[9] Only the Christian believer has a faith which completes and sets his reason free.[10] But as scientist or philosopher he is in possession of no *esoteric knowledge* which gives him an advantage over the non-believer. The question of the will and the sinful use of reason is relevant and must be considered in connection with this issue. But it is important first to see in what respects reason and faith are independent of each other.

Let us remember, in the first instance, that as Brunner states it, there is nothing sinful in the exercise of reason as such and, hence, nothing sinful in the enterprise of philosophy. Sin may and does infect philosophy and, when it does, inevitably stands in the philosopher's way. Hence, the pronouncements of faith are *relevant* and even crucially relevant to the human quest for truth in all of its aspects. But we must be careful to avoid an easy confusion on this point. Even though it is relevant to proclaim the sinful use of reason and to specify it in particular instances, it is not, from Brunner's position, relevant or legitimate to invoke such a judgment in attempting *to decide a proper scientific or philosophical question.* Revelation has nothing *directly* to say about questions that may arise in science or philosophy. Brunner is specific in stating that faith has nothing to say about questions of a factual or logical nature and, by implication, of a general philosophical nature. A logician may misuse his own reason and, for example, be unwilling to acknowledge a deficiency in one of his proofs. And this may be a result of his pride. But to point to his pride is not to exhibit the logical error, and Brunner is surely correct in distinguishing the two

[9] *Ibid.*, p. 213.
[10] *Ibid.*, p. 429.

procedures. There are logical questions that have nothing directly to do with the possible sinfulness of man, and to invoke religious categories in a discussion of purely logical matters is to adopt a comic role. The case of science and logic is much clearer than that of philosophy in general, since Brunner is willing to accept only a *critical philosophy*. But the principle is clear even if the status of metaphysical questions must remain for the moment in doubt. Insofar as a *proper* metaphysical question is stated within a philosophical context, it would be an illegitimate *ad hominem* to point to the sinfulness of one of the parties to a dispute. To assess the spiritual condition of the disputants, insofar as this might be possible, would advance us not one whit toward the resolution of the problem.

Brunner not only acknowledges the legitimacy of philosophy but, as we have seen, conceives of the possibility of a *Christian philosophy*. It is important to consider in what sense he regards philosophy as in any sense *Christian*. It is perfectly clear that he does not look upon philosophy as nothing but the expression of Christian revelation. Human reason, on Brunner's view, has its proper autonomy and engages in the quest for knowledge in at least relative independence of the disclosures of faith. To understand the Bible ever so well, even "through the eyes of faith," is by no means to qualify as a competent philosopher. Philosophy is not and cannot be *Christian* in the sense that it is merely theology. Philosophical knowledge can be achieved only through the vigorous exercise of the intellect as it works with the materials of experience. So far as the form or content of philosophical truth is concerned, the Christian engaging in philosophy has absolutely no advantage over the non-Christian. He cannot, in the first instance, come by his truths by deriving them from revelation, and, in the second place, he cannot defend them by appeal to faith. As philosopher he must justify his knowledge claims before the court of reason alone. Thus, there is no special *Christian philosophy* in the sense that any special set of philosophical doctrines may be regarded as distinctly Christian.

There is, of course, a very important question as to the compatibility of any given philosophical system with Christian revelation. Quite clearly, Christian theology is not compatible with, for example, a dogmatic materialistic metaphysics. The theologian or, indeed, the Christian believer, may insist that such a philosophy *must be* false because it disallows a truth of which he is certain. He thus pits his faith against the claims of the philosopher. Now this might be regarded as the end of the matter so far as the Christian believer is concerned; faith itself might be regarded as capable of establishing the limits of reason and, further, as the final arbiter in all matters of dispute. But Brunner does not adopt this position. His rejection of a *double truth* and his refusal to set faith above reason within the same sphere require him to find another solution. It is not faith which must be relied upon to limit reason, but philosophical reason itself. Brunner has confidence in the ability of reason to be critical of itself, to establish its own limits. But, it is important to add, *critical philosophy*, which Brunner regards as the only sound philosophy, is not to be embraced simply because it better accords with the pronouncements of faith, but rather because it *truly* and *realistically* assesses the scope and limits of human reason. Reason can know whatever it can know and, I take it, Brunner would consider it absurd to deny this proposition. To claim that reason is incapable of attaining knowledge only on the ground that for it to attain such knowledge would be to compromise the majesty of faith is wholly arbitrary. It is the philosopher alone who is expert in assessing the validity of knowledge claims.

On Brunner's view a critical philosopher like Kant, who was regarded by many as *the philosopher of Protestantism*, is either correct or incorrect in his claims as to the proper scope and limits of human reason. Kant himself stated in the Preface to the Second Edition of the *Critique of Pure Reason* that he was doing away with knowledge in order to make room for faith. Richard Kroner interprets this to mean that Kant was really *anti-intellectual* and considered it morally and religiously wrong for reason to obtain knowledge of God and the human soul. Kant doubtless thought that if knowledge were absolute it would leave no room for faith. But the argument of the *Critique of Pure Reason* is in no instance spoiled by any such ulterior concerns. The soundness of Kant's analysis of human knowledge in no way depends upon the validity of his conception of morality and/or religion. Reason must determine its own proper limits. This, I take it, is the view both of Kant and Emil Brunner. Neither of them embraces *anti-intellectualism* in any form. Kroner's interpretation of Kant and of philosophy generally reflects an element of Kierkegaard's anti-philosophical bias which Brunner rejects. There is but one truth in any given sphere and such truth must be determined by procedures appropriate to the context. This applies no less to metaphysics and ontology than to logic and science generally.

I want, in a moment, to examine Brunner's own view of the proper limits of philosophical reason and to argue that he has allowed too narrow a compass to philosophical speculation. But first we need to specify the sense in which philosophy may be Christian on Brunner's view. Brunner has stated the point with admirable clarity: "Only the Christian philosopher can think truly critically, and truly realistically, and only the critical philosopher can be a Christian." [11] By a *Christian philosopher* it is evident that Brunner means nothing more than the Christian believer who engages in the enterprise of philosophy. He is a *Christian philosopher* in the same sense in which he might be a Buddhist or a Hindu philosopher, that is, as a Buddhist or a Hindu who engages in philosophy. The adjective is meant to qualify the philosopher as a man, as an individual human being. In exactly the same way we might refer to the *Christian* physicist or the *Christian* biologist.

In asserting that "only the Christian philosopher can think critically, truly realistically" Brunner means to call attention to the fact that only the Christian fully understands and accepts his finite and sinful condition. He understands himself more profoundly than the non-Christian because God has disclosed to him his own perversity. But it is more than a matter of *understanding*, for the understanding itself is predicated on *faith* and *obedience*. In knowing for the first time that he is capable of sin and of a sinful exercise of his intellect and, further, in accepting this as the universal condition from which there is no escape save through God's grace, the Christian is in a position to be fully *realistic* about himself and the world. In knowing what faith is, in experiencing faith by living in it, he is able to distinguish more clearly between what is known or can be known and what can only be believed or accepted through faith. He can be realistic, first, because he knows himself more deeply and, secondly, because in and through his faith he is absolutely committed. If not above it, he is at least in a more favorable position to avoid the temptation to achieve salvation through *gnosis*. He has, in short, attained a new and higher freedom; he is free to recognize the truth about himself and the world for what it is. Since he has had an en-

11 *Ibid.*, p. 392.

counter with the one true God who, as pure subject transcends the world, he can more easily recognize the *idols* of reason. These are the conditions which, on Brunner's analysis, make it possible for the Christian to be truly critical and truly realistic.

It is much clearer why the Christian may be in a position to be realistic in his philosophy than why "only the Christian can think truly critically." Brunner believes, and regards this to be an essential tenet of the Christian faith that only through the historical revelation of God in Christ can the individual have a *personal encounter* with God. In maintaining this point he surely goes beyond a *confessional* statement to make a *dogmatic* affirmation. The possibility must be considered that although the Christian may have a personal encounter with God through His revelation in history and this encounter may be decisive for his own relation to God, it may not be the *necessary* condition for all personal encounter with God. If, as Kierkegaard was so fond of reminding us, "with God all things are possible," even the Christian is in no position to assert that God *can* reveal himself to man only in and through a special set of historical circumstances.

Such an assertion is either analytic, constituting nothing more than a definition of what is meant by personal encounter, or it is synthetic and dogmatic. We reach a point here, incidentally, where a question about the limits of theological knowledge must be raised. The *confessional* utterance which intends only to proclaim one's own faith can rest content with the analytic interpretation of the statement. It affirms that God has actually been encountered by the individual in a certain way, but does not attempt to transcend this experience altogether to make pronouncements about the possible ways in which God might be encountered. It is the *only* in Brunner's statement which is bound to trouble the philosopher, for it implies a knowledge of God that goes beyond anything that could be certified on the basis of historical revelation. How far can reason transcend the boundaries of faith without becoming speculative? And can it certify its more speculative utterances by appeal to faith alone? If critical philosophy is in order, is not a critical theology equally demanded? And have we not here found an instance of an *uncritical* or *dogmatic* gesture on the part of the theologian? Brunner abhors dogmatism in philosophy and I am sure can be no happier with it when it appears under the tent of theology. It is evident that a personal encounter with God in some context, historical or nonhistorical, other than the Christian revelation would have different features. But it is by no means evident that it would not or could not be the same God or that it could not be a disclosure of God in His subjectivity. My point is that in making such a dogmatic claim the theologian transcends a historically delimited encounter with God in order to make ontological pronouncements. He does not confine himself to the interpretation of the distinctive experience of the Christian believer, but asserts what is and is not *possible for all modes of encounter* with God. It is on precisely such a point as this that philosophy and theology must enter into discussion. Philosophy may prove invaluable in exhibiting the uncritical ventures of Christian theology.

It is apparent that Brunner favors critical philosophy not only because it is compatible with the Christian faith but, also, because he regards it as the soundest philosophical position. If it were on any count wrong or if critical philosophy were to be generally mistaken, Brunner would not want to support it. To endorse a mistaken philosophical position would be to introduce the sort of double-truth standard that Brunner rejects. It is important, then, to examine the limits which, on Brunner's view, are established by critical philosophy. An important case in point which he has discussed in detail is that of our knowledge of persons, both human and divine.

Brunner conceives of theology as dialectical. It is based upon a personal and existential encounter of the individual subject with God. Theology is founded upon this involvement of man with God and would be impossible apart from it. The Christian believer does not find it necessary either to produce the reality of God or to demonstrate His existence. He simply encounters God as his Creator and Redeemer, as the ultimate Subject with whom he is involved. Theology, as Brunner understands it, is *realistic, dialectical,* and *existential.* The primary basis of all theological reflection is the encounter with God and, of course, the being both of God and the individual human subject.

But whereas, on Brunner's view, theology begins with God and with faith, interpreted as fundamentally the relation of the believer to God, philosophy begins with man and the natural world and must *infer* the existence of God. Philosophy, on his interpretation of it, is markedly nondialectical and nonexistential.

But the hypotheses of metaphysics lack such [scientific] confirmation. They are purely logical extensions or augmentations of the picture of the world as presented by science or even by naïve sense perception. Their instruments are inference by causal regress and analogy, and these can never reach the unconditioned and absolute, but only a maximum of the finite. The God attained by metaphysics is never the almighty, but only a very powerful being, never the creator but only a demiurge.[12]

Now this is surely a fair characterization of some representatives of critical and, for that matter, even dogmatic philosophy. In the *Dialogues Concerning Natural Religion,* for example, Hume represents the task of natural theology in exactly these terms and reaches the same skeptical conclusion as that affirmed in Brunner's statement. If we must reach God by building Him up, as it were, out of the materials of the natural world and by a process which only goes a step further than the speculations of the natural sciences, the case is pretty desperate. A metaphysics which depends solely upon this type of causal inference cannot get very far beyond "the picture of the world as presented by science or even by naïve sense-perception." Moreover, the further it ventures the more dubious are its pronouncements. And so Immanuel Kant, the critical philosopher par excellence, also looked upon the role of reason in its speculative ventures. It leaves the full-bodied realm of experience only to beat its wings in an etherless void. We cannot reliably infer the existence of God from the facts of the world but only *postulate* His existence on the basis of our moral faith. If critical philosophy were the only sound philosophy, Brunner's claim that in the words of Luther, "the way of thought leads into the dark emptiness of reason" would be justified.[13] But we must question whether *critical philosophy* which involves only hypotheses "which are purely logical extensions or augmentations of the picture of the world as represented by science or even by naïve sense-perception" is the *only true philosophy.* Has Brunner, perhaps, prejudiced the issue somewhat in regarding theology as dialectical and existential while refusing to allow that philosophical reason might be capable of a similar involvement?

It is surely true, as Kant demonstrated, that we cannot know any reality as it is in and for itself through an objective apprehension

---

[12] Brunner, *The Philosophy of Religion, op. cit.,* p. 65.
[13] Brunner, *Revelation and Reason, op. cit.,* p. 409.

of it. To the degree that knowledge involves the appropriation of an object by a subject which insists upon its own purposes, interests, and categories, it cannot escape subjectivity. Science and a metaphysics, which models itself on science, cannot ultimately transcend appearance. As Hegel pointed out and as Kant knew, this amounts to saying that the object *qua* object cannot be known as a subject. And the converse of this proposition is that no subject *qua* subject can be known as an object. Insofar as Brunner is only reiterating this point he is on well supported philosophical ground. But when Brunner claims that a subject can never be known as an object, he is, I think, guilty of a confusion. It does not follow from the fact that a subject cannot *qua subject* be known as object, that a subject cannot be known as an object. Only if a being were *pure subject* would this inference be justified. In the case of God, of course, this is precisely what Brunner and others have maintained. And Brunner makes a similar claim with respect to human subjects. "The objective attitude toward persons is as wrong as a personal attitude toward things. Persons are not objects, but subjects; they have a claim on us to be known as 'thou.' " [14]

Now it is not at all clear to me that the "objective attitude toward persons is wrong" unless it is such as to regard persons *merely* as objects. To regard persons as objects *merely* would be, in effect, to deny that they are subjects in and for themselves. Such an attitude is not only *morally wrong* but *mistaken*. The attitude has the import of misrepresenting the being toward which it is directed. But it might be equally mistaken to regard a person as in no way an object. Surely every human subject has a body and expresses himself in and through his body, his actions, his words, and so forth. These are surely *objective* manifestations of the person and capable of being observed and described. I cannot disclaim my body any more than I can disavow my actions. For me to attempt this would be for me to put myself in the most acute form of *bad faith*, to use Sartre's term, and to pretend that I have a purely *private* and *subjective mode* of existence. The fact is that I am both subject and object and the unity of the two. I can be known *objectively* even though my inwardness can be revealed only insofar as I choose to reveal it through communication. It would be, I think, just as wrong to be treated as a *pure*

[14] *Ibid.*, p. 372; cf. Brunner, *The Philosophy of Religion*, *op. cit.*, pp. 89 ff.; *Philosophie und Offenbarung*, *op. cit.*, p. 50.

subject as a *mere object*. If I should be found lying in a ditch, I should want to be aided and, perhaps, taken to a hospital. This would surely be to treat me as an object, though not necessarily merely as an object. Moreover, one of the important and difficult lessons we each have to learn is that our bodies and our actions are our own and that we are responsible for them. We may be, as is well known, honest in thought and flagrantly dishonest in deed. In spite of my best efforts at disguise or concealment I reveal far more of myself in my appearance to others than I would like. I am an *object* for others as well as for myself, and this constitutes one of the most fundamental problems confronting me. And so, too, is the other an object for me. There is nothing wrong or mistaken in regarding oneself, others, or even God as an object. On the contrary, to do so is altogether unavoidable and necessary. It is only an attitude which regards human subjects or God as *merely an object* that is in error both morally and cognitively.

Brunner is fundamentally mistaken, I think, in assuming that reason must *infer* the existence either of God or of persons.[15] Reason begins with existence, be it that of God or of objects in the world. I do not have to infer that my neighbor is a person, a subject, by the observation of data. If that were the case, his reality as a person would never be more than *hypothetical*. I am from the first involved with him as a human subject and this is presupposed in all of my judgments about him. Existence here as elsewhere is *given* and *not inferred*. Kant knew this, I might add, in the case of empirical objects. Existence is given and could never be proved since all proofs begin with existence. But Kant was not a dialectical thinker and he did not see that in the cognitive situation the object is of as great an importance as the subject. Kant remarked that it is absurd to speak of an *appearance* without *something that appears*, but he neglected to analyze the relation between the thing as appearance and as thing-in-itself. Because for Kant the involvement is decisive only from the side of the knowing subject, it is necessary to conjecture as to the thing as it is in itself. But such conjecture is unnecessary if we are confronted from the first not simply with an appearance which is detached from its ground, but with an integral being which is as much involved as we ourselves in the experience. It was Hegel's

---

[15] Cf. Brunner, *The Philosophy of Religion, op. cit.*, p. 76: "But it is not only God who is unreal to us apart from revelation, but ourselves also."

great contribution to philosophy to recognize that the relation of subject to object is *internal* and *dialectical* and, hence, that the full being of both is involved in every experience. In other words, knowledge *requires* existential involvement and encounter. The fact that the deliverances of understanding never succeed in fixing the ultimate being of the one encountered in no way entails that existence *is only inferred from observed facts*. One need not adopt Hegel's view of absolute knowledge to reject the Kantian critical standpoint which permits only *shrewd guesses* about the ultimately real. It is important to note here that for Kant our knowledge both of God and empirical objects depends upon inference from our observations and for the same reason, namely that the knowing relationship is one-sided and nondialectical. If this basic presupposition of *critical philosophy* is questioned, we are no longer required to accept Brunner's characterization of the philosophical situation as having to formulate hypotheses on the basis of scientific or common sense observations. In short, Brunner completely fails to consider the possibility of either a dialectical or an existential metaphysics which begins with existence and involvement with other beings.

The fact of the matter is that knowledge is not based merely on *observation* and *inference*. I do not merely *look* at the world, but am involved in it in a variety of ways through feelings, volitions, actions, and so on. I do not take all the initiative in establishing the myriad relations presupposed by rational knowledge, for I respond as much as I lead. Feelings are my feelings but not merely that, for they refer beyond me and are clues to that to which I respond. My experience reflects my world fully as much as it reflects anything original with and internal to me. And because this is true, I am not put in the position of having to *infer* from subjectively ascertained facts what may lie beyond them. There is nothing presumptive or uncritical, in the sense of injudicious, about a philosophy which proceeds on such a basis. It does imply that metaphysics is prior both to ordinary knowledge and scientific theory in that it deals with the basic ontological relatedness underlying them. But it would be uncritical only if it were to deny that one term of the relation is always and inescapably a finite subject, namely myself.

The point I have attempted to make in this too brief discussion of critical philosophy is that Brunner's conception of philosophy is one-sided and itself *uncritical*. He seems to embrace a particular type of philosophy because it accords best with his own theological position without examining its intrinsic soundness vis-à-vis other philosophical perspectives. If Brunner is to defend his choice of a philosophical position, it is up to him to defend it against those who reject it for cogent reasons. Failing this, he must reconsider what he has said about the possibility of rational knowledge of God and human subjects. I hope I have made it clear that the limits he assigns to philosophical knowledge depend upon his conception of critical philosophy as nonexistential and nondialectical. If *critical philosophy* is not the only *sound philosophy*, which I am convinced it is not, then we have a right to question Brunner's statements as to the limitations under which philosophical theology and metaphysics operate in their concern with God.

It is, I think, both *bad theology* and *bad metaphysics* to maintain that God is pure subject.[16] The notion of a subject is surely a philosophical concept which has been assimilated by theology, or, if you prefer, even as it may have been independently developed by theology. We need not claim that we know God perfectly, either on the basis of natural knowledge or revelation. But if we are to talk or think meaningfully about God at all, we must reflect on what we mean or can mean in referring to God as a subject. Could He, for example, be in any sense a subject unless He were self-related, unless He were a self? And if He is, as a self, related to Himself, is He not necessarily an object to Himself? And if He is an object to Himself and necessarily so, how does this in any way militate against the possibility of our knowing Him as an object? In other words, in knowing Him as an object might we not in some way know Him as a self and, even, as a subject? Moreover, if God is related to the created world and to finite persons, must He not reflect this relatedness in Himself? Is not the creation some sort of expression of God in objective form and, if He is a living God who is present to His creation, does this not entail that God is more than pure subject? Hasn't Hegel given us a pretty definitive analysis of what it means to be a subject and delineated, if not exhaustively, at least some of the necessary modalities which pertain to a subject, whether human or divine? We cannot, to be sure, press any analogy too far in reference to

---

[16] Brunner, *Philosophie und Offenbarung, op. cit.*, pp. 50 ff.

God. But unless we take our analogy seriously, it becomes pointless.

The theologian *qua* theologian does not, I take it, concern himself with the analysis of such a concept as that of a *subject* for its own sake. He is concerned rather to employ it, on the basis of his understanding of it, in articulating the disclosures of religious faith. If that be so, then he may be guilty on occasion of working with poor metaphysical tools and is open to correction by the philosopher. Are Kierkegaard's, and after him Barth's and Brunner's, statements about God as the wholly transcendent subject to remain unanalyzed and immune to criticism? Critical philosophy might be content to leave theology to decide the matter and consider it beyond the limits of legitimate philosophical concern. But a dialectically oriented philosophy cannot leave the issue unexamined. It is, perhaps, through faith and revelation that God as subject is most adequately and authoritatively disclosed to man. But as soon as this revelation is interpreted, general philosophical questions are raised. And it is not merely futile controversy that results but, also, fruitful discussion. Religious revelation may be, indeed, the most important source of insight and knowledge of subjectivity, of the "hidden God." But metaphysics is of crucial importance in specifying the conditions for the understanding of this revelation. What is the relationship between the hidden and transcendent God of revelation and the God of natural theology and metaphysics? Surely it not only can be but must be *one and the same God*. Only Brunner's mistaken assumption that philosophical reflection cannot begin with the reality of God prompts him to deny this. God is related to man and the world as, also, to Himself in diverse ways. He is encountered not only in historically mediated revelation but throughout human experience. The fact that the historically mediated revelation is decisive for the Christian believer does not justify the *dogmatic* claim that *only* through this medium is personal encounter with God possible.[17]

Brunner recognizes that reason is required for the possibility of faith and as a primary instrument for theology.[18] He acknowledges, further, that theology does and must make use of philosophical concepts in interpreting and communicating insights of revelation. But so far as the theological use of reason is concerned,

---

[17] Cf. Brunner, *Revelation and Reason, op. cit.,* p. 409: "Outside this, His historical revelation, we do not encounter the personal God. . . ."

[18] "Reason is the *conditio sine qua non* of faith." *Ibid.,* p. 418.

it takes place within the context of a personal/existential encounter with God and, thus, has a primarily *instrumental* function. Although Brunner recognizes that philosophical reason does not furnish is own materials, but derives them from experience, he fails to see that philosophical inquiry begins with and transpires within man's encounter with reality in all of its modes. If God is real and, even more, ultimately and supremely real, it would be strange, indeed, if man's relation to God were not *presupposi- tional* to all reflection and inquiry. Brunner's view of philosophy would be far more adequate if he recognized that instead of revela- tion standing as the *sole* mode of man's encounter with God, it is but a special though decisively important relationship of man to God—a relationship which occurs and is possible only within the totality of man's relatedness to reality and its ultimate ground. It is nothing short of special pleading to reserve the dialectical func- tion of reason and existential encounter for theology. To give up this claim is not necessarily to obliterate the line between reason and faith or between natural or rational knowledge and revelation. But it is to recognize that man is, after all, a unitary being who can regard himself as philosopher or theologian only insofar as he abstracts from himself. He is at once all of these; and God, too, surely must be one God.

It is meritorious to insist upon the transcendence of God and the uniqueness of faith and revelation. But it is unfortunate if this emphasis either makes God *irrelevant* to the world or introduces a *bifurcation* between the God of philosophy and ordinary ex- perience, and the God of faith. If that occurs, the *transcendence* of God is maintained at the cost of His *reality*, and the purity of faith at the price of its *intelligibility*. The greatest single danger confronting Protestant theologians, a danger from which Brunner does not altogether escape, is that the *way* of apprehending truth may be regarded as more important than *truth itself*. It is, as Brun- ner correctly states, the common concern for truth that unites philosophy and theology. It is crucially important that the the- ologian not subordinate the God who is revealed to the mode of His revelation. Philosophy and theology can complement one an- other to their mutual enrichment only if *both* avoid dogmatism. If Brunner is mistaken in his assessment of the relation between philosophy and theology, he recognizes both the basis on which the issues must be formulated and the way in which it must be discussed and settled. There is only *one truth, one reason, one God,* and *one man.* It is only when these unities are forgotten or obscured that philosophy and theology either engage in fruitless controversy or, what is worse, become wholly irrelevant to each other.

GEORGE A. SCHRADER

DEPARTMENT OF PHILOSOPHY
YALE UNIVERSITY
NEW HAVEN, CONN.

7

Reidar Hauge

TRUTH AS ENCOUNTER

TRUTH AS ENCOUNTER *

I. Brunner's Concept of Revelation

The phrase "truth as encounter" points to one of the most basic concepts in the theology of Emil Brunner. To acquire a clear understanding of his theology, a consideration of the meaning of this important phrase is imperative. It should be pointed out, however, that this precise expression does not appear until a relatively late period in Brunner's theological development. This phrase, "truth as encounter," was first employed as the title for a series of lectures given in Uppsala in 1937.[1]

In the years which have since elapsed, Brunner has returned to this concept again and again. Particularly in his *Dogmatics* is this concept vigorously asserted and developed. But having recognized this, it should be clear to any student of Brunner's theology that this is hardly a new concept or recent innovation of his. From the beginning he had stressed the personal character of our relationship to God and had spoken of "the real meeting between our ego and the divine Thou." [2]

In order to clarify what is meant by the phrase, "truth as encounter," it seems to me that we can best begin by examining Brunner's concept of revelation. This approach appears advisable for two reasons. In the first place, the idea of revelation is the very heart of Brunner's theology. The whole problem of revelation has been one of his constant concerns. The designation of the the-

---

* Translated by I. John Hesselink, Basel, Switzerland.
[1] These lectures were published the following year, the original title being *Wahrheit als Begegnung*. The English translation which appeared in 1943 unfortunately used *The Divine-Human Encounter* as a title instead of the original and more significant literal equivalent of the German title, viz. "Truth as Encounter." Tr.
[2] *God and Man* (1936), p. 69.

ology that flourished after the First World War as a "theology of revelation" is particularly applicable to that of Emil Brunner. For him no task of theology is more fundamental and urgent than reflection on the nature and meaning of revelation. This concept is crucial for his whole theology. Secondly, he directly applies this emphasis on the personal character of revelation to what he has said about "truth as encounter." What he says about revelation in turn determines his understanding of faith. For he also describes faith as an encounter. Concerning the meaning of revelation and faith in the New Testament he has written: "Here revelation is 'truth as encounter' and faith is knowledge as encounter." [3]

In his explication of the Christian concept of revelation Brunner observes first of all that revelation must be understood as communication. This, he feels, is fundamental to the New Testament understanding of revelation. In the New Testament, revelation is a necessary and real communication, not merely an accidental or casual manifestation of a truth which could be apprehended apart from this manifestation. It is a communication in the deepest sense of the word, not just a pedagogical remedy. "Revelation is absolute communication [4] . . . revelation alone is absolute communication." [5]

The act of communication is absolutely decisive. According to Brunner this view of revelation has a specifically Christian character. It is true that in all religions revelation signifies something which was previously hidden and is now disclosed, but in the New Testament the idea of communication is radically transformed. Here we read about an absolute mystery and an absolute communication. This is true since God is the one who is revealed. Everything else, everything that in some way or another belongs to the world, is in principle already known, whereas God is the absolutely unknown. "Through God alone can God be known." [6]

We know about Him only when He makes Himself known. Accordingly, Brunner distinguishes sharply between revelation and reason, the latter being understood in its broadest connotation. Thus all autonomous knowledge—both rational as well as empirical —is included. A revealed truth cannot also be a rational truth. Ac-

[3] *Revelation and Reason*, p. 9.
[4] *God and Man*, p. 56.
[5] *Ibid.*
[6] *The Mediator*, p. 21.

cording to Brunner, there can be no *"articuli mixti"* (affirmations of
faith which are at the same time common to reason). Consequently,
the God of the Christian faith is always different from the God of
the philosophers. Not only the origin but also the content of the
idea of God is completely different. The first thing that must be
said about God is that He is known only where He makes Himself
known.

When Brunner speaks thus about absolute communications he
wishes to point out that revelation is an *event* in history. This, of
course, does not mean that history itself reveals God! Rather,
God reveals Himself in definite moments of history and above all
in Jesus Christ—in His person, life, death, and resurrection. True
communication is realized in and cannot be separated from the
historical person of Jesus Christ. Brunner lays great stress on this
once-for-allness of revelation. The revelation to which the New
Testament bears witness is neither general nor repeatable but is
absolutely unique. It is not an illustration of a truth which has
always been known or which apart from this revelation can be
known. The historical, therefore, does not act as a symbol. "Symbol
says nothing to me, but *suggests* to me what I ought of myself
to think [7] . . . it draws my attention to something which in principle
I can say to myself" [8] and therefore, has nothing to do with revelation.

Revelation in Jesus Christ is not merely the apex of potential
human knowledge. Jesus is not just a teacher, an example, a religious genius, or even a prophet, but the personal self-communication of God. By this identification of revelation with a person, the
idea of communication becomes categorically precise. To be sure,
the prophets also received the Word of God which they were to
proclaim. It is quite possible here as well to speak of a communication in a very real sense. But this communication is not absolutely
bound to the person of the prophets. It is not unconditionally
unique and therefore is not communication in the strictest sense
of the word. Jesus is more than a prophet in that he not only
speaks the Word but *is* the Word! Here there is no distinction between communication and person, nor between that which is
communicated and the one who communicates. Thus the nature
of revelation as communication is even more sharply underscored.

[7] *God and Man,* p. 55.
[8] *Ibid.*

Much remains, however, to be said about Emil Brunner's concept of revelation. Up to this point we have not spoken expressly about "truth as encounter." The ideas which we have discussed thus far, if considered in isolation, might appear to lead us in an intellectualistic direction. Precisely the opposite, however, is Brunner's intention! His concept of revelation, when rightly understood, could in no way be viewed as a form of intellectualism. For Brunner it is extremely important that revelation be not considered as the impartation of some doctrine. Nor is it a communication of truth which can be comprehended by human reason. Granted, there are instances in his earlier writings where Brunner appears to approach such intellectualistic expressions, but it is clear that they should not be so interpreted. His objection to intellectualism is essentially twofold. First, revelation is not doctrine but an act. Revelation consists of the acts of God for our salvation and above all His act in Jesus Christ. This same emphasis comes to expression in Brunner's later writings when he seeks to understand the significance of Christ, not first of all in His person but in His work, in God's act in Him. He repeatedly calls attention to the fact that the characteristic form of speech used in the New Testament witness to Christ is not the substantive, but the verb. Brunner's purpose here is to show that when revelation is understood as doctrine it cannot also be a historical event. For doctrine is essentially timeless.

His second reason for breaking with intellectualism is rooted in his conception of revelation as an encounter. Revelation is a "personal correspondence" [9] between God and man. "God does not reveal this and that—He reveals Himself by communicating Himself." [10] The goal of revelation is His Lordship over man and His fellowship with him. God reveals himself first as the Lord and secondly as the One who wills to have fellowship with man. It is in this context that Brunner first speaks of truth as encounter. It fol-

[9] This expression is used frequently in *The Divine-Human Encounter* but rarely thereafter, not even in *Revelation and Reason* which appeared only three years later and which is concerned with many of the same themes. This is not significant, however, in terms of any shifting of accent. By "personal correspondence" (*"personale Korrespondenz"* and occasionally *"personhafte Korrespondenz"*), Brunner seeks to indicate the formal relationship between God and man and more particularly the correlation between the Word of God and faith. He defines and illustrates this expression throughout *The Divine-Human Encounter*. Cf. especially pp. 47, 91, 95, 96, and 107. Tr.

[10] *Christianity and Civilization* I, p. 37.

lows then that faith also must be thought of in personal terms. Faith is not belief in doctrine [11] nor a belief in "something" but obedience to the God who has met us in Jesus Christ. It is "obedient trust" [12]—a phrase which he employs frequently. Faith always expresses itself in a "thou form," not in an "it form" or "he form."

In accord with his rejection of intellectualism, Brunner provides a sharp critique of the conceptions of revelation and faith in the theology of both the medieval and post-Reformation periods. "Of all the mistakes made by the Christian Church, this misunderstanding of revelation and faith may be said to have had the most disastrous results." [13] Brunner is convinced that from the outset intellectualism plagued Christian theology. Already when the church was engaged in a battle with Gnosticism in the second century, its quest for certainty led it to seek refuge in the notion of divine inspiration and thus in infallible doctrine. Brunner even feels that it is possible to detect this tendency in the New Testament period, for example, in the Pastoral Epistles, a tendency which eventually came to fruition in medieval Catholicism. Revelation has now become doctrine and faith doctrinal belief. Here we have a complete perversion of the proclamation of the New Testament. According to Brunner, it was first in the Reformation that the personal concept of faith was rediscovered.

At the Reformation this Catholic conception was perceived to be a misunderstanding of that which the church calls faith, and the biblical understanding of faith was restored. Indeed, this return to the biblical understanding of faith *constitutes* the essence of the Reformation. Its sole concern was this: that faith is a personal encounter with the God who meets us personally in Jesus Christ.[14]

Brunner maintains furthermore that almost immediately after the period of the sixteenth century Reformation, intellectualism reared its head again. In fact it can be detected already in the time of the Reformation and is clearly visible in the ensuing period of "Ortho-

[11] "Der Glaube ist kein Fürwahrhalten einer Lehre"—literally, "Faith is not the holding of a doctrine as true." Brunner is here tilting against any rationalistic understanding of faith where it is conceived of as primarily an assent to doctrine. The Reformers referred to such faith as a bare *"fides historica"* as over against saving faith. The positive relationship between faith and doctrine will be indicated later in this essay. Tr.

[12] Eg., in *Revelation and Reason*, p. 10.

[13] *Ibid.*, p. 8.

[14] *Ibid.*, p. 10.

doxy." The way was then open for a "paper pope." [15] Brunner thus speaks a clear and powerful "no" to any form of intellectualism, tendencies of which he regrettably perceives again in more recent "dialectical" theology.

We have seen that revelation is to be understood both as communication and as an encounter. One could ask whether something of a contradiction does not exist between these two concepts. Must one not posit a tension between the concepts of communication and encounter? In any case, is not personalism an adequate counterbalance to intellectualism which threatens to become a danger when one places the idea of communication so decisively in the foreground? Such a suggestion is quite possible in that Brunner very early designated revelation as communication; only later does he speak specifically of "truth as encounter." It cannot be denied that his battle against intellectualism has become increasingly sharper. When one looks closely, he will observe that a difference of accentuation has taken place, of which the expression "truth as encounter" is one indication. Although there has been a certain shift in emphasis, it should not be overlooked that the distinction was always absolute. The rejection of intellectualism is also clear in the early works, where the personal character of faith as well is stressed. In any case, Brunner himself could never allow one to speak of a contradiction between the concepts of communication and personalism. He would prefer to say that the latter concept is rather a consequence of the first.

It is only a personal God who is known through an absolute communication. The Absolute is not absolutely unknown; only a personal God is an absolute mystery. The "absoluteness" of communication is inseparable from its personal character and also from its "personal correspondence." Likewise, Brunner maintains that the radical New Testament concept of revelation implies the Lordship of God. That God is known only where He makes Himself known means precisely this, that He is Lord. But His Lordship is at the same time an expression of the personal encounter. When God encounters us, He makes known His sovereign will. Both His will to Lordship and His will to communion come to expression in this absolute communication. This comes out particularly clearly in Brunner's statements about forgiveness. Forgiveness is, on the

[15] *Ibid.*, p. 11.

one hand, a truth which can be known only through revelation. It is not something we can presume or demand. God Himself must declare to us that it is a reality. Brunner makes clear what absolute communication is precisely with this illustration of the forgiveness of sins. On the other hand, forgiveness is also an expression of personal encounter. It means that despite our sins God wills to have fellowship with us. Forgiveness signifies on God's side the absolutely personal.

II. Revelation and Truth

What Brunner says about the relationship between God and man is decisive for his concept of Christian truth. He speaks of *truth* as encounter. The encounter of God with man is also truth. It is evident then, on the one hand, that revelation is a communication of truth. This view was especially evident in his writings in the 1920's but is equally true of those of later periods. Truth is revealed in Christ; furthermore, Christian proclamation, properly conceived, is a proclamation of the truth. Brunner disassociates himself completely from any modern form of relativism concerning truth. On the other hand, it is precisely the act of God in Christ or "personal correspondence" which is also the truth. Christian truth, therefore, is not truth in the usual sense of the word. The Christian understanding of truth is quite distinct from the rational. In the first place, the truth which is spoken of in the New Testament is not static, timeless truth, for it "came into being." [16] Consequently, it cannot be the object of doctrine because it occurs in history. Truth is a person! For Brunner nothing is more certain than this, namely, the actuality and personal character of Christian truth. Secondly, he emphasizes that Christian truth cannot be corroborated by rational arguments and, therefore, is not generally acknowledged. He finds here a clear difference between the Christian and rational understanding of truth. It could be maintained that rational truth is likewise not generally acknowledged. Nevertheless, it is quite a different matter when Christian truth is accepted in obedience to the will of God, particularly when it is this will which is to be accepted.

When Brunner explicates the Christian understanding of truth,

---

[16] *The Divine-Human Encounter*, p. 140.

his main attack is against the familiar subject-object dichotomy in theology. He rejects both objectivism and subjectivism. Traditional intellectualism, which conceives of faith as an assent to doctrine, is labeled objectivism. Here the truth of God becomes a "thing," something within our grasp which we can manipulate. In this case it is no longer possible to speak of personal correspondence. All objective knowledge is impersonal. On the other hand, nothing is gained by emphasizing the subject at the expense of the object. Truth does not come from within man; nor is it to be identified with the human subject. In subjectivism also one cannot really speak of an encounter or personal correspondence. The whole subject-object approach is in itself false. Brunner does not deny that these categories are indispensable for philosophy, for there one is concerned with the question of knowing and being. The use of such categories to a certain extent is even necessary in theology insofar as theology is concerned with faith. But the antithesis between subject and object may not be applied to the correlation between faith and truth. The whole approach as such is open to objection no matter how the subject and object are defined. The net result in any case is that the personal character of truth is denied.

This personal conception of truth is of tremendous importance for Brunner's conception of the Word of God. On the one hand, it is important to recognize that God encounters us in his Word. Words are at the same time the means of communication between persons and the means for God's communication to us. "God is the kind of God who reveals himself in the Word." [17]

This idea, which was asserted by Brunner at an early stage, becomes explicit in his later emphasis on truth as encounter. For him the Word of God is not a "thing" which in some way or other can be objectified. Nor may it ever be directly identified with human words. It is no book and no doctrine; it is never anything which we could somehow control or manage. If we would understand Brunner's teaching about the Bible, it is essential to be very clear about this. It is impossible, he maintains, to speak of a direct identity between the Bible and the Word of God. We do not believe in the Bible as such in itself. Faith is always a "relation between person and person," [18] and consequently is not primarily belief in the Bible (*Bibelglaube*). True, the Holy Scriptures are an authoritative form

[17] *Ibid.*, p. 46.
[18] *Revelation and Reason*, p. 9.

of revelation. Christian faith is impossible wherever the Scriptures are bypassed. At the same time, however, Brunner rejects any a priori, axiomatic "belief in the Bible." "Christian faith is not faith in a closed Bible, but in an open Bible." [19]

We do not believe in something just because it is found in the Bible. It is much better to affirm that belief in the Bible is a consequence of faith in Christ!

At this point Brunner refers to the Christocentric emphasis of Luther's teaching about the Bible. Acknowledging his debt to Luther, he speaks again and again about Christ as the *dominus et rex scripturae*,[20] or asserts that the Scriptures are "the manger in which the Christ lies." [21]

It should be clear now why Brunner's view of the Word cannot be adequately explained either with the category of subjectivism or objectivism. In subjectivism human freedom is the only reality, and the Word of God is not even mentioned. Here the Word of God becomes only an expression of faith rather than a word from outside which is spoken *to us*. On the other hand, in objectivism the Word of God becomes an object which we can control. In this connection it is interesting to note that in recent years Brunner has become rather cautious about referring to revelation as a Word. For revelation is hardly a Word in the usual sense of this term. When we speak of the Word of God we are in reality speaking figuratively. The identification of revelation with human words is more characteristic of the Old Testament than the New Testament. Particularly in late Judaism, these two—revelation and a human word—are fused. In contrast, the Gospel of John expresses the uniquely Christian conception where it refers to the person of Jesus as the Word. By this no hypostatization of the Word is intended; instead the person of Christ has now assumed the place previously reserved for the Word. When Brunner rejects such "verbalism," his intent is only that of accenting the nature of the Word as personal communication. Here he remains firm and will retract nothing!

Note well, however, that this personal understanding of truth does not imply that knowledge is unimportant. Brunner can also

[19] *Ibid.*, p. 169.
[20] *Ibid.*, p. 276.
[21] *Ibid.*

stress this aspect with great enthusiasm. This is quite apparent, for example, when he writes:

It is not true that first of all there is a relation between God and man, between man and God, which can be known, even if it does not become actual. As a matter of fact, it is precisely in God's giving himself to be known and in this knowledge of God that the essence of the relationship between God and man lies. The event which is the relation between God and man is always an act of revelation, likewise, the event which is the relationship between man and God is always a relation based on knowing.[22]

What Brunner calls "personal correspondence" ("*personale Korrespondenze*") stands and falls with the recognition of this fact, namely, that God is known and acknowledged. Thereby he wishes first of all to realize his will to Lordship and communion. "Heat and motion can be communicated without revelation and knowledge, but not Lordship and the will to communion."[23] Brunner then is completely consistent when he says elsewhere that faith is "first of all an act of knowledge."[24] But he makes it clear that this knowledge is quite different from what we usually consider to be knowledge. God is known only where His Lordship and will to communion are acknowledged. Brunner even says of this knowledge that "one hesitates to call it knowledge at all."[25] This knowledge, therefore, is to be distinguished from ordinary knowledge in three ways. It does not make us masters over that which is known. It does not leave us unchanged. Nor does it render us solitary as all other knowledge necessarily does.

When Brunner speaks of truth as encounter it is thus decisive that God rules over man and wills to have communion with him. It is necessary then that God not only address man but also that man answer. This implies first of all that the relationship between revelation and faith is very close. It is a false antithesis when revelation is considered objective and faith its objective counterpart. Revelation always means that something is revealed *to me*. It is "a transitive event."[26] In a similar way Brunner insists that the Word of God is not only a past but also a present reality. "The Word in Scripture, Christ, becomes the same as the Word in the heart, the

---

22 *The Divine-Human Encounter*, p. 51.
23 *Ibid.*, p. 64.
24 *Revelation and Reason*, p. 34.
25 *Ibid.*, p. 26.
26 *Ibid.*, p. 33.

Holy Spirit." [27] Not only is the truth revealed to man but man is also obligated to respond in a responsible and active manner. He should not only listen, but also say, "yes." Of course, God's activity is primary. Revelation is God's activity and God acts spontaneously quite apart from conditioning. His priority is absolute!

However, this emphasis in no way denies the fact that we must also speak of an act of man. Man is not only an object but also a responsible subject. In fact, Brunner lays great emphasis on man's responsibility. For Brunner, responsibility is the distinguishing characteristic of human existence. This emphasis is inseparable from his view of the image of God and sin. Man is always active in some way over against God, either in faith or in disobedience. Sin is not merely imperfection, or something negative, but a negation. The revelation which is manifest in creation always calls out for human activity. But redemptive revelation also requires a human response. The simple receptivity of man must not be confused with an objective passivity. The importance with which Brunner regards the human response becomes apparent in his rejection of both sacramentalism and determinism. He rejects any form of sacramentalism where the Word of God in man is in any way interpreted as a physical phenomenon and where human responsibility is not taken seriously. This is obvious, for example, in his treatment of baptism. He points out that the act of baptism in the New Testament is a "two-sided happening," [28] which is an exact equivalent of what he has called "personal correspondence."

For the same reason he spurns any form of determinism. He maintains that determinism is of Stoic, not Christian, origin but that it nevertheless infiltrated Christian theology very early and unfortunately reappeared in Reformation theology. Note that here Brunner refuses to follow the reformers, even Luther, to whose personalism he otherwise especially appeals. It should be observed, however, that he criticizes only the teaching of the younger, not the older Luther! He finds that after 1525, Luther no longer taught determinism. Hence he has no objections against the later statements of the Reformer. But he has discarded the doctrines of the omnicausality *(Alleinwirksamkeit)* of God's grace and the denial of free will. He insists that these doctrines are incompatible with personal correspondence. For the same reason he will not accept the doctrine

---

[27] *The Philosophy of Religion*, p. 28.
[28] *The Divine-Human Encounter*, p. 178.

of universalism. Personal correspondence stands or falls with the possibility of saying something about the freedom and responsibility of man. This becomes a real issue in the question of the knowledge of truth. Since faith is obedience, not a mere acceptance of certain doctrines as true, and since truth is known only where man responds affirmatively to God's will to Lordship and communion, one cannot avoid speaking here of human activity.

The possibility of knowledge and the responsibility of man implies that man has a special place in God's plan of creation. One need not hesitate to affirm that God is also Lord of the impersonal creation. Perhaps He even has a real communion with this impersonal creation, but in the deepest sense His Lordship and communion are realized only in His relationship to man. From the outset God is the One "who approaches man," [29] just as man is the one "who comes from God." [30] Brunner has little sympathy for the cosmocentric theology which has come into vogue in certain circles today. For him this cosmocentric emphasis is just another form of objectivism.

What Brunner has said about the Christian understanding of truth should indicate that this conception of truth is not a purely formal concept. He emphasizes strongly that in the New Testament truth is an expression of rich content. Truth and grace, truth and life belong together. Brunner will make absolutely no distinction between a formal and a material principle: "The 'formal principle,' the Word of God, and the 'material principle,' redemption through Jesus Christ or justification by faith alone, are not two, but one and the same principle seen in two aspects." [31] When theology makes the formal principle the object of special investigation, it has the task of making clear "how this structural 'form' is determined by the 'matter' and the 'matter' by the 'form.'" [32]

Formal theology has the same object as the material, but it observes the same object from a different viewpoint. The fact that Brunner does not recognize a formal or neutral concept of revelation follows from his assertion that this problem is "the central problem of theology," [33] and that "the event which is the relation between God

[29] *Ibid.*, pp. 46 ff.
[30] *Ibid.*, p. 47.
[31] *Ibid.*, p. 46.
[32] *Ibid.*
[33] *Revelation and Reason*, p. 3.

and man," is always "an act of revelation." [34] He has always taught that the reality of revelation already has meaning in terms of content. Nevertheless, it is true that this emphasis has become more pronounced since the occasion when he first spoke of revelation as encounter. When revelation is understood as encounter, it is not only something formal. The personal is real—God's revelation is life. It is in and of itself redemptive revelation. But the real is also personal. Revelation has no other content than the encounter of God with man. Its only purpose is to realize God's Lordship over man and his communion with him. Brunner is thus quite consistent when at this point he calls attention to the unity of revelation and reconciliation. "In the New Testament revelation is simply Jesus Christ (Gal. 1:15) and reconciliation (Rom. 3:21)." [35] When God gives himself in order to have communion with man, it is precisely in this action that he has reconciled the world to himself.

In the above résumé I have indicated how Brunner's understanding of truth has been worked out in his dogmatic studies. At this juncture I would like to add a few brief observations. The true dogmatic norm is Jesus Christ himself, since he is the truth. In the final analysis it is not the Bible but the Christ witnessed to in the Bible who is the norm of dogmatics. The existential character of faith must be preserved also in dogmatic statements. Dogmatics, of course, involves the transition from the "Thou-form" to the "it-form" but it is nevertheless, "believing-thinking" and may never withdraw from the obedience of faith. What is meant by "truth as encounter" is illustrated throughout his dogmatics. In his *Christian Doctrine of God*, for example, Brunner breaks with the old metaphysics of being. Instead he emphasizes that God is the Lord who claims us for Himself. He is love in that He wills to have communion with us. The creation is viewed in the same way. God is only known as the Creator where He is first acknowledged as Lord. But the creation is also an expression of His love. He creates the world in order to realize His plan for Lordship and communion with man. Similarly, it is important to note that in Brunner's anthropology the basic thing that must be said about man is that he is a responsible being. Likewise when he speaks so emphatically about the universality of sin, it becomes clear that man is responsible for his sin. And when Brunner proceeds from the work rather than the person of Christ

[34] *The Divine-Human Encounter,* p. 51.
[35] *Revelation and Reason,* p. 4.

in his Christology, his intention once again is to understand God's encounter with us. Again, the first thing that must be said about the deity of Christ is not that Christ has a divine nature but that God encounters us in Him. I cannot deal with the question of the church here except to remark that Brunner regards as very significant the fact that God's truth summons us not only to an encounter with God but also to communion with other men.

III. Questions to Brunner

Brunner's exposition of the Christian understanding of truth is extremely suggestive and significant. Whether we agree with him or not, at least this much can be said—he has forced us to consider questions which in theology heretofore have not been given sufficient attention, questions of great import which must be thought through anew. I feel also that he has given a faithful expression of the biblical concept of truth. If we would venture an opinion concerning this exposition of Brunner's, we must always keep in mind his personalism. There is no point in either discussing or criticizing isolated facets of Brunner's understanding of truth unless we examine them in the light of his basic position, namely, personalism. Here I must refrain from raising the question as to what extent it is even possible to speak of Brunner's "personalism." More specifically, how closely in his personalism related to what is today known as theological personalism? What precisely does he mean by personalism? One thing is certain—his great concern is only to emphasize the personal character of our relationship to God. Revelation is not a doctrine but an encounter of God with man. Likewise, faith is not belief in something or belief in a creed but obedient trust in the God who has encountered us in Jesus Christ.

It has been alleged occasionally that Brunner's personalism really stems from philosophical presuppositions. It is claimed that his personalistic categories are actually foreign to biblical thinking and that in reality their roots are to be found in the new I-Thou philosophy rather than in the Bible. Brunner insists, however, that his only aim has been to take seriously the New Testament concepts of revelation and faith. It is undeniable that he is very appreciative of the contributions of Ebner, Buber, and Grisebach, and he has expressed his deep gratitude to Kierkegaard above all. But he hastens to add that Kierkegaard's sole purpose was to recover the New Testament understanding of truth and faith. Hence it seems to me that one can still maintain that Brunner's personalistic thinking is in accord with the witness of the New Testament. It is possible, of course, that he has tended to oversimplify the New Testament data; and the "intellectualism" which he claims to find already on the fringe of the New Testament may well be a more prominent and essential element in the Bible than Brunner is ready to admit. Yet I am convinced that in the main he substantiates his fundamental thesis very successfully. It is hardly controvertible that, in the New Testament, faith is not belief in a doctrine or truth about God, but faith is in God Himself as He makes known His will to us in Jesus Christ and offers us true communion. Faith, therefore, must never be understood as *primarily* belief in doctrine *(Fürwahrhaten)* but as trust. The importance of this insight becomes even greater when Brunner applies these ideas to the questions of truth and theological knowledge. If God reveals Himself not through a doctrine but through his self-communication in Jesus Christ, this self-communication must also be the truth. The truth then is not a truth *about* God's self-communication, but the self-communication itself. It is obvious that this whole approach has far-reaching consequences for theological thinking and methodology.

I feel, therefore, that basically Brunner deserves our unreserved and grateful concurrence in his particular form of personalism. But it should never be a glib, unreflective assent! Brunner himself is convinced that his understanding of the Christian meaning of truth is quite revolutionary. Consequently, he does not expect this approach to win immediate and unopposed acceptance. It is clear that this approach has profound and far-reaching implications which conflict with much traditional thinking. It is inevitable then that a host of difficult questions will arise. Therefore, we must now ask whether Brunner's contribution—correct and convincing though it may be—has not been achieved at the expense of other truths which cannot be surrendered. One could also ask whether all the problems and difficulties that occur in this connection have been adequately explained and solved. The nature of this essay does not permit even a cursory review of such possible problems and questions. But I would like to ask questions in three related areas.

1. In my opinion Brunner has a valid insight in the way he develops the personal understanding of truth against both objectivism and subjectivism. Yet it is still possible to query whether he is completely correct in his analysis of objectivism and subjectivism. By ob-

jectivism he means that truth is considered to be in the object; by subjectivism that truth is found in the subject. In objectivism God's truth becomes a present and disposable entity, a "thing" which we can master. In subjectivism truth is grounded in human freedom. Though these definitions may be philosophically accurate, the question still remains whether they apply to what is usually called the object and the subject in theological thought, in this case objectivism and subjectivism. This might be particularly doubtful in the case of objectivism. When a theologian refers to the objective, frequently his purpose is to point to God's act and the divine origin of truth. Brunner concedes as much when he says that objectivism, properly understood, is quite justifiable in insisting "that in the creation of His connection with man God's act is the first." [36]

Now it is certainly possible for such an understanding of objectivism to develop into a perverted objectivism where the personal character of our relationship to God is lost. Is not the principle error then that God's act is emphasized so exclusively that it is no longer possible to speak of a response of man? It is quite possible to assert that God's work and truth then become something which man controls. On the other hand one could argue that this is also the case with subjectivism which, like objectivism, can also be construed in such a way that a responsible decision by man is impossible. In a deterministic view of predestination, for example, Brunner sees an illustration of this kind of objectivistic error. In whatever form deterministic objectivism manifests itself, the net result is always the same, namely, that "man's independence and freedom" [37] are undermined.

He finds this to be the case again in an objectivistic view of the sacraments, especially with an objectivistic doctrine of baptism. This whole question also receives attention in the second volume of his *Dogmatics* which deals with the doctrine of reconciliation. Here too when he speaks of "truth as encounter," [38] in opposition to objectivism, he wishes to point out that the purpose of God's redemptive act—despite its objective reality and uniqueness (*Einmaligkeit*, literally once-for-all-ness)—is to bring man to a decision. It is indeed quite possible to understand the intellectualistic objectivism which Brunner particularly has in mind as an undue emphasis on God's

[36] *The Divine-Human Encounter*, p. 169.
[37] *Ibid.*, p. 54.
[38] *The Christian Doctrine of Creation and Redemption*, p. 290.

act to the exclusion of the human response. With regard to intellectualism, it is perfectly justifiable to maintain that here the Word of
God has become an object that can be manipulated. But that does
not prevent intellectualism from also being guilty of a one-sided
emphasis on the act of God. Revelation now is no longer an address
to man where an answer is required and responsibility is presupposed. When faith becomes merely a matter of belief in correct
doctrines, one can no longer speak of a responsible decision. For
me, the real inadequacy of both the subjective and objective tendencies is that in objectivism responsibility is not taken seriously and
in subjectivism God's act is not taken seriously.

What has been stated above becomes important also for the
question of where we actually find manifestations of objectivism
and subjectivism. I am convinced that Brunner has performed a
great service by delineating vigorously the objectivism typical of
medieval Catholicism. But is this the only thing that can be said
here? Must we not likewise point to a Roman Catholic subjectivism?
Was not the protest of the reformers directed against Rome's subjectivism as well as its objectivism? Is this not the case, for example,
when the reformers—particularly Luther—stressed that salvation is
God's work alone? One might well ask whether Brunner has ac-
curately evaluated the teaching of the reformers about the absolute
sufficiency of divine grace and the bondage of the will. The fact that
I raise these questions, however, is not to be taken as an indication
that I am not in agreement with Brunner's basic position. I realize
that when he emphasizes human freedom, he does so not in an
absolute but a dialectic manner. His purpose is only to give due
allowance to the stress on responsibility which, I believe, is solidly
rooted in the New Testament. Despite this legitimate intention, I
would still like to ask whether the Reformer's doctrine of the bondage of the will is not a valid protest against both Roman and hu-
manistic subjectivism; and whether, in any case, it must not be
conceded that this doctrine cannot be simply dismissed as a remnant
of objectivism but should rather be understood as an antisubjec-
tivistic doctrine? At any rate, a case could be made for the thesis
that the reformers' understanding of revelation and truth was a
judgment on subjectivism as well as objectivism. Brunner, in fact,
has emphatically taken this position. He has affirmed, for example,
that the reformers destroyed the medieval synthesis of biblical
revelation with philosophical speculation about God. When he pro-

ceeds to assert that they wished to restrict the true knowledge of God to God's self-communication [39] it appears to me that it could also be maintained that they were opposing a subjectivistic viewpoint.

The real problem then is how we can avoid both objectivism and subjectivism. It is self-evident that Brunner opposes both of these tendencies very effectively in his analysis of the Christian understanding of truth. Against the one danger he interprets revelation as a real communication and a unique event. Against the other he stresses that something is revealed *to me*. Thereby he avoids the pitfalls of both objectivism and subjectivism. If what has been said above about the nature of objectivism and subjectivism is correct, it is also crucial that he views revelation first as an act and secondly as a command and address. On the one hand, revelation is an act of God which is completely independent of any human activity. On the other hand, it is also a proclamation of God's will which demands a decision and appeals to man's sense of responsibility. Admittedly, it is a little surprising that Brunner is inclined to emphasize the character of revelation as an act *(Tatcharakter)* even against objectivism. After all, it is really subjectivism which fails to attribute any decisive influence to the divine act. Objectivism, in its own way, does just exactly the opposite, that is, by constantly pointing to God's act. Therefore it is subjectivism rather than objectivism which fails to do justice to God's act. When God's revelation is regarded as God's act, then not only an intellectualistic objectivism but also all subjectivism is shown to be false. Secondly, when one speaks of God's act, is not objectivism in effect thus overcome? It has become the vogue to a certain extent in contemporary theology to stress the historical character of revelation in contrast to revelation construed as doctrine. But this new emphasis in itself does not necessarily mean that Brunner's type of personalism is gaining acceptance because this emphasis of contemporary theology can also fit in well with a thoroughgoing objectivism—also in Brunner's sense! Even God's act can become a "thing," a disposable entity. There is no doubt that Brunner is right when he stresses that revelation in the New Testament is not a doctrine but an act; that the New Testament witness to Christ is characterized by its use of the verb rather than the substantive; but even a theology where verbs are predom-

[39] This is especially true in *God and Man*.

inant can be very objectivistic. It must be remembered that man's
responsibility—which is excluded in objectivism—is not preserved
and guaranteed as much in a concept of revelation where God's act
is emphasized, as in one where God's address is pivotal. And it is
precisely this which is decisive in Brunner's critique of objectivism.
He has stated as clearly as possible that revelation is both a manifestation of the divine will and an address. What I find important
here is that not only a doctrinal objectivism but also an "act objectivism" is opposed. Thus against subjectivism the emphasis must
be placed on the character of revelation as an act, whereas against
objectivism the stress must be on revelation as address. For me the
difficulty is always that either the act or the address is not sufficiently
taken into consideration. I would like to think that this could also
have significance in regard to the opposing sides in the so-called
demythologizing debate. Does not the essential point of conflict
consist in the fact that one side emphasizes God's revelation primarily as act, the other as address?

2. In his fight against intellectualistic objectivism, Brunner's
goal is to replace its concept of truth with an entirely different one.
The truth which is witnessed to in the New Testament is not "truth-
in-itself" *(an-sich-Wahrheit),* but truth in encounter *(Begegnungs-
wahrheit).* It is no "it-truth" but a "Thou-truth" and is not therefore
a truth which can be affirmed through mere doctrinal belief. Brunner never tires of proclaiming that faith may not be understood as
simple assent to doctrines. This also is one of his especially valuable
insights. Nevertheless, one cannot refrain from asking whether belief in doctrines is not also an aspect of faith? Such belief in itself,
of course, is not faith. Brunner is right when he affirms that faith
is always concerned with God's will and with the revelation of that
will, and that faith therefore is always obedience. According to the
New Testament, a belief in doctrine that is not at the same time
obedience and trust is not faith. Neither is the objective knowledge
of truth and acceptance of truth a necessary prerequisite for faith.
It is not true that faith as obedience and trust only becomes possible
after the recognition that such and such a fact is true. True as this
may be, it should still be possible to speak of an "assensus" of faith.
After all, it is impossible to be obedient to revelation without af-
firming that something is true! When we believe in the revelation
of God in Christ we believe also in a truth *about* God. When we
believe in Jesus Christ, we believe also *that* He is the Lord and the

Son of God. Having said this, there need be absolutely no fear that the personal character of faith will be weakened. The question is only whether faith *as* personal encounter does not also include belief in objective facts and doctrinal conviction. Since Brunner speaks so emphatically about a real communication and the knowledge of faith, it would seem that he would have to agree. It is to be hoped that he will have more to say about this particular issue.

Now Brunner has also spoken of the necessity and importance of faith in something *(Etwasglaubens)*. And he has spoken not only of a distinction in this regard, but also of a "positive relation" [40] between revelation and doctrine, between faith in Christ and faith in something. He says that when God addresses us and we respond in faith, "this address and this response can take place only by virtue of biblical doctrine." [41] Furthermore, we cannot have this experience except within this framework." [42] Doctrine, and more specifically the holding of a doctrine to be true, also has an instrumental and sacramental significance. "The tokens are not accidental to but necessarily connected with the content." [43] The question still persists, however, as to whether this is sufficient. If I see this problem correctly, it is not enough first to distinguish and then to unite content and form, a fact and a token. Objective truth has significance in terms of content as well as instrumental and sacramental significance. Faith, that is, the truth that Jesus is the Lord and that God encounters us in Him, is not only a form and a token but is also contained in the fact itself.

I feel that Brunner is right when he speaks of different concepts of truth. We must distinguish between personal truth and rational truth, the truth of encounter and factual truth, "Thou-truth" and "it-truth." Yet one wonders whether there is not something common to these two concepts of truth. In fact, it appears to me that precisely what Brunner says about the distinction between the two concepts in reality proves their essential unity! That the Christian truth has come in Christ and is known only in obedience to the will of God seems in no way to me to exclude the affirmation that it also includes a truth *about* God.

3. We must agree with Brunner in his sharp insistence on the

[40] *The Divine-Human Encounter,* p. 108.
[41] *Ibid.*
[42] *Ibid.,* p. 110.
[43] *Ibid.*

unity of the formal and the material principles. If truth is encounter, or a personal correspondence, it can never be only a formal entity. If so, it is pointless to speak of a separate material principle. I am convinced that this is a decisive point for Brunner's whole theological program. As soon as one distinguishes between a formal and a material principle, he has already opened the door for the old intellectualism to enter again. This means that we must also affirm the unity of revelation and reconciliation. But having said this, it must be granted that questions of considerable importance and difficulty must now be faced. It is not so simple to view revelation and reconciliation as a unity. Moreover, how is this unity to be understood? Is revelation also reconciliation, or is reconciliation by the same token revelation? Is truth reality or vice versa? Karl Barth in his *Church Dogmatics* has chosen the latter alternative. Where does Brunner stand here? I have the impression that his answer would be in favor of the first of these alternatives. But lacking definite confirmation, we must wait for Brunner himself to clarify his position here.

If the relation of God to man is basically a relation in revelation, and if the decisive thing happens precisely in God's revealing Himself, revelation of necessity is also reconciliation. Brunner, in fact, has stated explicitly that revelation as such is also reconciliation and Lordship. In view of his general position, it is quite logical that he should view revelation not only as an establishment of communion but also as reconciliation. In the first place, he stressed emphatically that forgiveness cannot be taken for granted as a self-evident truth. Forgiveness cannot be postulated but must be communicated from beyond. Secondly, we must recall that God reveals not only His will to communion but also His will to Lordship. When God forgives He makes it clear at the same time that His will to Lordship is absolutely binding. "God takes His own law seriously." [44] This means that Brunner understands and can take seriously the "must" [45] which is so characteristic and significant in the portrayal of the life and death of Christ in the New Testament. By virtue of the fact that God reveals and realizes in Christ both his love and his righteousness means—if I have understood Brunner correctly—that one can and must speak of the vicarious penal sufferings of

---

[44] "The Christian Doctrine of Creation and Redemption" *(Dogmatics II)*, p. 295.

[45] *Ibid.*, p. 287.

Christ. Occasionally, however, one gets the impression that Brunner could have stressed more emphatically the independence of the fact of reconciliation.

Occasionally he does appear to take a position that reconciliation is distinct from revelation, that the cross of Christ also has significance as revelation. This appears to be the case when he writes: "Here 'word' and 'revelation' are one; the vicarious suffering of Christ *effects* the reconciliation, but it also reveals the depths of sin and the love of God." [46]

This means that the vicarious sufferings of Christ, which effect reconciliation, also signify revelation, but not that this revealing is also a cause. There is certainly no contradiction here. If God's revelation signifies reconciliation, it can also be the highest revelation of his love. Nevertheless, it is still an important question as to how the unity of revelation and reconciliation is to be understood.

The questions which I have raised are intended in no way to detract from the great service he has performed in his attempt to restore and clarify the Christian understanding of truth. The significance of his accomplishment in this realm is so great that theology can ill afford to ignore it.

REIDAR HAUGE

THE THEOLOGICAL FACULTY
UNIVERSITY OF OSLO
OSLO, NORWAY

[46] *Revelation and Reason,* p. 106.

8

Tetsutaro Ariga

JESUS OF HISTORY AND CHRIST OF FAITH

JESUS OF HISTORY AND CHRIST OF FAITH

I. Western and Non-Western Situation

Before entering our theme itself a word may be needed about the situation from which this paper is being written. For unlike the other contributors to this volume I belong neither to Europe nor to America but to Japan. Nor have I ever been regarded by any person as an exponent of dialectical theology. I was trained in liberal theology first at Doshisha University in Kyoto then at Union Theological Seminary in New York. It was only after I came home in 1925 that I first heard the names of Barth and Brunner. But when their theology began gaining popularity within certain theological circles in Japan I was not quite ready to welcome it. Rather, I went on with my historical studies and tried to develop my thinking upon the foundations I had laid with the help of liberal theology. I even deplored the fact that my students at Doshisha Theological School were losing their interest in history due to the influence of dialectical theology opposing "historicism." Many a time I had to warn them that history should not be confused with historicism, that the nature of Christianity would not be correctly understood without knowing its manifestations and development in history. Such a warning was especially relevant in a country where Christianity did not form a part of its own historical heritage and yet where so many varieties of Christian faith were being introduced from abroad. Any person placed in such a situation finds himself obliged to ask: "What are the actual differences between various churches and denominations? Which will be the best one for me to choose? Or are there some essential qualities which would give a religious body the right to be called Christian? If so, are they to be found as features common to them all? Or are they to be sought in some other way and applied as criteria in evaluating various claimants to the title of Christianity?" But that is exactly the series of questions asked by liberal theologians such as Harnack and Troeltsch.

There is also another set of questions to be asked in our situation in Japan. Christianity here has to be confronted by Shinto, Buddhism, and Confucianism, which are integral parts of our cultural heritage. Naturally one would ask, "What meaning would be left to them if I accept Christian faith? Are they to be entirely discarded as heathenism? Or even from a Christian point of view do they have some virtues of their own? If so, what are their relative values? And how should one consider Christianity's relationship to them? Is Christianity a synthesis of all traditional religious teachings? Or does it pose itself as an antithesis to them all so that a still higher future synthesis should be awaited? But if Christian faith should really be absolute, in what sense can I consider it to be so?" Questions like these are again questions asked by liberal theologians, especially by those of the *Religionsgeschichtliche Schule.* Only, these questions as well as those mentioned above are to us in the Orient not merely academic but vitally practical questions which cannot be avoided. It was unfortunate indeed that the influence of dialectical theology had the effect of giving Japanese students of theology the mistaken notion that these questions themselves were part and parcel of liberal theology and therefore were to be discarded together with it. I was one of the few who protested against this kind of influence on the part of dialectical theology. Of course this did not mean that I had found satisfactory answers in liberal theology. Nothing final was to be found in "human experience" and "history." But there were at least indications in the development of liberal theology itself of an effort to overcome experience and history in one way or another. Those indications together with my dissatisfaction with solutions already offered by liberal theologians enabled me to see more clearly the point of dialectical theologians that faith is something radically different from religious experience and that revelation should never be confused with history.

Thus I came to be more and more appreciative of the revival of the theology of revelation without a radical break with my liberal background. When Dr. Brunner came to Japan in the fall of 1949, I realized how much influence I had after all received from the kind of theology of which he was a foremost spokesman. On a number of occasions I was his interpreter, but his words and thoughts were found so natural and familiar to me that it was a most pleasant experience to put them into my own language. His sole concern has always been with the presentation of the Gospel of Jesus Christ to modern man and that is precisely where my own vital interest lies. Our chief difference—ignoring for the moment the vast difference in scholarship and originality—lies in the fact that he has been chiefly addressing himself to the post-Christian man of modern Europe while in Japan I must grapple with the situation of the pre-Christian existence of man. Actually our situation here is complicated by the fact that contemporary Japanese civilization is a pre-Christian Oriental civilization which has been rather thoroughly permeated with the post-Christian, secularized civilization of the modern West.

II. Toward the Dialectical Understanding of Jesus

In his inaugural lecture as *Privatdozent* at the University of Zürich with the title *Die Grenzen der Humanität* (1922),[1] the earliest work of Brunner's that I know directly, he discusses the meaning of "the boundaries of humanity." By setting up such boundaries modern European man thought he could secure his own domain where his autonomous reason might legislate over the world with great dignity. According to this view, man is a spirit *(Geist)*, not merely a part of nature. All the resources necessary for the realization of his true humanity are to be sought within himself in his mind and will. Religion itself seems reasonable only when understood as something within the boundaries of humanity, that is, as a part of human culture. All reference to the beyond or the supernatural has thus become superfluous. But, Brunner says, the concept of boundary also has another meaning. Boundaries are limitations. That man has his boundaries means that he has his limitations. This fact modern man has had to realize despite all his expanding knowledge and increasing control over nature. The more he knows, the more he realizes his own ignorance; the more he accomplishes, the more keenly he has to admit his impotence. Thus the tragic character of human existence consists precisely in the fact that the same boundaries that once made man so proud have also made him feel so helpless. But this is not the end of the story. For the very relativity and finitude of which man is now so painfully conscious

[1] *Sammlung gemeinverständlicher Vorträge und Schriften aus dem Gebiet der Theologie und Religionsgeschichte* (Tübingen: J. C. B. Mohr [Paul Siebeck], 1922), pp. 102 f.

should make him realize that he can judge his existence to be relative and finite only in reference to the absolute, the truth itself, namely, God. Indeed, man's present *crisis* means that he stands under the *judgment* of God.

Here in this earlier work we can already discern Brunner's general orientation. Exactly twenty-five years later, on the occasion of his Gifford Lectures given shortly after another world war, he again discusses the crisis of Western civilization in these words: "This crisis at bottom is nothing but a consequence of the fact that the deepest foundation of this civilization, the Christian faith, has been shaken in the consciousness of European and American nations, and in some parts of this world has been more than shaken, in fact shattered and even annihilated." [2] What mankind had experienced during the ensuing quarter of a century only confirmed his earlier observation. It is to man in such a situation that Brunner has been addressing himself with his prophetic cry, Return! Return to your God in repentance and accept the Gospel of Jesus Christ! So his constant appeal is that man should recover his sense of sin and guilt and have faith in Jesus Christ as Mediator between God and man. He never wearies of pointing out that modern theology in its attempt to interpret Christian faith in terms of human experience has virtually removed from it the sense of sin and guilt and therefore rendered the notion of a Mediator unnecessary. To such a theology Jesus is, after all, a historical figure, a great religious "genius" or "hero" at most. As such "he represents nothing more than humanity raised to its highest point—no less, but also no more." [3] But it is not the human personality of Jesus that is truly meaningful to the existence and history of man. Christian faith ought to rediscover in Him the incarnate Word of God: not "Christ after the flesh" but "Christ in the flesh." [4] The former is only relative whereas the latter is absolutely decisive.

Brunner's intention is therefore none other than to reintroduce the faith of the Apostles—and of the reformers—to the modern world. But it would be misleading to identify him as a fundamentalist or to call him neo-orthodox. For unlike fundamentalists he is not at all opposed to historical research as applied to the Bible. He is in-

[2] *Christianity and Civilization*, (New York: Charles Scribner's Sons, 1948), Part I, p. 4. The lectures themselves were delivered in 1947.

[3] *The Mediator* (London: Lutterworth Press, 1934), p. 39. (German edition, 1927.)

[4] *Ibid.*, pp. 156 f.

deed ready to accept its results insofar as they are convincing from a purely historical point of view. But he rejects those presuppositions or categories of modern historians that do violence to the message the New Testament itself meant to convey. He is, however, equally opposed to orthodoxy because, whether in its older form or in its newer guise, it means an objectivization of living faith.[5] To Brunner Christian faith refuses to be subsumed under any form of objectivism, whether a formula or an institution.

To grasp this point is of cardinal importance for a correct understanding of Brunner's dialectical argument. On the one hand, Jesus of Nazareth is a historical figure and as such an object of historical science. The historicity of Jesus is indeed an essential part of Christian faith, which is incompatible with any sort of docetism. The following quotation from Brunner's *Dogmatics* will illustrate the point: "It is part of the Christian's belief in the Incarnation of the Word, that he believes in a 'Jesus of History' who is such that His historical existence is always being subjected to critical research. This, indeed, is involved in the 'flesh' in which the Word of God, the Son of God, came to us." [6] On the other hand, historical research alone cannot penetrate into the secret of His Person which is hidden behind his historically perceivable personality. Only by faith can we recognize Jesus as the Christ, as the Person who comes to us from the dimension "yonder"—as the incarnation of the Word of God.[7] To the judgment of faith the man Jesus is the incognito Son of God in the form of a servant. But the coming of the Word of God to us means nothing else than the coming of God Himself to us. "The coming of God" is indeed the very theme of the Bible, according to Brunner. That God comes in His Word is what is meant by revelation. That God comes finally in power is what is meant by the Kingdom of God. Jesus Christ, however, has come as the end of prophetic revelation in word and as the beginning of the coming of God in power. In Him God has come in the Word which is at the same time a Person.[8] Thus it is clear that to Brunner the meaning of Jesus Christ can be properly understood only *theo*logically while

[5] *The Divine-Human Encounter* (Philadelphia: The Westminster Press, 1943), pp. 30 ff. and 37 f. (German edition, 1938). Cf. "Toward a Missionary Theology," *The Christian Century*, LXVI, 27, July 6, 1949, p. 816.

[6] "The Christian Doctrine of Creation and Redemption," *Dogmatics II*, (London: Lutterworth Press, 1952), pp. 244 ff. (German edition, 1950).

[7] *The Mediator*, Ch. IX.

[8] *Ibid.*, p. 286. Cf. *Der Mittler* (Tübingen: J. C. B. Mohr [Paul Siebeck]), p. 254.

the meaning of God can only be truly grasped *Christo*logically. For in Christ we meet by faith not a man but God himself who comes to us.

III. The Self-Movement of God and the Category of Uniqueness

Although it is not the purpose of this paper to treat Brunner's doctrine of God in full, we cannot but touch it if we want to interpret his Christology adequately. As is expected, he is solely interested in the recovery of the biblical conception of God from all its distortions, ancient as well as modern. Over and over again he calls our attention to the fact that the Bible tells of a personal God of action, not a Being removed from all becoming. The title of Chapter 10 of *The Mediator*, "The Self-Movement of God," well characterizes this biblical conception. God here is not a timeless, impersonal, abstract Idea or Being but a living, personal God who acts, comes, and becomes, whose action really happens in time and history.

It is therefore quite understandable that he opposes any attempt to interpret God in terms of Being.[9] But the history of ontology in Christian thought goes back to the late pre-Christian era when Hebrew scriptures were translated into Greek and the Jewish Hellenists tried to interpret their faith in philosophical terms. As Brunner himself points out, the content of Hebrew biblical thought could be adequately expressed only by means of the Hebrew language.[10] So already with the Septuagint version, Greek influences began making themselves felt. There the name of God revealed to Moses, *'ehyeh 'ᵃsher 'ehyeh*, had been translated as *egō eimi ho ōn* ("I am He who is"). Since this seems to me to be a point of crucial importance, I might add a comment on what Brunner has already said in this connection on various occasions. It is indeed true, as Gilson has pointed out, that there is a world of difference between "He who is" of the Septuagint and the Vulgate and "That which is" of a Plato.[11] But historically speaking it was precisely this translation of the Septuagint that provided an opening for the infiltration of

[9] For his attitude toward Paul Tillich's ontology, see *Eternal Hope*, (London: Lutterworth Press, 1954), p. 116. (German edition, 1953.) For Tillich's appraisal of Biblical religion, see especially his *Biblical Religion and the Search for Ultimate Reality* (London: James Nisbet & Co., Ltd., 1955).

[10] *The Mediator*, p. 395 (*Der Mittler*, p. 355).

[11] Etienne Gilson, *God and Philosophy* (New Haven: Yale University Press, 1941), p. 42. His text is of course the Vulgate, where *'ehyeh*, etc., is translated as *Ego sum qui sum* while the following *'ehyeh* (Exod. 3:14b) is rendered as *Qui est*.

Greek ontology. Thus we find Philo of Alexandria interpreting the *ho ōn* of the text in the sense of *to on* (being) or to *einai* (to be); and it was primarily through his influence that the ontological theology of the Greek fathers was developed. In this way, then, our theological language itself has been "corrupted" by the Greek way of thinking.[12] Of course this observation should not blind us to the fact that in Christian thought ontology has been molded into something different from what it was in Greek philosophy. But, after all, the meaning of the Hebrew verb *hāyāh* cannot be adequately covered either by *to einai* or by *to be*. For *hāyāh* combines in itself all the meanings of "becoming," "happening," "acting," and "being." It is therefore impossible for any kind of *ontology* to do full justice to biblical thought which is based on what one might term *hayathology*, especially on the revelation of the subjective and irreducible *'ehyeh* (first person) of God.[13]

How difficult it is to give proper expression in English or German to this most basic Biblical thought may be illustrated by the writings of Brunner himself. For instance, on pp. 400 ff. of *The Mediator* he talks about "the Being of God" *(das Sein Gottes)* or "the eternal, unchangeable Being of God" while his real emphasis is clearly on the "coming" and "becoming" of God. This is, however, only a seeming contradiction, for we read on p. 402 the expressions "the Divine Being of God" and "the Divine Being of Christ." In this case the German original has *Gottes Gottsein* and *Christi Gottsein*, where emphasis falls on *Gott* rather than on *Sein* so that *Gottsein* means "being God," not "the Being of God." The use of the verbal noun *Sein*, often combined with other terms into one word, is, of course, quite common in German theology and sometimes invites the question as to whether it is copulative or ontological. In any event, to identify God with Being must have been far from Brunner's intention.

Another basic concept underlying Brunner's understanding of Jesus is the concept of *Einmaligkeit*. God's coming to us in Jesus Christ has happened only once in history as a unique event. It actu-

---

[12] *The Mediator*, p. 395; "The Christian Doctrine of God," *Dogmatics I*, 1949, pp. 128 ff. (German edition, 1946.) Of the writings of Philo, see especially *Quod Deterius Potiori Insidari Soleat* (44) 160; *De Mutatione Nominum* (2) 11; *De Somniis I* (39, 40) 230-231.

[13] For a fuller discussion of this problem, see Thorleif Boman, *Das hebräische Denken im Vergleich mit dem Griechischen* (Göttingen: Vandenhoeck & Ruprecht, 1952), pp. 25-37.

ally happened in history; it is not a myth devoid of historical foundation. However, unlike other historical events, it bears the character of uniqueness. Brunner discussed this concept of uniqueness in the sense of "once-for-all-ness" in *The Mediator*,[14] but it was in a short essay entitled *Das Einmalige und der Existenzcharakter,* 1929,[15] that the theme received special attention. In this essay he attempts to clarify the concept of uniqueness as "the category of the Christian religion" in contrast to the concept of uniqueness in modern philosophy of history on the one hand and in contrast with the same concept in mythology on the other. Windelband, Rickert, and Dilthey all regard the category of uniqueness or individuality as basic for the understanding of history. But "the unique" *(das Einmalige)* in this sense is never unique. Civilizations and epochs of history possess their own unique, individual characters. They are not, however, windowless monads. On the contrary, they are linked with each other by universal laws and structures of nature and culture. Great heroes of history are certainly great individuals but only as high peaks of the universally human. To them is applicable not the concept of the unique *(das Einzige)*, but only that of "the unique within its kind" *(das Einzigartige)*. For history cannot be considered apart from the law of causality or without reference to meaning. In history, therefore, individuality simply means particularity within generality.

Thus myth rather than philosophy seems to be the realm where the concept of the unique belongs. Indeed Cassirer in his analysis of mythological thinking has pointed out that its basic character lies in its relatedness to time. The time factor in mythology, however, should be sharply distinguished from the rational, homogeneous, quantitative concept of time of modern man. The time of myth is qualitative. It points to what has happened in time by telling a story about it. To this extent, then, its interest is in the unique. But mythical events cannot be unique insofar as they are not actual historical events but merely represent certain periodically recurrent phenomena of nature. Thus the mythological conception of time is circular rather than linear. Consequently the *Geschichte* told by a myth is not truly "history" but merely a *Geschichte* in the sense of a "story."

---

[14] *The Mediator*, pp. 377 ff.; see especially note 1 on p. 379.
[15] *Blätter für deutsche Philosophie, Band* 3 (Berlin: Junker und Dünnhaupt Verlag), pp. 265-282.

The prophetic religion of Israel and Persia, however, takes the meaning of time much more seriously. Cassirer calls it also a myth, but its concept of time is entirely different. Here time is no more circular and rotary but "stretched out" as it were between the absolute beginning and the absolute end. It thus obtains a direction; it is irreversible and therefore has the character of uniqueness. This concept of time, however, is conceivable only where there is faith in God the creator. But we know it is only in Israel that the concept of creation out of nothing was developed in its purity. There indeed time as well as the world, as the creation of God, is conceived to be unique and irreversible. The religion of Israel therefore takes history most seriously so that *Geschichte* means to it what has actually happened as *Geschehen*. The most important point about this is that history thus acquires a practical, existential significance for the self-understanding of man. For in history so understood man is encountered and spoken to by God the creator. This coming of God to man in history is what we call revelation; but as long as we remain within prophetic religion we do not yet find the unique. On the contrary, at the stage of prophecy not just one person but many persons receive their revelations so that none of these may be called final. Here finality is expected to come only at the end of history, in the Messianic time. History, for prophecy, acquires at the most a preliminary character pointing to its future fulfillment.

But precisely this ultimate revelation Christian faith finds in Jesus Christ. In him God has really come to bridge the gulf which lies between Him and man. The ultimate, Messianic time is already here with Jesus! In Him and His cross the Eternal has come on His own initiative to reconcile man, by sin estranged from Him, to Himself. Thus by the cross and resurrection of Jesus Christ the divine work of reconciliation has been accomplished once for all. It is final; no repetition is needed. This is the meaning of *ephapax* in the New Testament (Rom. 6:10; Heb. 7:27; 9:12; 10:10)—"once-for-all-ness" in its absolute sense. And in this absolutely unique event a personal encounter between God and man takes place which puts man in a "serious" situation, in the "critical now" where he finds himself obliged to decide whether he should by repentance accept the love of God thus revealed or remain in his estrangement and defiance under the wrath of God. Here man has to make a decision; and it is only by making his own decision that he becomes a truly responsible person. A person who has made such an existential decision is no more a mere onlooker, a theoretical, contemplative, or aesthetic being. He takes time and history in earnest and participates in the making of history in a most responsible way.

So much for the essay on "The Unique." I have tried to outline it because I see in it a major contribution of Brunner toward a better understanding of the meaning of Christ and His work. The uniqueness of the event of Christ is thus absolute in a twofold sense. On the one hand it sets the event apart from all the other events which are relative. On the other hand, however, this unique event alone gives human existence and history their true meaning. This is a point set forth in the concluding chapter of *The Mediator* where, among other things, the author says: "The perception of the real significance of history, and therefore the serious view of history, has come into the world through the Christian faith, faith in the Mediator. History in the qualified sense exists only through Christ." [16]

IV. Over against Schweitzer and Bultmann

Jesus is neither a mere religious and moral teacher nor simply a prophet. Jesus Himself said He was "more" than a prophet (Matt. 12:41 f.). He was sure that the Kingdom of God was actually coming with His activity (Matt. 12:28; Lk. 11:20). The synoptic record shows he was indeed conscious of his Messiahship. Brunner says this fact cannot be explained away as a reflection of early church theology or as simply due to the influence of Jewish apocalypticism. For Christian faith recognizes in Jesus—both the prophets and the Apostles bearing witness to him—precisely the Messiah as Mediator between God and man. Schweitzer is right in recognizing the eschatological-Messianic character of Jesus' preaching but errs in regarding his expectation of the speedy coming of the Kingdom as an apocalyptic illusion. This, according to Brunner, is due to Schweitzer's failure to understand the tensioned structure of time revealed to faith by the event of Jesus Christ. So he dismisses the theory of "consistent eschatology" and, together with it, the views of Werner and Buri which are based on Schweitzer's argument.[17]

Likewise he makes explicit where he disagrees with Bultmann's theory of demythologizing. He raises no objection against Bultmann's proposal to discard the ancient *Weltbild* (view of the physical universe) presupposed by the New Testament. But, Brunner

[16] *The Mediator,* p. 614.
[17] *Dogmatics II,* pp. 254 ff.; pp. 260 ff.

declares, Bultmann has confused *Weltbild* and myth. These are two different things; therefore the rejection of the one should not automatically mean the rejection of the other, especially the "myth" of the coming of the Son of God. Also, he is not against Bultmann's intention to make the New Testament message existentially relevant for men of today. His criticism is rather that the influence of Heidegger's philosophy has made it difficult for Bultmann to appreciate the once-for-all-ness of the event of Christ and the meaning of the history of salvation.[18]

This attitude to the problem of demythologizing is already anticipated in what Brunner writes in *The Mediator,* where we read among other things the following words about the ascension: "The Ascension has nothing to do with the conception of heaven, of the kind current in olden time, of a three-storied universe. For us who no longer hold this view this article of faith is just as necessary as it was for primitive Christianity." [19] In this connection, however, it should be noted that in his *Dogmatics* he distinguishes between "ascension" and "exaltation." Here he holds the latter rather than the former to be essential, chiefly on the ground that Luke's report concerning the ascension does not agree with what the rest of the New Testament, especially Paul, says about the appearance of the Risen Lord. But I believe he has gone too far when he says, "While the exaltation of Christ and His session at the Right Hand of God belong to the fundamental *kerygma* of the witnesses in the New Testament, the exaltation as 'Ascension' plays no part in the teaching of the Apostles." [20] It seems to me that "session" necessarily implies "ascension." Also, the Epistle to the Hebrews expressly says Jesus the high priest "has passed through the heavens" to enter the Holy of Holies of the heavenly sanctuary to pour His own blood there. Such a sharp distinction between the terms therefore seems to be unnecessary. If we are not bound to take "exaltation" and "session" literally, there is no reason why we should stick to the literal meaning of "ascension."

All in all, however, Brunner's acceptance of the results of New Testament criticism is quite sensible and discerning. When he says the accounts of the virgin birth in the introductory sections of Matthew and Luke are quite isolated in the New Testament and

[18] *Ibid.,* pp. 263 ff. Also *Eternal Hope,* Ch. 13.
[19] *The Mediator,* p. 585.
[20] *Dogmatics II,* p. 373.

therefore have small evidential value, he is talking like a good liberal historian. This, of course, does not mean that he has adopted a liberal view of Jesus. He firmly believes in the Incarnation of the Word of God, for which belief, however, texts such as Rom. 8:3, 2 Cor. 8:9, Phil. 2:6, and John 1:14 are most basic; and these simply state the fact without reporting "how" it happened. Likewise, for his belief in the resurrection of Jesus, Brunner finds his support in Paul rather than in the four Gospels with their accounts of the empty tomb. The Apostles are not eyewitnesses to a purely historical event of resurrection but are rather witnesses of faith testifying to their meeting with the Risen Lord. It meant a none the less real resurrection—of the body though not of the flesh.[21]

V. The Work of the Mediator

According to Brunner the Person of Christ cannot be understood apart from his Work, and he often quotes the words of Melanchthon found in the first edition of his *Loci:* "To know His acts of kindness is to know Christ" (*hoc est Christum cognoscere, beneficia ejus cognoscere*). In *The Mediator,* however, Brunner finds himself obliged to warn against the Ritschlian, pragmatic interpretation of the dictum, over against which he defends the concept of "divine nature" used by classical, Chalcedonian Christology. But in *The Divine-Human Encounter,* which appeared eleven years later, he says:

The old Christian theology converted the Biblical verb-theology into a Greek substantive-theology. . . . I must correct at this point certain emphases in my own book *The Mediator*. It was indubitably an unconditional necessity for the Church to defend the unity of God and man in Jesus Christ against all mythological, gnostic, and moralistic-rationalistic attacks. But the Church bogged (so to say) at that point. It gave the Christian faith a false orientation about the Being instead of the work of Christ. . . . The Person of the Mediator must also be understood as an *act* of God, namely, as His coming to us in revelation and redemption.[22]

And in this connection he again quotes the same dictum of Melanchthon, this time with unqualified approval. Perhaps by the time of his writing this book (1938) Ritschlianism had ceased to be a danger

---

[21] *The Mediator,* pp. 322 ff.; 573 ff.; *Dogmatics II,* pp. 350 ff.; 365 ff.
[22] *The Divine-Human Encounter,* pp. 142 f. Cf. *The Mediator,* Ch. VIII; also p. 268, note 1; pp. 407 f.

but he was facing another kind of danger, that of reverting to objectivistic orthodoxy.

I have no intention of entering now into the details of Brunner's view of the Atonement. Suffice it to say that he shows great appreciation for the Anselmic theory of satisfaction. Anselm certainly takes the problem of human guilt seriously. Man has sinned against God; therefore his guilt is infinite. There is no other way for man to be saved than through the satisfaction made by the God-man Jesus Christ. Anselm thus emphasizes the necessity of the Atonement. But, according to Brunner, he is mistaken in arguing for its *absolute* necessity. Over against this notion Brunner has a preference for Calvin's theory of *relative* or *conditioned* necessity, which he regards as more true to the teaching of the New Testament. Moreover, Anselm is convinced that his theory of satisfaction is sufficient by itself, whereas in the New Testament there is found not just one but a variety of conceptions all pointing to a fact that defies our penetration. But the most serious defect in this theory, according to Brunner, lies in the fact that Anselm has made the work of the Atonement purely objective and hence missed the Biblical truth of divine-human encounter.[23]

Now what place, one might ask, does the ethical teaching of Jesus have in connection with his work of atonement? Brunner, of course, emphasizes the eschatological character of the ethical demands of Jesus. They are the ethics of the coming Kingdom of God and hence impossible for sinful human beings to fulfill.[24] But are the ethical demands presented simply to drive man to despair? Indeed they are. Men despair of themselves and accept by faith the grace of Jesus Christ. But even as forgiven sinners, that is, as believers, they have within themselves a possibility to sin as long as they live in the body of death. We are reminded, however, that the Word of God gives us not only forgiveness but also regeneration. As Brunner says: "The Word of reconciliation would not be effective, it would not be the Word of God, if it were not the beginning of redemption. Faith is power, energy, the principle of life, the moral power of renewal."[25]

If this is so, the life of the Kingdom has already been started here—in faith and hope, to be sure, yet in all its seriousness. Brun-

---

[23] *Dogmatics II*, pp. 289 f.; *The Mediator*, p. 472; p. 481, note 1.
[24] *The Mediator*, pp. 418 f.
[25] *Ibid.*, p. 532.

ner makes his position in this regard even more clear by warning against a twofold error. On the one hand he calls our attention to the rationalistic error which makes the teaching of Jesus stand by itself apart from His Person. On the other hand there is another error whereby His teaching is converted into pure Christology. The latter is a misunderstanding which is even more dangerous than the former. Thus, neither the so-called synoptic Jesus nor a mistaken Paulinism! For the Kingdom of God as His gift has its imperative aspect. The gift *(Gabe)* of forgiveness is not simply a gift, but also presents us with the task *(Aufgabe)* of doing the will of God.[26] Faith cannot be separated from love. Without love faith is dead indeed.

Thus faith is dynamic. By faith man receives the power of the Holy Spirit to transform his personality. This power is also a community-making power: wherever the Spirit of God works there is formed a fellowship of faith and love. And this fellowship *(koinōnia)* is the Church. Although my present task is not to discuss fully Brunner's conception of the Church, a discussion of his understanding of Jesus would not be complete without a word about Jesus' relationship with his Church. Concerning this question, however, we notice some change has taken place in Brunner's thought. In *The Mediator* we read: "The question whether Jesus Himself founded the Church may be answered in the affirmative, not only in the dogmatic sense, but also in the historical sense. He founded the New Covenant, not as an *ecclesia invisibilis,* . . . but as a real community, a 'people,' . . . whose constitution is 'the blood of the New Covenant.' "[27]

That at that time, around 1927, Brunner meant by the Church the concrete historical church as well as the fellowship of faith is also clear in his *Religionsphilosophie protestantischer Theologie,* where he writes, "The invisible fellowship of those who know His name as their own becomes also a historically visible quantity, even one of the great historical powers: the Church, Christianity in its historical shape."[28] In the same essay he adds that the true Church remains invisible although it is never without its visible embodiment. But in the course of time Brunner seems to have abandoned

[26] *Dogmatics II,* pp. 276 ff.

[27] *The Mediator,* p. 559.

[28] *Religionsphilosophie protestantischer Theologie,* p. 75 (in the *Handbuch der Philosophie,* Abt. II, München u. Berlin: Verlag von R. Oldenbourg, 1927; translation mine). Cf. *The Mediator,* pp. 614 ff.

this distinction between the visible and the invisible Church. Instead, he now makes a sharp distinction between the original apostolic *ecclesia* as true Christian fellowship and the Church as an institution. And he says Jesus did not found the Church in this latter sense.[29]

Personally I do not see how we can be justified in severing the original *ecclesia* so sharply from the historical Church, for even the apostolic *ecclesia* suffered from the human weaknesses of its members. And who can say there is no Christian fellowship within the historical Church or churches? I might only add that the conception of the Church as the "body of Christ" is something unique among the religions of the Far East with which I am familiar. There are temples, shrines, and monasteries; but no "church" is found except in Christianity. And there is no other way to show to the non-Christian world what it is like except by building churches in all their concreteness.

VI. *The Meaning of Absoluteness*

The event of Christ is unique. Is He then absolute? If so, in what sense? Precisely this problem engages Brunner's attention in a brochure entitled *Die Absolutheit Jesu*. Christian faith finds in Jesus the in-breaking of eternity into history, which means no other than the *Aufhebung* of history in the midst of history. Stated in philosophical terms, which cannot by the nature of the case be adequate for our purpose, Jesus might be called "the absolute which all history seeks yet does not find, by which all history is moved yet which can never itself become history"—"the absolute in the midst of the relative." [30] This is indeed what Christian faith amounts to. But then does Christian faith stand alone in isolation? Brunner says, No. For even Christian faith cannot evade the task of clarifying its relationship to other viewpoints. Such a work of comparison and confrontation is not the primary concern of theology, for Christian faith is self-sufficient and hence does not need support from apologetic arguments. Nevertheless, there remains this "secondary task of theology," which should not be neglected because the Christian believer is still a member of the

---

[29] *The Misunderstanding of the Church* (London: Lutterworth Press, 1952), pp. 17 and 22 f. (German edition, 1951.)

[30] *Die Absolutheit Jesu* (Berlin: Furche-Verlag, undated), pp. 17 f. (translation mine).

human society at large participating in its culture and learning.

One's Christian faith, therefore, should not isolate him from the rest of society. On the contrary, he should be willing to clarify for himself as well as for others the relation in which his faith stands to human reason on the one hand and to the claims of non-Christian religions on the other. Brunner's answer to the first of these two questions may be summed up in the following way. Both faith and reason should respect the boundary between them. Reason has the right to operate withins its own limits without any interference from outside. This also means, however, that reason in turn should recognize its own limitations and admit that it can never by itself attain the absolute. Christian faith thus does not interfere with the work of reason; yet it offers fulfillment for human reason by accomplishing what the latter cannot do. In the first place, no philosophy can in the end avoid the problem of the absolute, hence the problem of God. But it is obvious that philosophical reasoning alone can never solve this problem precisely because the idea of God as an object of rational thinking is no true God. God is known only when He reveals Himself to us, that is, in the divine-human encounter. In the second place, faith also fulfills the practical reason by giving the right answer to its deepest problem, the problem of guilt. Christian revelation indeed shows the infinite gravity of human guilt but at the same time it also brings home to us the divine word of forgiveness.

As regards the second question, namely, that of Christian faith in its relationship with other religious faiths, Brunner first makes it clear that he does not agree either with the verdict of rationalism that all positive religions are equally superstitious, or with the view of romanticism that all religions are individual, historical manifestations of one essential religion. In marked contrast with this romantic view of religion, Christian faith holds fast to the absolute uniqueness of Jesus Christ. But Brunner says this should not make Christians blind to the moments of truth contained in other religions than their own. These moments of truth are scattered, not meaningfully brought together. Nevertheless they are there.

So Brunner turns to the history of religions and finds two different streams. There are, on the one hand, personalistic religions of the will and law. On the other hand, there are impersonalistic, mystical religions. In the former type we find the distance between God and man, man's state of sin and guilt, the divine wrath and judgment emphasized, whereas in the latter type the nearness of the divine and even divine love and grace are taught. The one is aware of its relatedness to history and the goal of history, although its chief concern is with the thought of divine retribution. The other removes this concept of retribution by emphasizing divine grace, but it knows nothing of the divine judgment, historical revelation, and the goal of history. It is only in the Christian revelation that these two types of religion can find their "synthesis," for in Jesus Christ the will of God has been revealed as both holy and merciful.

Of course this does not constitute rational proof. It is rather a judgment of faith for which the sole criterion is provided by the Christian revelation itself. Yet this attempt to clarify the meaning of Christian faith in confrontation with other religions as well as general human culture seems to me of great practical significance. As I said in the opening part of this paper, the particular situation in which I am placed cannot but make me sensitive to the problem of what meaning Christian faith possesses for man living in a land with a religious and cultural heritage which is other than Christian. Brunner himself has been addressing himself chiefly to the post-Christian man of Europe and America. No doubt during his visits to Japan he has become quite familiar with our situation here. He has already given us stimulating criticisms and helpful suggestions. But it is primarily the responsibility of Japanese theologians themselves to seek to clarify the meaning of Christian faith for Japanese people by means of a careful analysis of our situation. And studies of this sort should be continued not only here but also in all other mission fields. We have to note, however, that such studies involve much more than a quest for better methods of missionary and evangelistic work. Our problems lie far deeper. Confronted with the task of bringing the Gospel of Love to our fellow human beings, we are obliged to ask many, many questions—questions about ourselves as well as others, questions about our own religion as well as other religions. Thus the very fact that we believe in the absolute uniqueness of Jesus should make us humble rather than arrogant and our minds open rather than closed, in order that only the eternal word of love and truth may penetrate the hearts of all people and do its own work of reconciliation, illumination, and transformation.

TETSUTARO ARIGA

FACULTY OF LETTERS
KYOTO UNIVERSITY
KYOTO, JAPAN

9

Anders Nygren

EMIL BRUNNER'S DOCTRINE OF GOD

EMIL BRUNNER'S DOCTRINE OF GOD *

Dealing with the "Doctrine of God," one faces a difficulty at once. For this doctrine can hardly be treated as a separate dogmatic problem. The question could be raised: What does not belong to this theme within Christian faith? Actually, the situation is such that everything in Christian faith is included in Christian belief in God and receives its particular feature from it, just as, on the other hand, everything that Christian belief says gives to its doctrine of God its particular feature.

When I say in the Apostolic Creed: "I believe in God," this means that I believe in the almighty Father, creator of Heaven and Earth. It also means that I believe in Jesus Christ the incarnated, crucified, resurrected, and exalted Lord, and in the redemption won through Him, which approaches its completion in His *parousia*. And it also means that I believe in the Holy Ghost who leads us to Jesus and to right faith through the gospel in the church.

The point here is not a general belief in God which then is completed by something else—that is, that I believe first of all in God, and then in Christ as a second belief, and eventually in the Holy Ghost as a third. The point is rather the belief in God. The confession of faith in Jesus Christ and the Holy Ghost is nothing other than faith in God, and without the faith in Christ and the Holy Ghost it would not be the Christian faith in God.

Precisely on account of this, however, the doctrine of God seems to lead us astray. Everything is involved, nothing is excepted. In order to be able to treat our subject we have to restrict ourselves to what is usually treated under the heading of the "doctrine of God."

In addition to that, a second restriction is necessary. In the

---

* Translated from the German by Gero Bauer, Vienna, Austria.

rich output by Brunner there are contributions everywhere which belong to our subject. If all of these were to be taken into consideration, the question would inevitably be posed as to whether or not a development from one viewpoint to the other had taken place in Brunner, and this, again, would exceed the limits of this essay. We shall restrict ourselves, therefore, to Brunner's final presentation as it appears in the first volume of his dogmatics *The Christian Doctrine of God,* 1946.

I.

The problem of the doctrine of God is, to a high degree, the problem of the relation between the Christian revelation of God and the philosophical concept of God. Few contemporary theologians have comprehended the problem involved in this relation as clearly as has Emil Brunner. He shows an extraordinarily penetrating grasp of the fatal role which neo-Platonic ontology has played in the Christian doctrine of God. This is his main theme, and one to which he keeps returning in constantly new perspectives. It is sufficient to quote here one single passage. We read in Brunner:

Anyone who knows the history of the development of the doctrine of God in "Christian theology," and especially the doctrine of the attributes of God, will never cease to marvel at the unthinking way in which theologians adopted the postulates of philosophical speculation of the Absolute, and also at the amount of harm this has caused in the sphere of the Christian doctrine of God. They were entirely unaware of the fact that this procedure was to mingle two sets of ideas which were as incompatible as oil and water; in each view the content of the word "God" was entirely different; for each view was based on an entirely different conception of God.[1]

They did not perceive the sharp distinction between the speculative idea of the Absolute and the witness of revelation. This obliviousness of so many early theologians accounts for the extensive influence of this point of view—the speculative way of thinking which simply could not be combined with the biblical revealed religion—on the development of the doctrine of God, but above all on the doctrine of the Divine attributes. The extent of this influence is absolutely amazing. It is hardly an exaggeration to

[1] Brunner, *The Christian Doctrine of God,* translated by Olive Wyon (Philadelphia: The Westminster Press, 1940), p. 242. All subsequent quotations in this essay are from this work. Ed.

say that the theological doctrine of the Divine attributes, handed on from the theology of the early church, had been shaped by the Platonic and Neo-Platonic idea of God, and not by the Biblical Idea.[2] This influence of Neoplatonic ontology can be traced throughout the Christian theology up to our own time. If, however, one starts from the concept of God as the absolute being, the *summum bonum*, and the indifferentiated one, *to en*, as many theologians have done, then it is impossible to pierce through to the completely differently oriented biblical doctrine of God.

In contrast with this speculative thinking of absoluteness, Brunner wants to justify a pure theology of revelation concerning the doctrine of God. It is not possible to let revelation form our thoughts in various other points of dogmatics; in the doctrine of God, however, it is essential to choose the point of departure, of revelation. If we can say anything at all about God then this is based upon God's self-manifestation given in the revelation. Thus Brunner's presentation of the doctrine of God aims at giving —in the true sense of the word—a *Christian* doctrine of God, one which is based on the Christian revelation and is a clear expression of its peculiarity.

We can approve of all this, of the negative limitation as well as of the positive termination of the task. With that the basis is laid for the following critical examination of Brunner's doctrine of God. The purpose of such an examination can only be to investigate the degree to which the presupposed principles have been consistently carried through.

II.

1. It is wise to begin, as Brunner did, with a chapter on the "Name of God," which is followed by a chapter on "God, the Lord." In doing this he obtains an immediate connection with the Christian revelation in contrast with the philosophical doctrine of God, which starts out from quite a different perspective, namely a speculative one. He may also count on our approval when he draws upon the Christian revelation of God seen before the background of holiness. It is necessary to keep holiness and love together if one wants to speak correctly about God's love. It is not as though they were two things, independent of each other, which are to

[2] Pp. 242-243.

be added together. God's love is the holy love. A love which does not include holiness is not God's love. Many mistakes have been made in dogmatics by speaking of God's love without defining more fully its content, as though the word love itself were precise enough to be applied to God's love. Thus the divine *agape* could be confused with sentimental love, or the love which one finds in different spheres of human life.

Brunner is conscious of the fact that the divine love in its essence is something different from the usual human love. ". . . all we can say, at its best, is in the form of parable. It is not that we already know what 'love' is, and can then apply it to God; . . . rather, the situation is this: that the *idea*, the understanding of love—the Agape of the New Testament—can only be understood from what happens in revelation. The story of revelation, Jesus Christ, the Crucified really defines the meaning of the new conception: Love, which is *Agape*. Love is the self-giving of God; love is the free and generous grace of the One who is Holy Lord." [3] Love and revelation belong together. Therefore, all features of the divine love have to be drawn from the revelation. "Hence the perception of this love is bound up with the event of revelation, or, as we have already said, this love does not define itself in intellectual terms, but in an Event." [4] Only in Jesus Christ and in His self-sacrifice do we find the love which is the "truly causeless, unmotivated, incomprehensible; it springs solely from the will of God Himself; that is, from His incomprehensible will to give His very self to us." [5] In this love we encounter God Himself and not only a divine attribute. It was wrong, therefore, when the traditional dogmatics tried to define God's love as an "ethical quality." This love cannot be derived from the commandment of love. Rather, it is an offspring of the love which God has shown us. "Actually, the Moral Law does not come first, but second. It does not come before, but after the love which is given to us." [6]

2. All this proves that Brunner was serious about his principle, namely, to establish his doctrine of God upon the message of the biblical revelation. It indicates, however, we have reached the

[3] P. 185.
[4] P. 188.
[5] P. 187.
[6] P. 197.

point at which the question marks begin to pile up. The question may be raised whether or not even the concept of the revelation is understood in a way which brings in a speculative and ontological feature—one which is alien to the Bible. Brunner rejects the philosophical concept of God in its Platonic and Neoplatonic forms. But does he not base his doctrine of God on *another* philosophy, a personal I-Thou philosophy? And is it not also this philosophy which eventually is asked to carry theology? This question is inevitable if one considers the central concept of Brunner's dogmatics, the concept of God as the subject per se. How does he come to this concept? First through a formal analysis of the I-Thou relationship. This analysis proceeds in two phases:

i. The first phase consists in a separation of the *thou* from the world of objects, from the mere products of thinking, from the object. The *thou* is something different from the "non-self." The *non-self* is the world, the totality of the objects. The *thou*, however, is the non-self which is a self like myself, of which I only become aware when it is not thought by my own efforts, or perceived as an object, but when it makes itself known to me as self-active, self-speaking, as "I-over-against-me" (p. 122). The I-thou relationship is something completely different from the relationship of the self to the world, from the relationship of thinking to its object. In contrast to all that can be called "it," the "self" (or "I") is a subject, a personality. The contrast between subject and object is, therefore, fundamental for the I-thou relationship insofar as I am only concerned with the relationship of one subject to the other. Now the question is whether a human *thou* can ever be regarded as a mere subject and not, at the same time, as an object. Thus we have reached the second phase of our analysis.

ii. The second phase consists in a distinction between the subject per se, who is God, and the relative thou, the relative subject, which is man. Every "thou" we can know only if it reveals itself. Yet there is a certain possibility of recognizing a human thou ourselves. "The mystery of human personality is not absolute; it is only relative, because it is not only 'other than I' but 'the same as I.'"[7] Thus, I have two sources for recognizing a human thou, the self-revelation of the unknown *thou* and my being a subject, my being a person.

[7] P. 123.

With God the case is different. He is the Thou per se, the subject per se. This has certain consequences with respect to the question how I can come to know about God. "Therefore I cannot myself unconditionally think God as this unconditioned Thou, but I can only know Him insofar as He Himself, by His own action, makes Himself known to me." [8] Here I have only one source: God's revelation. The reason why a divine revelation is necessary is this: "God is only subject, He is not also Object; He is the absolute Subject, subject in the unconditional, unlimited sense." [9]

Summing up this analysis of the I-thou relationship one can say: The world is an object, man is a subject, but "a subject that, at the same time is object." [10] God is subject only, never object. This concept of God as the subject per se, the unconditional subject, according to Brunner, is not only the starting point for theological thinking, but its very content. Brunner says: "True theology, therefore, must not only begin with the knowledge of God as the absolute Subject; its one, its sole task, is to make this clear." [11]

There is a strange parallel between Brunner's process of thinking about God as the absolute subject, and Schleiermacher's *feeling of utter dependence*. Even if this parallel was not intended by Brunner, even if he was not aware of it at all and would reject it, still the similarity of structure is striking. In both cases the thought starts from the world and takes its way from the relativity of the world to the unconditional, to God. As in Schleiermacher the feeling of utter dependence is the subject matter of theology, so in Brunner the concept of God as the subject per se is the content of theology. This similarity of the structures could be analyzed at greater length. Of course, there are essential differences, also, which stands with Brunner's I-thou philosophy, partly also to the difference of their basic theological views. The reader should consult Brunner's treatise, "Mystics and the World," and observe its decided No to Schleiermacher.

We shall not dwell on this point any longer, however, but realize that for Brunner, the thought of God as the subject per se is immediately connected with the thought of revelation. Ultimately

[8] P. 122.
[9] P. 140.
[10] P. 140.
[11] P. 141.

these two are but one. God, who essentially *is* the absolute subject, is also the God of the revelation. There an indissoluble unity of God's essence and revelation, "not only in the sense that God's essence is made known through the revelation, but in the sense that it is the essence of the God of the revelation." [12] This again means that God's essence is the will to self-communication. In this connection Brunner uses in quotation marks the unusual notion of the "communicativeness" of God. Revelation means that God "steps from His sphere of His own glory and self-sufficiency" and imparts Himself to us.

Just as the concept of the revelation is included in the concept of God as the absolute subject, so also God's love is included in the revelation. For, as the revelation is God's self-disclosure, so also God's love is this self-disclosure. Thus Brunner can say: "Revelation as the self-communication of God, is the act of Divine Love. As the One who reveals, namely, as the One who reveals Himself, God is One who loves." [13] If the revelation of God's love in Christ is the center of Christian belief, then it becomes clear through our investigation how and to what degree Brunner can say that theology as a whole has no other task than to make clear the concept of God as the absolute subject. For this being a subject, an absolute subject, is expressed especially in God's will to revelation and self-communication in love. Through the love and self-sacrifice of Christ, the being Subject per se and the self-communication are definitely clarified.

The question that presents itself in this connection is whether or not Brunner, despite his clear insight in the fatality of the compromise between the metaphysical speculations and the biblical revelation, ended up in a similar compromise. With him it is not the Platonic, Aristotelian, or Neoplatonic speculation that provides the ideas in which the Christian belief in God is dressed. This speculation has been replaced by an I-thou philosophy and a kind of philosophical actualism, but in this case, too, the main point is the compromise between a philosophical thinking and the revelation.

III.

An instructive example of the mixture of philosophy and revelation in Brunner's doctrine is to be found on page 191 of his *Dogmat-*

[12] P. 130.
[13] P. 191.

ics. Because of the fundamental and, at the same time, illustrative significance, a longer quotation should be given as follows.

> Just as sovereignty is His Nature—the Being who is Absolute Subject— so also, to put it in an abstract way for once, so also His Being as Subject is "for-some-end," it is Being which goes forth from Itself, Being which communicates Itself. To use a parable: We cannot grasp or describe the nature of radium without speaking of radioactivity. Radium is the radiant element—that is its very nature. Even so the nature of God is to shine forth in His glory, communicating activity, personal being, which wills communion. There is nothing "more metaphysical" in the doctrine of God than this: that God's nature in Himself is precisely His being-for-us. If the doctrine of God as he is in Himself is the philosophical formula of "Being-Subject," then the Christian formula for the Being of God is "Being-for-us," or, as we have just said: "Being-for-something" (for some purpose). To think that it is correct *first of all* to deal with the metaphysical being of God, and *then* with His Love, as His "ethical attribute," means that the decisive element in the Biblical Idea of God has not been perceived. That is why it is so important to know the Love of God not as an "attribute," but as the fundamental nature of God. God's nature is the radiation of spiritual energy, an energy which is the will to impart Himself. In contrast to all other forms of existence, this is the Nature of God: the will to impart Himself. This is Christian ontology, this is the doctrine of the Being of God, and this is fundamentally different from that of speculation.[14]

In order correctly to understand this process of thinking, one has to take into account that Brunner's main task is to remove the traditional idea of love as an "ethical attribute" of God and here Brunner, of course, is right. In addition to that, it is our intention to abandon any thinking of God as "it," as the subject that we can direct by our own thinking. The development of his thinking, accordingly, aims at a greater emphasis on the revelation in which God is subject through and through, and on the necessity of this revelation. Undoubtedly Brunner is right here, too. Saying this, however, one has to turn one's attention to another side of the matter. If one lets end this fact that God is subject of the revelation in a philosophical definition of God as the subject per se, which then is defined by means of the revelation as "being to some end," as "energy of radiation," and as "will to self-communication," and if one wants to build up a Christian ontology and a doctrine of the being itself, then this may have advantages over the Greek meta-

[14] Pp. 191-2.

physical speculation. For in that speculative framework God was "it," an object. And yet this attempt, which is based on the I-thou relationship, remains itself a speculation insofar as one believes that God's essence can be defined by means of philosophical ideas and consequently can be made an "it," an absolute subject. Contrary to Brunner's intention, God becomes a "something" that can be embodied in an ontology.

If one stops with Brunner's way of thinking in which God is labeled as the subject *per se* and the subject-to-some-end one cannot but be surprised how far one has gotten away from Christian belief in the form in which it is given in the revelation. Philosophical reflection has greatly altered the Christian belief. Brunner is aware of that, yet takes it to be inevitable. This is due to Brunner's very conception of dogmatics. The dogmatic reflection according to Brunner, has to precede what is given in the very act of faith. If, however, the dogmatic reflection takes over, then his "thou" is changed to a "He," or, as we have seen, to an "it." What we find in the biblical message of the revelation "in poetic or childlike, unreflected form," this dogmatics has to present in a rationally investigated and more scientific form. This means to leave what is actually given and to transform it in rationalizing reflection. If faith and the message of faith contains a personal relationship to God as the "thou," then dogmatics is a stepping out of the thou-relation to God, almost a change of approach away from God to the world. Dogmatics makes God the subject of reflection and instruction. But the further we go in this direction, the further the doctrine gets away from the message of faith. The danger of dogmatic thinking, according to Brunner, is that it may lead to a rationalistic dissolution of faith unless it is restrained by the act of faith as such. "The more that reflection, exact definition, strictly logical argument, reasoned classification, method and system predominate in Christian doctrine, the more 'scientific' it becomes, and the further it moves from the original truth of faith from which it proceeds, and to which it must continually refer." [15]

Brunner clarified in the following parable how he understood the union of faith and rational thinking which is the condition for dogmatic thinking:

Thus the act of thought in dogmatics may be compared with a movement which arises through the activity of two differently directed forces, for

[15] P. 64.

instance, one tangential and the other centripetal. The purely rational element of thought, logic, has the tendency to go straight forward from each given point; but faith continually prevents this straightforward movement by its pull toward the center. So instead of a movement in a straight line there arises a circular movement around the center—and this is a picture of real theological thinking. Theological thinking is a rational movement of thought, whose rational tendency at every point is continually being deflected, checked, or disturbed by faith. Where the rational element is not effective there is no movement of thought, no theology; where the rational alone is at work, there arises a rational, speculative theology, which leads away from the truth of revelation. Only where faith and rationality are rightly interlocked can we have true theology, good dogmatics.[16]

It is the predicament of theology that it fails to deal properly with its very subject, the Christian faith, the more rationally it proceeds, and that logic and faith are played off against each other in the work of the theology in such a way that they "check and disturb each other in every point." Whether or not this should be the case depends on how the task of theology is defined. If one defines it, as Brunner does, in such a way that it is "not only a process of thought about that which is given in faith, it is at the same time *believing thinking*" (p. 76), then the above-mentioned predicament is inevitable. If, however, one gives to theology the more modest task of presenting the essence of faith in its context as truthfully as possible, then those difficulties do not arise at all. Faith remains faith, and theology remains "thinking about what is given in faith." What is given in faith is subject to the scientific investigation of theology. If theology transforms faith and makes it something different from faith then it violates its scientific task which consists in a truthful representation of its subject in its peculiarity. If, however, one makes dogmatic thinking a rational kind, the act of faith, then one will inevitably end in a speculative doctrine of God.

Emil Brunner has accomplished the magnificent work of freeing the doctrine of God and dogmatics from the fetters of Platonic and Neoplatonic speculation. The question that remains is whether or not one has to take a full step and free dogmatics from any kind of speculation. This, however, would necessitate a full-blown examination of the task of theology.

ANDERS NYGREN

LUND, SWEDEN

[16] P. 16.

10

Edward A. Dowey, Jr.

REDEEMER AND REDEEMED AS PERSONS IN HISTORY

REDEEMER AND REDEEMED AS PERSONS
IN HISTORY

Emil Brunner first appeared on the world scene as a constructive theologian in 1927 with the publication of his volume, *The Mediator*. The point of view was new and radical for that day, although the author honestly claimed "nothing new to say" but what "has been the faith of the church from the earliest days." [1] J. K. Mozley introduced the English translation with the remark that "British students of theology are no longer likely to imagine that every theologian of the first rank in Europe outside the Roman Catholic Church will most probably have given up the doctrines of the Trinity, the Incarnation, and the Atonement." [2] Theology was in a period of extraordinary conflict. Thus we should understand the heavily polemic tone of this great nonorthodox, nonliberal, neo-Reformation volume.

The themes of *The Mediator* appear again in Dr. Brunner's *Dogmatics*, Volume II, *The Christian Doctrine of Creation and Redemption*, published in 1950. Within this period he has worked continuously at stating all branches of Christian thought in terms of the new understanding that he and others achieved in the 1920's. He has not yet presented his full treatment of faith, justification, and related topics in the unfinished *Dogmatics*, so a discussion of his doctrine of redemption, which has been assigned to me, must be written without some very important constituents. Still, the "spiral movement" by which he characterizes his method of presentation and his strong drive to expose the unity among various theo-

---

[1] *The Mediator*, p. 14. All Brunner's works are cited from English translations where available at the time of writing. Several quotations have been altered freely.

[2] *Ibid.*, p. 9.

logical topics [3] may make it possible to write on redemption as the divine reconciling activity without being seriously misleading, or misled. The procedure will be to offer an interpretative account, stressing the general trend, and asking questions along the way.

I. General Considerations

Although the whole of theology may rightly be understood as falling within the term redemption, it is commoner to designate thus the "work" of Christ and its reception among men. In this, as in all topics of theology, Dr. Brunner has found the bête noire at work: abstraction. Whether in Anselm or Abelard, the Reformers or Ritschl, or in the double abstraction of orthodoxy (objective soteriology and subjective soteriology), the concrete reality of redeeming grace tended to become either impersonal transaction or pious dream. In The Mediator it was the latter abstraction in the form of Schleiermacher's mysticism and Ritschl's moralism (not to mention Harnack!) that Brunner attacked most passionately. If, however, orthodoxy with its inerrant Book of true propositions, its penal-satisfactory atonement, and its effectual call of the predestined was less severely persecuted, it is only because (as Mozley's remark above shows) it was already moribund theologically. In subsequent times, with the success of the former critique, the latter is returning, aimed against tendencies on Brunner's right.[4]

The language that served this polemic so well in 1927 was not biblical, but was Bible "translation," [5] according to a main tenet of Brunner's theological program. The names of Buber and Heim do not occur in The Mediator, and Ebner and Gogarten receive slight mention,[6] although all these were widely cited ten years later in Man in Revolt. Nonetheless the entire group of personalistic concepts in their characteristic expression were present throughout: person, decision, act, community, conversation, history, I-Thou, encounter, and once-for-all.[7] Except for the last, these are not biblical terms, and they did not belong to the general vocabulary of tradition or theology before the twentieth century, apart from Kierkegaard whose century, after all, is the twentieth. Today these terms are also common usage in standard theological works, and have un-

---

3 Ibid., p. 19.
4 Dogmatics II, Preface.
5 Dogmatics I, p. 71.
6 Martin Buber's I and Thou, first appeared in 1923.
7 Truth as Encounter, passim; Revelation and Reason, Chs. I-V.

happily become clichés of much substandard parlor theology. Brunner made these conceptions productive not only for understanding the Bible, but for exegeting his favorite Athanasius and Irenaeus, Luther and Calvin, and for extracting biblical insights from the best intentions of theologians of all ages. Another essay in this volume will deal thoroughly with these matters. But three preliminary comments about this manner of expression and understanding are needed to introduce this interpretation of "God's Redeeming Work in Christ."

First. Truth as an act of personal encounter of the believer with God in Christ is to be understood as Brunner's prime hermeneutic principle. His conception of biblical authority excludes propositional truth, scientific statements about the natural world, and certain legendary and mythical materials found in the Bible (the virgin birth and the empty tomb qualify on all four counts), not finally on historico-critical grounds, but because they are extraneous to Encounter. He offers no hindrance to any kind of serious and critical study of biblical materials, and he uses such research with great skill, and yet he does not expect a great deal of positive help from it. The historical events essential to faith are asserted irrefragably as components of the Encounter and they belong to the certainty of faith.[8]

There is no objective revelation "out there" in the Bible waiting to be perceived. Revelation, rather, is a "transitive event which proceeds from God and ends in man," and the man-side of the event is faith.[9] Faith is believing encounter, always involving the free trusting obedience of man to God as Lord, at the point where God bowed to man in the weakness of Christ. Revelation is found where Christ is set forth and received (Luther, *Was Christum treibet*). The Bible is its indispensable normative instrument, and under the norm are other instruments: preaching, sacraments, and the entire life of the church. Encounter is not an episodic, psychological state, as the word might imply, but a permanent new reality of the believing life. This conception, derived from the Bible and exercising its influence as the principle of interpretation, achieves for Dr. Brunner a vast simplification of soteriology. It prevents the *ordo salutis* proliferation that a scholastic type of thought usually produces in trying to deal precisely with the countless intricacies and incongruities of a

8 *Dogmatics II*, p. 259.
9 *Revelation and Reason*, p. 33.

Bible taken as errorless formal authority. It also precludes the emptying of biblical richness and variety, and of biblical history itself, in the oversimplification of Ritschl's conception of the atonement. Whether this is taken advantage of fully by Dr. Brunner in the development of the doctrine of redemption is a question to be raised further on.

Second. History understood as personal encounter "writ large" seems to me to be the central category of Brunner's thought. According to his conception of faith, in which faith's apprehension of biblical history is normative, person-ness is never to be understood in isolation from community. Persons-in-historical-community form a single conception as opposed to history seen either as an aggregate of individuals or as individuated substance. At the risk of a barbaric sentence, Brunner's conception might be epitomized in this way: History is made up of the relationships of persons in decision (person means *das in-Entscheidung-Sein*)[10] to whom the past is present as guilt, and the future is present as the hope of a redemption begun in the past, and the past and the *present* are apprehended in the paradoxical faith relationship of "no longer" guilty (the "gift" of the gospel, freedom from "law") and "not yet" redeemed (the "task" or "imperative" of grace).[11] That most of the human race has not known this, and that faith and Bible do not give any valid instruction about the vast age and extent of the race does not deter Brunner from asserting that this *is* history, and that it includes all history, even for the overwhelming majority of mankind who could not know about it. The assertion is not empirical and inductive in a sense acceptable or available to research. It is rather a way of stating a theological reflection upon the church's confession that God encountered in faith is God the Creator.

Creation, however, is presented in Brunner's thought in ways that seem to conflict with this conception of history, especially in the realm of social ethics.[12] The language of "orders" of creation and of the "formal" image of God in man (a term which he once abandoned, then adopted again)[13] tends to rigidify the more "rela-

[10] *Man in Revolt*, p. 440 (German ed., p. 457). This entire section is very important.

[11] Cf. *Ibid.*, Ch. XIX; *Revelation and Reason*, Ch. III; and *The Eternal Hope*, Ch. VIII-X.

[12] *Man in Revolt*, p. 513; *Dogmatics II*, Ch. II.

[13] Thus, Reinhold Niebuhr: "Brunner . . . tends to revert to an almost pure Thomism in seeking after a 'justice which transcends human caprice and convention,'" *Faith and History*, p. 194n.

tional" understanding of history. Brunner himself does not intend this to happen: [14]

It is indeed difficult for us to combine "structure" and "relation." And yet it is the unique quality of human existence that its structure *is* a relation: responsible existence, responsive actuality. The biblical witness is ruthlessly consistent on this point; it knows man only as he stands "before God," even when he is godless. The fact that man, misusing his freedom and denying his responsibility, turns his back upon God does not mean that he no longer stands "before God." On the contrary, he stands before God as a sinner . . . in a wrong attitude, hence he is "under the wrath of God." [15]

A view that combines structure and relation might seem to have outgrown the terminology that in the past has been used to separate structure and relation. But terminology aside, both the clear intent of Brunner and the difficulty of supplying him with better formulae lead us to reaffirm what was stated above: history is the central category of his theological reflection. Our question will be whether this is fully expressed in the doctrine of redemption.

Third. The new insights into person and history fully operative in the polemic of *The Mediator* were not so effective as they might have been in recasting the positive statement of the doctrine in Books II and III. This work exhibits the traditional topics in conventional arrangement, although repeatedly stressing the dangers of isolating "person" from "work." A decade later Brunner wrote:

I must correct at this point certain emphases in my own book *The Mediator*. . . . [Ancient dogma] gave the Christian faith a false orientation about the Being instead of the work of Christ. . . . The Person of the Mediator must also be understood as an *act,* namely as his coming to us in revelation and redemption. . . . Even the Person of the Mediator is comprehended with the verb, if I may so express it, not with the substantive. One could actually say: Jesus Christ, even and especially in his divine-human *being* as Person, is God's *act,* just as he is the *Word* of God.[16]

In *Dogmatics,* Volume II, we find the promised correction, which will be described below. Our question again will be whether even

---

[14] Brunner's intent is fully appreciated by Paul Ramsey, *Basic Christian Ethics,* p. 261.

[15] *Dogmatics II,* p. 60.

[16] *Truth as Encounter,* pp. 142 ff.

the final statement goes as far as it might in assimilating the traditional doctrine of the "person" to the very different concept of person as newly understood by Brunner and his friends.

II. The Fullness of Time

In expressing the historical center of the Bible as the unconditionally decisive act of redemption, Brunner uses the language of Paul, "when the time had fully come" (Gal. 4:4; cf. Rom., Chapters 8 and 10). Four motifs are prominent in this discussion: (1) the mystery of divine decision, (2) law and gospel, (3) the messianic interpretation of the Old Testament and of world history as "preliminary" to the gospel, and (4) hints and traces in world history of divine preparation for the gospel.[17] The first of these shows that despite some traces of divine planning "it lay wholly within God's mystery *when* the time was fulfilled. . . . In the idea of time fulfilled the eternal supratemporal decree of God and the historical reality of time meet together." [18] To determine the point at which history would be ripe to be the medium of revealing its own meaning is beyond the grasp and understanding of faith. That such a time has already occurred, however, is an essential feature of it. This statement about time is given content by Paul in the ideas of law, gospel, and adopted sonship. And this is the lead that Brunner, citing also Schlatter, follows. Adoption represents God's election or choice; law and gospel show the quality of human existence in time in the light of that choice.

Brunner insists that Paul's negative view of law is not merely directed against a misunderstanding of the Old Testament by Judaism, but against something that belonged unavoidably to it. The chief quality showing the Old Testament's temporary and preliminary status is that it did not and could not distinguish between the righteousness of works and that of faith, although the basis of the distinction was laid in the relation between covenant and law. A result, among others, was the inability to distinguish clearly between the nation as such and the believing community. This incompleteness is perceived when one looks *backward,* as Paul did. Paul's

[17] *Dogmatics II*, Ch. IX; cf. "La conception chrétienne du temps," *Dieu Vivant* (1949), pp. 17-30.

[18] *Dogmatics II*, pp. 236 f. I do not understand why Dr. Brunner uses the term "decree" *(Ratschluss)* here rather than "election," in view of his general treatment of the subject. *Dogmatics I*, Ch. XXII, seems to use the term only in the title.

nomos had in fact "come in between" God's grace and his people. Law under the conditions of sin had become and always becomes the instrument of self-righteousness rather than a path of believing obedience.

Law as frustrated self-salvation, according to Brunner, is that which binds together the Old Testament people and paganism. "The Lex, severed from the covenant, is a principle common to all religions, it belongs to the natural man as such." All religion outside of Christ, including the "Christian religion," is work-righteousness, a law wrongly understood. Law, thus, is a term describing universal human history where something has "come in between," fracturing the free personal relationship of men with men and with God. The "in between" is extremely important, for nomos belongs neither to the original nor the ultimate relation to God. As such it belongs neither to creation nor to consummated redemption, but to man in "contradiction between his true and his actual existence." [19]

Looking *backward*, again, with the aid of Paul's Romans, we see that the "in between" means also between the promise given and its fulfillment. Thus, while there is an unresolved conflict within the Old Testament taken in its own terms (part of its preliminary character) its true and basic meaning can be seen, through Christ, to have been the promised grace.

The relationship of law to gospel, of Old to New Covenant, thus is the relationship of the redeeming event in Christ to all history. "In this sense not only the Old Testament, but the whole of world history is to be understood in a 'messianic' way." [20] World history belongs to the time of promise and preparation under law and wrath. Not that we can ourselves trace these elements (see below), but we can look "backward" from the New to the Old (this would mean also, one presumes, from the new to the old "man" within ourselves) and confess that this is so. This insight is not the product either of Old Testament exegesis, nor of research in world religions, but of faith's grasp of the meaning of the decisive, once-for-all event in Christ.

These three motifs, if they have been rightly understood thus far, represent what is in my estimation an excellent understanding of biblical teaching, which is clearest in Paul, but also present in the Gospels. Among theologians this insight is especially well devel-

[19] Cf. German title of *Man in Revolt.*
[20] *Dogmatics II*, p. 237.

oped in Luther and Calvin. Parenthetically, I would like to comment that Oscar Cullmann, who is usually cited with approval by Brunner, pays almost no attention to the relation, or lack of it, between time and the law gospel theme. Even where Paul's classic passages are cited, it is mostly with reference to other themes that happen to be present.[21] Brunner gets a good deal more support in this matter from Bultmann's *Theologie des Neuen Testaments,* Chapters II and XVII,[22] where the theme is related both to the teaching of Jesus and to Paul's view of law.

I would be interested in having Dr. Brunner's opinion of the fruitfulness for theology of Cullmann's somewhat barren "redemptive line" of time, which seems mostly built around the unambiguously futuristic eschatology of the return of the Son of Man, and takes so little account of the law-gospel aspect of these teachings. In this connection, further, it would be interesting to have Dr. Brunner's opinion of the "time of the law and the time of grace" in Luther's comments to Galatians 3:23, 4:4, *et passim.* This matter is discussed by Theodosius Harnack, Brunner's favorite Luther interpreter, but with curious inattention to the Galatians Commentary, which he cites in this connection only in one trivial aspect.[23] Luther presents the two "times" running simultaneously:

This Paul speaketh in respect of the fulness of the time wherein Christ came. But we must apply it not only to that time, but also to the inward man. For that which is done as an history and according to the time wherein Christ came, abolishing the law, and bringing liberty and eternal life to light, is done spiritually every day in every Christian: in whom is found continually, some while the time of the law, and some while the time of grace.[24]

[21] Cf. *Christ and Time,* pp. 137 f; 140; 180-182; 222-230. The last place cited is the fullest treatment. Cullmann's rejection of Kierkegaard's "contemporaneity" may be well founded in part, but if a choice must be made, Søren Kierkegaard seems closer to Paul than the "time line." Cullman makes no use of the *loci classici* in which Paul relates time to law and gospel (Rom. 8:1-8; Gal. 4:1-7) except for one inconsequential reference to Rom. 10:4. In *Die Christologie des Neuen Testaments* the subject is scarcely broached. C. H. Dodd in *Gospel and Law* does not relate the two subjects. This is not so much a failure in W. G. Kümmel's *Verheissung und Erfüllung,* which is devoted chiefly to Jesus' preaching, and he does presumably deal with the problem elsewhere.

[22] Especially, pp. 18 ff.; 262 ff.

[23] *Luther's Theologie,* I, p. 299 ff.

[24] Quoted from English translation, ed. Philip Watson, p. 328 f.; *Weimar Ausgabe,* XL, Part 1, p. 514 ff., *passim.*

This teaching, unless I have quite missed the core of Dr. Brunner's thought, comports well with his conception that the covenant is original and universal in scope and runs, so to speak, concurrently with the time of law that "came in between." Yet he has not expressed himself in full accord with Luther, and it would be interesting to know why.[25]

The fourth motif of the fullness of time thus is one which seems to add nothing but seductive temptation to lead astray from the other three. Dr. Brunner makes use of the Pauline terminology of immaturity, the concept of preparation, and some biblical references to world events, to discover hints and traces in world history (other than law) of how God went about selecting the time for the Messiah. He cites political, intellectual, linguistic, and religious conditions of the Hellenistic world as a peek into the "divine workshop." This seems to me to deal with permanently interesting problems of research, namely, how did Christianity spread, how was it dependent on Alexander, on Augustus, on Plato, and on Hellenistic saviour cults. But can this lead to *heilsgeschichtlich* observations? The religious and theological significance is, to my mind, nil. Is it derivable from the revelatory function of Scripture, conceived as the instrument of Encounter? All history may be seen in the dialectic of law and gospel, and this is fruitful for the life and preaching of the church. But the working out of the preparatory "traces" as a theological task seems to be wide of the mark, except for unmistakably messianic expectations in the Old Testament.

III. The Redeeming Action

The basis of redemption and of the whole of Christian theology is *faith* in Jesus as the Christ, that is, as the fulfillment of messianic promises. All this is presupposed throughout nearly two volumes of Brunner's *Dogmatics* that progress nonetheless according to the traditional *ratio essendi*. The movement is from the periphera to the middle of concentric rings. The outer circle is the "eternal Ground," then follows the self-communication of God in creation and providence, next comes world history, then saving history, and finally the "fullness of time" in the single redeeming event of the Messiah. At this point (Volume II, Chapter X), the method consciously shifts to the *ratio cognoscendi*. From the questions about

[25] *Man in Revolt,* p. 123.

what God is and how he reveals himself, Brunner now changes abruptly to, "How does a man become a Christian?" On faith, where Personal Act meets personal act, where the Work receives its response, the whole matter rests like a cone on its apex. First, in this new disposition, is the picture of Jesus' life and the Apostolic witness to it, then the "work" and finally the "person" of Christ, ending with his deity and his "exaltation." The most obvious differences from *The Mediator* are the reversal of the order of "work" and "person" and the prominent appearance of the old orthodox scheme of three "offices." Calvin had originally developed this device in a few brief paragraphs of his *Institutes*.[26] Schleiermacher adopted the offices "to preserve a continuity" in theology.[27] They appear also in a favorite Lutheran theologian of Brunner, von Oettingen.[28] It should be noted also that, while the threefold office was not present in *The Mediator*, a good deal of the later content of that *locus* is found in Book III under the rubrics, "revelation, reconciliation, and dominion."

Faith as such will not occupy us in this essay. It is the subject of another chapter. Further, faith will probably receive much elaboration when the final volume of the *Dogmatics* appears. Suffice to say, in faith man "encounters" the very person of God at His redemptive work in Jesus Christ. This is at once knowledge of God and self-knowledge by which man receives his restored original relationship to God as a gift of the Spirit. The meeting or personal intercourse is such as to place emphasis on "verbs" rather than "nouns," on events in history rather than on a suprahistorical nature, on functions and offices rather than metaphysical status, on the Coming One who brought the new age rather than the eternal Being apart from history. All this is to be found predominately in the Synoptic and Pauline writings and especially in the names given to Jesus: Messiah, Eon, Lord, Saviour, Mediator, Immanuel. These names mean that God's redemptive activity was completely at one with this particular man's life in history. "The Christology of the New Testament . . . is thoroughly oriented to *Heilsgeschichte* [history of redemption], is not metaphysics. Anything to do with metaphysical being and substance is the background, not the foreground, of the message of the New Testament. To speak of Jesus is to speak

---

[26] *Institutes II*, xiv.
[27] *The Christian Faith*, p. 439.
[28] *System der christlichen Heilswahrheit*, II/2, Ch. III.

of His work: *hoc est Christum cognoscere, beneficia ejus cognoscere.*[29]

How to conceive theologically of the "benefits" and to do so without "substantive metaphysics" is now the problem.[30] As the whole conception is historical, Brunner chooses to present it through three principle figures in the religious and social history of the Old Testament people: prophet, priest, and king. These are historical realities and biblical terms used as theological concepts in what has been in the past a very popular tour de force among dogmaticians. How well does this old device serve Dr. Brunner? We shall not inquire into the biblical base in detail, but ask rather if, given the interpretative principles we have been discussing, these terms serve their purpose.[31]

Prophet. There is ample biblical basis to interpret Christ as prophet. His preaching and presence raised the question of whether He were one of the prophets "returned." He was clearly "more than" a prophet (Matt. 12:41; 13:17; cf. Luke 7:26) in His "but *I* say to you," His offer of forgiveness in His own person, and His identification with the fulfillment of prophecy. Brunner emphasizes that the prophetic "office" or function as revealer (the traditional doctrine) consists in the "identity of word and person" and of "work and person," and the inseparability of His teaching from the redeeming event of His having "come." Harnack denied the person of the Son in favor of Jesus' ethical teachings, and Thurneysen assimilated the "ethic" of Jesus to His redeeming work, robbing it of relevance to the believer. Brunner insists that Jesus as prophet meets men as both gift and task (*Gabe und Aufgabe*) respectively: the gift of forgiveness and the claim of a new righteousness. This is not law any more, but the divine Agape itself in the new age—the time having fully come! "This Kingdom or Rule of God, promised by the Prophets, ushered in by Jesus, and through him finally to be completed, is the essence of the message of Jesus." [32] It is a teaching

---

[29] *Dogmatics II*, p. 272 f.

[30] *Ibid.*, p. 273. Paul Althaus, in *Theologische Literatus Zeitung* No. 20 (1929), pp. 470-479, in an early review of *The Mediator*, called on Brunner to abandon fears of Ritschlianism and begin his Christology *von unten nach oben*. Several suggestions in this review seem to sense the direction in which Brunner's thought would go.

[31] The following material is largely a selective summary from *Dogmatics II*, Chapter XI; detailed citations will not be given.

[32] *Ibid.*, p. 291.

that has to do with "now" and "from now on" in the life of the Christian.

Still, we must recognize that Jesus as revealer in this sense of the fulfillment of the prophetic promise and the consequent transformation of legal righteousness into the claims of love is only partially presented. The death and resurrection are not part of his own teaching, but of the apostolic witness about him. Thus his revealing work reaches its summit in that which lay outside his "prophetic office," in his "priestly work of reconciliation."

Before going on, two comments: First, both the older orthodoxy and liberal theology related Christ to the prophets as revealer, teacher, and bringer of the divine command. The advantage of Brunner over the former is that by refusing to separate person and work, he avoids such trifling as the decision about when, how, and in "which" nature Christ functioned thus. In contrast to liberalism, he was preserved a biblical apprehension of time and history and the nonlegal, but absolute, demand of Jesus' "Ethic." His book, *The Divine Imperative,* seems to me in principle an expanded treatment of the prophetic office understood in this way. It is curious, however, that in *The Divine Imperative,* Chapter XIV, he adopts the "third use" of the law *(usus didacticus),* but has dropped it in the *Dogmatics,* without any real alteration in content. Is this a substantive or merely terminological change? Is it not possible to use the term "law" as the structure of positive personal relation, as well as heteronomous demand? Second, we merely note, provisionally, that the "prophetic office" is repeated in substance in *Dogmatics,* Chapter XII.

Priest. A wholesome clearing away of a vast mass of scholastic and legalistic, objectivistic and subjectivistic, in short, nonpersonal conceptions and a restatement of the center of the New Testament message in personal-historical terms is what we might now expect to find in Dr. Brunner's conception of the Atonement. And that is exactly what we discover. Overlapping with the prophetic office, the priestly is first presented as including the entire life and teaching as well as the death of Christ. This excludes the "unbearable pedantry" of "active" and "passive" obedience in orthodoxy. Jesus' life was self-understood by the first believers to belong to his significance. Death was the problem. Five quite different, but closely related and frequently intermingled methods of interpretation appear in the New Testament: the Old Testament sacrificial cult; legal punishment (drawn from public law); payment of a debt (from private law); victory over powers of darkness; and the new Passover, issuing in freedom from bondage. None of these are "theories" or demonstrations of calculable necessity, according to Brunner. They are pictures and images of great richness throwing interpretative light on the meaning of what actually happened in history. They all mean that man's condition is fatal, that man cannot finally help himself—hence they take the actual guilt of history with utter seriousness. The "necessity" of the atonement is a "conditional necessity": *if* man is to be saved, something "must" be done by God for him.

Man by himself knows only frustration and defeat. He may pretend, but not successfully, that guilt is nothing. A convincing act of forgiveness "must" come to him—in fact, it *has* come for the entire explanation is a posteriori. A convincing act of forgiveness has occurred, decisively (once for all), and the relation to God is restored. In all this man knows God as unconditional love, yet perceives that God takes His own holiness and justice seriously. Man sees his old situation in its very depths and knows his new state as righteous only by virtue of a gift (justification). That is to say, the times have really changed, history has a new quality, personal relations have a new principle: the time had fully come, finally, "under Pontius Pilate."

Briefly, and minus the debate with Anselm and with Abelard, the foregoing account is Brunner's doctrine of the priestly office. Two comments come to mind: First, the artificial organization of material is much more obvious than among the orthodox statements, because the orthodox achieved consistency by subjugating all the images to one, say, penal substitution. The priest image does not so obviously imply conceptions derived from civil and private law and ancient demonology so well as the prophet figure, for example, fits the former "office." At the same time, this is no longer important, since the whole matter has been appreciated in its symbolic import. The entire series of images might seem to belong to homiletics or liturgy rather than theology, but guilt and reconciliation are terms that could hardly be translated into yet more personal language. Secondly, this material, too, is repeated briefly in Dr. Brunner's presentation of the person of Christ.

King. Jesus' preaching of the kingdom as present in Himself is again a readily identifiable part of the teaching of the gospels. The kingdom thus present, however, was not the terrifying approach of divine majesty, but a gift of God. In this kingdom holy love overcomes evil by winning trust, love, service. This is a new kind of kingship that rules by "coming down" and offering forgiveness. Its law, which is the fulfillment of "the law," is love of neighbor, its true, factual extent is the community of faith's obedience. Its goal, which is the goal of all history, is the will of God: "You shall be my people and I shall be your God." "This is the voluntaristic-personalistic theme, which is the chief characteristic of the biblical view of God. Certainly, as in every religion, salvation is important; but this salvation consists in unity of will with, and personal communion between, God and man. Everything else is secondary, or is merely a conclusion drawn from this truth." [33]

Kingship is only briefly discussed within the context of the threefold office, and a large portion of space is devoted to rejecting the idea that Christ is already king, rather than, so to speak, *imperator designatus*. Christ's actual dominion, according to Brunner, is in the believing community and it is wrong to try to derive the form or powers of the secular state or social ethics directly from faith in Christ. These are matters of the structures of creation and of history where voluntary obedience to this King is neither actual nor intended. The Easter victory is not yet fully consummated.

This office is the least problematic of the three, to my mind. The figure or image of king fits the entire biblical frame of reference and the quality of the analysis is entirely according to the conception of person as seen previously in terms of law, gospel, and faith. But again we note this material repeated in connection with Christ's person—a matter about which we shall now have some questions.

In summary: The threefold office, although it is certainly not the only, and it may not be the best device for describing how Christ's "benefits" were provided for man's salvation, has the quality of versatility. Having formerly served Calvin, Turretin, Schleiermacher, *et alii*, it has now been turned successfully by Dr. Brunner into an expression of biblical truth understood as personal encounter. These images express the many-sided teaching of Scripture, notably in avoidance of objectivistic and subjectivistic eccentricities. The chief objection, I think, might be that these categories are devotional and liturgical rather than carefully wrought theological distinctions, and

[33] *Ibid.*

hence are too amenable to ringing prose rather than precise statement. The chief observation that I wish to make is that this section
of Dr. Brunner's theology seems to have been *too* successful and
to have made the subsequent *locus* superfluous.

IV. Act Plus Person?

It strikes the reader at first with some amazement that the rich
and creative flow of thought in Dr. Brunner's *Dogmatics* seems suddenly to turn back upon itself in the final chapter of the second
volume. This long discourse entitled "The Person of Jesus Christ"
contains some very interesting excursus on ancient christological
controversies and on biblical accounts of the virgin birth and the
empty tomb. But it fails to advance very much the understanding
of the Messiah that had already been expressed as Christ's work.
We have new titles,[34] but not new material. The opening presentation of "The Mystery of the Person of Jesus" contains little but the
content of the earlier Chapter X, "The Foundation of Faith in
Christ." A section called "The Deity of Jesus" is a forthright repetition of the threefold office, adding only that seen in its full import,
it must be interpreted to mean "God-man."

In His revealing, reconciling-redeeming, and royal work we feel compelled to express the mystery of His divine Person. Because He reveals
God to us as no human being could reveal Him, because He reconciles
us to God, as no human being could reconcile us to God, because He
makes us trustful servants of God as no human being could do, we know
that we must confess Him to be the God-Man, we must confess Him as
the one who is not only True Man, but at the same time—whether we
understand it or not—True God.[35]

"The Eternal Godhead of the Son" promises to follow the lead
of the Fourth Gospel which is also "the way marked out for dogmatic Christology: from the historical foreground to the 'suprahistorical' background." But the positive sections reiterate the threefold
office and the remainder is polemic against certain types of church
and biblical authority, and against Adoptianism, Sabellianism, and
Arianism. "The Incarnation of the Eternal Son of God" contains
previously described material about the "coming" One and the
Kingdom, and argues the unacceptability of the virgin birth stories

[34] The following references are to titles of subsections in *Dogmatics II*,
Ch. XII.
[35] *Ibid.*, p. 340.

both in fact and in their docetic tendencies. "The Doctrine of the Two Natures" is rejected as answering to a wrongly posed question, although "true God and true Man" without any theory of explanation is regarded as the correct formula. The final section on "The Risen and Exalted Lord" does bring new teaching, although this is so closely intertwined (as it must be) with the royal office that one wonders what purpose is served by the separation.

If this analysis is correct, we must seek some reason for it. The repetition can scarcely be inadvertent: Homer would not "nod" for the space of seventy-five pages. A possible reason is adumbrated in my comments above that the repetition was to occur and in my questions about whether Dr. Brunner has gone far enough in adjusting the traditional *loci* of theology to his own apprehension of truth as encounter. It seems to me as if the force of this apprehension has brought to the fore the subject of Christ's "work" in Dr. Brunner's theology, thoroughly restated and personalized. This he has realized and has expressed it systematically by correcting the arrangement and content of *The Mediator* as promised. But even more has happened, and he did not appear to be fully aware of it in writing his dogmatics. The concept of Encounter has really robbed the traditional *locus* on Christ's "person" of any *raison d'être* as a separate theological topic. The evidence of it is that the *Dogmatics*, Chapter XII, is reduced almost entirely to repetition and polemic. The next development may well be to take more seriously the *union* of work and person and give a fully integrated analysis. If not, the divine "person" will continue to hover over history as a metaphysical abstraction. Two recent volumes that have appeared in America make use of the personal-voluntarist categories with this tendency. One of them thus arrives at the felicitous expression that the gospel consists "in the work of His incarnate life." [36]

This criticism I take to be one that goes with rather than across the grain of Dr. Brunner's theology. Yet, if based on a genuine grasp of his thought, it is a matter of real importance, and a subject on which his comment will be interesting.

EDWARD A. DOWEY, JR.

PRINCETON THEOLOGICAL SEMINARY
PRINCETON, NEW JERSEY

[36] G. W. Hendry, *The Gospel of the Incarnation* p. 165; cf. W. J. Wolf, *No Cross, No Crown*.

11

Georges Florovsky

THE LAST THINGS AND THE
LAST EVENTS

THE LAST THINGS AND THE LAST EVENTS

Behold, I make all things new—Rev. 21.5

I.

E schatology was for a long time a neglected field in modern theology. The arrogant phrase of Ernst Troeltsch—*Das eschatologische Bureau is meist geschlossen* ("The bureau of eschatology
is for the most part closed")—was distinctively characteristic of the
whole liberal tradition, since the Age of the Enlightenment. Nor is
this neglect for eschatological issues fully overcome in the contemporary thought. In certain quarters eschatology is still regarded as
an obsolete relic of the forlorn past. The theme itself is avoided,
or it is summarily dismissed as unreal and irrelevant. The modern
man is not concerned with the last events. This attitude of neglect
was recently reinforced by the rise of theological Existentialism.
Now, Existentialism does claim to be itself an eschatological doctrine. But it is a sheer abuse of terms. Eschatology is radically inte-
riorized in its existentialist reinterpretation. It is actually swallowed
up in the immediacy of personal decisions. In a sense, modern
Existentialism in theology is but a fresh variation on the old Pietistic
theme. In the last resort, it amounts to the radical dehistorization of
the Christian faith. Events of history are eclipsed by the events of
inner life. The Bible itself is used as a book of parables and patterns.
History is no more than a passing frame. Eternity can be encountered and tasted at any time. History is no more a theological problem.

On the other hand, precisely in the last few decades, the basic
historicity of the Christian faith has been reassessed and reaffirmed
in various trends of contemporary theology. This was a momentous
shift in theological thinking. Indeed, it was a return to Biblical faith.

Of course, no elaborate "philosophy of history" can be found in the Bible. But there is in the Bible a comprehensive vision of history, a perspective of an unfolding time, running from a "beginning" to an "end," and guided by the sovereign will of God toward the accomplishment of His ultimate purpose. The Christian faith is primarily an obedient witness to the mighty deeds of God in history, which culminated, "in those last days," in the Advent of Christ and in His redemptive victory. Accordingly, Christian theology should be construed as a "Theology of History." Christian faith is grounded in events, not in ideas. The Creed itself is a historical witness, a witness to the saving or redemptive events, which are apprehended by faith as God's mighty deeds.

This recovery of the historic dimension of the Christian faith was bound to bring the eschatological theme into the focus of theological meditation. The Bible and the Creed are both pointing to the future. It has been recently suggested that Greek philosophy was inescapably "in the grip of the past." The category of the future was quite irrelevant in the Greek version of history. History was conceived as a rotation, with an inevitable return to the initial position, from which a new repetition of events was bound to start again. On the contrary, the Biblical view opens into the future, in which new things are to be disclosed and realized. And an ultimate realization of the divine purpose is anticipated in the future, beyond which no temporal movement can proceed—a state of consummation.

In the witty phrase of von Balthasar, *die Eschatologie ist der "Wetterwinkel" in der Theologie unserer Zeit* ("Eschatology is the 'eye of the storm' in the theology of our time").[1] Indeed, it is a "subtle knot" in which all lines of theological thinking intersect and are inextricably woven together. Eschatology cannot be discussed as a special topic, as a separate article of belief. It can be understood only in the total perspective of the Christian faith. What is characteristic of the contemporary theological thought is precisely the recovery of the eschatological dimension of the Christian faith. All articles of faith have an eschatological connotation. There is no common *consensus* in the contemporary theology of "the Last Things." There is rather a sharp conflict of views and opinions. But there is also a new widening of the perspective.

[1] Hans Urs von Balthasar, "Eschatologie," *Fragen der Theologie Heute,* Feiner, Trütsch, Böckle, editors (Zürich: Köln, 1958), pp. 403-421.

Emil Brunner's contribution to the current discussion was both provocative and constructive. His theology is a theology of hope and expectation, as it befits one who stands in the Reformed tradition. His theology is inwardly oriented toward "the Last Events." Yet, at many points, his vision is limited by his general theological presuppositions. Indeed, his theology reflects his personal experience of faith—what he himself calls—*die gläubige Existenz.*

II.

The mystery of the Last Things is grounded in the primary paradox of Creation. According to Brunner, the term Creation, in its biblical use, does not denote the manner in which the world did actually come into existence, but only the sovereign Lordship of God. In the act of Creation God posits something totally other than Himself, "over against" Himself. Accordingly, the world of creatures has its own mode of existence—derivative, subordinate, dependent, and yet genuine and real, in its own kind. Brunner is quite formal at this point. "A world which is not God exists alongside of Him." Thus, the very existence of the world implies a certain measure of self-imposed "limitation" on the side of God, His *kenosis,* which reaches its climax in the cross of Christ. God, as it were, spares room for the existence of something different. The world has been "called into existence" for a purpose, in order that it manifest the glory of God. The Word is the principle and the ultimate goal of Creation.

Indeed, the very fact of Creation constitutes the basic paradox of the Christian faith, to which all other mysteries of God can be traced back, or rather in which they are implied. Brunner, however, does not distinguish clearly, at this point, between the very "being" of God and His "will." Yet, the "being" of God simply cannot be "limited" in any sense. If there is a "limitation," it can refer only to His "will," insofar as another "will" has been "called into existence," a will which could not have existed at all. This basic "contingency" of Creation testifies to the absolute sovereignity of God. On the other hand, the ultimate climax of the creative *kenosis* will be reached only in "the Last Events." The sting of the paradox, of the *kenosis,* is not in the existence of the world, but in the possibility of Hell. Indeed, the World may be obedient to God, as well as it may be disobedient, and in its obedience it would serve God and manifest His glory. It will be not a "limitation," but an expansion of God's majesty. On the contrary, hell means resistance and estrangement, pure and simple. However, even in the state of revolt and rebellion, the world still belongs to God. It can never escape His Judgment.

God is eternal. This is a negative definition. It simply means that the notion of time cannot be applied to His existence. Indeed, "time" is simply the mode of creaturely existence. Time is given by God. It is not an imperfect or deficient mode of being. There is nothing illusory about time. Temporality is real. Time is really moving on, irreversibly. But it is not just a flux, as it is not a rotation. It is not just a series of indifferent "time-atoms" which could be conceived or postulated as infinite, without any end or limit. It is rather a teleological process, inwardly ordained toward a certain final goal. A *telos* is implied in the very design of Creation. Accordingly, what takes place in time is significant—significant and real for God Himself. History is not a shadow. Ultimately, history has a "metahistoric" goal. Brunner does not use this term, but he stresses strongly the inherent "finitude" of history. An infinite history, rolling on indefinitely, without destination or end, would have been an empty and meaningless history. The story is bound to have an end, a conclusion, a *katharsis,* a solution. The plot must be disclosed. History has to have an end, at which it is "fulfilled" or "consummated." It has been originally designed to be "fulfilled." At the end there will be no history any more. Time will be filled with eternity, as Brunner puts it. Of course, eternity means in this connection simply God. Time has meaning only against the background of eternity, that is—only in the context of the divine design.

Yet, history is not just a disclosure of that primordial and sovereign design. The theme of actual history, of the only real history we know about, is given by the existence of sin. Brunner dismisses the query about the origin of sin. He only stresses its "universality." Sin, in the biblical sense of the term, is not primarily an ethical category. According to Brunner, it only denotes the need for redemption. Two terms are intrinsically correlative. Now, sin is not a primary phenomenon, but a break, a deviation, a turning away from the beginning. Its essence is apostasy and rebellion. It is this aspect of sin that is emphasized in the biblical story of the Fall. Brunner refuses to regard the Fall as an actual event. He only insists that without the concept of the Fall the basic message of the New Testament, that is—the message of salvation,

would be absolutely incomprehensible. Yet, one should not inquire
into the "when" and "how" of the Fall. The essence of sin can be
discerned only in the light of Christ, that is—in the light of redemption. Man, as he can be observed in history, always appears as sinner, unable not to sin. The man of history is always "man in revolt."
Brunner is fully aware of the strength of evil—in the world and
in the history of man. He commands the Kantian notion of the
radical evil. What he has to say about the Satanic sin, as different
from man's sin, about the superpersonal Satanic power, is impressive
and highly relevant for theological inquiry, as much as all that
may inevitably offend and disturb the mind of modern man. But
the major question remains still without answer. Has the Fall the
character of an event? The logic of Brunner's own argument seems
to compel us to regard it as event, as a link in the chain of events.
Otherwise it would be just a symbol, a working hypothesis, indispensable for interpretative purposes, but unreal. Indeed, the
end of history must be regarded, according to Brunner, as "an
event," howsoever mysterious this event will be. "The beginning"
also has the character of "event," as the first link in the chain.
Moreover, redemption is obviously "an event" which can be exactly dated—indeed, the crucial event, determinative of all others.
In this perspective it seems imperative to regard the Fall as event,
in whatever manner it may be visualized or interpreted. In any
case, redemption and Fall are intrinsically related to each other,
in Brunner's own interpretation.

Brunner distinguishes clearly between the creatureliness as
such and sin. Creatures come from God. Sin comes from an opposite
source. Sinfulness is disclosed in events, in sinful acts and actions.
Indeed, it is an abuse of power, an abuse of freedom, a perversion
of that responsible freedom which has been bestowed upon man
in the very act by which he was called into existence. Yet, before
the abuse became a habit, it had to have been exercised for the
first time. The revolt had to have been started. Such an assumption
would be in line with the rest of Brunner's exposition. Otherwise
one lapses into some kind of metaphysical dualism which Brunner
himself vigorously denounces. In any case, creatureliness and sinfulness cannot be equated or identified.

Indeed, Brunner is right in suggesting that we must start from
the center, that is, with the glad tidings of redemption in Christ.
But in Christ we contemplate not only our desperate "existential

predicament" as miserable sinners, but, above all, the historical involvement of men in sin. We are moving in the world of events. Only for that reason are we justified in looking forward, to "the Last Events."

The course of history has been radically challenged by God—at one crucial point. According to Brunner, since the coming of Christ, time itself has been charged, for believers, with a totally new quality—*eine sonst unbekannte Entscheidungsqualität* ("an otherwise unknown quality of decision"). Ever since, believers are confronted with an ultimate alternative, confronted now—in this "historic time." The choice is radical—between heaven and hell. Any moment of history may become decisive—for those who are bound to make decisions, through Christ's challenge and revelation. In this sense, according to Brunner, "the earthly time is, for faith, charged with an eternity-tension"—*mit Ewigkeitspannung geladen.* Men are now unescapably called to decisions, since God has manifested His own decision, in Christ, and in His cross and Resurrection. Does it mean that "eternal decisions"—that is, decisions "for eternity" —must be made in this "historic time"? By faith—in Jesus Christ, the Mediator—one may, already now, "participate" in eternity. Since Christ, believers dwell already, as it were, in two different dimensions, both inside and outside of the "ordinary" time—*hoc universum tempus, sive saeculum, in que cedunt morientes succeduntque nascentes* (this universal time, or age, in which the dying give place to those being born. St. Augustine, *Civ. Dei,* XV.I). Time has been, as it were, "polarized" by Christ's Advent. Thus, it seems, time is related now to eternity, that is to God, in a dual manner. On the one hand, time is always intrinsically related to the eternal God, as its Creator: God gives time. On the other hand, time has been, in those last days, radically challenged by God's direct and immediate intervention, in the person of Jesus Christ. As Brunner says himself, "temporality, existence in time, takes on a new character through its relationship to this event, Jesus Christ, the *eph hapax* of history, the once-for-all quality of His cross and Resurrection, and is newly fashioned in a paradoxical manner that is unintelligible to thinking guided by reason alone." [2]

We have reached the crucial point in Brunner's exposition. His interpretation of human destiny is strictly Christological and Chris-

[2] Brunner, *Eternal Hope* (Philadelphia: The Westminster Press, 1954), p. 48.

tocentric. Only faith in Christ gives meaning to human existence. This is Brunner's strong point. But there is an ambiguous docetic accent in his Christology, and it affects grievously his understanding of history. Strangely enough, Brunner himself addresses the same charge to the traditional Christology of the Church, claiming that it never paid enough attention to the historic Jesus. It is a summary charge which we cannot analyze and "refute" just now. What is relevant for our purpose now is that Brunner's Christology is obviously much more docetic than that of the Catholic tradition. Brunner's attention to the historical Jesus is utterly ambiguous. According to Brunner, Christ is a historic personality only as man. When He "unveils Himself"—that is, when He discloses His Divinity to those who have the eye of faith—He is no more a historical personality at all. In fact, Christ's humanity, according to Brunner, is no more than "a disguise." The true self of Christ is divine. To faith Christ discards His disguise, His "incognito," to use Brunner's own phrase. "Where He discloses Himself, history disappears, and the Kingdom of God has begun. And when He unveils Himself, He is no longer an historical personality, but the Son of God, Who is from everlasting to everlasting." [3] This is a startling language, indeed.

Actually, Christ's humanity is just a means to enter history, or rather—to appear in history. God's relation to history, and to human reality, is, as it were, no more than tangential, even in the crucial mystery of Incarnation. Actually, Christ's humanity interests Brunner only as a medium of revelation, of divine self-disclosure. Indeed, according to Brunner, in Christ God has really found a firm footing in humanity. But this does not seem anything more than that God has now challenged man in his own human element, on his own human ground and level. In order to meet man, God had to descend—to man's own level. This may be understood in a strictly orthodox way. Indeed, this was the favorite thought of the ancient Fathers. But Brunner denies any real interpenetration of divine and human aspects in Christ's person. In fact, they are no more than "aspects." Two elements meet, but there is no real unity. Christ of faith is only divine, even if in a human disguise. His humanity is just a means to enter history, or rather—to appear in history. Is history just a moving screen on which divine "eternity" is to be projected? God had to assume a beggar's robe of man, for

[3] Brunner, *The Mediator* (London: Lutterworth Press, 1949), p. 346.

otherwise He would be unable to encounter man. There was no real "assumption" of human reality into the personal experience of the Incarnate. The role of Christ's humanity was purely instrumental, a disguise. Basically it is a sheer "Docetism," as much attention may be given to "historic Jesus." After all, "historic Jesus" does not belong, in this interpretation, to the realm of faith.

Real decisions are not made on the plan of history, says Brunner. "For that is the sphere in which men wear masks. For the sake of our "masquerade," that is, for the sake of our sinful mendacity, Christ also, if I may put it like this, has to wear a mask; this is His Incognito." [4] Now, in the act of faith, man takes away his mask. Then, in response, Christ also discards His mask, His human disguise, and appears in His glory. Faith, according to Brunner, breaks down history. Faith itself is a kind of a "meta-historic" act, which transcends history, or even discards it. Indeed, Brunner stresses the uniqueness of God's redemptive revelation in Christ. For man it only means that the challenge is radical and ultimate. Man is now given a unique opportunity, or occasion, to make his decision, to overcome his own limited humanity, and even his intrinsic temporality—by an act of faith which takes him beyond history, if only in hope and promise, till the final *kairos* has come. But is human history ultimately just a masquerade? According to Brunner's own emphatic statement, temporality as such is not sinful. Why, then, should divine revelation in Christ discard history? Why should historicity be an obstacle to God's self-revelation, an obstacle that must be radically removed?

In the last resort, the radical change in history—the New Age, released by Christ's Advent—seems to consist only in the new and unprecedented opportunity to take sides. God actually remains as hidden in history as He has been before, or, probably, even more than before, since the ultimate incommensurability of divine revelation with the human masquerade has been made self-evident and conspicuous. God could approach man only in disguise. The actual course of history has not been changed, either by God's intervention, or by man's option. Apart from the decision of faith, history is empty, and still sinful. The intimate texture of actual historic life has not been affected by the redemptive revelation. Nevertheless, a warning has been given: The Lord comes again.

[4] *Ibid.*, p. 346.

This time He is coming as judge, not as Redeemer, although Judgment will actually accomplish and stabilize redemption.

By faith we can now discern an "eschatological tension" in the very course of history, although it would be idle and in vain to indulge in any kind of apocalyptic calculations. This tension seems to exist on the human level alone. The eschatological *interim* is the age of decisions—to be taken by men. God's decision has been already taken.

As a whole, Christian history, according to Brunner, was a sore failure, a history of decay and misunderstanding. This is an old scheme, firmly established in Protestant historiography at least since Gottfried Arnold. The primitive Christian community, the ecclesia, was a genuine Messianic community, "the bearer of the new life of eternity and of the powers of the divine world," as Brunner puts it. But this primitive ecclesia did not survive, at least as an historic entity, as an historic factor. Brunner acknowledges partial and provisional "advents" of the Kingdom of God in the course of history. But all these "advents" are sporadic. Where faith is, there is ecclesia or Kingdom. But it is hidden, in the continuing "masquerade" of history. Ultimately, the ongoing history is a kind of testing ground, on which men are challenged and their responses are tried and tested. But does the "saving history" still continue? Is God still active in history, after the First Advent—or is history now left, after the great intervention of Christ, to man alone, with that eschatological provision that finally Christ comes again?

Now, history is obviously but a provisional and passing stage in the destiny of man. Man is called to "eternity," not to "history." This is why "history" must come to its close, to its end. Yet, indeed, history is also a stage of growth—the wheat and the tares are growing together, and their ultimate discrimination is delayed— till the day of harvest. The tares are growing indeed, rapidly and wildly. But the wheat is growing also. Otherwise there would be no chance for any harvest, except for that of tares. Indeed, history matures not only for judgment, but also for consummation. Moreover, Christ is still active in history. Brunner disregards, or ignores, that component of Christian history. Christian history is, as it were, "atomized," in his vision. It is just a series of existential acts, performed by men, and, strangely enough, only negative acts, the acts of rebellion and resistance, seem to be integrated and solidarized. But, in fact, ecclesia is not just an aggregate of sporadic acts, but a "body," the body of Christ. Christ is present in the ecclesia not only as an object of faith and recognition, but as her Head. He is actually reigning and ruling. This secures the Church's continuity and identity through ages. In Brunner's conception Christ seems to be outside history, or above it. He did come once, in the past. He is coming again, in the future. Is He really present now, in the present, except through the memory of the past and the hope of the future, and indeed in the "meta-historic" acts of faith?

Creation, according to Brunner, has its own mode of existence. But it is no more than a "medium" of divine revelation. It must be, as it were, transparent for divine light and glory. And this strangely reminds us of Platonizing gnosis of Origen and his various followers. The whole story is reduced to the dialectics of eternal and temporal. Brunner's own term is "parabolic."

III.

The notion of "the end"—of an ultimate end—is a paradoxical notion. An "end" both belongs to the chain or series, and breaks it. It is both "an event" and "the end of all events." It belongs to the dimension of history, and yet it dismisses the whole dimension. The notion of "the beginning"—first and radical—is also a paradoxical notion. As St. Basil has said once, "the beginning of time is not yet time, but precisely the beginning of it" (Hexaem. I.6). It is both an "instant" and more than that.

Of the future we can speak but in images and parables. This was the language of the Scripture. This imagery cannot be adequately deciphered now, and should not be taken literally. But in no sense should it be simply and bluntly "demythologized." Brunner is formal at this point. The expected *Parousia* of Christ must be regarded as "an event." The character of this event is unimaginable. Better symbols or images can be hardly found than those used in the Bible. "Whatever the form of this event may be, the whole point lies in the fact that it will happen." [5] The Christian *kerygma* is decisive at this point: "the ultimate redemptive synthesis has the character of an event." In other words, the *Parousia* belongs

[5] Brunner, *Eternal Hope*, p. 138.

to the chain of historic "happenings," which it is expected to conclude and to close. "A Christian faith without expectation of the
Parousia is like a ladder which leads nowhere but ends in the
void." At one point, in any case, we can go beyond images: it is
Christ that is coming. The *Parousia* is a "return," as much as it is
an ultimate novelty. "The Last Events" are centered around the
person of Christ.

The end will come "suddenly." And yet it is, in a certain sense,
prepared inside of history. As Brunner says, "the history of man
discloses radically apocalyptic traits." At this point he indulges
in metaphysical speculations. "The swing of the pendulum becomes ever faster." This acceleration of the *tempo* of human life
may reach the point at which it can go no further. History may
simply explode suddenly. On the other hand, and on the deeper
level, disharmonies of human existence are steadily increasing:
there is "an ever-widening split in the human consciousness." Of
course, these suggestions have no more than a subsidiary or hypothetical value. Brunner tries to commend the paradoxical concept
of the end to the modern mind. But they are also characteristic
of his own vision of human reality. History is ever ready to explode,
it is vexed and overburdened with unresolved tensions. Some
years ago a Russian religious philosopher, Vladimir Th. Ern, suggested that human history was a kind of "catastrophical progress,"
a steady progression toward an end. Yet the end was to come from
above, in a *Parousia*. Accordingly, it was to be more than just a
"catastrophe," or an immanent or internal "judgment"—a disclosure of inherent contradictions or tensions. It was to be an
absolute judgment, the Judgment of God.

Now, what is Judgment? It is no less "an event" than the
Parousia. It is an ultimate encounter between the sinful humanity
and the Holy God. First of all, it will be an ultimate disclosure or
manifestation of the true state of every man and of the whole mankind. Nothing will be left hidden. Thus, Judgment will terminate
that state of confusion and ambiguity, of inconclusiveness, as
Brunner puts it, which has been characteristic of the whole historic stage of human destiny. This implies an ultimate and final
"discrimination"—in the light of Christ. It will be an ultimate and
final challenge. The will of God must be finally done. The will
of God must be ultimately enforced. Otherwise, in the phrase of
Brunner, "all talk of responsibility is idle chatter." Indeed, man

is granted freedom, but it is not a freedom of indifference. Man's freedom is essentially a responsive freedom—a freedom to accept God's will. "Pure freedom" can be professed only by atheists. "To man is entrusted, of man is expected, merely the echo, the subsequent completion, of a decision which God has already made about him and for him." [6] There is but one fair option for man—to obey; there is no real dilemma. Man's purpose and goal are fixed by God.

All this is perfectly true. Yet, at this very point, the vexing question arises. Will actually all men accept, at the Last Judgment, God's will? Is there any room for radical and irreversible resistance? Can man's revolt continue beyond Judgment? Can any creaturely being, endowed with freedom, persist in estrangement from God, which has been persistently practised before, that is— to pursue its own will? Can such a being still "exist"—in the state of revolt and opposition, against the saving will of God, outside God's saving purpose? Is it possible for man to persevere in rebellion, in spite of the call and challenge of God? Is the Scriptural picture of separation—between the sheep and the goats—the last word about man's ultimate destiny? What is the ultimate status of creaturely "freedom"? What does it mean that finally the will of God must and will prevail? These are queer and searching questions. But they cannot be avoided. They are not dictated only by speculative curiosity. They are "existential" questions. Indeed, the Last Judgment is an awful mystery, which cannot, and should not, be rationalized, which passes all knowledge and understanding. Yet, it is a mystery of our own existence, which we cannot escape, even if we fail to comprehend or understand it intellectually.

Brunner emphatically dismisses the "terrible theologoumenon" of double predestination, as incompatible with the mind of the Bible. There is no eternal discrimination in God's creative design. God calls all men to salvation, and for that purpose He calls them into existence. Salvation is the only purpose of God. But the crucial paradox is not yet resolved. The crucial problem is, whether this only purpose of God will be actually accomplished, in all its fullness and comprehensiveness, as it is admitted and postulated in the theory of universal salvation, for which one may allege Scriptural evidence. Brunner rejects the doctrine of the *Apokatastasis*, as

[6] *Ibid.*, p. 178.

a "dangerous heresy." It is wrong as a doctrine. It implies a wrong security for men—all ways lead ultimately to the same end, there is no real tension, no real danger. And yet, Brunner admits that the doctrine of the forgiving grace, and of the justification by faith, leads logically to the concept of an universal redemption. Can the will of the omnipotent God be really resisted or, as it were, over-ruled by the obstinacy of feeble creatures? The paradox can be solved only dialectically—in faith. One cannot know God theoretically. One has to trust His love.

It is characteristic that Brunner discusses the whole problem exclusively in the perspective of the divine will. For that reason he misses the very point of the paradox. He simply ignores the human aspect of the problem. Indeed, "eternal damnation" is not inflicted by "the angry God." God is not the author of Hell. "Damnation" is a self-inflicted penalty, the consequence and the implication of the rebellious opposition to God and to His will. Brunner admits that there is a real possibility of damnation and perdition. It is dangerous and erroneous to ignore that real possibility. But one should hope that it will never be realized. Now, hope itself must be realistic and sober. We are facing the alternative: either, at the Last Judgment, unbelievers and unrepentant sinners are finally moved by the divine challenge, and are "freely" converted—this was the hypothesis of St. Gregory of Nyssa; or their obstinacy is simply overruled by the divine Omnipotence and they are saved by the constraint of the divine mercy and will—without their own free and conscious assent. The second solution implies contradiction, unless we understand "salvation" in a forensic and formalistic manner. Indeed, criminals may be exonerated in the court of justice, even if they did not repent and persevere in their perversion. They only escape punishment. But we cannot interpret the Last Judgment in this manner. In any case, "salvation" involves conversion, involves an act of faith. It cannot be imposed on anyone. Is the first solution more convincing? Of course, the possibility of a late "conversion"—in "the eleventh hour," or even after—cannot be theoretically ruled out, and the impact of the divine love is infinite. But this chance or possibility of conversion, before the Judgment-Seat of Christ, sitting in glory, cannot be discussed *in abstracto*, as a general case. After all, the question of salvation, as also the decision of faith, is a personal problem, which can be put and faced only in the context of concrete and individual existence. Persons are saved, or perish. And each personal case must be studied individually. The main weakness of Brunner's scheme is in that he always speaks in general terms. He always speaks of the human condition and never of living persons.

The problem of man is for Brunner essentially the problem of sinful condition. He is afraid of all "ontic" categories. Indeed, man is sinner, but he is, first of all, man. It is true, again, that the true stature of genuine manhood has been exhibited only in Christ, who was more than man, and not a man. But in Christ we are given not only forgiveness, but also the power to be, or to become, children of God, that is—to be what we are designed to be. Of course, Brunner admits that believers can be in communion with God even now, in this present life. But then comes death. Does faith, or—actually—one's being *en Christo*, make any difference at this point? Is the communion with Christ, once established by faith (and, indeed, in sacraments), broken by death? Is it true that human life is "a being unto death." Physical death is the limit of physical life. But Brunner speaks of the death of human persons, of the "I." He claims that it is a mystery, an impenetrable mystery, of which rational man cannot know anything at all. But, in fact, the concept of this "personal death" is no more than a metaphysical assumption, derived from certain philosophical presuppositions, and in no way a *datum* of any actual or possible experience, including the experience of faith. "Death" of a person is only in the estrangement from God, but even in this case it does not mean annihilation. In a sense, death means a disintegration of human personality, because man is not designed to be immaterial. The bodily death reduces the integrity of the human person. Man dies, and yet survives—in the expectation of the general end. The ancient doctrine of the Communion of Saints points to the victory of Christ: In Him, through faith (and sacraments), even the dead are alive, and share—in anticipation, but really—the everlasting life. *Communio Sanctorum* is an important eschatological topic. Brunner simply ignores it altogether—surely not by accident but quite consistently. He speaks of the condition of death, not of personal cases. The concept of an immortal soul may be a Platonic accretion, but the notion of an "indestructible person" is an integral part of the Gospel. Indeed, only in this case there is room for a general or universal Judgment, at which all historic persons, of all ages and of all nations, are to appear—not as a confused mass of frail and unprofitable sinners, but as a congregation of responsive and responsible persons, each in his distinctive character, congenital and acquired. Death is a catastrophe. But persons survive, and those *in Christ* are still alive—even in the state of death. The faithful not only hope for life to come, but are already alive, although all are waiting for Resurrection. Brunner, of course, is fully aware of this. In his own phrase, those who believe "will not die into nothingness but into Christ." Does it mean that those who do not believe "die into nothingness"? And what is "nothingness"—"the outer darkness" (what is probably the case) or actual "nonbeing"?

It is also true that full integrity of personal existence, distorted and reduced by death, will be restored in the general Resurrection. Brunner emphasizes the personal character of the Resurrection. "The New Testament faith knows of no other sort of eternal life except that of the individual persons." [7] The flesh will not rise. But some kind of corporeality is implied in the Resurrection. All will rise, because Christ is risen. Now, Resurrection is at once a Resurrection unto life—in Christ, and a Resurrection—to Judgment. Brunner discusses the general Resurrection in the context of faith, forgiveness, and life. But what is the status of those who did not believe, who did not ask for forgiveness, and never knew of the redemptive love of Christ, or probably have obstinately denounced and rejected it as a myth, as a fraud, as a deceit, or as an offense for the autonomous personality?

And this brings us back again to the paradox of the Judgment. Strangely enough, at this point Brunner speaks more as a philosopher than as a theologian, precisely because he tries to avoid metaphysical inquiry, and all problems which have been suppressed reappear in disguise. Brunner puts the question in this way: how can we reconcile divine Omnipotence and human freedom, or—on a deeper level—divine holiness (or justice) and divine mercy and love. It is a strictly metaphysical problem, even if it is discussed on the scriptural basis. The actual theological problem is, on the other hand: what is the existential status of unbelievers—in the sight of God, and in the perspective of the human destiny? The actual problem is existential—the status and destiny of individual persons. For Brunner the problem is obscured by his initial choice—his sweeping bracketing together of all men as sinners,

[7] *Ibid.*, p. 148.

without any real ontic or existential discrimination between the righteous and the unrighteous (Marcel Jouhandeau, *Algèbre des valeurs morales*). Indeed, ultimately, it is but an illusion, an aberration, a violence, and a mistake. But the sting of sin is precisely in the denial of the divinely instituted reality, in the attempt to establish another order or regime, which is, in contrast with the true divine order, a radical disorder, but to which one may give, in selfish exaltation, ultimate preference. Now, sin has been destroyed and abrogated—it can not be said that "sin has been redeemed, only persons may be redeemed. But it is not enough to acknowledge, by faith, the deed of the divine redemption—one has to be born anew. The whole personality must be cleansed and healed. Forgiveness must be accepted and assessed in freedom. It cannot be imputed—apart from an act of faith and gratitude, an act of love. Paradoxically, nobody can be saved by love divine alone, except it is responded by grateful love of human persons. Indeed, there is always an abstract possibility of "repentance" and "conversion" in the course of this earthly or historic life. Can we admit that this possibility continues after death? Brunner will hardly accept the idea of a "Purgatory." But even in the concept of Purgatory no chance of radical conversion is implied. Purgatory includes but believers, those of good intentions, pledged to Christ, but deficient in growth and achievement. Human personality is made and shaped in this life—at least, it is oriented in this life. The difficulty of universal salvation is not on the divine side—indeed, God wants every man "to be saved," not so much, probably, in order that His will should be accomplished and His Holiness secured, as in order that man's existence may be complete and blessed. Yet, insuperable difficulties may be erected on the creaturely side. After all, is "ultimate resistance" a greater paradox, and a greater offense, than any resistance or revolt, which actually did pervert the whole order of Creation, did handicap the deed of redemption? Only when we commit ourselves to a Docetic view of history and deny the possibility of ultimate decisions in history, in this life, under the pretext that it is temporal, can we evade the paradox of ultimate resistance.

St. Gregory of Nyssa anticipated a kind of universal conversion of souls in the afterlife, when the Truth of God will be revealed and manifested with compelling evidence. Just at that point the limitation of the Hellenic mind is obvious. Evidence to it seemed to be the decisive motive for the will, as if "sin" were merely ignorance. The Hellenic mind had to pass through a long and hard experience of asceticism, of ascetic self-examination and self-control, in order to overcome this intellectualistic naïveté and illusion and discover a dark abyss in the fallen soul. Only in St. Maximus the Confessor, after some centuries of ascetic preparation, do we find a new and deepened interpretation of the *Apokatastasis*. Indeed, the order of creation will be fully restored in the last days. But the dead souls will still be insensitive to the very revelation of Light. The Light Divine will shine to all, but those who once have chosen darkness will be still unwilling and unable to enjoy the eternal bliss. They will still cling to the nocturnal darkness of selfishness. They will be unable precisely to enjoy. They will stay "outside"— because union with God, which is the essence of salvation, presupposes and requires the determination of will. Human will is irrational and its motives cannot be rationalized. Even "evidence" may fail to impress and move it.

Eschatology is a realm of antinomies. These antinomies are rooted and grounded in the basic mystery of Creation. How can anything else exist alongside of God, if God is the plenitude of Being? One has attempted to solve the paradox, or rather to escape it, by alleging the motives of Creation, sometimes to such an extent and in such a manner as to compromise the absoluteness and sovereignty of God. Yet, God creates in perfect freedom, *ex mera liberalitate*, that is, without any sufficient reasons. Creation is a free gift of unfathomable love. Moreover, man in Creation is granted this mysterious and enigmatic authority of free decision, in which the most enigmatic is not the possibility of failure or resistance, but the very possibility of assent. Is not the will of God of such a dimension that it should be simply obeyed—without any real, that is, free and responsible, assent? The mystery is in the reality of creaturely freedom. Why should it be wanted in the world created and ruled by God, by His infinite wisdom and love? In order to be real, human response must be more than a mere resonance. It must be a personal act, an inward commitment. In any case, the shape of human life—and now we may probably add, the shape and destiny of the cosmos—depends upon the synergism or conflict of the two wills, divine and creaturely. Many things are happening which God abhors—in the world which is His work and His subject. Strangely enough, God respects human freedom, as

St. Irenaeus once said, although, in fact, the most conspicuous manifestation of this freedom was revolt and disorder. Are we entitled to expect that finally human disobedience will be disregarded and "dis-respected" by God, and His Holy Will shall be enforced, regardless of any assent? Or it would make a dreadful "masquerade" of human history? What is the meaning of this dreadful story of sin, perversion, and rebellion, if finally everything will be smoothed down and reconciled by the exercise of divine Omnipotence?

Indeed, the existence of Hell, that is, of radical opposition, implies, as it were, some partial "unsuccess" of the creative design. Yet, it was more than just a design, a plan, a pattern. It was the calling to existence, or even "to being," of living persons. One speaks sometimes of the "divine risk"—*le risque divin*, says Jean Guitton. It is probably a better word than *kenosis*. Indeed, it is a mystery, which cannot be rationalized—it is the primordial mystery of creaturely existence.

Brunner takes the possibility of Hell quite seriously. There is no security of "universal salvation," although this is, abstractly speaking, still possible—for the omnipotent God of Love. But Brunner still hopes that there will be no Hell. The trouble is that there is Hell already. Its existence does not depend upon divine decision. God never sends anyone to Hell. Hell is made by creatures themselves. It is human creation, outside, as it were, of "the order of creation."

The Last Judgment remains mystery.

GEORGES FLOROVSKY

HARVARD DIVINITY SCHOOL
CAMBRIDGE, MASS.

12

Dale Moody

THE CHURCH IN THEOLOGY

THE CHURCH IN THEOLOGY

What is the New Testament ecclesia? A church *(Kirche)* or a community *(Gemeinde)*? Is it an institution or a brotherhood? This is the question which Emil Brunner has raised in the contemporary discussion on the nature of the Christian ecclesia. His radical distinctions and proposals, which have not yet received the attention they deserve, are among the most hopeful signs that renewed interest in Christian unity will not be identified with institutional conformity. According to the published writings of Professor Brunner, and to some degree from private statements, this provocative thesis has been influenced by two major movements: the philosophical personalism that reaches back to Kierkegaard and a pneumatic dynamism that was associated with Christian Socialism. It will be noted how Brunner tends to identify the *Kirche*, the institutional church, with the *Es-Welt* (the "it-world" or the impersonal sphere), while the *Gemeinde* is the community of personal relations, the "I-Thou" relation of personalism. At the very roots of much that is best in Brunner are the Blumhardts, father and son, whose rare combination of social concern and spiritual power was felt by Brunner through Leonhard Ragaz, Professor of Theology, and Hermann Kutter, the great preacher at the Neumünster, both in Zurich. From this perspective both the *koinonia* and the *diakonia* of the ecclesia come to life in a fresh way.

The Koinonia of the Ecclesia

It is hazardous to reduce Brunner's complex thinking on fellowship to a few simple factors, but he does hang much on two things: the objective event of the past to which the apostles bear witness and the subjective experience of the Holy Spirit, who, in the present, produces personal faith and eschatological hope. God not only "sent forth his Son" in the fullness of time, but he also "has sent the Spirit of his Son into our hearts" (Gal. 4:4-6). Out of this revelation of God has come the ecclesia which is God's personal presence in history through the present activity of the Spirit.[1] Although Brunner's thought moves beyond the objective-subjective antithesis into the dimension of the personal, the idea of *koinonia* (fellowship) may be presented around these two points.

The objective embraces the historical and apostolic aspects of the Christian fellowship. The most positive emphasis on the historical *koinonia* is related to the concept of fulfillment. As in all of Brunner's mature theological exposition, the historical revelation which finds its fullness in Jesus Christ is central. On the one hand revelation is related to Israel as the people of God in the Old Covenant and on the other to the church as "the Israel of God" (Gal. 6:16) in the New Covenant. Holding that the Old Testament is promise, not fulfillment, extreme Christological exposition is rejected in favor of historical revelation.[2] Both continuity and discontinuity with Judaism are found in the faith of the early disciples. At first associating themselves with the worship at the Jerusalem temple without much sense of inconsistency, the consciousness that they shared the fellowship of the new age of the New Testament was soon recognized in distinction from the Old Covenant.[3]

Associated with this positive teaching on fulfillment is the negative attitude toward institutionalism. Holding that the ecclesia is a fellowship, all ideas that reduce it to a mere outward means toward an end must be rejected. The whole external institution, with all its paraphernalia, is in opposition to the fellowship of persons who participate in Christ through the Holy Spirit. Repeatedly he drives home the point that the New Testament ecclesia has nothing to do with organization and institution, though more recently he has been willing to say the ecclesia has institutions and needs organization.[4] Jesus did not "found the ecclesia" in any institutional sense. Had the early disciples thought of the ecclesia as an institution alongside the institutionalism of Judaism, it would

[1] *Dogmatik III*, Ch. 1.

[2] *Offenbarung und Vernunft*, 82-95 (81-95). References in this note, as in the following notes in this chapter, are first to the original and second, in parentheses, to the English translation. Ed.

[3] *Das Missverständnis der Kirche*, 21-25 (19-22).

[4] *Ibid.*, 12 f. (11); *Dogmatik III*, Ch. 3.

have been impossible for them to be considered a Jewish sect (Acts 24:5, 14). It is not too difficult to see how much Brunner here leans on the distinction between I-it and I-Thou. The apostolic aspects of the Christian ecclesia raise the problems of succession and tradition. Brunner's analysis of apostolic succession considers the distinction between the word of Christ (*Christuswort*) and the will of Christ (*Christuswille*).[5] The word of Christ deals with proclamation. The teaching ecclesia asks the question: What is the source of its authoritative message? An answer requires the examination of both the original eyewitnesses and the crystallized form of witness in the written Word. The apostles, by the significant fact that they witnessed the unique historical event, occupy a position which is untransferable. The concept of uniqueness (*Einmaligkeit*), which stresses the unrepeatable nature of the event to which the apostles bear witness, is one of Brunner's basic ideas.[6] Since the primal eyewitnesses to a once-for-all event can never be replaced, the position of the apostolic authority is essentially untransferable.[7]

In a surprising shift of appreciation, Brunner pays tribute to Anglican arguments for the recognition of the will of Christ in the function of the church. According to this view, administrative authority, so neglected by Protestantism, is transferable and permanent.[8] It soon becomes obvious, however, that the Spirit is given a place in the *koinonia* that neither Scripture nor succession can assume. The ecclesia "has become no synagogue of mere scriptural exegesis" even if the Scriptures are the crystallized norm which regulates its teaching.[9] The sorry spectacle of ecclesiastical institutionalism makes necessary "the power of the Word and Spirit of Christ."[10]

Apostolic tradition belongs to the very nature of the Gospel grounded in historical revelation. *Ohne Tradition kein Evangelium*[11] is Brunner's brief summary of this point, but his three distinctions in

---

[5] *Das Missverständnis der Kirche,* 36 (31).
[6] *Der Mittler,* 7, 129, 274, 339 f. (25, 154, 308, 379 f.); "Das Einmalige und der Existenzcharakter," 451; *Der Mensch im Widerspruch,* 451 (435); *Offenbarung und Vernunft,* 399 (404); *Dogmatik I,* 325 (305).
[7] *Das Missverständnis der Kirche,* 30 f. (26 f.); Fraumünster, *Predigten,* 25 (32).
[8] *Das Missverständnis der Kirche,* 36 (31).
[9] *Ibid.,* 39 (33 f.).
[10] *Ibid.,* 32 f. (28 f.).
[11] *Ibid.,* 40 (35).

the meaning of tradition make it clear that this is a return, not to Rome, but to Reformers.[12] The primitive Christian concept of tradition is related in a most vital way to both the event of historical revelation and the formation of the canon. It is related to the event of historical revelation because the preaching of the Gospel to other generations, in order that they too may participate in salvation, means necessarily the transmission of the Gospel—*paradosis, traditio*. The canon is necessary to protect the original revelation against later accretions that could change the Christian Gospel into something utterly different. There is no fundamental antithesis between this primitive Christian idea of tradition and the Scriptures, for the canon of Scripture secures the apostolic tradition.

Secondly, the early Catholic concept of tradition adds to the canon of Scripture the office of bishop to guarantee the genuineness of the apostolic tradition. Despite the recognition of considerable cogency in Anglican arguments for the office of bishop alongside the canon, Brunner is unwilling to accept any concept of administrative authority based on continuity in office. Aside from the doubtful validity of Hegesippus's succession lists, a "yes" and a "no" must be given to this theory. The validity of the idea of development may be established both in the New Testament and in the early history of doctrine, but along with the possibility of development is the danger of distortion.

Thirdly, the neo-Catholic Roman idea of tradition demonstrates how real the danger of transformation and distortion can be. Adopting the point of view of Rudolf Sohm, who held that the Gospel is incompatible with any legal order, the claim is made that the deviation of Rome takes the step by the completed *Codex juris canonici* of 1918 in which all matters of faith and morals are subordinated to the authority of the Pope. This is the triumph of institution over tradition, for "tradition is no more the witness of history, but the Pope's power of decree over past history." [13]

The more subjective aspects of the Christian *koinonia* focus on spiritual and eschatological ideas. It is in the realm of the spiritual that the Blumhardt background should be recalled and a certain stereotyped idea of Brunner should be forgotten. In his monumental criticism of Schleiermacher, Brunner thunders against all efforts to

[12] *Ibid.*, 39-52 (35-46).
[13] *Ibid.*, 52 (46). Note also the striking phrase: *Die Demission des Wahrheitssinnes vor dem geschichtlichen Prozess*, (p. 47).

substitute religious experience for revelation, but this is aimed at the philosophy of identity which removed the need for the Word of God.[14] His *Entweder die Mystik oder das Wort* must not be interpreted to mean *Entweder der Geist oder das Wort*.[15]

The spiritual phenomena of particular importance for understanding the *ecclesia* are related to the metaphor of the body of Christ.[16] The unity of the *ecclesia* as the body of Christ, metaphorically and essentially organic, is the work of the Spirit. The members of the body are given functions, not "offices," and all are in the ministry. The modern distinction between active and inactive members arises only when an institution is substituted for a vital fellowship. Organization and legal administration, compensating for the lack of spiritual power, are a false representation of the body of Christ. The ministry is primarily one that requires spiritual power.

At times the metaphor of the body is related to other definitions of the church. The most systematic statement appears in the last volume of the *Dogmatik* where three classical definitions of the church are summarized and evaluated.[17] The idea of the church as the *coetus electorum* signifies the eternal election of God in Jesus Christ and overcomes all isolationism as men are bound to God and to one another. The idea of *corpus Christi* is the historical aspect through which the transcendent origin of God's electing love is made known to the community. The idea of *communio sanctorum* points to the immanent work of the Spirit in adding members to the body. All three of the definitions are necessary, for any one without the other would lead to either an abstract spiritual individualism (*numerus praedestinatorum*), or a sacramental hierarchy (*corpus Christi*), or to an emotional-pietistic individualism (*communio sanctorum*).

In the specific application of eschatology to the understanding of the *koinonia* of the *ecclesia* both the Resurrection and the return of the Lord are central.[18] The Resurrection of the Lord transforms the ideas of mysticism and magic. As long as the death and Resurrection of Christ, the basic elements in New Testament faith, remain the point of departure for understanding the future consummation, the return of Christ cannot be dismissed as ancillary. The consum-

[14] *Die Mystik und das Wort*, 6, 48 f., 52, 85, 94, 191.
[15] *Ibid.*, 5, 399. Cf. *Dogmatik III*, Ch. 1.
[16] *Das Missverständnis der Kirche*, 54-59 (49-52).
[17] *Dogmatik III*, Ch. 2.
[18] *Das Missverständnis der Kirche*, 62-67 (55-59).

mation which dawned with Jesus (Matt. 12:28; Luke 11:20) creates the expectation of the future consummation. Two contrasts help to hold these two phases of the consummation in balance. The first is the contrast between the hidden and the revealed. The rule of God, hidden in the flesh of Jesus (Luke 17:21), which only began to dawn in the Resurrection, awaits revelation at the coming of the Lord in glory. The second contrast is between the pneumatic and the Messianic factors in this expectation. As long as the final consummation is not yet fully revealed, the present rule of God is understood in terms of the gift of the Holy Spirit.[19] This pneumatic expectation, as a pilgrim life on earth, awaits the Messianic fulfillment in the future consummation. This is the eschatological perspective which emerges in *The Misunderstanding of the Church*.

A more detailed picture of this *Schwellenexistenz* (threshold existence) appears in *The Eternal as Future and Present*.[20] The tension between *jetzt-noch-nicht* (now not yet) and *doch-jetzt-schon* (yet now already), which was applied to the understanding of the *ecclesia* in *The Misunderstanding of the Church*, is here elaborated, as the very title of the book would indicate.

The resolution of the tension between consistent and realized eschatology is found along the lines of such New Testament scholars as Oscar Cullmann, W. G. Kummel, and Eduard Schweizer who advocate an intermediate position between the extremes of Albert Schweitzer and C. H. Dodd. This "inaugurated" eschatology, while agreeing with realized eschatology in recognizing the decisive nature of the once-for-all event in Christ, looks forward to a future consummation. Realized eschatology is right in grasping the center of gravity for primitive Christian faith in the grace of divine presence bestowed upon the ecclesia in the Holy Spirit, but it is wrong in failing to grasp the Messianic life of the believing community waiting for the revelation of the Lord in glory. Again the chief point is the proper balance between the pneumatic and Messianic factors in the ecclesia. Brunner discerns a sort of law in Christian history "to the effect that, the more lively becomes the hope of an imminent end, the more intensely the church lives in the power of the Spirit of God, so that the possession of the Spirit and expecta-

---

[19] "*Das Pneumatische ist das Eschatologische und das Eschatologische ist des Pneumatische*" (*Ibid.*, 65).

[20] *Das Ewige als Zukunft und Gegenwart*.

tion of a near end go together as in the primitive Christian community." [21]

This positive presentation of the ecclesia's eschatological existence would not be in proper proportion if some recognition were
not given to two movements for which Brunner has both antipathy
and affinity. The first is the demythologizing *(Entmythologisierung)*
movement which centers around the writings of Rudolf Bultmann.
According to this interpretation, the eschatological orientation toward the future is a mythological expression of the new character
of the present. Bultmann's controversial writing on the *New Testament and Mythology* groups the biblical ideas of space and time
together without adequate distinction, according to Brunner. [22] At
one place Brunner's distinction is sharp: "Every myth uses symbol-
ical elements, but not every religious symbol is mythological. Myth
is symbol in movement; symbol is myth without movement.
Symbolism in the representation of God makes him visible in
space; mythology makes him visible in time." [23] It is difficult to
determine how rigid this distinction is to be made, but it seems
fundamental in determining the point at which Brunner parts
company with Bultmann. Brunner gladly departs from the biblical
picture of a three-story universe, [24] but he thinks it disastrous to
include God's action in nature and history in this discarded picture. [25] Bultmann, according to Brunner, substitutes a symbolism of
the impersonal and timeless for the symbolism of personal life and
action in time. [26] The Christian understanding of time is not primarily chronological but has to do with what has happened once
for all *(Einmaligkeit)*. The ecclesia has its foundation in the unique
event and finds fulfillment in a glorious consummation. A timeless
eschatology fails to comprehend the *Schwellenexistenz* of the ecclesia. "The eternity to come has become a present reality, the
existence of the community of Christ is a Messianic or eschatological
existence; it is life in the divine presence at the heart of temporality,
the Kingdom of God in the midst of the world of sin and death." [27]

[21] *Ibid.*, 143 (130). English translation quoted.
[22] *Dogmatik II*, 311 f. (264 f.).
[23] *Offenbarung und Vernunft*, 395 (400).
[24] *The Word and the World*, 98; *Der Mensch im Widerspruch*, 439 (423);
Offenbarung und Vernunft, 273-277 (276-281); *Dogmatik II*, 312 (265); *Das
Ewige als Zukunft und Gegenwart*, 133-140 (120-127).
[25] *Dogmatik II*, 312 (265).
[26] *Das Ewige als Zukunft und Gegenwart*, 130 (117).
[27] *Ibid.*, 160 (145). English translation quoted.

The second movement, for which Brunner has far more antipathy than affinity, has developed from Schweitzer's consistent eschatology. It is known as de-eschatologization *(Enteschatologisierung).* Martin Werner, the most voluminous advocate of this development sees the delayed *parousia* as the direct cause of the rapid Hellenization of the early church.[28] In some ways Brunner's emphasis on the misunderstanding of the church resembles the thesis of Werner, but there are important differences. Brunner thinks the process of Hellenization was the cause rather than the result in this radical transformation.[29] Furthermore, for New Testament writers the decisive event of salvation has already taken place, and Paul clearly faced the possibility of a delayed parousia.[30] But even with these protective arguments, it is difficult to overlook the similarity between Werner's "illusion" and Brunner's "misunderstanding" of the church. Was the transition as radical as either supposes?

The Diakonia *of the Ecclesia*

Koinonia is expressed through *diakonia* (service). Two principles, which form a frame for the new life of fellowship, are of central importance. The first is that of the congregation. The place where the word is heard, prayer is made, and the sacraments celebrated becomes God's congregation and the most vital unit of the common life in Christ. The congregational concept, rooted in the classical meaning of the ecclesia, attaches great importance to the assembled people. The second principle is that of cooperation, which removes the barriers to the common life. Brunner points out how both the removal of the distinction between priests and laymen and the refusal to set the sacred and the profane in opposition are attended with tension in the New Testament, so much so that the *Agape,* associated with the feeding of the poor, became separated from the Lord's Supper.[31]

The sacraments of the ecclesia are distinctive in nature and definite in number. The nature of the sacraments presents a delicate balance requiring both negative and positive discussion, if misunderstanding is to be avoided. On the negative side the very term

---

[28] *Die Enstehung des christlichen Dogmas* (Bern: Verleg Paul Haupt, 1941, 1954).

[29] *Dogmatik II* (263).

[30] *Das Ewige als Zukunft und Gegenwart,* 141 f. (128 f.).

[31] *Das Missverständnis der Kirche,* 67-70 (60-63).

"sacrament" is suspect. The word, belonging as it does to the heathen world, was unfortunately taken over by the reformers. Although Brunner suggests no other collective term such as "ordinance," he strongly asserts that the use of this heathen word became the starting point from which the *Gemeinde* of Jesus was transformed into a *Sakramentskirche*. It should be noted, however, that this criticism of sacramentalism does not lead him into a concept of "mere symbolism." In his lectures at the University of Helsinki the sacraments are described as the visible word, much in the manner in which the reformers, following Augustine, spoke of the *verbum visible* as an accommodation to our sensuous nature; but even here, as early as 1936, the interpretation does not fully fit the phrase.[32] In 1951, in *The Misunderstanding of the Church*, the interpretation of the reformers is declared unsatisfactory in itself, even though there is a measure of truth in their argument. It is an effort to rationalize the irrational.[33] Sacramentalism and symbolism alike fail to grasp the New Testament reality.

On the positive side the sacraments are interpreted as a two-sided event.[34] On one side the sacraments are the act of the *Gemeinde*. In the sacraments one is joined to the concrete congregation by an act more unmistakable than listening to God's word in preaching. They are a *verbum communale* in which the individual is really incorporated into common life of the community. They are also a *verbum activum* in which communion with Christ is realized through the common action of the congregation. One may remain a spectator in hearing the proclaimed word and in seeing the sacraments as *verbum visible*, but participation in the sacraments requires *action* as well as hearing and seeing. Out of the role of a spectator into the role of a participant one comes in the performance of baptism and the Lord's Supper.[35]

On the other side the sacraments are the act of God. Even before the act of the *Gemeinde*, God acting in his prevenient grace, forgives sin and cleanses and regenerates in the act of baptism.[36] The Lord's Supper is more than a mere symbol; it is an integral part of the saving act itself. The bread and wine are signs *(Zeichen)* of

---

[32] *Das Wort Gottes und der moderne Mensche*, 99-104.
[33] *Das Missverständnis der Kirche*, 77 (67).
[34] *Wahrheit als Begegnung*, 136 (128); *Das Missverständnis der Kirche*, 77 f. (68).
[35] *Das Missverständnis der Kirche*, 76 (66).
[36] *Wahrheit als Begegnung*, 136 (128).

the presence of the Lord not only with the first disciples in the Upper Room but always wherever baptism and the Lord's Supper are received in faith.[37] "It is not an as if," Brunner concludes, "but it is the reality of saving history." [38] But it should be carefully noted that the sacraments are associated with saving history, not *identical* with it. They are, as the reformers understood Scripture, only a *necessitas relative*, not a *necessitas absoluta*.[39] One may receive the saving benefits of Christ with no sacraments at all!

The number of the sacraments are two: baptism and the Lord's Supper. Baptism is not easy to clarify. There is no question that the original mode of baptism was immersion,[40] but the meaning is clouded by the problem of infant baptism. At first Brunner's consideration reaches the point of caustic criticism. These criticisms spring from the application of two principles: personal correspondence and justification by faith.[41] Baptism, according to the principle of personal correspondence, is two-sided; but infant baptism, in both Catholic and Protestant practice, has become a one-sided event.

These caustic criticisms expressed in the Olaus Petri lectures (1937) are considerably softened in *The Misunderstanding of the Church* (1951). On the ground of the causative characteristics of baptism, which Brunner locates in the paralogical, a renewed effort is made to justify infant baptism. On the left Karl Barth follows the purely cognitive interpretation and calls for a return to baptism on a profession of faith,[42] and on the right hand is Heinrich Schlier, whose acceptance of the *opus operatum* led him to become a Roman Catholic.[43] Across the narrow ledge between symbolism and sacramentalism Brunner follows the light in his paralogical penumbra. This position, difficult as it is to maintain, attempts to find the way which can distinguish between pagan magic and genuine mystery.

Against the background of saving history, the Lord's Supper may be described as esoteric, edificatory, and eschatological. It is esoteric in that it is strictly confined to the initiated. At this point Oscar Cullmann's arguments fail to persuade Brunner that all serv-

[37] *Das Missverständnis der Kirche*, 78 (68).
[38] *Ibid.*, 78 (69). Cf. *Unser Glaube*, 126 (110).
[39] *Ibid.*, 82 (71 f.).
[40] *Unser Glaube*, 124 (108).
[41] *Wahrheit als Begegnung*, 136-140 (128-132).
[42] *Die kirchliche Lehre von der Taufe*, 3 Auflage (Zollikon-Zurich: Evangelischer Verlag, 1947).
[43] *Die Zeit der Kirche* (Freiburg: Herder, 1956), 47-56, 107-129.

ices, aside from baptism, centered around the sacramental meal. The evidence of the New Testament would suggest two types of services, one for the cultic celebration of the Lord's Supper (I Cor. 10, 11) and the other for prayer and the proclamation of the word to unbelievers (I Cor. 14). In this way Brunner holds to a type of esoteric "close communion." [44]

The edificatory factor pertains both to the present and to the past. The present participation in the Lord's body was more real at the Lord's Supper than at any other time, yet this is only *intensively*, not *exclusively*, the experience of communion with Christ. A modern sectarian prejudice that often gives the impression that the Lord is present everywhere save in the Lord's Supper could profit as much by this delicate distinction as those who make the Lord's Supper the sole channel of communion. This present sense of participation was strengthened by the recollection from the past of the crucified and risen Lord who ate and drank with the disciples. What had once happened was recalled in a manner in which the presence of the Lord was repeated.[45] In other words, this is his "real presence." [46] His sacrifice was once-for-all, but his presence is repeated in participation and recollection.

The eschatological meaning, which furnishes the future perspective, is of supreme importance, for in the Lord's Supper the believers, in festive joy, look beyond the horizon of death to the festal meal in the Kingdom of God.[47] Thus the Lord's Supper means the present communion of believers with the Lord and with one another as the saving events of the past are recalled in the eschatological hope of the future.

It is clear that Brunner's principles of personal correspondence and justification by faith involve him in no little difficulty with the practice of infant baptism.[48] His appeal to the idea of the covenant and New Testament references to household baptisms reflects the uneasy position which results. Colossians 2:11 and following contrast rather than compare baptism and circumcision, and no passage

---

[44] *Das Missverständnis der Kirche*, 71, 73 (63 f.) Cf. Brunner's cherished quotation from Luther's *Deutsche Messe und Ordnung des Gottesdienstes, Ibid.*, 130; *Dogmatik III*, Ch. 5.

[45] *Ibid.*, 72 f. (63, 65).

[46] *Ibid.*, 148 (126).

[47] *Ibid.*, 79 (69).

[48] *Wahrheit als Begegnung*, 136 (128); *Das Missverständnis der Kirche*, 74 f., 147 f. (65 f., 126 f.); *Dogmatik III*, Chs. 5, 6, 8.

238   ESSAYS OF INTERPRETATION AND CRITICISM

could make faith more explicit. In the case of the household baptisms the context makes clear that this is the baptism of believers. In every instance there are functions incapable for infants. The household of Stephanas "devoted themselves to the service of the saints" (I Cor. 1:16; 16:15). Lydia's household (Acts 16:15) was perhaps her servants, and the household of Crispus (Acts 18:8) "believe in the Lord." The jailer's household heard the "word of the Lord" and "rejoiced" (Acts 16:32, 34). Mark 10:15 may give some grounds for the dedication of infants, but Brunner's presuppositions seem logically to rule out the practice of infant baptism.

The orders of the church are associated with the administration of the sacraments. In the New Testament no word is given about who may perform baptism and administer the Lord's Supper,[49] but this becomes a major issue in what Brunner calls the shift *(Verschiebung)* in the life of the ecclesia.[50] This shift becomes the starting point *(Ansatzstelle)* in the ecclesiastical development which transforms the *Gemeinde* of the New Testament into the *Kirche* of Catholicism.[51] In the transformation the sacramental shift brings into focus the office of bishop and ordination so that that church order becomes "a substitute for the Spirit" *(Pneumaersatz)*.[52] Sacramentalism, especially as it found expression in the writings of Ignatius of Antioch, transforms the spiritual unity of the body of Christ into a sacramental unity that requires the exaltation of an authoritative leader. The bread and wine, intended to be signs of the Word and the Spirit, are now looked upon as "the medicine of immortality" *(pharmakon athanasias)*.[53] Brunner's blistering phrase asserts: "they now *receive* the Body of Christ, instead of *being* the Body of Christ." [54] Priestly functions, centered in the office of bishop, displaces the preaching of the Word in the power of the Spirit. Institutionalism is interlocked with sacramentalism, and the two together produce an ecclesiasticism with the claims of apostolic authority.

The union of sacrament and office gives rise to ordination, the

[49] *Das Missverständnis der Kirche,* 75 (66).
[50] *Ibid.,* 90 (79).
[51] *Ibid.,* 84 (74).
[52] *Ibid.,* 103 (90).
[53] A phrase from Ignatius (Eph. 20) that looms large in Brunner's polemic. Cf. *Wahrheit als Begegnung* 16 (15); *Das Missverständnis der Kirche,* 87 (77).
[54] *Das Missverständnis der Kirche,* 87 (72).

sacrament of office. It is not until administration becomes related to *cheirotonia* that spiritual gifts *(charismata)* are subordinated to institutional administration. In this process of transformation Brunner traces three links in the sacramental chain.[55] At first the laying on of hands represents the transmission of a special spiritual grace. Brunner points out that in the Acts the performance of this act mediates the Holy Spirit (8:17), restores Paul's sight (9:17), consecrates Barnabas and Saul for their mission (13:3), and imparts the Holy Spirit to the twelve men at Ephesus (19:6). The second link appears when the transmission of a special spiritual grace qualifies Timothy for a specific office (2 Tim. 1:6). Then comes the link which makes sacramental slavery possible: the transmission of the apostolic *charisma* to the bishop. The formula of Cyprian, which asserts that whoever has the office receives the spiritual grace requisite for its fulfillment, completes the process.

The tension between official position and charismatic power is obvious in the early history of the church.[56] Even the Old Testament reflects a similar conflict, but the two are allowed to exist together (Num. 11:16-30). Professor Brunner pushes the distinction to the point of contradiction so that the letters of Paul and the presbyterial order of Acts lead in different directions. The difference is great, but the New Testament holds them together. In the ministry of Christ the balance between the anointment of Jesus and the appointment of the twelve has some official implications. When Jesus is anointed with the Spirit (Mark 1:10 f.) the role of the servant is fulfilled (Luke 4:18), and this becomes for the disciples the pattern of future *diakonia* (Mark 10:44 f.).

The twelve, first sent on a mission to Israel (Matt. 10), are finally after the Resurrection sent as the eleven on a mission to all nations (Matt. 28:16-20), and this seems to be a functional ministry. Some official suggestions may be drawn from the words of appointment *(epoiesen)* in Mark 3:14 and following, but the eschatological role the twelve are expected to fulfill (Matt. 19:28) makes it more evident that the number twelve is related to the new Israel. This is confirmed by the election of Matthias (Acts 1:21 f.). The terms on which the replacement of Judas is made rules out any successors to the twelve among those who were not eyewitnesses,

---

[55] *Das Missverständnis der Kirche,* 91-95 (80-83).
[56] Hans von Campenhausen, *Kirchliches Amt und geistliche Vollmacht in den ersten drei Jahrhunderten* (Tübingen: J. C. B. Mohr, 1953).

but another type of ministry arises among the disciples. The appointment of the seven, who are to perform the *diakonia* of the tables that the apostles may be free for the *diakonia* of the word, is made by prayer and the laying on of hands (Acts 6:1-6). The laying on of hands, which also has Old Testament background (Num. 8:10, 12; 27:18, 23; Deut. 34:9), is not completely ruled out in the appointment *(cheirotonesantes)* of the elders at the conclusion of the first mission by Barnabas and Paul (Acts 14:23). It is certainly a fatal step to conclude with Cyprian that the office and the gift have a necessary connection. It is as possible to ordain Simon Magus as it is to baptize him, but this does not destroy the importance of either baptism or ordination. As long as *cheirotonia* presupposes *charismata* the two need not conflict. The danger arises when the conclusion is drawn that he who holds the office necessarily has the power.

After the point of departure in Ignatius a process of development, supported by roots in the New Testament as well as by reasons drawn from the life of the early church, completes what Brunner believes is a transformation.[57] The roots in the New Testament reach back to three widely divergent trends in the life of the ecclesia. At one extreme is the quasi-gnostic anti-authoritarian spirit reflected in the Johannine writings, a point of view that rebukes all official authority with the picture of mutual service in the foot-washing scene. Over against the Johannine writings is the quasi-Judaic authoritarianism of the Jerusalem "pillars." The Pauline view is in between. Hebrews stands closer to Paul, and the pastoral epistles represent the spirit of the Jerusalem community. With all of the variety in the New Testament, how did the authoritarianism of the Jerusalem community triumph? Three reasons have been given: the threat of heresy, the growth in numbers, and the delay of the *parousia*. All the arguments have some justification, but Brunner thinks they can all be traced to one root: the sacramental shift. This inward transformation is the real difference between the *Gemeinde* and the *Kirche*, and the result is the center of Christianity.

The unity of the church illustrates in many ways the radical nature of Brunner's distinction between *Kirche* and ecclesia. The transformation of the early centuries, established in the *Volkskirche* of Constantine and the *Zwanskirche* of Theodosius, resulted in replacement of the Word and the Spirit by the sacraments, the hin-

[57] *Das Missverständnis der Kirche*, 95-106 (84-93).

drance of fellowship by the institution, and the stifling of vital faith by dogma. This led to disunion in two major rifts. According to the metaphor of the seed and the tree the rise of the Roman Catholic Church, through the process of transformation, led to the schism of Photius in 858 and to the final cleavage between the Latin and Greek forms of Christianity in 1054. Greek Orthodoxy, with its undeviating loyalty to tradition, represents the first stage of a completely sacramental institution.[58] It should not be forgotten, however, that the preservation of tradition in both the Latin and Greek forms, was of great value despite this transforming process.[59] Perhaps the most significant factors in the process were certain retarding movements which slowed the growth from the small seed to the great tree. Illustrating this with the metaphor of the kernel in the shell, such schismatics as the Montanists, Novationists, and Donatists are looked upon as reminders of the early ecclesia. Even the spiritual Franciscans, with their strong sense of brotherhood, are sparks of fire from New Testament love.[60]

The second rift is the Protestant Reformation, and this breakthrough of the New Testament ecclesia resulted in three forms. The first is the state churches (*Landeskirchen*) of Europe, in which the attempt to purify papalism soon fell into the pattern of Constantine's *Volkskirche* and even the *Zwangskirche* of Theodosius. Here, as on so many other points, Luther came nearest to the New Testament, especially in his writing, *Deutsche Messe und Ordnung des Gottesdientes* (1526), in which the idea of a gathered church and a disciplined community is proposed as his ultimate purpose. Earlier, December 10, 1520, Luther started at an important point by burning the sacred canon law (*Corpus juris canonici*), but his famous "not yet" (*noch nicht*) in regard to setting up a New Testament congregation flickered out when he allowed the territorial princes to organize the church.[61] Brunner also nettles the Lutheran theologians for their strange silence on this writing by Luther.[62] Calvin was more concerned with a sacred church polity, which he worked out on the basis of his powerful exegesis of Scripture, but the result was a unique thing in history: a confessing church and a compulsory

---

[58] *Ibid.*, 107-110 (94-96).
[59] *Ibid.*, 115-117 (101 f.); *Dogmatik III*, Ch. 7.
[60] *Dogmatik III*, Ch. 5.
[61] *Das Missverständnis der Kirche*, 110 f. (97).
[62] *Dogmatik III*, Ch. 5. Cf. *Das Missverständnis der Kirche*, 152 (130).

church united in one.[63] All the compromises between the New Testament ecclesia and the inherited ecclesiasticism can be defended on the basis of the Augustinian distinction between the visible and the invisible church, but the result is not the New Testament ecclesia united in the Word and in the Spirit.

The second form which arose out of the Reformation is the free churches. Brunner's point of chief concern is his mother church in Zurich where in 1523 Zwingli, without the least scruple, took over the heritage from Constantine and Theodosius.[64] Only those who know Brunner's deep love for the people of Zurich and the esteem in which he is held as a preacher and as a man will fully understand the almost pathetic overtones with which he pleads for the church to throw aside the handicaps of a state church and give herself to the type of ministry found in the New Testament ecclesia.[65]

It is in this connection that his appreciation for the free churches, especially for the Anabaptists and American Christianity, becomes surprisingly strong, if not startling. The Anabaptists in Zurich and other places in Europe wanted not *reformatio* of the *Volkskirche* but *restitutio* of the New Testament ecclesia. The name *Wiedertäufer* (rebaptizer) was applied to them in order to make them subject to the ancient penalties against the Donatists, and the death penalty was reaffirmed by the Imperial Edicts of Charles V in 1528, 1529 at Speyer. Yet in these despised *Schwarmgeister* and *Rottengeister*, against whom not only Zwingli but also Luther and Calvin waged war, Brunner finds many of his ideas of the *ecclesia*.[66] Yet they too fell into Calvin's error by thinking a sacred church polity could be found in the New Testament.[67] Brunner sees the vindication of the free church tradition in the contrast between the situation in Europe, where there is a virtual crisis in church life, and that in America where the churches enjoy popularity.[68] With much discernment the errors of the *Papstkirche* and the *Volkskirche* have been exposed, but Brunner still belongs to Luther's *Noch-nichtkirche*.

The third form is that of the brotherhoods which weave Bible

---

[63] *Das Missverständnis der Kirche*, III, 118 (97 f., 103); *Dogmatik III*, Chs. 5, 6.

[64] *Dogmatik III*, Ch. 5.

[65] *Ibid.*, Ch. 6.

[66] *Ibid.*, Ch. 5.

[67] *Das Missverständnis der Kirche*, 119 (104).

[68] *Dogmatik III*, Ch. 8.

study, prayer, and meditation into daily life. The economy organized around some form of farming or handcraft attempts to imitate the common life of the early Christians, although the lack of eschatological perspective usually leads to decline. These brotherhoods are usually superior to the life of the cloister, since the latter does not overcome the boundary between the sexes.

The long history of conformity and compulsion has resulted in discord rather than unity, and this has left a deep longing for community. In this situation the dangers of collectivism, both political and religious, may be grasped as substitutes for true fellowship. The political aspect appears most obviously in modern Communism which offers collective tyranny to individualistic chaos, especially among the people who have suffered under a capitalism unconcerned for the poor. Sparked by the hope for a classless society which would guarantee the good life, Communism had the character of a Messianic faith, but this enthusiasm soon disappeared and a method of force took its place. A political totalitarianism now stands over against the religious totalitarianism of the Roman Catholic Church. This situation Brunner calls the problem of *Paragemeinde*.[69]

Contemporary man, fearing the anarchy into which the rationalistic and individualistic philosophy of the enlightenment has led him, is anxious to seize totalitarian collectivism which appears to him the opposite of anarchy whether it be in the political form of atheistic Communism or the religious form of the sacramental papal church.[70] Brunner does not propose an organic union of Protestantism to meet this challenge, but rather the recovery of the ecclesia which transforms collectivism into community and individuals into persons existing in love for God and men. Many years of ecumenical activity and interest have failed to persuade him that a superorganization is the remedy for disunion and the answer to man's longing for community.

The ecumenical movement, which grew out of the insight that the church is one, has reached the point where again institution may threaten fellowship. After the "movement" became an "institution" in 1948 serious misgivings have developed in Brunner's mind. Although there is much value in ecumenical conversation, there is now real danger that institutional unity will be confused with the unity of the body of Christ. This type of unity, which the

[69] *Dogmatik III*, Ch. 9, B.
[70] *Das Missverständnis der Kirche*, 131 (114).

Roman Catholic Church already offers, has within the idea of a world organization the seeds for a new "misunderstanding" in a superchurch. The multiplicity of churches, often enriching and corrective, is far better than a false ecclesiasticism and clericalism.[71]

Over against political and religious collectivism new forms of fellowship, both civil and Christian, have arisen to meet the spiritual needs of modern men. Lodges and clubs are not without significance, but a whole series of Christian "movements" offers signs of hope. The most important listed by Brunner are: the *Innere Mission* (home mission) of Johann Hinrich Wichern in Germany, the Danish Fold High School of N. F. S. Grundtvig, the Y.M.C.A. and Y.W.C.A., evangelism of the last century, the Oxford Group Movement (M.R.A.), the Evangelical Academy in Germany and Switzerland, and the *Mukyokai* movement in Japan.[72] The movements are able to reach people who are beyond the appeal of the churches. Much good has been done by all these groups, but it is difficult to see that they are free from the handicaps of the churches. The fellowship, if it is to work in an organized manner, is unable to avoid some type of institutional form. Is it not better to vitalize forms through spiritual power than to end in unorganized chaos?

DALE MOODY

SOUTHERN BAPTIST THEOLOGICAL SEMINARY
LOUISVILLE, KY.

[71] *Dogmatik III*, Ch. 7.
[72] *Ibid.*, III, Ch. 9, A.

13

N. H. Søe

THE PERSONAL ETHICS OF EMIL BRUNNER

THE PERSONAL ETHICS OF
EMIL BRUNNER *

It seems to me no exaggeration to state that the famous ethics of Emil Brunner, *Das Gebot und die Ordnungen* (1932), more than any other book marks the beginning of modern works on theological ethics. There are to my opinion three main reasons for this fact:

(1) The chief reason is that the author came from that insight which had enabled him in 1927 in his *Religions-philosophie protestantischer Theologie* to delineate a new approach to the problems of philosophy of religion. No longer were we given a philosophical introduction into religion and finally into Christianity. The way was the directly opposite one. The starting point was the fact that we have met and had to submit to the wonder of revelation, which, being a wonder, has no foundation in any philosophical reasoning. *Offenbarung begründet sich selbst, oder es ist keine Offenbarung* (p. 6). And so the truth of revelation is the light that shines out upon all achievements of human thinking and religious experiences, not, however, to disclose that they are entirely without any value or truth, but that all of them are only enclosing strange fragments of truth, particles, as it were, from a broken mosaic, particles which no philosopher nor religious genius could fit together so as to produce the true picture. From this it is clear that Brunner would only be able to write a Christian Ethics which was entirely orientated

---

* The English-speaking reader faces a fair amount of German words and phrases in this essay. Most of them are titles of books, and if these have been translated they appear in German and in English in the Bibliography. We considered it unwise to translate titles that have not appeared in English. A few sentences have been freely translated, the editor, not the author of this essay, being responsible.

from and illuminated by the light of revelation, and yet so that philosophical ethics (the phrase taken in its broadest sense) was not disposed of as of no importance but taken seriously as containing odd and displaced fragments of the Christian teaching. So it is evident that to Brunner, Christian ethics is possible only as part of Christian dogmatics. He emphatically proclaims *ein unauflösliches Ineinander von "Ethik" und "Dogmatik"* (*Gebot u. Ordn.*, p. 71). And he very earnestly strives to keep true to that program.

(2) The second main point is that the author of *Das Gebot und die Ordnungen* came from a very definite dogmatic position. He had previously written such works as *Die Mystik und das Wort* (1924, second revised edition, 1928), and *Der Mittler* (1927). This means that he had been one of the leading figures of that thoroughgoing new orientation in the understanding of Christian doctrine which at that time often was labeled as "dialectical theology." This involved a definite break with the anthropocentricity of the previous generations. The gulf between God and fallen man was taken seriously. The whole of salvation was found in the miraculous gift of divine grace in the person and act of the Mediator. And it was understood that grace was not a kind of supernatural force which in certain experiences of conversion or in a gradual process of sanctification came to be the possession of a sincere Christian, but that grace always remains divine in the strict sense of that term, so that everything depends on whether God ever and again will turn his face in favor to us and never let us alone with our more or less "reborn" capacities of leading a new life. Influence from Søren Kierkegaard is here and elsewhere noticeable and readily admitted by the author. This means that it has become impossible in the footsteps of Schleiermacher or the *Erlangerschule* to develop a Christian ethics as a description of what it means to be reborn, this considered as an empirical fact. Everything must be understood from the divine revelation, that Word of God which is never in our safe possession, but which comes to us whenever God wills and takes hold of us to use us as instruments of that divine love which is God's gift in Christ.

(3) But Brunner's great achievement in the field of Christian ethics results from the fact that he had reached a new approach to the problem of what it means to be a human being. He is an ex-

ponent of what may be called a new anthropology which, however, as he maintains, is only a rediscovery of that understanding of man possessed by the reformers and the Biblical authors, but which had been lost, or at any rate seriously obscured, by the influence of classical philosophy and modern idealism. The author of *Das Gebot und die Ordnungen* feels himself deeply indebted to philosophical thinkers like Ebner, Buber and Grisebach, and to a theological scholar like Gogarten who has rediscovered the truth that the "I" is only *vom Du her* (p. 279). Brunner therefore protests against the concept of an autonomous I, a self-sufficient individual, the ideal of a spiritual Robinson Crusoe. Such a concept of man is a gross misunderstanding. Our being is never an isolated existence, but always, whether we acknowledge it or not, an existing together with the Other, the Thou. *Unser Sein ist . . . ein Mit-sein.* Only through a Thou can man be a human I. From this anthropology we understand also that Brunner is a reformer of Christian ethics because he, like Gogarten (see for example, Fre. Gogarten: *Politische Ethik,* 1932), and others, explicitly turns against that tradition which divided the "material" of Christian ethics into an individual ethics and a social ethics. Only in total misunderstanding of what it means to be a man can there be a place for an individual ethics, an ethical existence of a human being in its (impossible) isolation. We may, however, speak of a personal ethics as different from a social ethics, when we keep in mind that a person always means man in his relation to "the Other," *Sein als Mit-sein.* The borderline between the two parts of ethics can therefore never be drawn sharply. The distinction is more a matter of convenience than of principle. We may, however, distinguish between spheres of human existence where man is more directly related to his neighbor, and others where he is definitely "in office" *(im Amt),* enclosed in social orders *(Ordnungen).* Even so, we must also keep in mind that in our most "private" relations, say to our friends, we are always in a certain status as married or unmarried, Swiss or German, having a definite vocation, and so on. In this connection the decisive point can be stated thus (p. 288): *Das wahrhaft personale Selbst und die Gemeinschaft entstehen und vergehen im selben Akt.* [The truly personal self and the community arise and cease to exist in the same act.]

If this threefold insight is rightly taken as characterizing Brunner's approach to our subject, one important problem immediately turns up: That which here is taken as the two first points was the result of new theological insight. But the new anthropology (point three) asks: Was not that the gift of philosophers who were able to grasp a truth which had been hidden in the philosophical tradition from Socrates and Plato to Kant and Fichte and their modern followers? And if so, how is this insight related to the new theological understanding?

The answer does not seem easy, not even if we take into consideration the fuller statements given in *Der Mensch im Widerspruch* (1937). It is evident that according to Brunner our *humanum* is so created that our being is inevitably a togetherness with "the Other" and that this not only means a relation to but even a responsibility toward our neighbor. Love as the fulfillment of the Law is a statement not only of some moral law but of the very law of life as such. In Brunner's view, there seems to be no difficulty in building a bridge over the gulf between a simple statement of what man is (an indicative) to a statement of what is man's duty (an imperative), a gulf which, according to David Hume and several modern thinkers, can carry no bridge whatsoever. At any rate in *Das Gebot und die Ordnungen* we get the impression that the simple fact of man being unavoidably related to his Thou is synonymous with the "fact" that he is responsible toward him (see, for example, pp. 279 ff.).

But how does man attain knowledge of this right anthropology? We rather get the impression that we might rationally discover the structure of humanity as a *Mit-sein*, a *Sein-in-Verantwortung*, whereas it is only through revelation in Christ that we come to know that this responsibility means that we are created to love our neighbor, and only here we discover what this really means (see especially p. 280). And yet it is of course important that Brunner explicitly states in this book that the relationship of the individual to community *(Gemeinschaft)* is to us no philosophical but a theological problem (p. 278). And in *Der Mensch im Widerspruch* (see pp. 333 ff.) it is plainly and explicitly stated that only through divine revelation in Christ the true understanding of *humanitas* is "revealed and founded" (p. 338). Of course Brunner knows that his opponents will point to the fact that non-Christian philosophers seem to have acquired the same anthropology. This question is already touched in a discussion with Grisebach in *Zwischen den*

Zeiten, 1928, pp. 219-232, and 1929, pp. 90-106, and more carefully dealt with in *Der Mensch im Widerspruch.* Here he very definitely maintains that every modern "I-Thou philosophy," as opposed to the idealistic tradition, makes use of Christian categories although perhaps without clearly knowing this. It is not even enough, as might have been gathered from *Natur und Gnade* (1934), to distinguish between the "formal" and the "material" aspects of the image of God, and leave it to philosophy to discover the pure "formality" that humanity is characterized by *Wortmächtigkeit* and *Verantwortlichkeit,* and then maintain that theology and theology alone can discover the right "materiality," the right content to fill out this "form." No, there is no common concept of responsibility that might be subdivided into an idealistic and a Christian one. "But the concept of responsibility is either a Christian or a non-Christian, a legalistic-autonomous one or a concept born out of Christian faith" (p. 556).

It may be questioned whether this is tenable. But in this way, at any rate, the consequence of reasoning is kept in Brunner's thinking. Only through Christ can we know what true responsibility, real communion, and therefore true love means. Brunner states this last consequence very definitely. We are told that there exists no real love or true fellowship outside the "body" of Christ. "Natural" man has toward his neighbor either a relationship of legalistic correctness (the idealist who knows what is his duty to his fellow man and fulfills it, for example, in a Kantian spirit), or he practices a partial, a biased love, like the mother's love for her own child (p. 290). It is explicitly stated that if the self-centeredness of natural man is broken and he is thrown open for the Thou, this is the mystery of faith as seen under the ethical aspect (p. 304). Even the seemingly so unselfish love of a mother for her child is only an analogy to or an indication in the direction of this unconditional love.

We pause one moment to examine this result. Is this description of non-Christian love a just one? Or has Brunner to a certain extent succumbed to the temptation to depict the non- or pre-Christian attitude in such a way that the glory of Christian love may shine in its full splendor on this rather gloomy background? When Anders Nygren in his *Eros and Agape,* I (1930) had made much the same statement of a Christian agape, which in a qualitative way was distinctive from non-Christian *eros* or *philia,* he was rather severely criticized by Friedrich Karl Schumann in his *Um Kirche und Lehre* (1936, pp. 180 ff.). Schumann points out that it is a simple fact that "natural" man in certain cases quite spontaneously, without any selfishness or any biased, partial love, performs acts of "unerotic agape," to use Nygren's terminology. It is well known how Søren Kierkegaard deals with this same problem in his *Deeds of Love*. Often he argues on the line of Brunner or Nygren. But his main thesis is that Christian love is different in kind from all other love, because God comes in between as the *Zwischenbestimmung* (determinating intermediary) and calls us to love in a way that is so opposite to ordinary friendly behavior that the Christian runs the risk of being actually hated because of his curious love which, nevertheless, is the only true and pure love. Schumann, on the contrary, reaches the conclusion that we can by no means point to any visible difference between Christian and "natural" love. The only difference is that God in his wonderful and hidden way may graciously use his children's acts of more or less miserable love as instruments of and channels for his divine love. To me it would appear that a certain combination of that which Schumann stresses and certain elements from Kierkegaard would come as near to the truth as we are able to.

But—would not Emil Brunner agree to this—at any rate the Brunner of *Das Gebot und die Ordnungen*? He has laid himself open to the critique of Schumann. But is not his ultimate aim to emphasize that Christian love is never a human possibility, not even of a very "Christian" and reborn man? Christian love is possible only when Christ Himself is present and makes that possible which, without His presence, would remain impossible. Indeed Brunner very strongly claims that divine love alone is the condition *sine qua non* of Christian love. We should not ask, he stresses, *who* the man is who performs deeds of true love, but *where* he is. And so the only possible answer is that he is "in Christ." "God alone shines in His own light, He alone has *aseitas*. We are planets that shine only in borrowed light, in His light" (p. 148).[1]

But now as to Kierkegaard's special point: Is Christian love, according to Brunner, in a visible way different in kind from

[1] May I add that this, as far as I can see, holds true also of Nygren, at any rate from his *Eros and Agape* onward, although he also is rightly criticized by Schumann.

"natural" love even when this, as far as we can judge, is "unerotical agape"? What is the content of the Christian commandment of agape? What has, to this point, been outlined of Brunner's position seems to indicate that what we receive in Christ is not so much a new commandment as it is a true understanding of that "responsibility" into which man was created and which is his essence of being. But it soon becomes clear that this does not mean that a Christian has only to conform to the orders of creation as, in the light of revelation, he now understands them. We are here confronted with the famous dialectics of listening to and obeying the commandment of the Creator and obeying that of the Redeemer. Not that we here are facing a clearly dualistic situation. It is the same triune God who is Creator and Redeemer, and it is the same law of love that is our guide in both cases. Nevertheless, we can see and ascertain a dialectic movement between a conservative and a critical, yes, even revolutionary attitude toward what is given *(die Gegebenheiten)* of this world and also what our "neighbor," as he meets us, really is (see especially pp. 99 ff.). A fuller evaluation of what this means must, however, be given in a study of Brunner's social ethics. Here we may confine ourselves to stating that Brunner most definitely emphasizes that true love of our neighbor never can forget what has in Christ been disclosed to be his destination, the goal of his existence. It is almost as if we were hearing the voice of Kierkegaard when Brunner says that true love can only mean the will to lead the other into the love of Christ. And yet a certain duality remains. On the one hand, we have learned through God's revelation in Christ what it is to be human beings, and, on the other hand, we have been called into the reality of a new creation. And this dialectics of duality and unity permeates Brunner's concept of love.

And now if we proceed to the last treatment of these problems familiar to me, that of *Dogmatik II* (1950), how is the solution of these problems to be found? Because the treatment is very short it is extremely difficult to come to a clear answer. It seems, however, that now the dialectics of the commandment of the Creator and that of the Redeemer is replaced by a certain duplicity which is a kind of graduated series. First we have the obedience to the law of the Creator incarnated so to speak in the orders of Creation. Simply *behavior* in these relations is demanded of everybody, and what it means is more or less known to every normal human being.

Also, non-Christians have a *cognitio legalis,* obscured to a certain extent through sin, but nevertheless an important reality, and now clarified through special revelation. From here even the Christian learns the material content of that which he has to do. The material direction *(die materiale Vorschrift)* comes from the order of Creation (p. 267). Even what the good Samaritan had to do he recognized from the order of Creation of a healthy human body (p. 266). The content of that which is demanded is always known in that way, a way which is also to a large extent open to the pagans. The motivation, however, has become a new one to the Christian. As to motivation, all comes from Christ. But all this is only the lower stage of Christian behavior, lower but always indispensable. Over and above that stage we have that spontaneous love which surmounts all commandments. This love is the fulfillment of all commandments but it breaks asunder the very concept of commandment. It can exist only where it is received as a gift.

This seems to be along the same lines as those which Brunner had worked out in 1943 in his *Gerechtigkeit,* especially in the paragraph on "justice and love." It is not an easy task to state in how far he now has deviated from what he taught in 1932. But perhaps it would not be unjust to say that the previous tendency to speak of a recognizable law of the Creator as more or less distinct from the new commandment of Christ has now become so far victorious that we are running the risk of leaving the whole content of concrete ethical teaching to those resources which are common to all humanity. The "specific" Christian ethics, apart from the new motivation, is now more or less explicitly limited to that indefinable spontaneity that transcends that which the order of creation exacts. These questions, however, are more important to the problem of the social ethics of Brunner. So here we omit an examination of the question in how far what we have here noticed is already to a certain extent present in *Das Gebot und die Ordnungen,* where he deals with the concept of a *justetia civilis,* to which only the Christian can and will attain. I only permit myself the following question: Is the Brunner of *Dogmatik* II in accordance with that remarkably clear statement of 1932 (p. 202): "It is a fatal dogma of a certain Lutheranism that the 'orders of created world' are not subject to the commandment of Christ but only to reason"?

But at any rate, Brunner remains true to his very strong opposition to all kinds of legalistic ethics. God has not given us a law which now we, eventually by means of a finely elaborated casuistry, could handle and from which we could derive knowledge of the "right" procedure in any case. In *Dogmatik* II it is as clearly stated (pp. 261 ff.), as in his previous writings, that Christian existence is not a performance of certain "Christian" acts, but it is the state of being in and under and directed by the love of God, the fellowship of the Holy Spirit. He never turns out a *Situationsethiker.* In *Dogmatik* II he seems, as far as I can judge, to come pretty near to the position claimed to be that of Luther (see especially Ragnar Bring: *Gesetz und Evangelium und der dritte Gebrauch des Gesetzes in der Lutherischen Theologie,* 1943). Luther claims that a Christian is as well a *homo vetus* as a *homo novus.* As the new man the Spirit has taken possession of him; Christ dwells in him; and so he performs acts of love transcending every law, in spontaneous and joyful activity, whereas, as "the old man," he remains under the discipline of the law which enforces of him just behavior. However that may be, in his major work on ethics after 1932 Brunner quite definitely, in continuation of the tradition of Lutheran and Reformed orthodoxy, teaches the so-called *usus tertius legis,* that is, that the revealed will of God may be known by us, not to be sure, as a definite rule that we can follow, but as giving us positive instruction to come to a general knowledge, a provisional guidance, a sort of outline of that which divine love can be expected to claim or to lead us into. Elaborating this further, Brunner keeps close to the tradition from the orthodox period in stating that to the reborn the Law is no longer the order of the lord to his slave but the regulation of the father to his son. If we actually believe (belief is never present if not *in actu*), the Law has become a sort of road guide, an indication of the route to be taken, so that the Law has come to be our delight. Here Brunner also is in fundamental agreement with men like Kohlbrügge and Alfred de Quervain, whereas Calvin was more inclined to speak of the Law even in the life of the reborn as a whip to arouse the sluggish man.

But now the question arises: what is the content of the divine Law? You are bound by divine order to the Thou, your neighbor, and the "new commandment" calls upon your love. But what as to your own person? Is there any possibility of continuing the old Christian tradition of speaking of a love of ourselves, our own person? Have we, perhaps, duties to our self, virtues belonging to our own being, to be cultivated?

First Brunner most emphatically does away with the old concept of virtue derived from Aristotle. It is individualistic and therefore opposed to true humanity. All true virtue is openness for, readiness for "the Other One." This does not mean that man should fall into self-contempt, despair of his own existence, engage in a negation of his own individual being. Brunner clearly sees the danger of turning the call to self-denial for the sake of the Thou into this caricature. That would be rebellion against God. The "I-Thou" relationship claims that the "I" is not blotted out or obliterated but preserved for service. And the fact that God wills us as single persons, that he in Christ says his Yes to our individuality and even wishes to preserve us as individual beings through all eternity, makes it clear that we are not to throw away our own selves in despair or contempt or long for that individuality-devouring unification of which the mystics dream. Brunner even speaks not only of self-respect but of "thankful self-love" (*dankbare Selbstliebe*, p. 154), a dangerous phrase which, of course, has exposed him to severe criticism, but which, read in the context, is not only defensible but perhaps even necessary, at any rate in the period around 1932.[2]

Therefore not only is suicide an impossible solution for a Christian, but, according to Brunner, man has to accept the fact that God not only wills our existence but also the special form of each individual human existence. Not only our *Dasein,* but also our *Sosein.* A flight away from our given individuality is prohibited (p. 155). We have a dignity, not in ourselves, but in God's acceptance (p. 156). If we accept Grisebachs' "hard sentence": "The I is the Evil," it is right when we think of the I as self-sufficient, in its No to the Thou. In that sense we have to deny our selves. But this has nothing to do with ascetic seeking for individual sanctification. The old self has to die not through exercises in self-abnegation, but through self-giving in love.

From this it should be understood that Brunner, though he

---

[2] See, for example, the way in which Brunner in *Der Mensch im Widerspruch* admits that Nygren may be right in his protesting against the manner in which Harnack spoke of "the infinite value of the human soul," but immediately adds (rightly) that the human soul through divine love receives an infinite value (p. 288). See also his opposition to a naturalistic determinism, *op. cit.,* pp. 259 ff.

explicitly states that the Good according to the New Testament is fully defined in the word love, that is, love to your neighbor, yet can introduce two small sections in which he deals with "the religious exercise" and "the moral exercise."

Obviously this causes him some trouble. When he speaks of the double commandment of love, he very definitely explains that love of God is not something on the same level as love of the neighbor. That is not indicated when Jesus says that these two commandments are like each other. They are alike as are the tree and the fruit, the fountain and the stream. He therefore states that there are no duties toward God in the same sense as we have duties toward our neighbor. There exists no action directed toward God, no religious exercises that are ethical duties. Nevertheless he naturally teaches the necessity of prayer, of church-going, Bible-reading, meditation, and can even, not quite consistently, say that we must (sollen) pray; God desires that we seek Him in prayer. What Brunner safeguards against is the danger that a religious exercise which is necessary, not for the sake of God but for our own sake, should become a "pious work" (pp. 293-299). Thus far, I think he is right, though it seems to me that particularly in a period when the tradition of Kant and Ritschl, and the influence of existentialism, combine in telling us that love of God simply means love of your neighbor, it would have been desirable if Brunner had emphasized the simple exegetical fact that such an interpretation is contrary to the text of the gospels. There is a commandment of love of God relatively distinct from love of our neighbor. And it is important that this is made clear (see, for example, Karl Barth: Kirchliche Dogmatik, I. 2, p. 480).

As regards the "moral exercise" (sittliche Uebung) in relation to the person's own self, Brunner is very anxious to make clear that this can only indirectly be a good work. Cultivation and domination of self is not of any final value, but can be valuable, yes indispensable, as a means to certain given ends. We are here in the domain of technics. But this domain is of great ethical relevance, though indirectly. So Brunner claims the necessity of self-examination, in some cases even as far as psychoanalysis. But the goal is not, as in the main line of philosophical tradition, the building up of a certain habitus, but the readiness for certain acti, that is, acts of unselfish love. It is noteworthy that Brunner in this connection

protests against certain tendencies to speak of the "positive" character of Christian ethics. Here Christian ethics is confused with the
philosophical ethics of Greek origin. And Nietzsche noticed here
more clearly than many of his Christian opponents the true character of Christian life.[3] At any rate, Brunner accepts the fact that
a "Christian character," a sort of residuum for ethical activity,
exists, and that here we may even speak of an increasing or a de-
creasing. But these, he claims, are questions that pertain more to
the field of pedagogics than to that of ethics. He therefore also
opposes that attitude which has been called "life-reform as a
principle" (p. 186).

Of course Brunner remains true to the famous Lutheran doctrine *simul justus et peccator*. How should man, being a new creature only in the ever-new, ever-gracious presence of his Lord,
reach a state where he, in his own being, is only partially a sinner?
And yet, certainly, Brunner is, as early as 1932 (before that he was
influenced by the group movement) eagerly emphasizing that we
are under a divine imperative that exacts of us a "better righteousness," yes—to be perfect. The difficult question of the relationship
between the divine indicative (the new life as a gift) and the
divine imperative (the new life as a challenge) he at any rate
attacks in a helpful way, eager not to lose either side of this
double truth.

In this connection we notice the fact that Brunner is aware of
the strange truth that although our Lord always expects of us the
perfect, the absolute, all His concrete commandments to us concern, and must concern, relative ends (see pp. 169 ff.). This problem, which has been attacked so well by Reinhold Niebuhr in *An
Interpretation of Christian Ethics* should, however, have been
treated more explicitly. And it is in my opinion directly misleading
when Brunner in this connection quotes Kierkegaard, and, following
in his footsteps, says that God does not exact the relative as such
from us, but only that we "perform the movement of faith." This
indicates that Brunner has not noticed how strongly Kierkegaard
is determined by a "Christianized" (but really very Kantian)

---

[3] This appears to me to be essentially correct. And in 1932 it had to be
emphasized. The question is, however, whether there is not more to be said.
Is not Brunner here one-sided? Has not the time come when it must be said
that the great Christian thinkers have been too exclusively claiming *mortificatio
carnis* and have almost forgotten the God-given *vivificatio*? See especially,
Karl Barth, *op. cit.*, IV. 2, pp. 649 ff.

Gesinnungsethik. Brunner has, as previously stated, most clearly seen one danger of a "Christian" *Gesinnungsethik,* namely, that it tends to make the "reborn" man the source of the new life. But has he clearly seen the second danger, that this type of ethics makes everything depend on the motivation of the action and leaves the actor finally disinterested in the result?

And yet, that Brunner knows at any rate something of this danger is especially visible in the paragraph on *Erfolg und Fortschritt* (pp. 268-272). He knows that he who acts out of love must act with the intention really, actually, to reach results. He also knows that effective results must be the consequence of actions in true belief. And he also is right in observing that such an assertion is a statement of faith, not of experience, and that the real fruits are hidden to the day of the Lord. So one might say that the bricks for building the house desired are all there. But the house is, I think, left unfinished.[4] Because the influence of Kant is so dominant in the German-speaking part of Protestantism, it would have been more valuable if Brunner here explicitly had criticized the tradition of the *Gesinnungsethik.*

When we deal with the problem of ethics as a striving to reach certain definite ends, relative in themselves, but in the special case under the absolute obligation of divine commandment, we touch the problems of ethical compromise and of the relation of means and ends.

Helmut Thielicke has recently stated (*Theologische Ethik,* II. 1, 1955, p. 65) that the problem of ethical compromise, as far as his knowledge goes, has received remarkably little attention in theological works. I can not see that this holds true of Brunner. Here he has a very definite position, namely, that we should either have to flee from the world or enter into compromises with the sinfulness of the world if it were not because of our trust in justification by faith, and the conviction, inseparably connected with this, that we, in all our actions, are placed in a divinely-given vocation (*die Rechtfertigung allein aus Glauben und damit der Berufsgadanke*). Brunner here advocates the confident joy of the Christian who trusts

---

[4] Nevertheless, the peril of an idealistic *Gesinnungsethik* is much more apparent in Karl Barth's writings, not only in his earlier ones, but even, for example, in *Kirchliche Dogmatik* I. 2, p. 487: "I will nothing and I dare not will anything, when I testify to my faith. I only live the life of my faith in the concrete confrontation with my neighbor." This is nearer to Fichte than to the New Testament.

that when he acts under the vocation from God and seeks to exercise love for his neighbor, God takes upon Himself all responsibility
for the unavoidable (the given) sinfulness of the situation wherein
the action is, so to speak, placed (pp. 186, 190). The Danish professor of Christian Ethics and the well known Kierkegaard scholar,
Ed. Geismar, always spoke in this connection of our being forced
into a situation from which we could get out only "with a wounded
conscience," because there was no possibility of finding the right
way; every choice was sinful. In contradistinction to this, Brunner
proclaims that a Christian can trust God even in the most en-
tangled plights and so gladly obey. "How should it be tragic to
obey God?" (p. 189). Of course this does not mean that we, by
means of certain methods of casuistry, can once and forever define
the right choices. Neither does it mean self-righteousness, nor does
it deliver us from the anxiety of a difficult and serious and perhaps
terrible choice. But it gives us that free conscience which is the
gift of divine justification.

This also holds true as to the problem of means and ends.
Brunner is, of course, far off from that rightly abhorred doctrine
that the end always sanctifies the means. But he is far too much
aware of the corruptness of the present world to teach that we
should avoid all use of means that are not quite pure and holy.
Pure and holy means we never find. Everything we may touch is
tainted with sin. "We can in this world do nothing without using
sinful means" (p. 261). But Brunner risks the dangerous, but to my
opinion necessary sentence: "The necessary end sanctifies the
necessary means" *(ibid.).* Of course he knows that certain means are
so corrupted that the use of them will almost inevitably spoil the
goodness of the end pursued. Then these means are to be avoided
even at the cost of sacrificing certain very good ends. We are to be
very careful in our deliberations as to the relationship of ends and
means. But here Brunner also teaches that a joyful obedience is
possible—because of divine forgiveness.

It may seem almost contradictory to this, but it certainly is
not, when Brunner speaks of the suffering of a Christian when the
gulf between that which he should like to perfom as testimony
to divine love and that which, under the given circumstances, he
is forced to do becomes terribly evident, and the guilt of our whole
being is, as it were, manifest in these particular actions which we
had to perform. Brunner, who previously said that it cannot be

tragical to obey God, now quotes Kierkegaard's phrase: "a Christian is recognizable through suffering" (p. 259). And Brunner rightly points to the fact that this becomes a stimulus to fight for better conditions of society, and that it makes the Christian long for Christ's final victory.

In his ethical writings Brunner does not have a great deal to say explicitly of eschatology. But the Christian hope permeates all his works, to such an extent that without this nothing would be really sensible.

And by this statement I might close this very brief outline of that part of Brunner's ethics with which it is most easy for me to agree. And I cannot come to a conclusion without expressing my indebtedness to a book like *Das Gebot und die Ordnungen,* not to speak of *Der Mittler.* A new perusal has confirmed my thankfulness and my not uncritical admiration.

N. H. SØE

THE UNIVERSITY OF COPENHAGEN
GENTAFTE, DENMARK

14

Reinhold Niebuhr

THE CONCEPT OF "ORDER OF CREATION" IN EMIL BRUNNER'S SOCIAL ETHIC

THE CONCEPT OF "ORDER OF CREATION" IN EMIL BRUNNER'S SOCIAL ETHIC

I well remember the excitement and gratitude to which I was prompted when Emil Brunner published his *Das Gebot und die Ordnungen* a quarter century ago. We were in America just emerging from the illusions of a pure liberalism, which in Christian ethics attempted to derive a social ethic from the gospel commandment of love. This could not be done without sentimentality for the agape of the gospel is too pure to provide for the standards and calculations of an adequate social ethic. Brunner's was the first, and in my opinion still the best exposition of a social ethic from the standpoint of a Reformation theology which disavows the Biblicist tendencies of some so-called neo-orthodoxy to derive all moral and social standards purely from Scripture. This Biblical legalism, usually of Calvinist origin, frequently turns out to be more capricious and irrelevant than Catholic legalism based upon classical natural law concepts. Brunner followed the Reformation in his distrust of the moral intuitions of natural law because he agrees that "reason is involved in the Fall" which is to say that reason is not as incorruptible as the classic and medieval ages assumed. Therefore moral law, relying either on intuitions of reason or deduced from the proposition that one must do good rather than evil, is not the true guide of the conscience as Catholicism assumed.

Brunner follows Luther and builds a social ethic upon the concept of *Schöpfungsordnung* or "order of creation." He is essentially true to the Reformation principle that love is not a counsel of perfection added to the natural law, but that all laws are tentative and relative and that, ultimately considered, there is only one law—the law of love, which gives Brunner the phrase for his book *Das Gebot*. In all these elaborations one follows Brunner's exposition gratefully for he has given many fresh insights into the intricacies of community life and the life of the Christian by applying Reformation principles to modern problems.

Nevertheless my chief point of criticism of Brunner's social ethics concerns the adequacy of the Reformation concept of the order of creation or, as Brunner sometimes defines it, following Augustine, the "natural order." This is supposed to be the order that God intended, though Brunner never tires of reminding us that everything in history is corrupted by sin and we have no sample of the original purity. But there must be something in the order of creation which makes it normative. But it is difficult to find this normative principle because man is a historical creature and there are no purely "natural" forms in his life which have not been subjected to both the freedom and the corruption of history.

Brunner, following Luther, makes monogamy the chief example of the order of creation not only because monogamy is the most primordial and perennially valid of human communities, but because it is the one institution which is validated by a Scriptural appeal to the order of creation. It will be remembered that Jesus in rejecting divorce which Moses had allowed "for the hardness of your hearts," declared that "in the beginning it was not so." He then proceeds to derive from a genuine order of Creation, heterosexuality, ("male and female created He them") and from the fact that the marriage bond merges two personalities into one ("And they shall be one flesh") the conclusion that the ideal law for such a union is its indissolubility. "Now what God hath joined together let no man put asunder." It is just in this ideal example of the natural order (in which, incidentally, Catholic natural law and Reformation concepts of natural order agree) that prompts some questions about the validity of the concept. Undoubtedly, every Christian would agree that the indissolubility of the marriage bond is the ideal solution for the actual intimate mergence of two lives, physically and spiritually. But this mergence is not a fact of nature but an achievement of history and is tolerable only when grace sustains the partnership. Significantly, the Reformation continues to permit divorce, as Moses did, for "the hardness of your hearts," while the Catholic Church insists upon the absolute indissolubility of marriage. If we move from the problem of the indissolubility of marriage we find that everything is touched by history and is relativized by historical circumstances. Brunner rightly calls attention to the fact that the order of Creation refutes all abstract feministic equalitarianism (which forgets the fact that the woman has a biologically determined vocation) which a man does not have, fatherhood being only an avocation. But he does not deal adequately with the fact that the Christian community was tardy in recognizing the fact that a woman in a modern culture must have the freedom to add another vocation to that of motherhood because it regarded the biological limits as more fixed than they are.

Luther rightly derives the authority of the parent from the order of Creation but wrongly derives the authority of government from the supposed extension of the authority of the parent. It is historically correct that government is derived from the growth of the family to clan, and clan to nation. But the chief and the king have historically elaborated forms of power and authority and John Locke was quite right in challenging the idea that government had an inherent authority upon the basis of natural order.

The fact is that the natural order gives us only minimal conditions for social life. It establishes the foundation as the law of love furnishes the pinnacle for the moral life. Between the minimum and the maximum, we must reach hazardous and historically relative standards of justice which must be more flexible than Catholic natural law theories allow, and it must have more body in its conceptions of justice than the Reformation theory permits. Thus, Brunner follows the Reformation theory which gives the state the negative function of preventing anarchy and is too complacent toward the peril of injustice and tyranny. "It is true, of course," he writes, "that every order of the state which prevents anarchy is good even though it may be wholly injust . . . even an imperfect system of law is better than anarchy," (*The Divine Imperative*, p. 449). This judgment expresses the Reformation's rather too extravagant fear of anarchy which inevitably betrays it into complacency toward tyranny. It would be better to regard anarchy and tyranny as the Scylla and Charybdis between which mankind must steer toward justice, fearing the one evil as much as the other.

The failure to give sufficient body to the concern of justice prompts Brunner to be rather too critical of revolutionary movements that resist injustice and he fails to profit by the truth in the sectarian Christian tradition, particularly of the seventeenth century. Brunner remains consistently critical of all existing social

orders but consistently pessimistic about the possibility of changing them. Thus, he declares, "The first question a Christian must
ask is not how can I alter it but how can I serve within it" (*ibid.*,
p. 401); or again: "Love is content to do what comes to hand
and not primarily to make great plans. Work on the grand scale
is not the primary concern of love" (p. 285). Brunner rightly
objects to the Christian "antirevolutionary parties" and declares
that in principle, "Revolution stands exactly upon the same
footing as obedience to superior authority"; but he adds that, "All
political activity must aim at order and peace and thus revolution
can be allowed only as an exception" (p. 618). The emphasis upon
order and peace rather than justice perpetuates the Reformation's
basic mistake of finding no standard of justice between the pinnacle of love and the base of order. In another context, Brunner
practically rules out revolution by the assertion that a system
"which actually maintains order is the best as long as a better order
can not be maintained without a break in continuity" (p. 230); or
as in the German original, the new order must be established
Pausenlos. That rules out every revolution for a Christian. This
conservatism may seem justified when we measure the effects of
the French and Russian Revolutions; but it hardly does justice
to the fact that the revolutions were prompted by the collapse
of the old order, and to the creative consequences of the many
revolutions in history. In the same category of complacency is
Brunner's advice that a judge must not be too concerned to pass
judgment upon the basis of a law which he regards as unjust since
there are no completely just laws (p. 255). This is certainly in conflict with the English Common Law tradition in which the conscience of generations of judges has contributed to the gradual
emergence of just laws.

The real crux of the defect in the conception of the order of
creation is revealed in Brunner's approach to the concept of
equality. For equality is the regulative principle of justice, though
Brunner is quite right in asserting that equality is not the simple
possibility which the seventeenth century Christian sectarians regarded it as being, or the eighteenth century philosophers assumed
it to be. "The egalitarian law of nature," declares Brunner, "does not
belong to the world of the Bible but to stoic rationalism. Now the
creation, quite apart from sin, simply leads to incomprehensible inequality, conditions for which we cannot account. The egalitarian

idea does not arise out of reverence for the Creator but out of the desire to dictate to the Creator how things ought to be" (p. 407). This dictum suggests the dangerous idea that all efforts to correct historic inequalities are presumptuous. It also embodies the Reformation's rather too uncritical reverence toward any *status quo*, including natural contingency, as divinely ordained. Brunner's polemic against abstract egalitarianism has betrayed him into a disregard of the principle of equality as a regulative principle of justice.

Fortunately there has been a real development in his thought on this issue from his *The Divine Imperative* to his *Justice and the Social Order*. In the second book, the very title of which reveals the author's growing interest in justice rather than order and peace, Brunner declares: "Justice is closely akin to equality. . . . Justice is equality. Just treatment means equal treatment to all and equal wage for equal work and equal praise for equal achievement" (p. 27).

Nevertheless, Brunner has difficulty with the concept of equality even in *Justice and the Social Order*, largely, I think, because he derives inequality from the order of Creation and because he is in such strong and justified reaction to the abstract egalitarianism of Stoic and eighteenth century thought. He rightly observes that equal treatment for unequal situations and needs is not justice.

That is why Marx rejected "bourgeois equality" as the final norm. On this point, Marxist utopianism and Christian orthodoxy agree that love is a more transcendent norm than equality. But Brunner fails, I think, to do justice to equality as a regulative principle of justice as a transcendent principle, if you will, as one implements love with the *calculi* of justice, and tries to "give each man his due." This Aristotelian principle which Brunner strongly emphasizes gives us, of course, no clue about what each man's due is. Brunner's rightful rejection of abstract equalitarianism leads him to a rather wholesale rejection of all schemes. He writes: "God does not create schemes, He creates individuals. . . . The inequality which is the consequence of individuality is just as much created by God as that which is common to all mankind" (*The Divine Imperative*, p. 40). It may be that "God does not create schemes" but it is necessary for men, when dealing with problems of justice, to create schemes and structures of justice. Aside from the fact that it may be dubious to equate individuality with inequality, it seems that the excessive emphasis upon inequality in the "order of creation" leads to confusion in dealing with the various aspects of inequality. There are, first of all, inequalities resulting from natural contingencies such as the health and sickness of two children in the same family, or the brightness of one and the mental retardedness of the other; or the inequalities between nations due to the fact, for instance, that China is lacking in the mineral resources of either Russia or the USA. Is it not rather dangerous to regard these contingent inequalities as willed by God? It would be better to make Thomas Jefferson's mistake and to say that "All men are created equal," which is obviously absurd but which may really mean that we ought to treat them in such a way as to eliminate fortuitous inequalities among them. The second form of inequality is derived from the necessary social hierarchies and gradations of authority. Sectarian Christian radicalism and the equalitarians of the eighteenth century were completely oblivious of the necessity of these gradations and Brunner is right in emphasizing their function. He also calls attention to the sinful corruptions in these social hierarchies, as Luther did. But in common with Luther, he fails to recognize that an adequate social ethic must deal with both the necessity of social gradations and with the prevention of excessive forms of power and privilege, not justified by function. In this respect, one feels that the acceptance of the Reformation concept of the order of Creation has betrayed Brunner into a perpetuation of the complacency of both reformers toward excessive and socially preventable inequality.

The adoption of this complacency, or more properly of the defeatism of the Reformation in regard to the possibility of establishing a more perfect justice which overcomes the inequalities of both nature and history, prompted Brunner to speak of the "hardness" of every scheme of justice and of making too rigorous a separation between love and justice. Love is reserved purely for personal relations; and the "orders" seem designed only for the sake of order and a very rough justice. Any extant scheme of justice is, of course, very rough, judged by the standard of love. But the standard of love should not be merely a principle of indiscriminate judgment upon any and all possible historic systems. It should also be a source of discriminate judgment upon various systems of justice. For justice is the servant of love and there are more indeterminate possibilities of love approaching the standard of love than Brunner realizes. It is insufficient, for instance, to speak of the necessary hardness of penal justice when secular penology has added psychiatrists to act as *amici curiae* to the court in dealing with child delinquency, a perfect example of a more living contact between love and justice than Brunner assumes.

Though Brunner stands in the general Reformation tradition rather than the specifically Lutheran one, I suspect that Luther's doctrine of the "Two Realms" plus the influence of Martin Buber's great work, *I and Thou* has persuaded Brunner to make this too radical distinction between the realm of the personal and the institutional and to reserve love only for the realm of personal, indeed, individual relations. It was a great achievement to make this distinction between the personal and the institutional in the days when it was necessary to counter the sentimentalities of Christian and secular liberalism. But sober second thoughts should prompt all of us to reexamine the social outlook of the Reformation, recognize the defects of its defeatism in matters of social and political justice, and be grateful that later Calvinism, sectarian Christianity and, yes, the Enlightenment with all its illusions contributed to the relative justice which we now enjoy in Western civilization. We will also be grateful that the free society which was established through various providential events in history made it possible for Western civilization to winnow truth from error both in the excessive pessimism of the Reformation and the utopianism of the radical perfectionists, whether Christian or secular.

These critical remarks about some aspects of Brunner's thought where I have been unable to follow him scarcely do justice to the greatness of his whole system of thought and to the debt we all owe to him, particularly the Protestants of the Anglo-Saxon world who have always found his exposition of Reformation theology so much more sympathetic and relevant than any other version of what has wrongly been defined as "neo-orthodoxy." Brunner has been one of the seminal theologians of our generation.

REINHOLD NIEBUHR

COLUMBIA UNIVERSITY
NEW YORK, N. Y.

15

Werner Kägi

EMIL BRUNNER'S CONTRIBUTION TO LEGAL AND POLITICAL THOUGHT IN A THREATENED AGE

EMIL BRUNNER'S CONTRIBUTION
TO LEGAL AND POLITICAL THOUGHT
IN A THREATENED AGE *

A systematic theologian has to be interested in everything; it is, in fact, his profession to combine his diverse knowledge into a system. For Emil Brunner this task has become a profession through vocation. His lively spirit has always been interested in everything; his systematic spirit has with great effort thrown a light on the connections between and the structure of the whole system. His universality, however, did not prevent him from devoting a special interest to certain fields during many years. This applies primarily to the field of law and justice, of freedom and power—the problem of the political order in the larger sense of the word. These were not simply favorite questions, freely chosen, but rather problems which our time brought forward so urgently that they were decisive for our destiny; it happened that they also appealed to Emil Brunner strongly. He has always followed the political events passionately; passionately he adopted also a definite attitude to the problems of domestic and foreign policy. Moreover, this passion for political affairs urged him to give the legal and political thought in a radically threatened time a more solid foundation and a clear aim. This he endeavored to do in innumerable lectures, sermons, and writings; he has written down his major systematic reflections in his ethics, *The Divine Imperative* (1932) and in his theology of law and social orders, *Justice and the Social Order* (1943).

This is neither the place nor the time to attempt complete appreciation of Emil Brunner as a legal and political philosopher. He is

* Translated by Ursina Campell.

still active among us, and we are unceasingly reminded that our time calls us to put our hands to the plow and look forward. Although the troubles of today leave us little time to look back, we still believe that something may be said about the importance of Emil Brunner in political and especially in legal thought. At some future time, a retrospective glance will certainly give a more carefully considered judgment; but perhaps the view from the battlefield of today—once Emil Brunner himself compared the Christian dogmatists and ethicists to "front-line officers"—would give a more lively and essential insight into the man. In addition, a backward glance from a greater distance is generally much influenced by the prevailing theology. Nowadays we are not only alarmed by the role that fashion plays in theology, how quickly—restlessly and faithlessly—something is praised today and cast away tomorrow, but also by the fact that the verdict on a certain theology as "out of date" may often mean that even the attainments in a single field are no longer taken seriously, considered, or duly appreciated. I, as a lawyer, shall attempt to estimate the significance of Emil Brunner's legal and political way of thinking quite independently of the prevailing theological currents.

According to my opinion Emil Brunner's most significant contribution is based primarily on the following:

I. Knowledge of a Primeval Order of Belonging

In the great crisis of our time and particularly during the origin of the totalitarian regime, the decline in legal thinking—the lack of resistance of a relativistic positivism—has played a big role. Nevertheless, we may not simply make positivism responsible for the great catastrophe. A positivism existed in legal thought which knew a last ethical reason of human law and which took it seriously. During the great trial, however, certain positivists opposed injustice and illegal supreme power, whereas, on the other hand, some apostles of the Law of Nature not only concealed their credo but betrayed it.

And yet it is true that positivism weakened the power of resistance and paved the way for the totalitarian regime. The positivist doctrine made an important contribution to the situation which led to the events of the first half of our century. Positivists' claims that "all values are subjective," that "law could have any contents," that justice is "an object which has nothing to do with logos" cannot remain without influence on the respect for constitution and law.

Thus, if everything has the same validity, it follows that all becomes indifferent. In this sense we can, like Emil Brunner, designate positivism as one of the great path makers of totalitarianism. Thus, lawyers failed in the great crisis, because they had already raised to their dogma the idea of justice as being something relative. "What is justice?" has become the juridical "question of Pilate" of our century. As a result, a lawyer is no longer a protector of justice but a mere "technician of the social" (H. Kelsen).

This decline was inevitable as one no longer believes in a "divine law," in an "eternal justice." For in that case, the law becomes simply the command of the stronger, whether this is an individual, a group, or a majority. During the Second World War, Emil Brunner sought *de profundis* to revive the significance of absolute justice. He based his studies on the great tradition of the antique-Christian idea of justice—which was maintained and unfolded in a long tradition of Roman Catholic legal thought, but early abandoned by Protestant thinkers. Emil Brunner himself emphasized the imperfection of his attempt, but nevertheless he endeavored to conceive a new normative idea for the positive code of law, justice—especially "earthly justice" which is the opposite of "justice of the faith." What is to be said "from the point of view of Christian faith"? The dim consciousness of justice, which is the constant basis of our feeling for what is right, should be raised to a clear principle, a clear idea.

Basing his ideas on the classical definition of justice by Ulpian in the *Digest* (1, 1, 10 pr.): *Justitia est perpetua et constans voluntas, ius suum cuique tribuendi,* Emil Brunner determines justice as a "primeval order of belonging" which is "original and not created by a human legislator." Thus, man sees himself placed again in an order; he forms "part of a structure" that regulates his sphere of life. This normative idea of justice does not belong to personal ethics but is the supreme principle of ethics concerning orders and institutions. It is the "critical instance above every human law." The primeval order of justice is of a superhuman, superterrestrial, and supertemporal kind. It is a principle of "valid, normative, and holy obligation."

In the subtitle, the work *Justice and the Social Order* is called "A Theory of the Principles of the Social Order." This work actually attempts to show in detail the just order of the family, of the profession, of the state, and of the community of nations. But the guiding principle of justice is the "primeval order," the order of Creation.

II. Personalism versus Individualism and Collectivism

Personalism has been a permanent concern of Emil Brunner and an important basis of his theory of justice. It is the narrow track between an anticollective individualism and an antipersonal collectivism. Emil Brunner often gratefully referred to Søren Kierkegaard, Martin Buber, and Ferdinand Ebner (who is still unknown) from whom he learned this direction.

His starting point is the doctrine of *imago Dei:* Man is—contrary to all other creatures—"created not only by God or through God, but in and to God" (*Man in Revolt,* p. 82). As a result, the meaning of man lies not in himself, neither has he simply derived it from any collective, but he finds it in his counterpart, in Christ, who is the original image *(Urbild).* The divine Word calls man into existence: this is the "answer" to that "call." For this very reason, the core of his existence is responsible existence. The person is the responsible being. Responsibility is what makes man as an "individual" (in Kierkegaard's sense of the word) select and independent. The collective as such can never be responsible.

Man as a person is absolutely not interchangeable. Man has this unique dignity, because the Creator "called him by his name" (Isa. 43, 1). Exactly for that reason he is not a mere part, a limb or a number, but an "individual," that is, the unconditional holder of responsibility.

Emil Brunner has repeatedly pointed out the strange "paradox of the Christian thought of independence" which gives man an unconditional value in itself on the one hand and makes him an individual, but sets him not less unconditionally in the community on the other hand. The individual can only become through the other, the "I" through the "Thou" (Martin Buber). Unconditional communion, however, is communion through love. God has created man for communion with Him, but at the same time also for communion with his fellow creatures. Responsible existence is existence in communion. Only through communion with God can real communion with fellow beings be possible.

During many years Emil Brunner struggled for the right understanding of communion. By this he made a considerable contribution to the basis of legal and political thinking in a radically threatened time.

In the last few years legal and political thought lost the normative idea of man. Emil Brunner revived it again in his anthropology [1] (*Man in Revolt*), starting from the great Western tradition. This, however, is a hedgehog position in the struggle against a solipsistical individualism on the one hand, which is not inclined to give the community what it deserves, and against an antipersonal collectivism (in different forms) on the other.

This basic work was naturally chosen as general theme of the volume presented to Emil Brunner on the occasion of his 60th birthday: "The image of man in the light of the Gospel" (Zurich 1950), which gives some idea of the world-wide echo which his wakening and arousing thinking has produced.

III. *The Totalitarian State and the "Right" State*

Another important theme in all the writings, lectures, and sermons of Emil Brunner of the last few years, dealing with legal and political questions, is a challenge to the totalitarian state. He considered the struggle against the totalitarian state as the struggle of our time.

Contrary to many other theologians who considered the totalitarian state just as a new "absolutism" or a "dictatorship," he recognized early the radically novel and revolutionary aspects of totalitarianism. As early as 1937 he rejected offhand in a contribution to an ecumenical volume, "The Totalitarian State and Christian Freedom," the idea of the totalitarian state as a governmental order that is "absolutely incompatible with the Christian faith." He showed that the totalitarian state is something radically different from a new form of absolutism: it is a state that desires to have "unlimited competence," that tolerates neither freedom nor autonomy of individuals or of smaller groups, but, on the contrary, claims to standardize and control all spheres of life. It is the Leviathan, the all-absorbing monster, *Allstaatlichkeit*, the *société close* in the sense of Henri Bergson.

In the thirties, Emil Brunner adopted a firm attitude against the brown totalitarianism of the "Third Reich" at a time when many Christian theologians were making bigger or smaller concessions to

[1] Cf. *Der Mensch im Widerspruch*, 1937.

the blood-and-soil mysticism and to the national god. Emil Brunner continued this struggle against the red totalitarianism which many theologians liked—and to some extent still like today—to consider as something completely different, although its very essence became more obvious every day.

In *Justice and the Social Order* Emil Brunner explained the genesis of totalitarianism as a consequence of the decline of the Western-Christian idea of justice. The totalitarian state is the final product of the decay of the Western Christian idea of the Law of Nature, it is "the necessary consequence of a faithless, antireligious and antimetaphysic positivism." It is not just a state that governs in an absolutist arbitrary manner, but it is "injustice made into a system." In a totalitarian state no human rights exist, no "eternal" norms "preceding the law of the state."

When the Commission of the Churches on International Affairs (CCIA) was founded in 1946, Emil Brunner referred, in a vote, to the dangers of the Bolshevik totalitarian state. The majority of the participants, especially those from England and the USA (with the notable exception of John Foster Dulles, who, as President of the Conference, had to be a bit careful) were then still impressed by the comradeship-in-arms with the Soviet Union during the Second World War. (We do not criticize this, we just mention it.) The diagnosis of totalitarianism was violently rejected with reference to the evolution under way in the Western and Eastern worlds. The sequel proved John Foster Dulles, who published exactly at the time a noteworthy series of articles in *Life* (which revealed the facts but also made him at once the most hated man in the Kremlin), and Emil Brunner to be right. Many persons revised those illusionary concepts long ago in view of their experiences; others have stuck to them even after Korea, Hungary, and Tibet, and they will probably still stick to them after the summer of 1960.

This struggle against the totalitarian state not only meant a purely defensive antipolicy for Emil Brunner, but it followed the image of a right state as a great and obligatory ideal. In his Ethics of 1932 he had already showed the necessity and the right of the state against all anarchic illusions, but at the same time he pointed out the limits of the state against all totalitarian tendencies. In 1942, in the midst of an overshadowed Europe, he called again to mind in a rectorial address, "The human rights according to the Protestant reformed theory," the origin and the significance of the rights of freedom. Man's fundamental rights are engrained in the likeness to God, these rights being primary to political law. The radical threat of the totalitarian state called the apology of the inviolable human rights which also guarantee personal freedom toward the state. At the time it was—necessarily and inevitably—also an apology of the ancient right of resistance. In *Justice and the Social Order* he laid down in 1943 the full and fundamental proof for these theories and postulates. He never doubted the necessity of the state —also in view of the noblest illusions of Christian anarchism—but he has shown and defended the order of a right state—as a limited and limiting state based on law *(Rechtsstaat)*. The state exists for man and not man for the state. It is nothing more than a subsidiary order, framework, and protection for a free and responsible community. The right state can be recognized especially by the fact that it guarantees inviolable fundamental rights.

Thus it was not quite by chance that his son, Andreas Brunner, as a lawyer, made a structural analysis of the state based on law in antithesis to the totalitarian state ("Right State versus Totalitarian State," Thesis, Zurich, 1948).

IV. Right Understanding of Democratic Order

Emil Brunner has defended democracy all his life, although not in the ordinary manner with conventional formulas and slogans, but critically and often provocatively. Once he recalled a time which gradually lapsed into a light democratic optimism that democracy could not be created overnight and that it was not always "absolutely the best form of government" for every nation, but on the contrary that it could under certain conditions be the "worst of all governmental orders." It is the "best form of government" as far as and because it takes the individual seriously as somebody who shares the responsibility; it is a bad form of government if it simply covers up the real power and if the citizens only seemingly have the right of being consulted. Emil Brunner put forward and defended repeatedly some of the fundamental norms and conditions of the right democracy.

(a) Emil Brunner wanted to safeguard democracy *against a wrong absolutist misunderstanding.* Law is not only the command of a specific majority without any consideration of its contents. A democratic majority is also bound to the limits indicated above—

especially to the limits of the fundamental rights. Democracy can only exist as a limited democracy, that is, as a state ruled by law. Long before J. L. Talmon, in *The Origins of Totalitarian Democracy* (London, 1952) had proved in detail that the absolutist-decision-istic misunderstanding of democracy would finally lead to the totalitarian state, Emil Brunner had referred to these dangers. An unlimited sovereignty either of a nation or of a state does not exist. Both are subject to a higher law which binds them both. Sovereignty in the strict sense of the word belongs only to God. This he considers decisive: "For without the limitation by the will of God, a people declines into anarchy and mob rule or the State into totalitarian tyranny." [2]

(b) On the other hand, Emil Brunner realized clearly that liberal democracy also requires *authority*. "Authority" is something different from "a claim on unlimited competence." Authority is necessary for the sake of liberty and the law. In a time when everything calls for freedom and equality, the postulate of authority is not very popular—it is even tabooed and suspect. Nevertheless, Emil Brunner has—again with courage to incur unpopularity—repeatedly come up against demagogy for the sake of the necessary authority. The state is a necessity, a foundation of God (Rom. 13). "Its prime duty, however, the duty which takes precedence, is to exercise authority, to have power to command" (*Justice and the Social Order*, p. 69). During the war, when our small nation was radically threatened, he expressed himself in favor of the death penalty (cf. *Death-Penalty, Two Voices of the Church*, Zurich, 1942, pp. 19 ff.; *Todesstrafe, Zwei Stimmen aus der Kirche*). At the time when "Christian" was always mistaken for "charity" and "grace" and "love" in the sense of mildness, it was a delicate task for the Christian theologian to call in mind that the authorities do not govern with the sword without good reason (Rom. 13). Moreover, Emil Brunner has never ceased to defend the necessary authority against an "excessive development of formal democracy." [3] Nevertheless, he required of the government in democracy that it should better take justice instead of the will of the people as a leading principle, and that it should really be a "government" and not merely an "executive."

2 *Justice and the Social Order,* p. 71.
3 *Ibid.,* p. 192.

(c) According to his personalism, Emil Brunner has always opposed centralism and unitarism and advocated *federalism* (*Justice and the Social Order*, pp. 120 ff., 218). This struggle naturally culminated in his contest with the totalitarian state: in the defense against the absorption of all orders and all rights by the state. Accordingly, federalism is the right structure of the orders; only in a federative structure the originality and the personal rights of the members are respected. But the ultimate foundation of this stucture consists again of the "primeval communion of the family" and the "individual" (in the personalistic meaning). More than once Emil Brunner said, quite rightly: "Not democracy but federalism saves us from the totalitarian state."

(d) Finally, Emil Brunner also adopted—again in an elucidating and pioneering manner—a definite attitude to the other basic question of the constitutional and legal development of democracy which Alexis de Tocqueville in his *De la Démocratie en Amérique* realized a hundred and thirty years ago to be the great problem of democracy: the distinction *between true and false equality*. The idea of equality belongs to the great idées-forces of our century. In the large masses of the population it doubtless found an evidence much stronger than liberty. But exaggeration of the idea of equality —the egalitarian misunderstanding—becomes a great danger to the democratic order. In *Justice and the Social Order* Emil Brunner clearly distinguished between two conceptions which tend to be fatally confused in discussion: the ultimate inviolable equality of personal dignity and the unlikeness of kind and function. The biblical understanding of man and community does not require an all-leveling egalitarianism; "The secret of the Christian idea of justice is not equality but the combination of equality and unlikeness." [4]

V. The Limits of the Legal Order

One thing political and legal thought owes to Emil Brunner is his contribution to its foundation as mentioned above in a few examples. The other is his steady reminder of the limits of all legal and institutional order. But still it might seem that, especially at a time when justice was so radically threatened (and keeps on being!), basic studies were and will remain necessary; nevertheless,

[4] *Ibid.*, p. 41.

these are only possible if the limits are permanently envisaged. Besides, the problems vary for each field of law.

In *constitutional law* Emil Brunner has emphasized that the pure legal form is insufficient. It must be borne toward fellow men as a liberal order through the will to freedom which also means through the will to justice. All these problems rose up again urgently for Emil Brunner during his professorship at the International Christian University in Tokyo. There he confronted the Christian conception with the Marxist and emphasized that the "political formal democracy" must be completed by the "social democracy" if a young democracy is to exist and grow.[5]

In *international law* Emil Brunner made an important contribution toward founding an international ethos—based upon the knowledge to which Max Huber referred to during several years, namely, that international law cannot exist without a leading ethos. He emphasized that the first answer must be that only the Gospel of Jesus Christ as the Saviour of the world, and the Kingdom of God that was revealed by Him can be the final and total answer to the international problem. Only on this basis, the second task which consists of helping toward the constitution of a human and just order of the community of nations—belonging to different religions—is possible. The Christian Church has to elucidate and "call to mind" the "Divine Law" where it is blurred. The "idea of communion" representing the kernel of Christian faith can also in the community of nations, which lies furthest away from the core of biblical revelation, lead beyond the "unfruitfulness of a mere legal aspect" (see especially "in search of an international ethos").[6]

And finally in *ecclesiastical law* Emil Brunner called forth by his work *Misunderstanding of the Church* (*Missverständnis der Kirche*, 1951)—through consent and opposition—a new and deepened reflection of the fundamental questions. He proved in a manner similar to that of the great canonist Rudolf Sohm before him, that often the Church has turned from a vessel of *ekklesía* into an obstacle to Christian community, in fact into a governing institution. Opposite this, he recalled in a passionate pleading that the very essence of new testamental *ekklesía* consists in the unity of communion with Christ in faith and brotherhood in love. This is pointed

[5] Cf. *Justice and Freedom in Society*, lectures, 1954-1955.

[6] "Auf der Suche nach einem internationalen Ethos," *Reformatio*, Sixth Year (1957) pp. 347 ff., 411 ff.

out in detail on pp. 41-51 and 234-36 of this volume, but it is worth referring to also in this connection. For far beyond ecclesiastical law, that ultimate, deepest communion is explained which must also be a permanent and last guiding principle for political thought —between individualism and collectivism.

Emil Brunner's legal and political thought is generally characterized by two features: First by his closeness to the present, that is, the lively interest he has always shown for the problems of today, which gave him the courage to face hot irons and dangerous problems such as the totalitarian state, the death penalty, the question of authority, equality/unlikeness, and so on. Second, there is his striving after clarity and simplicity. Emil Brunner has never said in a complicated way what could be said simply. His way of thinking does not simply analyze and contemplate, but it wants to be effective.

Innumerable persons—in the ecclesiastical and political field, in Switzerland and Europe as well as all over the world—have witnessed the influence of his thought. And there are many lawyers among them who owe to the theologian Emil Brunner a new and clear direction in their thinking and activity.

WERNER KÄGI

DEPARTMENT OF JURISPRUDENCE
THE UNIVERSITY OF ZURICH
ZURICH, SWITZERLAND

16

Peter Vogelsanger

BRUNNER AS APOLOGIST

BRUNNER AS APOLOGIST *

B runner's entire theology has an apologetic character. This is expressed even in the peculiar impetus of his thinking and speaking. His theology always tends to aggressiveness, encounter, criticism, dynamic decision. Particularly when it is presented as a sermon or as a "discussion with the other faculties," it has an aggressive, missionary feature. Its domain is the service in the church militant. It reveals errors, misunderstandings, hiding places in which the modern man usually entrenches himself against faith. It is in its whole tendency and aim a continuous encounter with the way in which the modern man thinks and understands himself. Thus it affects man in his reasoning, his responsibility, his personality. In addition to all this, however, Brunner has given a thorough theological foundation to this particular task in evangelical theology within the entire framework of theological thinking. Yet he energetically denies that, besides the primary, objective role of what is called his "special concern," there is a particular secondary task, namely the pedagogical and methodological posing of questions. For him, this apologetic encounter with disbelief is a goal of evangelical theology which is directly and necessarily connected with the preaching of the word.

Incorrect Apologetics

Brunner is aware, of course, of the difficulties of the idea of Christian apologetics, difficulties that become evident in the past and present again and again. With him apologetics is not what it used to be: an attempt to prove and to substantiate faith by means of thinking, a defense of Christianity against its modern enemies

---

* Translated by Gero Bauer, Vienna, Austria.

and despisers, an "apology for faith before the forum of human reason," an annexation of faith to a scientific system of thinking by harmonizing the oppositions and rational contradictions, however these sometimes ingenious, sometimes futile attempts may end, often amounting to the cheap exploitation of the weaknesses of the opponent, or to the questionable oversimplification of faith by means of a complete attenuation of its essence. Brunner, in approaching his task, occasionally reveals such false points of departure of an incorrect apologetics. In particular, he keeps his distance from two forms of a faulty apologetics.

1. He clearly separates himself from the undertaking of Roman Catholic fundamental theology, both in its classical Thomistic and in its modern forms, the latter as it appears in Przywara, for example. Brunner does not decline to express the proper human respect for the achievements of thinking which are contained in this undertaking. As a whole, however, this fundamental theology with its separation of reason and faith, with its claim to establish the supernatural truth of faith upon a rational basis, and to demarcate the truth of faith, if not as being rational, then at least as not being in contradiction to reason, is an attempt to destroy the *scandalon* of faith and to remove it. This attempt is based, on the one hand, on a wrong idea of revelation and faith, and deprives faith of its personal character. On the other hand, it is based on a wrong conception of human reason. To be sure, in Brunner's as well as in Thomistic theology, reason takes an essential part in establishing faith, and Brunner devotes persistent attention to this aspect. Yet reason does not create a natural basis of faith for the irrational truth of revelation; it is, rather, the means of accepting God's Word; it is on the basis of reason that it is possible to appeal to the natural man with the message of mercy, of revelation. The part reason plays in establishing faith is not constituent but receptive. It was, therefore, a total misunderstanding of Brunner's intention to equate his doctrine of the "point of contact" or the *theologia naturalis* with this Catholic fundamental theology. He in no way has the intention to attenuate or to eliminate the contrast between faith and the rational thinking of man himself, between the "wisdom of the cross" and the "wisdom of the world"; on the contrary he energetically insists on putting this contrast in its proper place. Nor, further, is faith proved by reason, not even subsequently, for this would be a "proved faith."

Nor, again, does reason as such stand in contradiction to faith. It is only the misunderstanding of reason concerning itself, its failure to recognize its own limitations and functions, that occasions the so-called rational contradiction to faith.

2. Likewise Brunner separates himself from the undertaking of apologetics, the intention of which is to defend the message of the revelation, together with its corresponding dressing in historical, ideological, philosophical, and scientific conceptions, notions, and forms of thinking, against a critical form of thought that is considered a process of dissolution. This attempt is evident in different variations, from the new-orthodox apologies of Luthardt, for example, in the nineteenth century, to the fundamentalism and biblicism of the present time. Brunner's central objection to this approach is the following. The message of faith is always embedded in the medium of historical, mythical, geographical, objectively urgent communications which are not the thing itself but only its form of communication. As such, these forms, therefore, do not have to do directly with God or with the absolute dependability of this message of faith, but are subject to the change of man's comprehension. It may even be the case that one form of communication, one "dressing of faith," not only becomes no longer serviceable but even an obstruction, especially when it becomes mixed with ideas of *Weltanschauung* which are alien to the gospel. Such an incorrect apologetics then assumes that it has to defend unimportant nonessentials or hopelessly obsolete ideas together with what is essential. Vice versa, it is afraid that by abandoning these nonessentials, the main work itself, the truth of faith, might be endangered. Thus it not only comes dangerously close to being misguided, it compromises faith itself. It promotes a misunderstanding about the essence of faith, shifts it out of the personal sphere, out of the realm of the subject into the sphere of objects, into the intellectual realm. This is especially fatal if this orthodox misunderstanding of faith is connected with clericalism, and with a decision about the question of truth by claims based on power, however concealed those claims may be. In contrast to this whole standpoint, a valid apologetics, in Brunner's sense, has to exercise a critical function on the very notion of faith. It has to separate, in the comprehension of the truth of faith, the form of existence of faith itself from the respective forms of thinking in which it is expressed. A classical example of this is

Brunner's interpretation of the Creation and the Fall of man; the biological and mythical form is carefully peeled off from the message that is relevant for faith, and thereby the way is opened for a full comprehension of the creation.

Eristics

In contrast to these inadequate attempts, Brunner defines the conception and the goal of a Christian apologetics in a new way. It is not an absolutely new definition though, for he deliberately recaptures essentials in the great traditions which lead from Augustine's *City of God* through Pascal's *Pensées,* to the total outlook embodied in Kierkegaard. He retains the term "apology" only for traditional reasons, and he prefers to substitute for it the term "eristics." This, he believes, is more appropriate to the proper goal of apologetics because it emphasizes at the same time the aggressive rather than defensive attitude in his service of the church. For real apology means the attack of faith on the strongholds of disbelief (II Cor., 10:4); the attack on human reason insofar as reason obstructs faith; and this latter involves an attack on the idols of modern thinking as these are expressed in contemporary "-isms." For the opposition to faith does not stem from reason as such, but from the abuse of reason, from the authoritarianism of the reason which regards itself and its creations as absolute. This autonomy of reason is expressed in the respective ideologies of the time, the "-isms." The primary concern of a Christian apologetics, by contrast, is to reveal this misunderstanding of reason about itself, to trace the false steps by which reason advances to autonomy. The second concern, however, is to disclose the results of this misunderstanding. Brunner soon recognized this as the "other task of theology." What he meant by this definition was not a task independent of or even secondary to the statements of the message, and the dogmatic reflections on the content of the message. Rather, he regards the other task as one contained in the message and necessarily connected with it. Revelation is divine self-disclosure, the coming of God to man. Thus it becomes human and seeks out man where he is. The word of the church is an instrument of the divine message and the word of the church has to subject itself to God's coming to man where he is, and to the discovering and grasping this man where he hides from God. This, therefore, is the passion of the divine agape itself that forces us to apologetics. It is not some independent humanistically motivated concern, but it is the zeal about God Himself that necessarily becomes a zeal about man. In this respect every attempt at preaching and theology which is not concerned about this other task, which does not take man seriously, is wrong from the very beginning. By reflecting about the initiation of the divine Word we necessarily recognize this apologetic task. It is the reverse side of the dogmatic task. Whoever approves of this one and takes it seriously, finds himself confronted at the same time with the other one. Since the truth of revelation aims at man, the dogmatic reflection on the essence and the contents of the truth of revelation leads to a confrontation with the pre-, non-, and anti-Christian ways of thinking. This, one might say, is the concern of a Christian humanism. At all times, and especially in its high periods, genuine Christian theology always has been, therefore, also apologetic. The reason why the apologetic character does not appear immediately in the theology of the Reformation is simply that the intention at that time was directed entirely toward doctrinal and similar altercations within the church, and the whole truth of revelation was dealt with only as concerns its interpretation, not its validity. Especially at the present time, however, a thoroughly understood Reformation theology is seen not only to mean an encounter with the heresies within the church, but also as a fight against the errors of the time and the world outside the church. Kiekegaard, before all others, has most deeply understood this. His entire thinking is nothing other than a simple, powerful attack on modern rational thinking. It is an attack which has not yet sufficiently been evaluated for what it is, namely, a "single, artistically designed attack on the ideologies of his time which contrast with the Christian faith, such as the idealism of Hegel, the romantic aestheticism, the self-contentedness of bourgeois morals embodied in the spirit of the rising masses. But we must not stop with Kierkegaard. The confrontation constantly changes, and therefore the task for the church is ever new. Brunner directs his far-reaching attack, as he follows Kierkegaard's penetrating thinking, yet he is completely independent in his confrontation with the typical contemporaneously characteristic ideologies of our time: that is, against the relativism, positivism, skepticism, and totalitarianism of modern thinking. We may conclude this section of our study by defining apologetics or eristics as an attack of faith on the respective contemporary ideologies. It is not a prelude to Christian theology. But it is an essentially inherent concern that is always incorporated into theology and the gospel. This is why we said at the beginning that Brunner's theology has an apologetic character.

The Interior Way of Christian Apologetics

The interior way which has to be pursued by a Christian apologetics, in the sense in which Brunner conceives it, will not become clear except through this definition, which excludes any danger of the assimilation of faith by disbelief and by the contradictions of the world, and which at the same time emphasizes the impregnation of revelation into the ideas and the thinking of the world. The path apologetics follows is precisely the path followed by revelation to man. Accordingly, the following items and limitations have to be taken into consideration.

1. Revelation is absolutely transcendent, unavailable to natural man, unprovable, inexplicable, the very mystery of God's self-revelation in Jesus Christ. This is an established fact for Brunner, and all different interpretations of what he calls *theologia naturalis* are false. His theology is a pure theology of revelation. Only in the Christian revelation is the true existence of man comprehensible. Christ is the *ratio cognoscendi* of all understanding. This understanding occurs only in faith. Faith is to be understood as the "truth in encounter," as a personal act of giving and receiving. This separates faith from the traditional categories of objectivism and subjectivism.

2. Precisely because the comprehension of the truth of the revelation is a personal act, however, the whole personality of man is involved. Christ never encounters man in a "vacuum," but always in a concrete situation. This situation is the situation of the sinner, the "man in the contradiction." Revelation involves the defeat of this contradiction in such a way that the natural self-understanding in which man entrenches himself against God's claim is annihilated. Together with that, the question of man's life, as that is contained in the contradiction, receives its answer. The distress or sickness of life which is hidden in sin is cured. This fact and its significance,

however, is comprehensible only for someone who himself "decides for faith."

3. The possibility and necessity of eristics is based upon this personal character of faith. Only because he has the gift of reason can man believe, as belief is understood in the Holy Scriptures, that is, receive the revelation, the divine self-disclosure of God. In receiving this disclosure of God he is not *truncus et lapis,* but he is claimed in his being as a person, and this includes his gift of reason. As a sinful man he bears an image of God in him, an image that is spoiled and reduced to a formal image. This image of God is the *lumen naturale,* the fact of being a subject, the having of the gift of reason. Only on account of this image can he sin; on it is based the character of guilt of the human sin. Only on account of this image, however, is it also possible to believe. For on it depends man's capacity to accept the revelation.

4. But at the same time the real resistance and opposition of man against the revelation stems from the reason which is dominated by sin. Disbelief is to be taken seriously only insofar as it is an offspring of the reason and is connected with the essence of man. Sin has spoiled reason, or man is sinfully spoiled by reason. This is the same thing. At any rate, there is no pure reason but only a rationality spoiled by the self-assumption of man. This is visible only through faith, of course. Thus it is seen that all statements that man makes about the world and himself are not direct, essential statements. All these statements are distorted. They are among the "-isms" of natural thinking as seen in culture, science, or in the ideologies. They are different at different times but they all originate from the same source, the sinful self-misunderstanding of reason. In the same way man is always the same in his self-security, which is founded on reason; at all times, however, he is different in the particular form of this self-security.

5. Apologetics or eristics is therefore a defense against the attacks on the fundamental revelation, attacks that originate from sinful self-misunderstanding, or more simply: It is a direct encounter with the objections to faith originating in natural reason. It takes place dialectically in such a way that it shakes this self-understanding of autonomous reason and at the same time claims man's

reason. It shakes it; that means that it proves that those objections do not originate at all from reason itself but from a reason which is formed by a particular *Zeitgeist*, from an understanding of life and of oneself in rivalry with the gospel, from a secret dogmatics and metaphysics of the natural man. Eristics uses reason; that means that by examining critically the fact that this contradiction of reason does not concern faith at all but rather a misunderstanding of faith, eristics shows that the true intentions of a critically purified reason have to end in faith, in Jesus Christ. Therefore it is necessary to show what is true and what is false in the human self-understanding. To complete this separation and to explain the true meaning of the Christian message by completing it—this is the aim of Christian apologetics.

6. One has to keep in mind that those objections do not originate only from "outside," from the world, from disbelief, but they are identical with the temptations with which one who believes always has to struggle. The temptations of faith are nothing but the temptations that proceed from the ideas of the world and are present in faith itself. By this insight apologetics is saved both from self-righteousness and from the tendency to "black-and-white" thinking. Apologetics, according to Brunner, essentially means that somebody who believes is aware of his disbelief, that he constantly prays: "I believe, Lord; help my disbelief." Therefore Barth's objection to Brunner's claim is in itself a failure. Apologetics, Barth objected, is not necessary and is unimportant because the false objections of reason against faith, on the one hand, and the contemporary ideologies, on the other hand, collapse in themselves. Disbelief is overcome where the revelation is preached and believed, where faith takes effect. This is wrong psychologically as well as theologically, because it presupposes a faith in the purest form. Just as dogmatic theology is constantly necessary as an encounter of faith with the heresy in the church, apologetics is necessary as a constant encounter with disbelief in the world, and, as disbelief persistently infiltrates from the world, also it is necessary in the church.

Forms of Apologetics

From this observation, the conclusion follows that Christian apologetics has to proceed inductively, not deductively. It must not start from general statements according to the method *quod est demonstrandum,* and explain these statements through concrete situations. It must not, from the very beginning, put the opponent to the wall so that he cannot but be defeated. It must not try to improve its chances of gaining a tactical success by merely pretending to deal with the objections of the different ideological points of view. Rather, it has to affect the listener, to appeal to him in his very abode, and to take him seriously. It has to start from the spiritual situation of the opponent and to attack that situation at the same time. It must start from the distress and the danger of the modern man, and show him at the same time that the gospel gives the rescuing answer to his question. Only this is the method of the divine agape, whereas any kind of preaching that just throws the gospel at the listener's head disagrees not only with the biblical understanding of faith but is also separated from agape.

Brunner, therefore, in a comprehensive process of thinking and with an amazing capacity to draw upon all the relevant spheres of thought, follows the true patterns and forms of human life in marriage, state, law, labor, economics, culture, the arts and sciences, in order, first of all, to complete the above-mentioned "separation of true and false things" in these forms of thinking and living. For in these the helplessness, skepticism, and egotism of the modern man becomes concretely evident. Brunner's doctrine of the "point of contact" does not mean anything but this effort. It is only the expression of this pertinent claim of an inductive discussion. It did not, however, as was imputed by certain writers, have anything to do with the assertion of a capacity of receiving the revelation which is inherent in the natural man.

This discussion naturally takes place on different levels. If it is supposed to be a vital discussion, if the church is supposed to be led out of the self-sufficiency of its monologue and to attain to a dialogue, to a real and ever new concretion of its message, then it must have the courage to leave the sphere of the church and with a missionary intention pierce through the walls of its tradition. Brunner's entire work in the church is motivated by this endeavor, and quite frequently out of this motive he sharply criticizes the church, perhaps at times too sharply. He demands and personally directs the discussion in three forms.

1. As a "discussion between the faculties." It is impossible to

show here how Brunner during his whole life has led this discussion in a most intensive and fruitful way. His principal doctrine, precisely formulated, comes about to this: The conflict between faith and scientific criticism, between theology and the rest of the faculties or academic disciplines proves to be a pretext which has been brought about either by the unjustified dogmatizing of traditional opinions on the part of the church or by skeptical distortions of the critical sciences. Real faith and real scientific thinking can never come into conflict. It is, therefore, the task of eristics to show by critical investigation of scientific statements what is genuine science in it, and what may be a hidden dogmatic presupposition which such science employs and by which its statements are dimmed, and so turned around until they become an obstacle to faith. The following are classical examples: The change of the physical picture of the world, the history of evolution, the historical biblical criticism; none of these is able to disturb the message of the biblical revelation. They only free them from the verbal clothing of inadequate notions. Vice versa, eristics has to warn the church-theology against crossing the boundaries, the motive of which is not missionary zeal but clerical claim of power or the faint-hearted, orthodox confusion of real faith with traditionally consecrated histories. At this point Brunner's thinking is particularly daring and unbiased, but also particularly honest and self-critical. Again and again a liberating ethos of truth predominates. He restrains theology from encroaching upon fields with which it has nothing to do. He may declare: "God has not given to the church D. F. Strauss to no purpose." And on the other hand he may state: "The total outcome of historical criticism of the preservation of the gospel, if seen in its main points, is absolutely nil." A particular role in this clearing up of the boundaries between the faculties is played by the idea of the "nearness of relation," which Brunner has introduced. A human idea of reason, or a statement of science touches faith, and is the more subject to severe critical investigation, the closer it comes to the personality of man. The reverse is also true. An objective mathematical statement will hardly ever get in touch or even in conflict with faith, while, for example, the philosophical idea of freedom enters an almost severe competition with the Christian message of faith. The closer a statement of science and natural reason comes to dealing with the personality, the more faith becomes relevant; the less relevant, however, is reason. The function of faith is changed from a regulative to a constituent one as the nearness of relation is increased. Of course, this "nearness of relation" cannot be stabilized by law; but by observing this principle the independence of science is protected against theological guardianship, on the other hand, and at the same time science is saved from hidden metaphysical encroachings of its field. It also keeps the lively discussion going.

2. As a sermon. According to the two tasks of theology which Brunner distinguishes, there are what might be called the "community sermon" and the "missionary sermon" or "evangelistic sermon." This is a relative matter, of course, for one rarely if ever finds these in their pure form, but rather blended, just as the listener to the sermon will never be exclusively a member of the community or an object of evangelization, or, to put it differently, never only one who believes or does not believe. The community sermon is essentially an enfolding of the gospel for the community founded in faith. It is an edification in the best sense of the word and it starts out from the text of the Bible. The missionary sermon is essentially an attack on disbelief, or the *Zeitgeist,* and has in mind that the modern man is formed by that *Zeitgeist.* It is of secondary importance, and a question of pedagogy, whether it is based upon a biblical text *expressis verbis,* whether it leads to a text, or whether it avoids the reference to it completely at the beginning. At any rate, it is no less a *praedicatio verbi divini,* providing that the one aim of the preaching of the gospel to the modern man is kept in mind steadily and without any concessions. Brunner's primary interest is that the preaching church recognize the difference between the two tasks theoretically in order to beware of illusions and the continued raising of illusions in its present structure of a *Volkskirche,* which is largely dominated by the situation of the mission. Also, in intact, living communities there is the kind of listener to the sermon whose thinking and ethical way of action are to a great extent motivated by pre-Christian skepticism. For him a mere declamatory repetition of Christ's message to the world, or even a "speaking in tongues" which does not refer to concrete situations and to human capacities, is not satisfactory. Therefore Brunner warns his students of homiletics to read carefully the newspaper as well as the Bible, a modern novel as well as books on dogmatics. Far-reaching practical conclusions and postulates which he has established out of this theoret-

ical distinction in his talks and lectures are still to be realized in the practice of the church.

It is interesting to observe how Brunner personally draws the conclusion in his own manner of preaching. He still preaches regularly in the Zurich Frauenmünster Cathedral before a large audience, the social structure of which reaches from the bourgeois to an academic circle and from the man on the street to the capitalist. Brunner never artificially separates the two concerns of the community sermon and the missionary sermon. He continually lets them blend into each other. His sermon is more and more a preaching of the elementary ideas of Christian faith and its confrontation with the contemporary ways of thinking and living. With his advancing age it becomes a highly charismatic mixture of fatherly admonition and lapidary evangelization. He renounces not only all bombast, but also all theological details. One could say: It is appropriate for the community in its concentration on the main things; it is missionary in its aggressiveness. It does not leave man in his equanimity; it stirs him out of his pious or worldy self-confidence, reveals his excuses, and pursues him to his hiding places in order to deliver him to the One who alone is his rescue and his peace. And with all this it does not exclude thinking but utilizes it fully. And this, not an exercise in rhetorics, is what makes his sermon so impressive.

3. The ministerial address. Ministerial work, according to Brunner, is the application of the sermon on the individual man with his problems, and the leading of man to the message of the sermon. It has its place in the entire context of the apologetic endeavor, but the emphasis is shifted from the intellectual to the ethic question. Very often what is opposed to the truth of faith as an intellectual doubt turns out to have an ethical background: the burden of fault and feeling of guilt in the heart. It is the task of ministerial work to reveal this background, not neglecting, hereby, the help of psychology in its proper limits. The *cor inquietum* at the same time is the *cor incurvatum in se,* its desire and its restlessness originates in its egotism; and man can be redeemed from this evil only by the miracle of the revelation in Christ. Only a lively, loving faith is aware of how many obstacles have to be removed to reach this miracle. Again, it would be a principal mistake to play off the ministerial and apologetic endeavors which patiently

and discriminatingly remove those obstacles to clear the way for the comfort and the admonitions of the gospel, against the miracle of the Holy Ghost in the decision for faith. This would amount to the inappropriate tearing apart of law and gospel. Only in a ministerial work, the limits of which are respected and the success of which is put in God's hands, is taking the concrete man seriously.

With that the ring of apologetics as Brunner presents it and practices it is finished. Finally, the question about the possibility and the limits of such an apologetics has to be raised. Apologetics constitutes no attempt to lead from faith to disbelief by the very process of argumentation. Also the possibility of a mere negative preparation of faith by disturbing the human self-understanding is not satisfactory. The former would dissolve the annoyance of the cross, the latter the unity of dialectics of judgment and mercy. Brunner circumvents these two dangerous points, on account of which many a well intended attempt at Christian apologetics failed, and comprehends even more clearly its primary task. Apologetics is not a forecourt of the Christian message or a useless defense of unimportant outposts. Apologetics is an endeavor that constantly accompanies the entire Christian message, that directs and at the same time claims human self-understanding on the basis of faith. In every single question, seemingly irrelevant, in every single situation, seemingly accidental, the main point is the decision of faith. It is the task of the apologist who is also a preacher to be aware of this. Apologetics, therefore, is and remains the "other task of Christian theology."

PETER VOGELSANGER

EDITOR, *REFORMATIO*
ZURICH, SWITZERLAND

17

Theodore A. Gill

EMIL BRUNNER AS TEACHER AND PREACHER

EMIL BRUNNER AS TEACHER AND
PREACHER

Emil Brunner is my great teacher and my great friend. That is not a boast—though I am glad to brag of the connection—but a clear statement of the context in which all my remarks about Emil Brunner are set down. It is, moreover, the kind of statement which would be interesting and significant from every essayist in the whole *Library of Living Theology* series. For theologians do not, any more than anyone else, write as disembodied minds unaffected by personal affections and disaffections. Theologians, almost more than anyone else, are personally partisan, jealous for their own teachers, sensitive about their own leads, always defending their own analysis in all their analyses. So to future thesis writers, researching this volume for clues suggested by contemporaries of a virtuoso theologican who will be thesis subject for many centuries, I confess my bias, insisting, however, that it is no more distorting than may be the private bent of any other commentator.

As student and friend, then, still too close to my beloved mentor to be able to distinguish criticism from disloyalty, I report on a living theologian often attended in class and in congregation. And very full classes and congregations they were. Since the books in this series will stand (as long as libraries last) as records of how things looked to those who were there to see, let the record show that Emil Brunner lectured for a long academic life to full classes and for an even longer pulpit life to overflow congregations. In the semesters when Dr. Brunner lectured "to all faculties," the university's largest auditorium was not adequate for the crowds. And the crowds of students and teachers held on to the end of the semester, too, not dropping off or, as happens sometimes now in other Swiss universities, yielding to invading phalanxes of firm-hatted townswomen playing at significance. On the regular Sundays of Dr. Brunner's preaching in the great Fraumünster the congregation always gathered early, year in and year out filling the sanctuary long before the service started, lapping out of distant balconies into hallways and onto stony staircases completely out of sight of the handsome, intense man in the high pulpit but within earshot of his compelling preaching.

The lectures and the sermons so eagerly heard have become the books from which the learned essayists in this volume elaborated their articles. Each writer has investigated an aspect of Emil Brunner's thought and each author has documented his reflections and criticisms from Dr. Brunner's very considerable published work. What has been so ably analyzed by my colleagues then, is Dr. Brunner's teaching and preaching. For me to fulfill my assignment, therefore, I need not repeat such an analysis of content but must report on the accent, the shading, the center of weight given his thought by the living voice of the teacher and preacher.

And this is not a lesser obligation than the other. For what is more wanting in any scholar's published production than some plain statement about the main weight or the creative center of his thinking? The more seriously a thinker is taken, the more diverse the topics on which his printed opinion is sought. The more systematic a theologian is, the broader the doctrinal spectrum he is expected to cover in print. Repetitions, recurrences of ideas within the published work will suggest what the author himself thought most important—what really got him going and kept him going as a thinker. But what would have been most helpful from each and every theologian who got by before a *Library of Living Theology* came along, was some succinct statement from the theologian himself (entirely personal, quite nontechnical, completely spontaneous) about what got him going, what kept him going as a theologian. Why *really* did you theologize, John Calvin? What were you *really* after, Friedrich Schleiermacher? What particular itch were *you* scratching through volume after volume, Origen? Academic dignity is given this flip question when it is related to the currently very fashionable interest in "method." What we need, what would set the search for each theologian's "method" way ahead, would be some preliminary hint from the theologian himself, or at least from those who knew him in the flesh, about what *he* thought he was after, what *he* thought he was up to.

It is the genius and virtue of this series of volumes that the theological titans of a generation that stands like a redwood grove above the shrubbery of the surrounding centuries, here have their chance in autobiographical essay and in rebuttal to their commentators to speak *vive voce* about what they thought the most vital center of their theology was, what their most personal motivations were. And for what it is worth, those of us who learned from these voices, living, can give our testimony on the same point, too.

I do not know what Dr. Brunner's own account of his life locates at his theological center. I do not know what my fellow essayists suggest herein about his theological drive. But I am so sure of the main point of his preaching and teaching and the main force back of them both, that I would challenge the honored subject himself and all my collaborators besides if they did not agree with my informed hunch—my settled conviction that Emil Brunner has first, last, and always driven to protect and to italicize human responsibility. That insistence was forced on me in the glorious years when thesis research under his direction led me through all his writing. And the idea was confirmed, at least for then, when he responded to my hesitant statement of the thesis, "Yes, yes, on this point I will always risk being *schulmeisterich*. I am a pedant in always coming back to the question of responsibility." Whoever misses that, in any volume or lecture or sermon, misses all.

The psychoanalyst would have to do whatever interior accounting is possible for the particular fix of any theologian's sights (Karen Horney has an especially arresting theory about all of us who worry much over responsibility!). But it takes no special technique to give an outside accounting for large concern about responsibility these days. Emil Brunner matured and wrote in a world and time where most of the sciences of man battered individual responsibility with determinist bludgeons. It was not just materialist physicists who pressed the attack on the notion of an even relatively free self. Some of them at least were reckoning with a "principle of indeterminancy" that seemed to breach a steely causation.

It was the sciences and the quasi sciences nearest the soft, personal, human reality that were pressing the most troubling attack on individual responsibility. Sociologists and anthropologists were describing patterns and trends and tendencies that located everyone in cultural and historical currents that absorbed all accountability. Environment of time and of space set decisions, however individually we announced them. Chronology and geography and meteorology and the neighborhood decided, however energetically we went through the motions of deciding.

Meanwhile, psychologists explained individual personality and action in terms of happenings too early and too accidental to be our responsibility, and of an unconscious activity by definition and description beyond our responsible control. And though the wisest and most careful analysts sought by their explanations and their explorations to free the individual, in explaining decision they explained away freedom to most who read while they ran and listened in a hurry.

At the same time, European politics featured totalitarian developments. Tyrannies of class or race or blood or party or despot fastened themselves on whole nations. Decision belonged to the tyrants, and people fleeing from freedom frantically abdicated their own responsibility. Those who resisted were stripped of theirs.

And during all of this, serious, sophisticated, contemporary theology was rediscovering Paul and Augustine and the Reformers and the mighty doctrines of the grace of God and original sin and justification by faith and with them the whole possibility of a theological determinism—or, at least, drastic enervation—closer to ultimacy than any of the others. Emil Brunner, understanding himself, the world, the claim of the Church best of all in terms of the Paul-Augustine-Reformers line, and therefore determined to develop that line, nonetheless saw the threat to freedom in the misconstruction and misappropriation of the massive formulations on which he would depend.

In every word of the teaching and preaching, in every line of the writing, Dr. Brunner's theology is a protest against every positivistic interpretation of the human soul as a by-product of physical or environmental process, against every resignation of responsibility to history, to the masses, to nation, to state, to class, or even to church authority. "Today our slogan must be: No determinism, on any account! For it makes all understanding of man as man impossible" (*Man in Revolt*, p. 256).

The claim I am making should now be tested in every area of Dr. Brunner's reflection. The other essayists in the present volume, however, have done the careful analyses of the various elements in his teaching which therefore need not be recapitulated here. It is still my brazen claim, however, that the description of each Brunner doctrine discussed is as accurate and as faithful to the great theologian's fundamental intent and as knowledgeable of his personal method, as it is related to his indefatigable defense of individual responsibility. Responsibility is the only stout cord on which the Brunnerian notions, causes, and doctrines can be strung in graded order.

Think, for instance, of his doctrine of God. Document it as you will, peel it and parse it and be meticulous in all footnote pagination: the special character of the doctrine will still be its emphasis on the independence, the separateness of the Almighty. The indwelling presence is not slighted, the God for us, with us, in us is not ignored, but always the guard is up against any mystical confusion of divinity and humanity, any simple continuity between God and man. There are good biblical reasons for such an emphasis, of course. And there was, in the sloppy subjectivism of the theologies written in the generations just before Brunner's, ample reason for his paying special attention to the objective "out-there-ness" of God. Besides which his persuasive teachers and colleagues— an Otto, a Barth—were bearing down hard on the same point.

Even so, the clue to Brunner's pushing the point so repeatedly, the clue to his maintaining the emphasis so consistently is his concern for our responsibility. His theology may not be derivative from his anthropology, but his doctrine of God is certainly intimately corollary to his doctrine of man. God's being is not affected by our theorizing on it. Truth, of course, is served by our getting a right understanding of God's own nature. But the principal advantage in seeing God straight, as he is, in his separateness and independence, is in the understanding this gives man of his own situation vis-à-vis God, before God, over against God. No mush of divine-humanity here, no confusion of essences, no commingling of motivations to start with, no undecided deciding—but God and man, unmerged, *confronting* each other, *meeting* in the Christ who alone bridges the universe-deep cleft of divine-human discontinuity. There stands God, active in the bridging, active in the encounter, but still God and not man. And so, there stands man, responsible because still himself and not God.

No single element in all Brunner's teaching has held longer, more repeated attention than his treatment of the *imago Dei*. Book after book by other authors makes reference to Brunner's discussion of the doctrine. And Brunner himself has repeatedly renewed the analysis. For it is a description of the creation of man in the likeness of God that makes men not just Godlike little centers of individual and independent consciousness, but free persons deliberately (because made able to) returning, reflecting, "imaging" the love of God. Man is not a spark from the divine fire, still aglow with heat not his; he is not a chip off the old block, marked with Another's grain. Man is men, separate, original, unique, distinct creations of God, whose most central reality is their ability to respond to His love and address, their response-ability, their *responsibility*.

So man in his creation is marked above all by his freedom, not autonomous freedom, but freedom to respond in love to the God with whom he is always face to face but by whom he is never forced, displaced. Yet the record is that men misuse their created freedom to reject the God who made them free to be whole when they choose to affirm Him. Not some men, but all men; not occasionally, but repeatedly; not accidentally, but deliberately. Brunner, with his colleagues in the New Reformation, found illumination on all this in the biblical doctrine of Original Sin. Their problem was to explain how it could be that though sin is not necessary (for if it is completely fated, then personal accountability is gone and sin washes out—or if it remains, sin deserves only sympathy, certainly not judgment) still it is demonstrably a fact that everyone does sin. How to explain that sin, though not inevitable, is invariable? This is the problem for all the New Reformers.

With them all, Brunner found important suggestion in the biblical account of the Fall with its implication (so often distorted into a biogenetic determinism) of a fateful element in all men's decision about God. Sin, if it is sin, is each man's own fault. Each man's revolt against God is his own revolt. But he lives in a revolution begun long ago and now in full flame. He is born to traitors and brought up in sedition. His rebellion, which is his own rebellion, lands him in contradiction, existence-unto-death, existence-in-the-wrath-of-God. The distortion of men's relation to God is a dominating element in the context of each man's decision. So there *is* a fateful element in our sin.

But never, never does Brunner let the Fall turn into a crawl-out.

Neither the idea of the power of sin nor the conception of its universal hold makes the single individual one whit less accountable for his sin. Nor do the conceptions of the Devil and evil power mitigate man's responsibility. Nowhere in Brunner is there any hint of innocence overwhelmed by superior evil. Man's lot is not that sympathy saved for the victimized, but that judgment and redeeming compassion visited upon responsible sinners. Sin is slavery, yes. To be sunk in sin is to be incapable of righteousness, agreed. But this is not the cause of sin, it is its consequence. Each man is "jointly responsible for the entire history of sin." If he is the slave of sin now, "he himself is to blame for his condition." Even the idea of slavery to sin cannot be allowed "to conceal that of freedom of decision and the concomitant responsibility" (*The Divine-Human Encounter*, p. 136).

It is a "formal" freedom that remains. American students of Brunner always have most trouble with this analysis. In discussion with their teacher he has sometimes been quite colloquial in his illustration of the philosophic abstraction. "Formal" freedom is the structure of freedom, the shape, the instrumentality of freedom, the container. And it remains. But without the appropriate contents, the free, consistent affirmation of God for which freedom was given. Like a milk bottle with nothing in it, formal freedom stands. It is not doing, delivering what it was meant and made to, so it is not itself what it was meant and made to be. Yet it is *something*. It is "formal" freedom; even the slave of sin has a free will; "free will is the presupposition and the essence of his human existence" (*Man in Revolt*, p. 269). So, while man cannot justify himself, he can be just; he cannot be righteous, but he can be right. He can be moral, but not good; ethical, but not sinless; honest, but not holy. He is fated and free: free to contribute to the fate, but free too to be and do more than he yet has. Responsible. The discussion is an endless vollying of alternative statements, a ping-pong of affirmations on both sides of the stiff net that logic sets up between the alternatives. Free-fated. Fated-free. But for Brunner, predictably, the heaviest strokes are on the side of our responsibility.

So God and man stand over against each other, not merging, but in "divine-human encounter." The title of what may turn out to have been his most important book (how remarkably it adumbrates the three-volume theology that crowns Dr. Brunner's publications) is no happenstance. The Brunnerian vision is of the encounter of Creator and human creature, the encounter of two discrete, responsible persons: one disappointed, the other maimed, but the first still concerned, and the second still accountable. "God the Giver, in sovereign freedom, face to face with man; man who responds with derived freedom, face to face with God" (*The Divine-Human Encounter*, p. 132).

The grace of God, in which the Creator reaches out to the creature, is on the initiative of God's responsibility. Yet "it is not forced on man, but submitted to him. He is not overwhelmed by it, but he is treated as one who can and should make free decisions" (*The Divine-Human Encounter*, p. 128). God's love, his forgiveness, his offer of new life, these *are*—but they come to man not peremptorily but as "the great invitation" (title of a famous Brunner sermon). God's love (which a man cannot let or hinder) comes to life in a man only when that man answers with love. God's Word, which is His alone, nonetheless becomes a blessing to a man only when that man hears and retains it. God binds Himself to man, but awaits too man's responsive binding himself to God. This is the "divine conditional," the "divine-human if" which is helped to the fulfillment God wills by our gratitude for what God has given, and by the trust awakened in us by His forwardness and fidelity, and by the gift of His Spirit—but which is still not forced, always awaiting our own decision.

Making the same point all over again is Brunner's emphasis on faith as community rather than unity and on eternal life as an abiding communion rather than a mystic union. Distinctness, separateness, paired freedoms responding voluntarily, these are the Christian anticipations. Individuality of being and of decision, this is not what is wrong but what is right about the human creation. Merging, loss of individuality, shucking off identity, subsuming wills under Will, this is no consummation devoutly to be wished by Christians, but the abrogation of creation. Community, meaning God and I and the other in eternal, vibrant encounter and relationship—that is our hope. Unity, meaning everybody sucked into some vast mush of divinity, that is what others, bewilderingly, call their *hope!* For Brunner, to the End beyond ends, responsible men face their Maker and one another in inviolable individuality, inescapable responsibility.

If the main point being insisted here were to be fully documented, another book would be in order wherein each subject treated by Brunner would be examined for signs of the main theme. Many of those subjects *are* treated in the present volume, however, and it is left for the reader to determine whether other men's studies corroborate this man's conclusion. But this man, as he has already warned, is not shaken in his judgment even if that is not shared by all his collaborators.

How else, for instance, account for the sturdy, but for many, disturbing, defense of the "orders" in *The Divine Imperative,* and of natural law in *Justice and the Social Order.* Brunner's ethics begins in as uncompromisingly a Christological, even Christocentric stance as any other theologian's of his time. God claims us for His love. "This is His Command" (*The Divine Imperative,* p. 116). First of all it is a Command simply to "Come and believe!" Only when we do that can we know what our next step will be. The law can't predict that for me. Only God can show me. And He does this by placing Christ before us, giving us in Him His own life, enabling us to know His loving will and to do it. The true basis for our Christian conduct, therefore, does not lie in rules, orders, or values, but in our absolute readiness to obey the commandment of love, whatever that turns out to be, reinterpreted for every new occasion by God as His part in the act of faith which is our free acceptance of God's free gift.

So far, so good. But now the question is how to recognize God's will, concretely? Well, His will is hidden in this world with all its individual aspects, its innumerable irrationalities and riddles. In this concrete world we discover certain traces of the will of the Creator. There is a hierarchy of values. The world is not entirely plastic to our designs as idealism is inclined to think. It is braced instead upon a fairly stable rib-work of immanent forms which we can only discover and respect. God's law does not hover over the world as an abstract ethical ideal; we meet it in this concrete world in that fateful moment when His call definitely challenges us.

But now wait a minute. First there was only Christ and the command to love, reinterpreted always by the God who orders and enables. Yet now there is evidently an immutable "given," too: hierarchies of values, natural laws, orders of creation. And where did they get into the picture? Brunner's critics have often asked. Is the Command defined by God in Christ—or in the Creation?

You begin with one, but wind up now with the other. And much ill-natured comment at this point has accused Brunner of theological schizophrenia or suggested that he has been fooled by his own ethical sleight of hand.

To which Brunner replies that it is after all the same God who commands us to love who made the world. And He doesn't ask us to love in principle or in the abstract, but in the world as it is. So he who orders and enables in Christ is only served, not scorned, if we acquaint ourselves with the conditions and the structures of the creation within which we are to seek to act in love. And if that world does have certain "created orders," then it is not Christian valor to ignore them, it is not Christian integrity to accuse Emil Brunner of having invented them, it is not Christian logic to set them up as *alternative* sources of God's ethical revelation—it is simply Christian responsibility to discover what can be known of those orders and to determine what love means here and now, the orders being what they are. As for their being an *alternative* to Christ's revelation, Brunner never can take quite seriously the competitive element insinuated into the godhead by such a suggestion, as if God the Father and God the Son were engaged in a vast one-upmanship on each other and we had to choose sides! The same Logos in whom the world was created and has its order is of course the very Logos who became flesh in Jesus Christ. It is not necessarily contradictory that the Christ in whom we hear that we are to love was quite privy to all the realities within which we have to determine and press that love. And it is not necessarily contradictory that the God who built in whatever constant structures there are in society or immutable orders in the world knew that these were just the ground realities within which love must come to actualize itself as something besides a mood or a sentiment.

So logically, theologically, Brunner has every right to add *die Ordnungen* to *Das Gebot*, to end with Book III in his great ethics text. Saying which, it is still possible to worry about those orders. For without them the command to love is excitingly more open to radical possibilities. When love and love alone is demanded, and Jesus Christ is its only illumination, definition, then brand new possibilities for decision, for action, for resistance, for construction are imaginable. When, however, the vast energy and excitement of love must always be somehow poured into and contained in relatively static forms of marriage, family, state, or economic order, the glow is unmistakably dimmed. Especially is this so when on occasion the orders of creation coincidentally parallel so closely the Zurich *status quo* (much as I love that). And most particularly when they square solidly with the indomitable *Frauenverein!*

But the Brunner ethic is not a product of his more conservative maturity. He was working at it in his more radical youth. And the "orders" got in not because they were a familiar part of classic Protestant theological education but because Emil Brunner, before he was a teacher was a pastor, and before he was anything else, was concerned for responsibility. And Emil Brunner knew in the beginning what all his sharpest younger critics have only very latterly discovered: that the nakedly, austerely Christological ethic was utterly incomprehensible to the congregation of Christians, useless in their decision and action. In daily Christian life, in regular decisions, principles and orders as hoary as any natural law were smuggled back into the ostensibly strictly Christological ethics, thinly disguised as spontaneous, particularized biddings of the Lord—which satisfied the purists and gave Brunner (and God?) a laugh. Or else, for the more sophisticated, the ethical decision itself became *the* ethical problem: never actually deciding anything, but always deciding on what terms one might decide something. With Christological integrity, of course.

Fortunately for us, if not for the world, social ethical issues are at the moment so massive and the pressures toward immediate decision so irresistible that Christian instinct is sufficing for choices and action. But the most promising new voices in Christian ethics are still feeling for new articulations which will fill the conceptual void which inhibits moral action for many. It is clear now that the command alone does not enable, that guidelines of some kind must be invented, deduced, or relocated. We are investigating the "context" of ethics, the "structures" of decision, the "shape" of ethics, "middle axioms," and so on. And we are perhaps learning a new appreciation of what Emil Brunner was up to in the 1920's when he would not wait till the 1960's to set the responsible Christian in a place of decision where the demand was apparent, the options decipherable, and the probabilities and precedents at hand. His teaching here met a practical necessity for responsibility that is more than a word.

Over and over again, the practical requirements of real responsibility have pressed themselves on the logical and the psychological pull of Brunner's theology. In his ecclesiology, just to check the system at one more place, the primary weight is put where it must be, on the ecclesia, the fellowship, "the oneness of communion with Christ by faith and brotherhood in love" (*The Misunderstanding of the Church,* p. 118). The Christian fellowship is what God is after, what he works through, what he will have. It is this ecclesia (and *not* the Church which is only the vessel of the ecclesia) which is given the promise of invincibility and eternal durability. The ancient and familiar churchly framework of the ecclesia may yet be utterly destroyed (since his Japanese experience Dr. Brunner is even more radical on this in private discussion than he has yet been in print), or at least completely reordered. And this will be small loss, for "not the hostility of the unbelieving world, but clerical parsonic ecclesiasticism has ever been the greatest enemy of the Christian message and of brotherhood rooted in Christ" (*ibid.,* p. 117).

The critique of the institutional church flares and crackles. The pull is as hard on the honest and disenchanted and impatient Brunner as it ever was on Rudolf Sohm, for whom, of course, the institution of the church is absolute contradiction of the ecclesia, is simply *wrong*. But Brunner draws back from so flat a judgment. Utterly unstructured fellowship would be to him as irresponsible a teaching as was absolutely unprincipled ethics. After all, it was the institutionalized church which maintained the Christian communion against misleading heresies and divisive fanaticisms long ago, and more recently it was the official Church which gave the communion protection and stability in a menacing Hitlerian state.

Again, it is his concern for responsible Christian thought and action that sets the doctrine for Dr. Brunner. It is false to say that in any essential way the real church *is* structure, *is* institution. The church *is* fellowship and nothing else. But the church *has* structure, it *has* institution. Which is what makes life and growth possible, Christian development possible, ecumenical progress possible. What the church *is* it may not alter, may not compromise. (What it *has,* it can adjust, accommodate, envisage changing.) And so again a doctrine finds responsible statement for the goading and directing of Christian responsibility.

The pattern is consistent, and the clue offered is unavoidable. The very first book was an all-out attack on mysticism (*Die Mystik und das Wort*), and the concern was for the unmingled, disparate, unqualified responsibility of each man before God. The first strain in the relationship between the great leader, Karl Barth, and his admiring but independent reader and friend, Emil Brunner, came when the young Brunner published an article on "the third use of theology." He dared there suggest that theology had an apologetic function—not, I take it, an apologetic that tried to *prove* the Christian faith, but a theological description of the faith that let it *approve* itself. This was anathema to Barth, who was still in his *Sturm und Drang*, just proclaim and let-the-chips-fall-where-they-may period. Yet as every Barthian who has ever taught or ministered on any campus could testify if he would, his responsible practice has involved him in more of the apologetics responsibly described and accepted at the beginning by Brunner than in flat declaration (which, however, was always good with the voguish and the faddy students).

That early acceptance of responsible address is of a piece with Brunner's lifelong practice. Latterly he has described his as a "missionary theology." By that he means just what he meant in the early articles already mentioned. His concern is not just for those within the church, though it does not leave them out. The church, as he sees it, cannot just talk to itself, letting the world eavesdrop on the soliloquy. The church must speak directly to the world too; the church must take responsibility for the discussion. Hence the famous interest in an *anknupfungspunkt;* hence the interest in natural law, on which all might agree and where not just action but wooing discourse could begin.

Responsibility was not a doctrine for Emil Brunner. It was a charge he took seriously, to himself as Christian and not just as systematic theologian. Sometimes it was a charge that took him adventuring in strange places. His brief flirtation with the Oxford Movement must be understood in this context of resolution and action. With a splendid and invincible naïveté, the wonderously sophisticated Emil Brunner assumes that everything of which the Christian theologian treats is *real,* is really *true.* That includes the Christian fellowship advertised but not often enough met in the church. Yet for a while such true fellowship was met in the Movement, and to this day Brunner remembers some of his Oxford evenings as a judgment on the church and an earnest of what might be more consistently possible under profounder auspices. The experience is not mentioned in the relatively recent *Misunderstanding of the Church,* yet along with his later acquaintance with the Japanese No-church it probably accounts for some at least of his emphasis there. Another explanation for the short episode with the Oxford Movement was his approving encounter there with a group effort to demonstrate that the power of conviction is a real force and has a real role to play in world affairs.

That was a concern and a certainty that was finally to swing Brunner's theological attention from the systematic development of the bases of our responsibility to a close inspection of the arena of our responsibility. From the time of *Justice and the Social Order* (1943) and especially in the ensuing Gifford Lectures, Brunner's main preoccupation (long prefigured, to be sure, in separate articles and pamphlets) was with culture-analysis and the specifics of Christian action in the community. Here enters his vigorous, disputatious, unremitting anti-Communism, too. Because his critique at this point now frequently allies him with conservative, even fundamentalist cohorts whose theology he would not be caught dead espousing (nor they, his!), his friends are more than a little discomfited, embarrassed by his insistence. But they should hardly be surprised. The stance is consistent with all we have known of him, and I speak now not of his politics or his economics, but of his theological drive for responsibility. His rejection of Communism is not just in defense of those "principles" by which he usually justifies his attitude. His real rejection is a rejection of any "wave of the future," of any self-advertised inevitability, of any historical determinism. He ends (though not soon, we pray) as he began, resisting in loud utterance what he originally countered in balanced scholarship, every threat to individual responsibility.

Confirmation of all of this comes not just from the lectures, articles, and texts, but from the sermons, too. There best, perhaps. The Brunner homiletics is a subject for another paper. For now, let us only be reminded that in the sermons the preacher makes colloquial, compelling, and clear precisely what the teacher taught. In the sermons the vernacular is baptized, and no one can miss the meaning, and responsibility, confirmed and directed, is laid on every listener. The clarity is not limited to the sermons, of course, for clarity of expression is a large part of Brunner's genius (*Brunner is immer klar,* said someone to Barth. *Ja, unheimlich klar,* said Barth. Which is not unrelated to an authenticated exchange: "They tell me I am the best known theologian in America," Barth twitted Brunner.

"Yes, you certainly are," Brunner replied. "And I am the most read.") But in the preaching the exhortation is direct, and the preacher's fine face, and the silver plume of his hair, and the vocal gold are somehow still in the lofty Fraumünster pulpit for many of us who accepted a task in that congregation from a greatly consistent teacher.

An afterword seems called for by all the above. For without this more personal note, a quite skewed impression could go through the earlier lines to all who do not know Emil Brunner as he is, in his person. The emphasis on responsibility, the strenuous affirmation and reaffirmation of our responsibility may have left a picture of a hard, positive, uninflicted, driving personality. Which would be in terrible error.

For Emil Brunner, always publicly so sure, so systematic, so quick to state and to defend, so eloquent in his own explication, is at home a winsome, sometimes even wistful, humble man. While other theologians and their defenders struggle against every evidence to prove that their hero has never deviated by a hair's breadth from his self-appointed line, Dr. Brunner talks ruefully but readily about such a detour as the Oxford Group episode. Late in his publishing career he confessed complete dissatisfaction with the order of his production. Full of admiration for Reinhold Niebuhr, he longs for a reversibility in history which would permit him to begin again so he could start as Niebuhr began, with the Christian treatment of specific issues, working back from the ethical enterprise to a theological system appropriate to that enterprise. Meanwhile, it is no secret, Dr. Niebuhr regrets not starting with the system! Two humble men are not impressed with a quantity and quality of work that the rest of us find overwhelmingly impressive.

Considering all that has been made of their disagreement, there is humility in Dr. Brunner's evaluation of Dr. Barth as a virtuoso theologian, a teacher and writer of absolutely unmatchable, unchallengeable information, insight, originality, weight. "Far out ahead," I recall my teacher saying. And when I repeated that to another teacher and friend, Dr. Reinhold Niebuhr again, he agreed at once, characteristically adding, "That's just Barth's trouble. He's so far out ahead he has no one to ride herd on him from either side. So he gallops all over, undisciplined, irresponsible . . . But great." It was another sign of a special goodness when a very sick and weary Emil Brunner climbed onto the train in Zurich in December, 1960, to take the third and last volume of his system to Karl Barth in Basle. And it was a splendid, typically juicy old Barth who loved the afternoon, and who has worried out loud to many subsequent visitors about "dear Brunner's" health.

Two last recollections that place Brunner for me. One comes from a night, now fifteen years off, when my vigorous mentor, after a long evening colloquium, was musing over his *süssmost*. We had just spent hours on the system; he had put a life into it. But then he reminded us of that passage in Matthew (25:34-40) where the King says "Come, O blessed of my Father," to those who had fed and clothed "the least of these," and banished those who had not —and never a word anywhere in the ultimate judgment about confessions or creeds or doctrines or *systems!* "That passage ticks like a time bomb in the basements of my system," said the great systematic theologian, and sent us all home.

The other remark comes from an afternoon a few months back. Then the older Brunner, who planned no more books, fretted about his failure and his generation's failure to reckon with philosophy, wished he could yet state the teaching with philosophic sense, meet the mounting philosophic critique. The remark is doubly illuminating. It is indicative of the searching *awareness* of Emil Brunner, knowledgeable as ever about what is going on. For of course it is a reckoning with philosophy, especially language philosophy, that comes next for theology. And the remark is a suggestion too why some of Dr. Brunner's later interests and utterances risk turning dated before the earlier more systematic writing does. For the concern for responsible reckoning with currents and events of his own time will naturally lose some relevance when new times bring new currents and events. The timely is soon dated. And yet, better the reach for the passing timely than an un-Christian try for the timeless. The only Christian timelessness is an everlastingly essayed timeliness.

As a matter of fact, I have a strong but undocumentable hunch that what will last longest of Dr. Brunner's teaching and preaching is a subsidiary element in its present development: his affirmation of Creation. It never gets a rounded statement, it stands always only in bas-relief, but there it is. It lurks in the defense of general revelation, it is involved in the attack on sheer Christo-centrism, it is a part of the concern for points-of-contact, it sounds in the support for orders-of-creation and natural law, it comes clear in the more philosophic discussions of time and matter, it is very lively in all the "worldly" interest. Barth has it when he sings about Mozart. Brunner has it everywhere: when he whirls through his Beethoven sonatas, never losing *élan* even when accuracy yields; when, as he once confessed, all Christian truth sprang into form and color for the young Emil as he first saw Michelangelo's Sistine "Creation of Adam"; when he writes theology; when he preaches.

The affirmation of the Creation may be a second theme in Brunner's composition. I suspect, though, that it may finally dominate in the long coda of historic reflection. Maybe that is just what *I* hope? But Emil Brunner is my teacher. He helped shape whatever hopes I have. And I am everlastingly grateful to the very good God for that.

THEODORE A. GILL

PRESIDENT
SAN FRANCISCO THEOLOGICAL SEMINARY
SAN FRANCISCO, CAL.

III

REPLY TO
INTERPRETATION AND CRITICISM
BY
EMIL BRUNNER

III

REPLY TO
INTERPRETATION AND CRITICISM
BY
EMIL BRUNNER

REPLY *

General

Above all else I feel an obligation to thank those who had the kindness to take part in this symposium. Nowadays even a university professor suffers from the evil of our age of having no time. I value it most highly therefore, honored men, that you were willing to perform such selfless service. All of you were moved by no other motive than that of finding the truth together with Emil Brunner. I am particularly shamed by the distinguished contributions of Messrs. Tillich and Niebuhr, because they did not make me suffer for my extremely modest contributions to the volumes devoted to their thought.

A critical analysis of my own theology has not only been welcome by me—as all my students would certainly testify—but it has also been a necessity for me. I can develop my own thoughts best in answering different or opposing views, and I am of the conviction that the truth, especially the truth of God's word, can be found only by common effort. All monologic thinking has become to me more and more suspect. Therefore the answer I would give initially to all the authors jointly is this, that my theology is not a finished one, but is rather "theology on the march." Being finished seems to me almost identical with being dead. The time of finished systems is past.

It is possible that some of the questions directed to me in these essays are answered in the concluding volume of my *Dogmatics*. With only one exception the authors of these articles did not know this third volume when they wrote, for it did not appear until the fall of 1960. (The English translation appeared in the fall of 1961.)

* Translated by Marle Hoyer Schroeder.

There I have raised and sought to answer many of the questions which have been expressly directed to me. I therefore beg leave to refer to that work occasionally and even to indicate particular chapters, for I do not think it good to repeat here in the short space allotted to me what has been treated there in greater detail, more thoroughly and with more circumspection.

All of us—not only Karl Barth, but also Paul Tillich, Anders Nygren, Rudolf Bultmann, Friedrich Gogarten—are thinkers whose thought circles around a common center, the revelation of God in Jesus Christ. Each of us, led by his peculiar basic intuition, seeks in his own way to break through to this center. Thereby each of us has probably succeeded in some way in coming closer to that center. But again and again it appears that a man's special strength is revealed simultaneously at certain other points with his weakness. Certain questions are put and answered more clearly than before, but at the same time others are thereby obscured. It is perhaps similar to the field of physics, where it has become clear to us since Heysenberg that when the full light of knowledge is allowed to fall on one point, others become all the more enveloped in darkness. The mere confession that such is necessarily the case shows an open mind for the other thinker and for the truth which comes to us through him. This recognition and this attitude are perhaps somewhat new in the history of theology, but they are indeed nothing but a necessary consequence of what St. Paul says in I Corinthians 2 about the supplementary gifts of the Spirit in the *ekklesía*. Herewith the program of an ecumenical theology is articulated. That with such a view one hardly initiates a theological "school" but rather exposes himself to the unwarranted reproach of eclecticism is something one must calmly accept. On this point I gladly stand with my antipode, Schleiermacher, who autographed a book for a student with the words, "David Friedrich Schleiermacher, *studiosus theologiae.*"

One final remark: part of my answers supplements my autobiographical sketch. This should indicate not that my thought and life are one unity—which would be a frightful overstatement—but rather that a relationship of mutual influence exists between my theology and my life. Again and again I have seen that decisive theological ideas have come to me while preparing a sermon, and on the other hand how the depth of my sermon has been conditioned by my theological work. My decision to resign prematurely my professorship in Zurich and devote myself to a missionary task in East Asia resulted from the basic missionary motive of my theology. What prompted me to accept this call was the fact that it involved the development of an academically trained Christian laity, in other words an "Evangelical Academy" in Japan.

Wilhelm Pauck

The masterly analysis of the most recent church history which Pauck's essay contains comes to the same conclusions as my depiction of the *Krisis der Kirche* (Crisis of the Church) in *Dogmatics,* Vol. III (pp. 115 ff.). However, there is a certain difference between his American and my European evaluation of organized ecumene, the World Council of Churches, of which he thinks more positively than I would. For us European Christians, the *ecumene* does not have the same meaning as it does for Americans. Our problem is not the variety of churches in one country, but rather the comparative irrelevance of the church as such.

On one detail I should like to comment. Among the authors whom Pauck names as the leading theologians of today is one who is missing in my appendix to *Dogmatics,* Vol. III, p. 245, *Ueber die theologische Lage der Gegenwart* (On the Theological Situation Today), namely, Reinhold Niebuhr. This omission is not based on any lesser evaluation of him, but rather on the fact that I regard Niebuhr less as a theologian than as a Christian philosopher. I have scarcely ever read any article or book by him on a matter of technical theology. All the more I value him as a Christian thinker—I was almost tempted to say layman. His prophetic criticism; his untheological language; his ability to awaken the interest of his contemporaries in every calling, since he is not limited by theological categories which have become alienated to men of today; his virtuosity in filling with Christian content the abstractions in which men think in our century; his outstanding knowledge of social and political problems of the present day—all of this makes him the ideal evangelist for the intellectuals of our time. On the other hand, on hardly any point of Christian dogmatics do I know the exact thought of Reinhold Niebuhr. I am therefore greatly satisfied by his statement about my theology: I may say that Brunner's whole theological position is close to mine and that it is one to which I am more indebted than any other (Reinhold Niebuhr, *The Library of*

Living Theology, Vol. II, p. 431). This corresponds to my feeling about him.

Since Professor Pauck neither directs any questions to me nor brings up any criticism, I think it may be interesting to the reader if I may supplement his historical survey. I have the English-speaking readers particularly in mind. To them I became known first of all under a double name: Barth and Brunner. Since Karl Barth himself did not speak English at the time and therefore went neither to England nor to America, I was regarded more or less as the English mouthpiece of this Barth-Brunner theology, until suddenly the well known controversy over natural theology made it evident that Barth and Brunner were not identical twins. When Karl Barth was spotlighted by the world press as the leader of the church's opposition to Hitler in Germany's *Kirchenkampf,* my situation was just as Ursula Berger describes it in her abbreviated paperback edition of *Der Mensch im Widerspruch* (Man in Revolt): "In the heat of the *Kirchenkampf,* Brunner was completely unjustly labeled and outlawed as a representative of natural theology, so that especially for young theologians Brunner's theological importance almost disappeared behind a screen created by the misunderstanding resulting from the controversy with Karl Barth" (*Gott und sein Rebel, Rowohebs deutsche Enzyklopaedie,* p. 138). It is understandable then that Eberhard Mueller's essay, "Church in Action," should begin with the sentence, "Emil Brunner is a suspicious phenomenon for many theologians and churchmen of today." On the other hand, it may well be said that the Anglo-Saxons would hardly ever have accepted the new theology, known under the name "dialectical theology," in its extreme Barthian form, as the Scandinavians also reject it to this day, while for the most part they acknowledge the relationship of my theology with the one of their genuine Luther.

After the World War the discussion of Bultmann's theology of demythologizing held the interest of German theologians almost exclusively. The motto then became, "Either Barth or Bultmann." I could not identify myself with one or the other of these extreme systems. I stand in the middle between them, so to speak, which makes it appear that my theology is an attempt at mediation. Actually this is not the case at all, because I simply have consistently pursued my own line, already unfolded in 1936 in *Man in Revolt* and in 1938 in *The Divine-Human Encounter.* At this time I knew

Bultmann merely as the founder and representative of the *Formge-schichte* school of New Testament research.

If there are resemblances with Bultmann's theses in my later works, *Revelation and Reason* and *Dogmatics*, Vols. I and II, they are due to a common inheritance from Kierkegaard. It was my own understanding of faith as existence, which I derived from Paul, Luther, and Kierkegaard, that differentiated me from Barth and Bultmann just as much as it brought me close to them. It was already evident in my article, *Die Frage nach dem Anknupfungspunkt als Problem der Theologie* (1932) and in my short book, *God and Man* (1930). Since I have been working on my *Dogmatics* (1946-1960), the concept of God's self-communication, decisive for overcoming the subject-object distinction, has become the basis of my theological thought. This has been expounded in all three volumes, but most clearly in *Dogmatics*, Vol. III.

Eberhard Mueller

If we now place Eberhard Mueller's article, "Church in Action," next in line, we do this because the basic orientation of my theology is most clearly evident therein. Certainly all theological effort is directed toward truth. However, it is a truth which is not theoretically discerned, but only grasped "in faith," that is, in an event which transforms the individual and integrates him into a fellowship. This concentration on a truth which happens is what distinguishes theology from philosophy. Its point of orientation is the *ekklesía*, the kingdom of God in the process of becoming, the "church in action." That is the first thing which Eberhard Mueller makes clear. The other is that theology is the science of communication. The self-communication of God is its theme. But this is at the same time the essence of the *ekklesía*. And yet it is astonishing how seldom theology has considered until now the essence of communication. Only today's crisis in preaching has urged theology to give this theme the attention it deserves. The "Evangelical Academy" is a new form of communication proceeding from the idea that no communication can take place unless the hearer himself is taken seriously for what he already is and knows. This is true in particular about his relationship with God, which is the center of the self. At this point Mueller touches the center of my theology. Its two focal points are the self-communication of God and the responsivity of man.

Allow me to make one small correction of Eberhard Mueller. From the very beginning I was actually called to Zurich as professor for systematic *and practical* theology, with systematic theology logically also including ethics. This thoroughly unusual combination of theological disciplines was impossible from an academic and scholarly point of view. But it met my own thinking insofar as it is my conviction that the task of theology is to clarify both the relationship of faith in Christ to all areas of life and also the grasp faith has on the totality of life. This interpretation of theology became the program of the "Evangelical Academy." It was my endeavor to steer a course between the Scylla of dilettantism, which wants to be everywhere at home, and the Charybdis of a theological intellectualism which has lost all relationship with the life of the church. The theologian must be on the one hand conversant with every area of life, showing that they are all open to that one thing which no science can grasp; on the other hand he must devote his most extreme concentration to that one thing as the source of faith. The first of these tasks, however, no one person can accomplish, but only a study group of Christian specialists (for example, sociologists, psychologists, lawyers) with theologians. The latter are fit to be included, however, only when their theology brings to the meeting that openness which makes them conversant, but conversant from that center which is the revelation of Christ. This theology is only developing today. It alone can become instrumental as we hope, in helping the church to fulfill its *Task in Our Times*.[1]

Hugh Vernon White

I have learned more from Professor White's article, "Brunner's Missionary Theology," than I have from any other. He offers much more than he promises. In fact, it is Professor White who has independently developed from my various works a missionary theology which exists in me only in its initial stages. He is so modest, however, that he is silent on this fact. Only one who has spent a great part of his own life as missionary is able to do this.

Since what White presents is much too comprehensive to be treated justly in a few lines, and since he directs no question to me

[1] Title of the *Festschrift* for my seventieth birthday.

or brings up any criticism, I should like simply to pull out one point and spotlight it. On pages 58-59 and following he demonstrates why the Old and New Testaments belong together in missionary proclamation, even saying that the non-Christian can come to faith in Jesus Christ only by going the way from the Old to the New Testament himself. This thought, which I have up to now only hinted at, but which White formulates clearly, formed a part of one chapter of *Dogmatics,* Vol. III, *Der Weg zum Glauben* (The Way to Faith). However, it could not pass the censorship of my co-workers, because it was not equal to the tremendous problems hidden in this theme. And yet I should like to prove here how deeply White grasped my whole theology by disclosing that this chapter began with that very idea of Israel's way being the way of every individual today, just as White distilled it from my works. Such a chapter, I realized, cannot be written by a theologian alone, but demands the cooperation of the Christian philosopher, psychologist, and sociologist with the theologian. Then it could be perhaps not only the most interesting, but also the most important, or at least the most relevant, chapter in Christian doctrine as a whole. It is a theme that has never yet been treated in theology, but which definitely must be treated—a task for future generations of theologians.

David Cairns

Professor Cairns, who thirty years ago attended my seminar on Pascal and Kierkegaard, has studied intensively not only my theology, but also those of Karl Barth and his antipode, Rudolf Bultmann. His essay deals with the cardinal point of my theology, the doctrine of man. It seems to me very fortunate that he focuses on a formal concept, the law of contiguity. Many have considered this an expression of relativism, but that is not at all the case. Only the center, but definitely that, is absolute. Cairns correctly sees in this idea a basic tenet of my theology. This also means that I cannot simply juxtapose reason and faith. It is precisely here that the rule applies: inasmuch as an assertion of reason approaches the center it loses its validity, and the assertion of faith steps into its place. Here the Either/Or is replaced by the Both/And. The absolute given, the true personhood in Christ, renders all other things relative, to be sure, but it also renders a simple juxtaposition of reason and faith impossible. From this law of contiguity one can see why there is indeed a Christian understanding of history characteristically different from that of idealism (Hegel) and also from that of naturalistic positivism (Spencer), but there is no Christian chemistry; why there is Christian marriage and family, but not a Christian economy or government.

The two questions which Cairns directs to me are of the greatest importance.

1. What does Emil Brunner mean by "created *in* love"? This is indeed an urgent question, which bothered even Augustine and which he sought to solve by differentiating between *non posse non peccare, non posse non mori,* and *non posse peccare, non posse mori.* The same question is at the very foundation of Karl Barth's concept of *wirklicher Mensch* (real man). My answer is different from both. Man is *really* the responsible one; in him, in his very being, dwells the destiny to love, which manifests itself in this, that wherever love encounters him he feels "at home" there. Christ therefore reveals man's creaturely being. He is "the Word which was in the beginning" and that therefore comes "to his own home." God created man in love, from love, toward love. But—and this is what is meant by the word sinner—man lives in contradiction not only to the will of God, but also to his own creaturely nature, in contradiction with himself. This is expressed in the German title, *Der Mensch im Widerspruch,* but does not become clear from the English translation *Man in Revolt.* We have no reason to talk of a *historical* existence before sin. We must be content with recognizing and acknowledging this contradiction between God's creation and its creaturely opposition, and not try to reinterpret it through Platonic-dualistic or evolutionist-monistic perspectives. The historicizing conception of Creation and Fall also falsifies the character of this contradiction, by changing it into a determinism. Only in the claim made by the word of Christ and only in faith, not via theoretical understanding, is this contradiction exposed and at the same time overcome.

2. The second question deals with the essence of freedom. As Cairns formulates the problem, however, it appears too much as an "academic" question. Actually there stands behind it a primary problem of mankind, and in addition a question of extreme relevance, the relationship between formal and material freedom. All culture rests on formal freedom, and atheistic nihilism is based on

the exclusive valuation of formal freedom (see Sartre). But because material freedom—the identity of our will the divine will—is split from formal freedom, culture itself is something formal, that is, from the point of view of divine love, something neutral. Just as a genius can be good or evil, so can also a high culture. This split between formal and material image from God's point of view should not be; it is the result of the "fall into sin," the contradiction in man. Faith in Christ conquers this split, but even then only in a preliminary way. The definitive conquest is the content of (eschatological) hope. In faith, or in being claimed by the God revealed in Christ, material freedom, namely, existence in the love of God, is added to formal freedom of decision. *Dogmatics,* Vol. III, treats this somewhat more extensively in various places (for example, pp. 25 ff. and pp. 323 ff.).

Paul Tillich

At the beginning of his essay Tillich identifies a common ground among the best known theologians of our time. I, too, have presented this view in my treatment *Ueber die theologische Lage der Gegenwart* (On the Theological Situation Today) (*Dogmatics,* Vol. III, pp. 245 ff.), and thereby also sketched my relationship to Tillich. Because of the unfinished state of his *Systematic Theology,* I stated my reservations there in the form of questions to him. Tillich has now done something similar. His question on "Brunner's Epistemology" allows me to answer one of these questions more precisely.

1. I have not developed any "epistemology," because I regard this as a problem for Christian philosophy, not theology (see, for example, *Revelation and Reason,* Ch. 25). I have never claimed to be a philosopher, but I have postulated a Christian philosophy and given an outline of its program. I must leave it to philosophers who are Christians to carry out this program.

2. On the other hand, my interpretation of revelation and faith sets certain limits to philosophy, whose precise formulation I must leave to the philosophical critics. I thereby gladly follow the approach of Tillich, who uses my book, *Wahrheit als Begegnung,* as starting point. In the English translation, *The Divine-Human Encounter,* the implied concept of truth is scarcely recognizable. It should be expressed more exactly, *Truth as Encounter.*

My thinking is oriented differently from that of Tillich. I do not ask philosophically if in this concept, "Encounter," there are still other relationships contained than the I-Thou, but I content myself with selecting this one as the only one meant in the Biblical witness. In contrast to Tillich, I understand encounter only as the truth which comes to us in faith in the self-communication of God. This truth creates a knowledge which rises above the subject-object distinction. We cannot make it an object of epistemological discussion, except by referring it back to its own source, God's self-communication. (This problem in its entirety will become clearer in the enlarged edition of *The Divine-Human Encounter* which is soon to appear.)

This reference back to the source results in this: God, the living God, can be grasped as such only in his communication of himself. *Dieu d'Abraham, d'Isaac et de Jacob, non des philosophes*—this confession of Pascal is also mine. The Systematic Theology of Tillich has to this day not succeeded in convincing me that combining faith in God with philosophical ontology gives an advantage to the former. I take the liberty to remind the reader of this book of what I wrote in *Dogmatics*, Vol. I, on the devastating effect of ontological thought in understanding the attributes of God (for example, Chs. 17-21 and appendices). The God of the Bible simply is not the "Being" of Tillich's ontology. That I have titled my book *Revelation and Reason* and not *Reason and Revelation*, as it is usually done, expresses the fact that it distinguishes the Christian philosopher from every other in that he sees from the perspective of faith what reason can accomplish, and not vice versa. Thereby the theologian willingly submits to philosophical criticism all philosophical statements he has experimentally set up. He will leave the question open whether and to what extent and in what way a rational metaphysic is possible and necessary. But in no case will he be able to incorporate faith into or subordinate it to a philosophical epistemology, since the latter stems from an It-world and not, as does faith, from a Thou-world. Since the essay by Professor Schrader brings up similar problems, my answer to him will say something further on the relation between revelation and reason.

And yet it is necessary to view Tillich's theology from another, positive perspective. The transformation of Christian faith arising from the introduction of ontological concepts surely has its positive side, for Tillich has thereby caught the ear of the many who reject faith precisely because they regard its personalism as anthropomorphism (here see *Dogmatics,* Vol. III, pp. 449 ff.). The Bible is starkly personalistic; this cannot be denied any more than that for this very reason it is hard for the contemporary thinker to gain access to it. On this negative fact rests the great "apologetic" significance of Tillich's theology. His function is eminently missionary, indeed precisely by virtue of what we must reject on theological grounds.

Modern man is estranged and alienated from all personal thinking because he is oriented toward the relationship of man to nature, to the It. His understanding of truth is that of "objective knowledge." But this is the polar opposite of "truth as encounter" (see *Dogmatics,* Vol. III, Ch. 17: *Glaube und Erkenntnis*). Here Tillich's synthetic theology performs a valuable service of mediation. It creates, so to speak, an emergency bridge from faith to impersonal rational knowledge or philosophy. More than that, indeed, it cannot do, and the question still remains open whether it is really faith or Biblical truth which comes to the modern man over this emergency bridge, and whether that so necessary connection might not be accomplished in some other way. I think I may answer this last question with Yes, although I have given only the abstract formula, so to speak, to this other solution, but not the concrete proof. As the essay by Professor Schrader shows, however, my book *Revelation and Reason* meets with more rejection than acceptance from philosophical thinkers. Perhaps the attempt will succeed not through any systematic work at all, but rather only in the reality of life: for as he approaches his own limits, the It-thinker becomes aware that his own problems are not thought problems at all, but rather problems in living, with which his thought cannot cope. This is the meaning of the so-called I-Thou philosophy. It is no philosophical system, but rather a signal appearing over and over again that as responsible beings we stand in another dimension than we do as thinkers. It is this problem of diverse dimensions to which Karl Heim dedicated his life work.

George Schrader

To my regret it was not granted me to meet Professor Schrader personally. However, what he writes in his essay I regard as precisely that which he considers impossible, a piece of Christian philosophy. I could hardly wish a better, more understanding, or, to me, more interesting conversation partner. His presentation and his critique derive from a basic view common to both of us, which does not need to be elaborated here. Personally I have never claimed to be a philosopher, although I agree with Schrader from the outset that I have probably often overstepped my limits as theologian, and that in my writings concerning critical philosophy I am very probably too uncritical. I am glad to let the philosopher "rap my knuckles" when he catches me crossing such a boundary. But I should like to have Professor Schrader reflect on this, that in addition to him I have two other renowned philosophers as conversation partners, who now and then give me a word of criticism with great philosophical competence, but whose critique sounds completely different from that of Schrader. One of them is the Basel philosopher Heinrich Barth, who recently published a work which I consider highly significant, his *Philosophie der Erscheinung* (Philosophy of Appearance), behind which stands the philosophy of Plato, Augustine, the medieval scholastics, and the neo-Kantian tradition of the Marburg school. The other is the Lausanne philosopher Pierre Thevenaz, who recently died, unfortunately much too soon, and who left two posthumously published volumes, *L'Homme et sa Raison* (Man and His Reason). In conversation with both of these—who also differed widely from each other—whatever I may have brought up philosophically has been critically elucidated from a completely different philosophical point of view. But one thing has become very clear to me in conversations with all three; the task of the theologian is completely different from that of the philosopher.

Now after I have fundamentally admitted, with full conviction and truthfulness, my limits and occasional boundary crossings, I may perhaps also be allowed to point out to Professor Schrader the limits of his competence. (Indeed, I know of no thinker who combines both competences. The one who comes closest to this idea is perhaps Paul Tillich. But I have just shown what sort of reservations I have to register as theologian against his *theology*). Professor Schrader would probably not have written several of his statements if when formulating his essay he had had available not only my book, *Revelation and Reason,* and the very early lecture, *Philosophie und Offenbarung* (1924), but also several others of my later works, above all *The Divine-Human Encounter* and *Man in Revolt,* as well as the anthropological portion of my *Dogmatics* (Vol. II,

Chs. 2-4). There, for example, I have explained very clearly that man is not pure subject, but simultaneously object and subject.

As theologian I have recognized it as my duty to look at the standpoint of philosophy from the standpoint of faith. Thereby it proves unavoidable that the theologian himself philosophizes, that is, that he thinks as much as possible without presuppositions. That he still remains dilettante in this, however, is just as clear to me as that the same applies to the philosopher who writes about faith. Epistemology, perhaps also metaphysics, is secondary from the perspective of faith, no matter how primary they may appear to the philosopher. It may well be that in an uncritical way I have up to now drawn the limits too narrowly around philosophy. But there is one point I now would make emphatically: the God grasped by faith is not the same as the one who can be grasped by man with his reason. The God of faith can only be grasped in his self-communication, through faith. Thus there remains the basic question whether what the philosopher says about God on the basis of his thinking and experience can be acknowledged by faith in any form that will not do violence to the thinking of the philosopher, or whether it is perhaps possible that what the philosopher as such can validly know can be included or incorporated into what faith says about God. From the perspective of faith only the first of these two possibilities can be accepted. But this does not mean the same as the medieval expression, *philosophia ancilla theologiae*. Philosophy is not subordinated to the theology, but to faith, which, however, self-critically restrains itself in *philosophicis* and at the same time leaves the philosopher every freedom of thought without prejudicing his results. This is precisely what I understand by a Christian philosopher. He is not one who thinks within the boundaries laid upon him by theology, but on the contrary, one who follows only the laws of thinking and whose faith gives him the ability to use his freedom rightly.

The relationship between philosophy and theology is endangered by an uncritical concept of reason as well as by a false understanding of faith. It is incumbent on us theologians to do away with the false understanding of faith—faith as intellectual acceptance of Biblical or ecclesiastical doctrinal propositions—for the sake of the right understanding. It is incumbent on the philosopher to do away with the false concept of reason. In this double endeavor the philosopher who is a Christian and the theologian who is a thinker come together somewhere in the middle. There are still few philosophers who see the situation in this way, just as there are few theologians who have recognized the false understanding of faith. Only for such a philosopher and for such a theologian does faith make a radical critical philosophy possible. Not a Christian's theology, but his faith, is presupposed, and that means the radical self-criticism of reason. At that point, in the middle of the tunnel, where critical philosophy and self-critical faith meet, it is evident that both are under God, and therefore have a new concept not only of critical philosophy but also of self-critical faith. This point is sighted in *Revelation and Reason*, but perhaps (philosophically) it is not adequately defined there.

Reidar Hauge

Professor Hauge has understood my book, *The Divine-Human Encounter*, very well, and has also grasped its importance for theology. The main theme contained in the title, truth as encounter, is unfortunately not recognizable in the translation *The Divine-Human Encounter*. Truth as encounter is a concept of truth unknown to philosophy. Hauge rightly sees that it is not an I-Thou *philosophy* which is at its base. Far rather does it express the quintessence of the gospel: Grace and *truth came through Jesus Christ* (John 1:17). It contains a critique of the whole idealistic and intellectual Greek tradition of the Western world (see *Dogmatics*, Vol. III, Ch. 17, *Glaube und Erkenntnis* and the second edition of *Wahrheit als Begegnung*).

The questions which Hauge raises, he himself did not mean to be objections. He merely wishes clarification on two points.

1. In opposing objectivism one must not sell objective history short. That, I think, is clarified in *Dogmatics*, Vol. III. In the New Testament witness it is the historical Jesus and the history of salvation that are involved. But these as such cannot be grasped objectively, but only through faith, which for that very reason is on the one hand "radical historicity" and on the other hand something above the subject-object distinction.

2. Does not faith contain also an intellectual acceptance, a "belief-that"? This point is also clarified in *Dogmatics*, Vol. III (see chs. 13 and 16). Objective history, that which a person accepts in

faith, is indeed contained in faith but does not precede it. Faith includes historical perception within itself. But one does not need first to perceive this history and then to believe in it. The kerygma of the crucified and risen Jesus Christ, the kerygma which brings forth faith, includes history, but not in that isolation which the historian demands, that is, not separated from the witness of Christ. Faith is even imbedded in the history of revelation.

Professor Hauge also brings up the additional question concerning the unity of the formal principle (revelation) and the material principle (reconciliation). And rightly so. The answer must be: The self-communication of God rises above this distinction. It is the unity of revelation, itself an act of grace, and reconciliation, the revelation of the merciful God.

Peter Vogelsanger

Dr. Vogelsanger, by examining one aspect of my theology, namely, theology as apologetics, understands masterfully how to present the whole at the same time. Only a man who thinks theologically and simultaneously formulates my view and his own view could do this successfully. There is nothing here to respond to except to express my gratitude and to say that in every theological path I have followed I feel he has always understood me completely. This understanding, however, does not rest only on this essay, but on the lifework of Peter Vogelsanger, who founded and up to now is directing *Reformatio*. This monthly magazine for evangelical culture and politics is probably the only one of its kind. Its high level is well known, and many Christians regard its existence as a necessity. The viewpoint that Christian faith involves the whole of life has always been a main emphasis of my whole theological work. In *Reformatio* Vogelsanger represents a realism which simultaneously asserts the unconditional truth of Christ and the relative autonomy of culture and the state, and does not think that cultural, social, and political life can or should take its norms from certain faith as long as a certain "Christological ethics" holds. For thirty years I have fought for recognition of this insight, and I have found a straightforward as well as brave comrade in the person of Peter Vogelsanger.

Tetsutaro Ariga

1. The essay by Professor Ariga of Kyoto, Japan, is significant first of all because it is the only one which is formulated from the perspective of a pre-Christian situation. A Japanese must view the problems and task of theology differently from a European or an American. To be sure, Ariga is aware that the Japanese situation, too, is not simply pre-Christian but at the same time also post-Christian. This is not primarily because there is also a Christian church in Japan—even though extraordinarily small—but above all because Japan participates in modern Western civilization and culture which as such is post-Christian. There are ideas active in Japan which would not exist without Christ, and at the same time there is a dominant mentality which has arisen in conflict with Christianity. Secularism, existentialism, and nihilism are all typical post-Christian phenomena. They have spread widely among the intellectuals as well as among laborers, so that one might even ask whether a dispute with the Japanese religion (Buddhism, Shintoism, Confucianism) is relevant any more. In any case it is strongly subordinated to the confrontation with these modern currents. Perhaps it is for that very reason that my dialectic view of the relationship between Christianity and non-Christian religion, distinct from religious relativism (Troeltsch) as well as from orthodoxy and Barthianism, has become important to Ariga.

2. This is even more significant since Ariga comes from a background of complete theological liberalism (Harnack, Troeltsch). He sees the importance of my theology above all in this, that it is a *Theology of Crisis*,[2] that is, one which understands the deepest cause of the crisis of culture to be the shattering of religious foundations. Liberal theology proved to him disappointing in this very connection. Above all he was moved by two questions, the question of the historical Jesus and the question of the understanding of history. To be sure, it is well known that the question of the historical Jesus played a central role in liberal theology. But this Jesus was not the Christ of faith. In Karl Barth's theology, on the other hand, he found a message of Christ, but the question of the historical Jesus was scarcely raised. He encountered this same one-

[2] This is the title of my first publication in the English language.

sidedness in the theology of Bultmann, who considered only the Christ kerygma valid, not the historical Jesus.

Therefore my article, *Das Einmalige und der Existenzcharakter.* (The Once-ness of the Christ-Revelation and the Character of Existence, 1923-1929), showing my understanding of history and at the same time of Christian faith as the *historical* faith, gave him the lead for the proclamation of the gospel in his situation. The historical event of Jesus is unique, first of all in the relative sense of the historian, secondly also in the absolute sense of faith, the *eph hapax* of apostolic proclamation. This central point proved to him that in my dialectic understanding of history lay the answer to the problem of Japanese Christianity. But how the gospel must be proclaimed to the Japanese people on the basis of knowing Jesus as the Christ, only the Japanese themselves can say in view of their religious tradition even in its present-day forms and their modern secularism.

Anders Nygren

All of us, even those who do not say it, owe the greatest thanks to Anders Nygren for his pioneering book, *Eros and Agape.* I felt certain that he should agree with my theology as a whole, for both of us stand on the same foundation of the gospel of Jesus Christ and of the *dikaiosyne theou* as understood anew by Luther. His objection to me, in spite of all better intentions, that I, too, make theology dependent on a philosophy, namely the I-Thou philosophy of Ebner and Buber, rests on an obvious misunderstanding. What he calls I-Thou philosophy is no philosophy at all, but the center of Biblical revelation, made evident as such and formulated theologically: the name of God. This is nothing else than what Nygren himself did when he wrote *Eros and Agape:* he made clear as a criterion of Biblical thinking a central concept of the Bible which does not appear there in this sharp antithesis to the other and placed it in contrast with the idealistic Greek thought world. There can hardly be any doubt that the divine "I" and the address "thou" characterize the Biblical kerygma just as much as they are unknown to the ontological thought of the Greeks. This last applies also to the theology of Schleiermacher, above all for his *Dialectic,* in which it is especially clear that he does not think personalistically but pantheistically. My opposition to Schleiermacher is just as sharp today as it was in my book, *Die Mystik und das Wort* (Mysticism and the Word, 1924). I have nothing further in common with him than that I would not want any more than he to see an open chasm between theology and philosophy, with the uneducated believers on one side and the scientifically educated unbelievers on the other. On the contrary, however, I do believe that recognizing the fundamental distinction between the I-Thou world and the I-It world is of greatest philosophical significance. This belongs not in theology, but rather in philosophy. It is an especially important example of what I mean by Christian philosophy.

Edward A. Dowey, Jr.

There is no greater joy for a theological teacher than to see his former students become independent teachers of a kind who practice the same critical freedom toward their former professor which it was his endeavor to teach them. Radical criticism of ourselves and of our theology becomes more and more bound together with my understanding of faith. Professor Dowey can therefore be assured that his critical questions to Emil Brunner are also accepted by him with joyful satisfaction.

His first question is whether my new formulation of Christology (*Dogmatics*, Vol. II, Chs. 9-12, especially Ch. 12) in contradistinction to the formulation in my book, *The Mediator*, carries out my newly won knowledge of the truth as encounter, that is, the historical understanding of Biblical truth. This is an excellent question. Dowey begins by examining the concept, *Erfuellung der Zeit* (fullness of time) (ch. 9). (Incidentally, I think his critical comment on Cullmann is thoroughly correct.) He summarizes his observations in the negative conclusion that the facts I present on the preparation of the gospel have no theological significance. Here one can see how hard it is for a theologian to acknowledge something which —by definition—cannot be grasped in theological concepts. It is the point where Biblical realism must show itself. If it is true that God prepared the way in history for the gospel of Jesus Christ, then these preparations are facts which contribute nothing to *doctrine*. In truth, the theological significance is nil, just as the fact that Jesus was born in the year one in Galilee. But if we are serious about the Incarnation, there must be a whole series of such coincidental facts of history. To call them theologically irrelevant is nothing else than Docetism. The Christ could not have been born in China in the Han dynasty instead of in the Jewish nation, nor in Periclean Athens. God does not work in such a way that he ignores historical continuity. That is why many New Testament scholars have already called the contemporary history of Jesus the fifth gospel. The life of Jesus cannot indeed be interpreted *from* the contemporary history, but neither can it be understood *without* the contemporary history, or else he would not be true man. The historian must be able to verify that Jesus was a child of this time and of his people. This is just what is meant by the words in Galatians, "born of woman, born under the law," the continuation of "when the time had fully come . . ." (Gal. 4:4). The historian explicates this by stating the contemporary history. The believer cautiously follows the clues of divine providence. I should like to reply to my former student Dowey: Do not despise the *historical* meaning of the words, "when the time had fully come," since this meaning is the recognizable side of the preparation of world history for the coming of the Redeemer.

Dowey's chief objection concerns the doctrine of the Redeemer's person (*Dogmatics,* Vol. II, Ch. 12). In the previous chapters —Dowey maintains—Emil Brunner has carried out his personalistic program, and thereby the chapter on the person of Christ is superfluous. It consists only in repetitions and polemics. But what Dowey calls polemics is actually the proof that orthodox doctrine replaces the verb with the substantive, the act of God with the doctrine of the divine nature of Christ. This proof is necessary and not at all superfluous, bringing new insights into the *beneficia Dei*. Even if its contents are of a negative sort, these negations are still necessary as supplement to what precedes them. Dowey's challenge, "Take more seriously the union of work and person," corresponds precisely to my own opinion. Orthodox dogmatics hinders the right understanding of the New Testament. That is why the destruction of the orthodox concepts is the necessary correlate to the positive work in the chapter, *Ueber das Werk Christi* (On the Work of Christ). The books by Hendry and Wolf which Dowey cites are unfamiliar to me. Perhaps they have both done what I should have done and which since has been included in *Dogmatics III*.

Dowey's expression, "personalist voluntarist," I do not understand. If he thereby means that the truth involved is identical with the act of God, then I agree. But if voluntarism should mean an ethicism, I must object. It is primarily God's and only secondarily man's action which is involved. However, in his whole critique Dowey rightly perceives that this chapter needs a new revision more than any other.

Georges Florovsky

I would need a large book to answer Professor Florovsky's questions adequately. He attacks mainly two major errors of my theology: the gnostic conception of history and the lack of any doctrine of hell.

1. First of all, concerning my conception of history, I should like to emphasize above all that I have indeed not treated this theme sufficiently, since I do not regard it as one belonging to dogmatics but to (Christian) philosophy. It is a theme unknown to the Bible. And yet I should like to point out—as the article by Ariga has already shown—that as early as 1929 in my essay *Das Einmalige und der Existenzcharakter* I sketched a Christian philosophy of history in discussion with the Neo-Kantian Cassirer (*Blätter für deutsche Philosophie*, 1929). On the other hand, I agree with Florovsky's criticism of my book, *The Mediator*, in which, as I had already acknowledged long ago in my answer to Althaus, my view of the humanity of Jesus was indeed Docetic. Since then, especially in *Dogmatics*, Vol. II, I have established my modified view and applied it in Christology.

Although Florovsky reproaches me with not taking history seriously enough, it appears to me that our interpretations are actually very similar. Most recently (*Dogmatics*, Vol. III, Part 4, Ch. 4) I have expounded my view as being determined by the parable of the tares among the wheat. The kingdom of God grows in the midst of human history, especially in the *ekklesía* but also wherever something of Jesus' Spirit has penetrated the world and its history, for example in the form of (worldly) justice and the recognition of human dignity. But it is not only the kingdom of God which grows, but simultaneously also the seed of the devil. This distinguishes the Christian view of history from every kind of idealistic view (Hegel). If Florovsky reproaches me with Docetism, that is, that the divine-human character of the historical process does not receive full treatment, then I for my part would conjecture a certain Hegelianism in him, paying too little attention to the diabolical traces in the course of history. And yet these are differences in accent more than any basic distinction. On the other hand, I should like to point out that the doctrine of parthenogenesis, which is close to the heart of every Greek Orthodox for the sake of the *theotokos,* contains a decisive Docetic tendency, since a man who has a human mother but no human father is not true man. This Docetism infects the whole theology based on the Apostles' Creed. The New Testament proclamation of Christ, as is well known, does not contain this singular idea, neither in Paul nor in John, the latter witnessing most powerfully to the deity of Jesus.

2. Florovsky's other objection concerns eschatology. Before I answer his critical statements, I should like to emphasize that they come from a viewpoint for the most part common to both of us. What unites me with Florovsky is the conviction that we must not "interpret" the New Testament's own futuristic eschatology whether with the "realized eschatology" of Dodd or with that of Bultmann, because this interpretation finally amounts to nothing else than *replacing* eschatology with a "radical understanding of *history*" (see Bultmann's *Geschichte und Eschatologie* [Theology and Eschatology], 1958). As important as the latter may be, it is obviously something different from the eternal life in perfect sonship with God, as the apostles proclaim it. This must be said especially to the American theologians, who reject every such futuristic eschatological proclamation as an invitation to flee the world and to withdraw from the tasks of social ethics.

Florovsky's criticism refers to the doctrine of Judgment Day and/or hell. Judgment is indeed to be taken seriously if one would take "redemption" seriously. But a doctrine that there *is* a state of eternal perdition appears to me incommensurate with the meaning of the judgment passages. The existence of a hell is no element of Christian hope. When Florovsky says that God does not simply break human opposition against his will, the idea that the kingdom of God is God's fulfilled will stands in contradiction to it. If God has done away with *my* opposition without doing me violence, why should he not do away with *all* opposition in the same way? That is why I teach both the *apokatastasis,* the universal reconciliation as expressed by Paul *and* the ultimate judgment. How both are to be thought of together I have expounded in *Dogmatics,* Vol. III, Part 4, ch. 10.

Dale Moody

The essay by Dr. Moody puts me into a rather embarrassing situation. I shall never forget how our acquaintanceship and friendship began. When I was at McCormick Seminary in Chicago holding the Zenos Lectures on "The Scandal of Christianity," suddenly a group of hearers appeared whose leader introduced himself as Dr. Dale Moody from the Baptist Seminary in Louisville. They had flown up from the South just for my lectures. In his enthusiasm Moody persuaded me to give lectures with discussion at his seminary, too, which was familiar to me as the largest of all theological schools, but strongly fundamentalistic. Dr. Moody has since then fought a brave and successful battle for an open-minded and ecumenical theology. From this it is understandable that he has worked out the theme, "The Church in Theology," in a way which reveals not only his thorough knowledge, but also a great understanding for my theological intentions. I think I would not be in error if I call him the theologian best informed on my theological works.

On the other hand, his essay is different from all the others in this book in its thoroughness of a kind the others in this symposium did not attempt, which allows it to reveal more of his fundamentalistic Baptist past than it was his own intention to do. The fundamentalists, to whom Dr. Moody otherwise in no way any more belongs, think in terms of theological tenets which can be taken out of any context (see, for example, the book *Revelation and the Bible*, ed. by F. H. Henry). This makes itself felt in Moody's essay, for instance, when he can cite these individual "tenets" with chapter and verse.

Small errors in regard to facts are scarcely worth mentioning (for example, I did not learn to know Blumhardt through Kutter and Ragaz, but knew him from my youth), but the following weighty error is completely incomprehensible to me. Moody asserts there is an unmistakable parallel between the view of Martin Werner (Bern) who considers the Christology of the New Testament an illusion, and my teaching in *The Misunderstanding of the Church*. In point of fact, the distinction between *ekklesia* and church is founded on the New Testament, namely on Paul (see *Dogmatics*, Vol. III, chs. 2 and 3). What Moody's critique probably rests upon is the following. As a convinced Baptist he has read into the New Testament the idea of the free church, consequently identifying the *ekklesía* with the Baptist free church, and therefore he must view my *Misunderstanding of the Church* as church-destroying. This false understanding was indeed suggested by that book, but is now no longer possible since *Dogmatics*, Vol. III, has appeared. What I call *ekklesía* is the Pauline *idea* of church which is critical of all church institutions as such, but should absolutely not be understood as rejection of organized churches. I am concerned with the Biblical *self-understanding* of the *ekklesía*, next to which the question of organization takes second place. The evil I turn against is the confusion of any church at all with the *ekklesía* of the New Testament, that is, the life in community with each other based on communion with God generated by God's Spirit.

I am in full agreement with his concluding sentence, that it would be better "to vitalize [church] forms through the Spirit than to end in unorganized chaos." And yet the second part of this sentence proves precisely that Moody has interpreted the meaning of my *ekklesía* concept not as a critical idea, but as a demand to reject all organized churches, as I already stated above. Here I can only give assurance of something which is unmistakably clear in *Dogmatics*, Vol. III, that I am no enthusiast who forgets that the life of the *ekklesía* fellowship cannot exist without organization. I only want to show that the organizational form as such, whether it be church, free church, or brotherhood, is not what is understood in the New Testament, more precisely in Paul, by the word *ekklesía*, and that the basic evil in all ages has consisted in viewing these organized forms as something holy.

On this basis one must also understand my criticisms of the Catholic and Protestant concepts of sacrament, for it was and is, after all, their false view and emphasis upon the sacrament which necessarily led to this misunderstanding. The question of infant baptism, which is part of the Credo for Baptists, has no decisive importance for me. As soon as one does not view it as a sacrament, that is, an imparting of salvation, I have nothing to say against it. On the contrary, I agree with the Baptist that the New Testament, whenever it *teaches* about the meaning of baptism, is always and only thinking of the baptism of believers.

N. H. Søe

In his essay on "Personal Ethics of Emil Brunner," Professor Søe has pursued the chief motives of my ethical works with greatest exactness and competence, and I must consequently declare unreservedly that he has done me justice. Therefore the questions he asks are not foreign to me, but are such as I myself ask again and again. One of the most important he himself has answered (p. 251), indeed in full agreement with me. It is the question whether the Christian and the non-Christian understandings of responsibility are the same. He cites as answer a sentence from *Man in Revolt:* "But the concept of responsibility is either a Christian or a non-Christian, a legalistic-autonomous one or a concept born out of Christian faith." This sentence I would formulate today in a somewhat more differentiated way. The non-Christian cannot indeed know what the *full* meaning of agape is, nor that it is nothing other than agape to which man is called. Only the Christian knows that self-giving love is the end of the law, in the double sense of the word *telos,* as purpose and as end. Only he knows the source of this love that only in Christ is it given and therefore real. But it would be foolish to maintain that the non-Christian knew nothing at all of agape, of self-giving love. While the representative of autonomous ethics tends to confuse agape with human love in general, Protestant, specifically Lutheran, ethicists usually fall into the opposite mistake of positing a crass opposition. Søe sees very well that neither the one nor the other is right. "Only through Christ we know what *true* responsibility, real communion, and therefore what *true* love means." The difference between Christian and non-Christian lies not so much in knowledge as such, but in the radicality of their understanding of love and in the assertion of its sole ultimate validity.

A second question (p. 252) asks whether it is true that "love of God simply means love of your neighbor." Søe is right to deny this. Jesus' double command is not only clearly double, but also "there is a commandment of love of God relatively distinct from love of our neighbor" (pp. 252-53). The question Søe raises in a footnote on page 252, whether at our time it would not be necessary to emphasize the positive meaning of agape, I answer in the same way as he does.

Finally, the problem brought up on page 259 is indeed of the greatest significance: motive and deed. It is clear above all in my social ethics that I do not succumb to the danger that Søe calls by the name *Gesinnungeethik*, that is, an ethics in which the purity of one's motive alone is important. On the contrary, in ethics I am so concerned about practical realization that I have dared to make and elaborate on this statement: The necessary goal demands the necessary means. For this very reason I take a sharp and clear position against totalitarian Communism; for this very reason I am not a pacifist and I am against a unilateral disarmament even of nuclear arms. Thereby my ethics gains the reputation among many of not being "Christian enough." My opposing thesis is this: The love of Christ should be the *motive* of all action, but not the *rule* for the action. The latter is rather to be derived from the situation. That is why my ethics is titled *Das Gebot und die Ordnungen*, the meaning of which the title of the translation, *The Divine Imperative*, does not make sufficiently clear. *What* is to be done results from the given situation; *why* something is to be done results from the love of Christ. Therefore the Christian may not stand under the law, which always normifies the situation in advance. This is particularly clear in social ethics. The Christian must assent to the state, in spite of the fact that he thereby assents to police, to military, and to retributory justice. Agape in its purity can be applied only in individual and personal areas, but even there only brokenly by virtue of the relationships in which we humans always stand. The agape active in faith in Christ can and must, so to say, be transformed into what we call justice. The principle then is this: Appropriate action out of love.

Reinhold Niebuhr

Although I have always respected Reinhold Niebuhr as a great Christian thinker, above all as a prophetic awakener of the social conscience, I regret to say that I cannot agree completely with any of his critical statements. Much of what he brings out in his essay on my social ethics appears to me to rest on misunderstandings. Above all he takes offense in my concept of *Schopfungsordnung* that is ("order of creation"), which appears to him too static, too little related to the changing historical situation. Perhaps the English translation of my book, *The Divine Imperative*, is partly at fault. It does not reveal, as did the original title, *Das Gebot und die*

Ordnungen, that the commandment (of God) stands *above* the orders of creation, and on the other hand that these are to be understood as pointing only to the commandment of the moment. And yet I must agree with Niebuhr's critique in this, that this concept is not clearly enough formulated. On the other hand, I have always thought Niebuhr's identification of my social ethics with the Roman Catholic doctrine of natural law was a false interpretation of my intentions. In *The Divine Imperative,* indeed more strongly in *Justice and the Social Order,* I have already emphasized that the orders of creation are always to be discerned anew from the historical situation, and therefore may never be considered as rigid law. They are a revolutionary as well as a conservative principle.

What is meant by this concept becomes most clear from the use Jesus made of it in Mark 10:1 ff. in regard to marriage. I have no desire hereby to repristinate Luther's ethics, as Niebuhr believes; he views Luther's ethics much too strongly in the light of Ernst Troeltsch's interpretation, who notoriously did not understand it properly. From Mark 10, however, it is clear that Jesus derived the essence of the sex relationship from the given facts of creation and thus elevated them to a normative ethical principle. Not out of agape, but out of this material principle is monogamy established as the idea of marriage, but this itself may not be interpreted, as do Roman Catholic ethicists, as law. Jesus does not mean to say that marriage is legally undivorceable. His words give an explanation of the essence of marriage based on the will of the Creator, and they are therefore not to be understood as law.

In a similar way I establish in *Justice and the Social Order* my rejection of egalitarianism. Not that equality is not an essential aspect of justice, but that this equality must be tempered and modified with creaturely unlikeness (not inequality!). This distinction between inequality and unlikeness is the main thought of my concept of justice. Niebuhr pays no attention to it at all. The first is related to the *essence* of man and is therefore fundamental; the second is related to his *function* in society and is therefore always subordinate to the first.

Niebuhr rightly objects to my sentence, "A system which actually maintains order is the best as long as a better order cannot be maintained without a break in continuity." As Niebuhr interprets this sentence, every revolution would thereby be ethically excluded, but this is not what I mean at all. However tyranny and anarchy are indeed on different levels. Even revolution desires a better *order*. Anarchy, on the other hand, is chaos, and as such it is absolutely reprehensible, being also, by the way, only transitorily *possible*.

Revolution as principle *(la révolution permanente)* leads, as we see today, to the totalitarian state.

In conclusion, may I say that I stand much closer to Niebuhr's own ethics than he supposes, closer than his picture of my ethics reveals. Perhaps this will be clearer from the chapters *Das Liebesgebot und das Gesetz* and *Der Christ in der Welt* (*Dogmatics*, Vol. III, pp. 344 ff. and 353 ff.). There I have said in detail that the law of love creates no standard and that no social-ethical system can be derived from it. Such a thing is possible only when agape is replaced by the rational principle of respecting the equal human dignity in every man. This rational principle of Stoic and Kantian ethics is indeed suitable to become the basis of a social ethic, and this is what most American theologians mean when they speak of the commandment of love.

Werner Kägi

When Max Huber, the great Christian jurist, former president of The Hague Supreme Court and president of the International Red Cross, retired from public life, it was an unusual stroke of good fortune for Switzerland and for ecumenicity that there was a man ready and capable to fill the great gap: Professor Werner Kägi, called from the University of Zurich to the chair of Max Huber and elected by the ecumene as vice-president of the Church Commission for International Affairs (CCIA). From his essay, "Emil Brunner's Contribution to Judicial and Governmental Thought in Times of Threat" we can recognize the important jurist, the admonisher in the confused din of voices, the courageous and clear-thinking Christian which he has proved himself to be in the last decade and a half.

As in all times, it is also true today that precisely the serious Christians are tempted to misunderstand the gospel of love and peace in the sense of Communism and pacifism, and thereby to betray humanity to the totalitarian state striving for world control. In the intellectual battle against this fatal confusion I am completely united with Werner Kägi, the Christian jurist and statesman, and for more than ten years I have fought beside him to prevent the flow of political defeatism into the Christian church. At the base of our thinking were the statements of the apostle Paul, who wrote Romans 13:1-7 from his understanding of the love of God. In the same way the reformers also based their political ethics on Paul.

The pacifism which thinks to be a necessary consequence of the gospel—now in the form of the demand to *unilateral* nuclear disarmament—would necessarily have the effect that Christians, without knowing or even wanting it, would be spearheading the world-rulership plans of anti-Christian powers. That is why today there is nothing so necessary as clear thinking based on faith, and more exactly, clear political thinking based on Christian faith. Nothing less is at stake than the future of free proclamation of the gospel and the *ekklesía* of Jesus Christ together with the whole humane heritage of humanity.

EMIL BRUNNER

ZURICH, SWITZERLAND

IV

BIBLIOGRAPHY OF THE WRITINGS
OF EMIL BRUNNER

BIBLIOGRAPHY OF THE WRITINGS
OF EMIL BRUNNER TO 1962 *

1914

Das Symbolische in der religiösen Erkenntnis. Beiträge zu einer Theorie des religiösen Erkennens. V–XI, 136 S., Tübingen, Mohr, 1914.

1915

Von Gottesreich und Weltreich. Ein Gedankenaustausch. E. Brunner und L. Ragaz. In: Neue Wege. 9, 1915, Nr. 7.

1916

Geist (Zum Pfingstfest). In: Gemeindeblatt für die ref. Kirchgemeinden des Kantons Glarus. 3, 1916, Nr. 6.

Grundsätzliches zum Kapitel «Die jungen Theologen.» In: Kirchenblatt für die ref. Schweiz. 31, 1916, Nr. 15.

1917

Ein offenes Wort an die Männer und Frauen von Obstalden und Filzbach. Zum Bettag, 1917. 8 S., Obstalden, Selbstverlag, 1917.

Das Unbedingte und die Wirklichkeit, unser Problem. In: Neue Wege. 11, 1917, Heft 7.

* This bibliography was prepared in its entirety by Margrit Brunner-Lauterburg. The basic listings appeared in the *Festschrift for Emil Brunner on His Seventieth Birthday,* (Zürich: Zwingli Verlag, 1959). We gratefully acknowledge the permission granted by Zwingli Verlag to use that material. Frau Brunner has not only made certain minor changes but has prepared two additional sections, one of which brings the bibliography into 1962, the other of which lists the main works which appear in English. Because we believe the latter will be especially useful to English-speaking readers throughout the world, it is included as a separate and closing section. The numbered items—books, articles, lectures, interviews—are available in English.

C.W.K.

1918

Etwas vom Konfirmandenunterricht. In: Gemeindeblatt für die ref. Kirchgemeinden des Kantons Glarus. 5, 1918, Nr. 3.

Mädchenbund. Stimmen zur Frauenbewegung. In: Korrespondenzblatt studierender Abstinenten. 22, 1918, Nr. 5.

Konservativ oder Radikal? In: Neue Wege. 12, 1918, Heft 2.

Die Kirche und die sozialen Forderungen der Gegenwart. In: Glarner Nachrichten, 1918, (16. Dezember).

1919

Worauf es ankommt. In: Glarner Nachrichten, 1919 (3. März).

Rezension von: Karl Barth, «Der Römerbrief.» In: Kirchenblatt für die ref. Schweiz. 34, 1919, Nr. 8.

Denken und Erleben. In: Vorträge an der Aarauer Studentenkonferenz, 1919. Basel, Kober, 1919, S. 5–34.

1. "Religious Socialism in Switzerland." In: *The Social Preparation.* 1919/20, 14/15.

1920

Das Elend der Theologie. Ein Nachwort zum Zürcher Ferienkurs, zugleich ein Vorwort. In: Kirchenblatt für die ref. Schweiz. 35, 1920, Nr.50/51.

Aus dem weniger bekannten Amerika. In: Kirchenblatt für die ref. Schweiz. 35, 1920, Nr. 37–39.

Die denkwürdige Geschichte der Mayflower-Pilgerväter. 88 S. Mit 9 Illustrationen nach zeitgenössischen Darstellungen. Basel, Reinhardt, 1920.

1921

2. *Rezension,* unter dem Titel *The Decline of the Occident,* von: Spengler, «Untergang des Abendlandes.» In: *The World Tomorrow,* November 1921.

Erlebnis, Erkenntnis und Glaube. VII, 127 S., Tübingen, Mohr, 1921. 2. und 3. neubearb. Auflage, VII, 132 S., 1923. 4. und 5. unveränd. Auflage, 1933. Zürich, Zwingli-Verlag, 1938.

1922

Die Grenzen der Humanität. Habilitationsvorlesung an der Universität Zürich. 27 S. Sammlung gemeinverständlicher Vorträge und Schriften aus dem Gebiete der Theologie und Religionsgeschichte, Tübingen, Mohr, 1922, Heft 102. Trad. Tokyo, Kobundo, 1952.

Die Krisis der Religion. In: Kirchenblatt für die ref. Schweiz. 37, 1922, Nr. 17.

1923

Ist die sogenannte kritische Theologie wirklich kritisch? In: Kirchenblatt für die ref. Schweiz. 36, 1923, Nr. 26/27.

1924

Auch eine Geheimschrift. Biblische Betrachtung. In: Gemeindeblatt für die ref. Kirchgemeinden des Kantons Glarus. 11, 1924, Nr. 2.

Die Mystik und das Wort. Der Gegensatz zwischen moderner Religionsauffassung und christlichem Glauben, dargestellt an der Theologie Schleiermachers. IV, 396 S., Tübingen, Mohr, 1924. 2. stark veränd. Auflage, VIII, 399 S., 1928, Zürich, Zwingli-Verlag, 1938.

Vom Dollar, vom Christentum und einigem andern in Amerika. In: Zwinglikalender 1924, Basel, Reinhardt.

Das Grundproblem der Philosophie bei Kant und Kierkegaard. Vortrag vor der Kantgesellschaft in Utrecht, Dez. 1923. In: Zwischen den Zeiten. 2. 1924, Heft VI.

1925

Was heißt: Erbaut auf dem Grunde der Apostel und Propheten? In: Verhandlungen der Schweiz. ref. Predigergesellschaft. 1925, S. 34–53.

Reformation und Romantik. Vortrag, gehalten bei der Tagung der Luthergesellschaft in München. 27 S., München, Kaiser, 1925. Trad. Nagoya, Ichiryusha, 1934.

Philosophie und Offenbarung. Die Offenbarung als Grund und Gegenstand der Theologie. Antrittsrede an der Universität Zürich, 17. Januar 1925. 2. Gnosis und Glaube. 3. Auf das Buchzeichen des Lesers. 52 S., Tübingen, Mohr, 1925. Zürich, Zwingli-Verlag, 1938. Trad. in: Philosophie und Theologie. Tokyo, Shinseido, 1936.

Gesetz und Offenbarung. Eine theologische Grundlegung. In: Theologische Blätter, 4, 1925, Nr. 3.

Geschichte oder Offenbarung? Ein Wort der Entgegnung an Horst Stephan. In: Zeitschrift für Theologie und Kirche. 6, 1925, Heft 4.

Von guten und von schlechten Predigten. In: Zwinglikalender 1925. Basel, Reinhardt.

1926

3. Die Absolutheit Jesu. In: Vorträge, gehalten auf der 29. Aarauer Studentenkonferenz, 1926. Berlin, Furche-Verlag, 1926, S. 39–64. SA. 2. Aufl., 28 S., Stimmen aus der deutschen christlichen Studentenbewegung, Heft 47. Berlin, Furche-Verlag, 1932. 3. Aufl. 1934. Trans. In:

The Union Seminary Review. 46, 1935, Nr. 4. Trans. Tokyo, Shinseido, 1935.

Die Erde dreht sich. Eine Erwiderung. (Betrifft einen Aufsatz von Ludwig Köhler über den Sündenfall.) In: Kirchenblatt für die ref. Schweiz. 41, 1926, Nr. 29.

Duplik. (Betrifft die Auseinandersetzung mit. L. Köhler.) In: Kirchenblatt für die ref. Schweiz. 41, 1926, Nr. 36, (vgl. Nr. 29).

Christlicher Glaube nach reformierter Lehre. In: Der Protestantismus der Gegenwart. S. 235–269, Stuttgart, Bohnenberger, 1926.

Theozentrische Theologie? Eine Bemerkung zu Schäders «Geistproblem der Theologie.» In: Zwischen den Zeiten. 4, 1926, Heft 2.

Der Sündenfall und die alttestamentliche Wissenschaft. In: Christliche Welt. 40, 1926, Nr. 20.

Die Aufgabe der Christen an der Welt. Ansprache in der St. Annakapelle an der Allianzwoche 1926. In: Monatsblatt der Evang. Gesellschaft des Kantons Zürich. 9, 1926, Nr. 2.

Gibt es geistliches Recht? In: Kirchenblatt für die ref. Schweiz. 41, 1926, Nr. 9.

Der Geist und die Triebe in der Geschichte. In: Neue Zürcher Zeitung, 1926, Nr. 999, (Juni).

Vom Rätsel Mensch. In: Gemeindeblatt für die ref. Kirchgemeinden des Kantons Glarus. 13, 1926, Nr. 6.

Religion oder Glaube? In: Zwinglikalender 1926. Basel, Reinhardt.

Die Kerngedanken der Reformation. Vortrag, gehalten an der Generalkonferenz des deutschschweiz. Hoffnungsbundes in der Stadtkirche Thun. Schweiz. Agentur des Blauen Kreuzes, Pflugschar. 19, 1926, Nr. 11/12.

1927

4. *Der Mittler.* Zur Besinnung über den Christusglauben. X, 565 S., Tübingen, Mohr, 1927. Zürich, Zwingli-Verlag, *1938. Trans. London, Religious Tract Society, 1934.* Trans. Tokyo, Shunyodo, 1944 (1. Buch: Voraussetzungen). *Trans. London. Lutterworth Press, 1946. Trans. Philadelphia, The Westminster Press, 1947.*

Gibt es eine allgmeine neutrale Staatsmoral? In: Neue Zürcher Zeitung. 1927, Nr. 77, (Januar).

H. Kutter. Beitrag zur Rundfrage der Neuen Zürcher Zeitung «Die Schweiz im Buch.» In: Neue Zürcher Zeitung. 1927, Nr. 641 (April).

Der wiedergefundene Bauplan. In: Zwinglikalender 1927. Basel, Reinhardt.

Inspiration und Offenbarung. Vortrag. In: Der Kirchenfreund. 61, 1927, Nr. 1, 3, 4.

5. *Religionphilosophie protestantischer Theologie.* In: Handbuch der Phi-

losophie. 99 S., München, R. Oldenbourg, 1927. 2. unveränd. Aufl. München, Leibniz-Verlag, 1948. Trans. (Umschreibung) Tokyo, Hyoronsha, 1934. Trans. London, Ivor Nicholson and Watson. International Library of Christian Knowledge, 1937. Trans. Seoul, Methodist Theological Seminary, 1949.

Der Zorn Gottes und die Versöhnung durch Christus. In: Zwischen den Zeiten. 5, 1927, Heft 2.

1928

Gibt es eine religionslose Moral? Vortrag, gehalten an der Maiversammlung 1928 der ehemal. Schüler des Seminars Unterstraß, Zürich. In: Schweiz. evang. Schulblatt. 63, 1928, Nr. 6.

Glaube und Erziehung. In: Zwinglikalender 1928. Basel, Reinhardt.

Grisebachs Angriff auf die Theologie. In: Zwischen den Zeiten. 6, 1928, Heft 3.

6. Zachäus der Zöllner. Predigt, gehalten in der Kirche Oberstraß. In: Zwischen den Zeiten. 6, 1928, Heft 4. Trans. In: The Christian Century, 1930, Nr. 13.

Gnade Gottes: V. Dogmatisch. In: Die Religion in Geschichte und Gegenwart. Handwörterbuch für Theologie und Religionswissenschaft. 2., völlig neu bearbeitete Auflage. Tübingen, Mohr, 1928, Sp. 1261–1268.

Die Krisis im Protestantismus. In: Süddeutsche Monatshefte. 19, 1928, Nr. 9.

1929

7. The Theology of Crisis. XXVI, 118 p., New York, Scribner, 1929. Trans. Amsterdam, W. Ten Have, 1932. Trans. Tokyo, Shinseido, 1931. Trans. Seoul, The Chungku Press, 1949.

Von den Ordnungen Gottes. Vortrag im Berner Münster. IV, 16 S., Bern, Gotthelf-Verlag, 1929.

Ein seelsorgerlicher Brief. In: Zwinglikalender 1929. Basel, Reinhardt.

Rezension von: Friedrich Karl Schumann, «Der Gottesgedanke und der Zerfall der Moderne.» In: Kirchenblatt für die ref. Schweiz. 85, 1929, Nr. 20.

Zu Epprechts Kritik über «die Mystik und das Wort.» In: Kirchenblatt für die ref. Schweiz. 85, 1929, Nr. 9.

Die junge Schweiz—was wir von ihr erhoffen. In: Junge Schweiz. 5, 1929, Nr. 1.

Die andere Aufgabe der Theologie. In: Zwischen den Zeiten. 7, 1929, Heft 3.

Ein reformiertes Wort zur Feier des Marburger Religionsgespräches. Vortrag, gehalten in Marburg 1929. In: Reformiertes Kirchenblatt (Frankfurt a.M.). 10, 1929, Nr. 19. In: Neuwerk. 11, 1929, Nr. 7/8.

Psychologie und Weltanschauung. Vortrag in der philosophischen Gesellschaft Zürich, 13. Febr. 1928. In: Neue Schweizer Rundschau. 22, 1929, Heft 1.

Das Einmalige und der Existenzcharakter. In: Blätter für Deutsche Philosophie. 3, 1929, Heft 3. Trans. Tokyo, Kobundo, 1952.

Theologie und Gemeinschaft. In: Neue Wege. 23, 1929, Heft 9.

Der heilige Name. Predigt, gehalten am 18. Nov. 1928 in der Kirche Oberstrass in Zürich. In: Zwischen den Zeiten. 7, 1929, Heft 1.

Zur Sozialethik. In: Kirchenblatt für die ref. Schweiz. 85, 1929, Nr. 21.

Glaube und Leben. Zwei Vorträge aus der Vorlesung an der Volkschochschule Zürich, Wintersem. 1929/30. In: Der Kirchenfreund. 64, 1930, Nr. 10, 11, 14.

Rezension, unter dem Titel *Zur evang. Ethik und Wirtschaftsethik,* von: Georg Wünsch, «Evang. Wirtschaftsethik.» In: Kirchenblatt für die ref. Schweiz. 85, 1929, Nr. 7.

1930

8. Gott und Mensch. Vier Untersuchungen über das personhafte Sein. Vorträge. 1. Die Gottesidee der Philosophen und der Schöpfergott des Glaubens. 2. Der Rechtfertigungsglaube und das Problem der Ethik. 3. Kirche und Offenbarung. 4. Biblische Psychologie. 100 S., Tübingen, Mohr, 1930. *Trans. London, Student Christian Movement Press, 1936.* Zürich, Zwingli-Verlag, 1938.

9. Der Säkularismus als Problem der Kirche. Eingangsvortrag zu einer missiontheologischen Konferenz, Basel, Frühjahr 1930. In: Unser Blatt. 1, 1930, Nr. 3. *Trans. in: The International Review of Missions, 19, 1930, Nr. 76.*

Die Botschaft Sören Kierkegaards. Rede vor dem Lesezirkel Hottingen Zürich. In: Neue Schweizer Rundschau. 23, 1930, Heft 2.

Gott und das Brot. Predigt über Mat. 4, 1–4. 14 S., Bern, Gotthelf-Verlag, 1930.

Jazz und Grammophon im Gottesdienst. In: Kirchenblatt für die Schwiez. 86, 1930, Nr. 10.

Der christliche Glaube als Grundlage der Erziehung. In: Schweiz. evang. Schulblatt. 65, 1930, Nr. 46.

10. Die Bedeutung des Alten Testamentes für unsern Glauben. In: Zwischen den Zeiten. 8, 1930, Heft 1. Trans. in: Philosophie und Theologie. Tokyo, Shinseido, 1936. *Trans. in: The Lutheran Church Quarterly. July 1947.*

Aus der Tiefe. Predigt in der Universitätskirche Marburg am 15. Sept. 1929. In: Zwischen den Zeiten. 8, 1930, Heft 2.

Der Erfüller. Predigt, gehalten in Basel am 25. Mai 1930. In: Zwischen den Zeiten. 8, 1930, Heft 4.

Theologie und Kirche. In: Zwischen den Zeiten. 8, 1930, Heft 5.

Begegnung mit Kierkegaard. In: Der Lesezirkel (Zürich). 17, 1930, Heft 3.

11. The Crisis of Psychology. *In: The Student World. 23, 1930, Nr. 1.* World's Student Christian Federation, Geneva.

1931

Das Grundproblem der Ethik. 30 S., Zürich, Rascher, 1931. Trans. Tokyo, Shinseido, 1933. Kobundo, 1952. Trans. Aarhus, Unges Forlag, 1935.

Erhalt' uns Herr, bei deinem Wort! Evangelische Andachten für jeden Tag. Berlin, Furche-Verlag, 1931, S. 240–262.

Volk und Kirche. In: Zwinglikalender 1931. Basel, Reinhardt.

Simon der Zauberer. Apg. 8, 9–24. In: Kirchenblatt für die ref. Schweiz. 87, 1931, Nr. 13.

Theologie und Ontologie—oder die Theologie am Scheidewege. In: Zeitschrift für Theologie und Kirche. N.F. 12, 1931, Heft 2.

12. The Word and the World. *IV, 127 p.,* London, Student Christian Movement Press, 1931. Trans. Amsterdam, W. Ten Have, 1931. Trans. Aarhus, Kobenhavn, De Unges Forlag, 1931. Trans. Tokyo, Shinseido, 1932. Trans. Lausanne, La Concorde, 1937. Trans. Seoul, The Chungku Press, 1949.

Das Haus Gottes. Andacht anlässlich der Pfarrkonferenz am 9. April 1931. In: Kirchenblatt für die ref. Schweiz. 87, 1931, Nr. 12.

Rezension von: Oskar Bauhofer, «Eine Religionsphilosophie vom Standpunkt der Offenbarung aus.» In: Kirchenblatt für die ref. Schweiz. 87, 1931, Nr. 11.

Die Christusbotschaft im Kampf mit den Religionen. 20 S., Stuttgart, Evang. Missionsverlag, 1931.

13. Is Jesus Coming? In: *The Christian Century, 1931, Nr. 51.*

1932

14. Das Gebot und die Ordnungen. Entwurf einer protestantisch-theologischen Ethik. XII, 696 S., Tübingen, Mohr, 1932. 3., unveränd. Aufl., Zürich, Zwingli-Verlag, 1939. *Trans. London, Religious Tract Society, 1934. Trans. London, Lutterworth Press, 1947. Trans. Philadelphia, The Westminster Press, 1947.*

Das Geld und der Haushalt Gottes. Ein seltsamer Katechismus. In: Zwinglikalender 1932. Basel, Reinhardt.

Die Frage nach dem «Anknüpfungspunkt» als Problem der Theologie. In: Zwischen den Zeiten. 10, 1932, Heft 6.

Rezension von A. Sannwald, «Der Begriff der 'Dialektik' und die Anthropologie.» In: Zwischen den Zeiten. 10, 1932, Heft 6.

Familie und reformatorischer Glaube. In: Atlantis. 4, 1932, Heft 12.

Meine Begegnung mit der Oxforder-Gruppenbewegung. In: Kirchenblatt für die ref. Schweiz. 88, 1932, Nr. 22/23. SA. 31 S., Basel, Reinhardt, 1932.

1933

Der Staat als Problem der Kirche. 20 S., Bern, Gotthelf-Verlag, 1933.
Eros und Liebe. In: Neue Schweizer Rundschau. N.F. I. 1933, Heft 5. SA. 45 S. Furche-Bücherei Nr. 32, Berlin, Furche-Verlag, 1937. Trans. Amsterdam, H. J. Paris, 1938.
Das wahre Volk. Predigt am Reformationssonntag 1933. 7 S., Bern, Gotthelf-Verlag, 1933.
Die reformatorische Botschaft und die Wirtschaftsfrage. 16 S., Bern, Gotthelf-Verlag, 1933.
Die Bedeutung des Abendmahls. 16 S., Bern, Gotthelf-Verlag, 1933.
Die Bedeutung der missionarischen Erfahrung für die Theologie. In: Die deutsche evangelishche Heidenmission, Jahrbuch 1933 der vereinigten deutschen Missionskonferenzen. Hamburg, Selbstverlag der Missionskonferenzen, 1933, S. 3–11.
Hochschule und Gymnasium. In: Jahrbuch des Vereins Schweiz. Gymnasiallehrer, Jahrg. 1932, Aarau, Sauerländer, 1933, S. 40–44.

1934

15. *Natur und Gnade. Zum Gespräch mit Karl Barth.* 44 S., Tübingen, Mohr, 1934. 2., erweiterte Aufl., VII, 60 S., 1935; dasselbe Zürich, Zwingli-Verlag, 1938. *Trans in: Natural Theology, comprising «Nature and Grace» by Professor Dr. Emil Brunner and the reply «No!» by Dr. Karl Barth. London, Geoffrey Bles: The Centenary Press, 1946, S. 15–64.*
Das Übernationale. In: Neue Schweizer Rundschau. N.F., 2, 1934, Heft 2.
Die Kirche als Frage und Aufgabe der Gegenwart. Vortrag im Kantonalzürcherischen Pfarrverein, 20. Mai 1934. 27 S., Bern und Leipzig. Gotthelf-Verlag, 1934. SA. aus: Um die Erneuerung der Kirche. 1934.
Um die Erneuerung der Kirche. Ein Wort an alle, die sie lieb haben. 60 S., Bern, Gotthelf-Verlag, 1934. Trad. Genève, Labor, 1934.
Sollen sie also untergehen? Ansprache vom 12. Nov. 1934, als Werbung für «Kinderhilfe.» In: Gesundheit und Wohlfahrt. 1934, Heft 12.
Das grosse Wunder. Predigt, gehalten in St. Gallen am 10. Febr. 1934. 8 S., St. Gallen, Buchhdlg. der Evang. Gesellschaft, 1934.
16. *Die Unentbehrlichkeit des Alten Testaments für die missionierende Kirche.* Vortrag am Basler Missionsfest 1934. 24 S., Stuttgart und Basel, Evang. Missionsverlag, 1934. *Trans. in: The Lutheran Church Quarterly, 1947.*
Imago Dei. In: Neue Schweizer Rundschau. N.F. 2, 1934, Heft 8.

Der Christ in Staat. In: Neue Schweizer Rundschau. N.F. 1, 1934, Heft 9.

Gemeinschaft. In: Zwinglikalender 1934. Basel, Reinhardt.

Kirche und Staat (1. Artikel). *Die Kirche und das Übernationale* (2. Artikel). In: Kirche und Welt. Studien und Dokumente. 3. Bd. Die Kirche und das Staatsproblem in der Gegenwart. Genf, Forschungsabteilung des Oekumenischen Rates für praktisches Christentum, 1934, S. 11–15, 16–24. Zweite, erweiterte Auflage, 1935.

Der christliche Staatsmann. In: Festgabe für Max Huber zum 60. Geburtstag. Zürich, Berichthaus, 1934, S. 240–249.

D'abord le règne de Dieu. Trad. libre et abrégée d'une prédication à Thoune au mois d'août, lors d'une réunion nationale des groupes d'Oxford (Ch. Béguin). In: Les Cahiers Protestants. 18, 1934, Nr. 8.

1935

Was ist und was will die sogenannte Oxfordgruppe? In: Zwinglikalender 1935. Basel, Reinhardt.

17. *Unser Glaube.* Eine christliche Unterweisung. 174 S., Bern, Gotthelf-Verlag, 1935. Zürich, Zwingli-Verlag, 1940. Trans. Lausanne, La Concorde, 1935. Trans. Budapest, Sylvester Kiadàs, 1935. *Trans. New York, Charles Scribner's Sons, 1936. Trans. London, Student Christian Movement Press, 1936.* Trans. Tokyo, Shinseido, 1936. Tokyo, Shinkyo Shuppansha, 1949. Trans. Aarhus, De Unges Forlag, 1936. Trans. Amsterdam, Ten Have, 1938. Trans. Prag, SCME/YMCA, 1938. Trans. Stockholm, Svenska Kyrkans Diakonistyrelses Bokförlag, 1939. Trans. Rom, Edizioni di «Religio,» 1940. Trans. Sèvres (S. & O.), Editions «Pro Hispana,» 1949. Trans. Seoul, Chungku Press, 1949. Trans. Bandung, Badan Penerbitan, G. Kolff & Co., 1950. Trans. Oslo, Forlaget Land og Kirke, 1953. Trans. Madras, The Christian Literature Society for India, 1953. Trans. Hong Kong, The Council on Christian Literature for Overseas Chinese, 1956. Trans. Bangkok, 1958. Trans. Lahore, Punjab Religious Book Society, 1953.

Verantwortlichkeit. In: Festschrift Heinrich Zangger. Zürich, Rascher, 1935, S. 1000–1007.

Vom Werk des Heiligen Geistes. 74 S., Tübingen, Mohr, 1935. Zürich, Zwingli-Verlag, 1941.

Das Ärgernis der Oxford-Gruppenbewegung. In: Neue Zürcher Zeitung, 1935, Nr. 1951 (November). Trans. Genève, Labor, 1936.

1936

18. Die Kirchen, die Gruppenbewegung und die Kirche Jesu Christi. *IV,* 56 S., Berlin, Furche-Verlag, 1936. *Trans. London, Hodder & Stoughton, 1936.* Trans. Genève, Labor, 1937. Trans. Kirisutokyo Shisoyosho Verlag, 1937.

Die Beichte und die protestantische Kirche der Gegenwart. In: Der Kirchenfreund. 70, 1936, Nr. 20–22.

Biblische Psychologie als Grundlage der Erziehung. In: Die evangelische Pädagogik. 5, 1936, S. 121–136. Trans. Osaka, Shinseikatsusha, 1954.

Das Vermächtnis Calvins. Vortrag bei der Calvinfeier im Grossmünster am 28. Juni 1936. 22 S., Bern, Gotthelf-Verlag, 1936.

Die Kirche und der Krieg. In: Neue Schweizer Rundschau. N.F. 4, 1936, Heft 6.

Was sollen wir tun? Predigt. 12 S., Bern, Gotthelf-Verlag, 1936.

Warum Christus? Predigt. 12 S., Bern, Gotthelf-Verlag, 1936.

Weihnachtsgruss an alle Gruppenfreunde der Schweiz, mit Theo Spörri. 4 S., Zürich, Fretz, 1936.

Antwort an Herrn Heinrich Marti (Betrifft die Oxfordgruppenbewegung). In: Neue Wege. 30, 1936, Heft 2.

19. Continental European Theology. *In: The Church through Half a Century.* Essays in honor of William Adams Brown. *New York, London, Charles Scribner's Sons, 1936, 133–144.*

1937

Das Wort Gottes und der moderne Mensch. Vier Vorlesungen an der Universität Helsingfors. IV, 109 S., Berlin, Furche-Verlag, 1937. Zürich, Zwingli-Verlag, 1947. Trans. Helsinki, Kustannusosakeyhtiö Otava, 1937. Trans. Amsterdam, W. Ten Have, 1938. Trans. Tokyo, Shinseido, 1938.

20. Der Mensch im Widerspruch. Die christliche Lehre vom wahren und vom wirklichen Menschen. IV, XVI, 576 S., Berlin, Furche-Verlag, 1937. 3. unveränd. Aufl., Zürich, Zwingli-Verlag, 1941. *Trans. London, Lutterworth, 1939. Trans. Philadelphia, The Westminster Press, 1947.* Studienausgabe unter dem Titel: Gott und sein Rebell. Eine theologische Anthropologie. Bearbeitet und herausgegeben von Ursula Berger-Gebhardt in der Reihe «rowohlts deutsche enzyclopädie,» mit freundl. Genehmigung des Zwingli-Verlages Zürich. 157 S., Hamburg, Rowohlt, 1958. Trans. Tokyo, Shinkyo Shuppansha, 1956.

Kirche im Alltag. In: Kirche und Staat. 4 Vorträge im Fraumünster. Zürich, Leemann, 1937, S. 29–32. Trans. in: Les Cahiers Protestants, 1938, Nr. 1.

Reformierter und katholischer Glaube. In: Zwinglikalender 1937. Basel, Reinhardt.

Die Ernte ist gross, aber wenige sind der Arbeiter. Missionspredigt. In: Zu einem Zeugnis über alle Völker. Stuttgart und Basel, Evang. Missionsverlag, 1937, 5–14.

Abrahams Glaube. In: In Extremis. Cahiers périodiques, 3, 1937, 1.

Totaler Staat und christliche Freiheit. In: Kirche und Welt, Studien und

Dokumente, Bd. 7. S. 37–59. Genf, Forschungsabteilung des Oekumenischen Rates für praktisches Christentum. 1937.

1938

21. Der Römerbrief. 151 S. Bibelhilfe für die Gemeinde. Neutestamentaliche Reihe Bd. 6. Hamburg, Schloessmann, 1938. Neuauflage: 142 S. Stuttgart, J. G. Oncken, 1948. Trans. Tokyo, Shinyko Shuppansha, 1954. *Trans. London, Lutterworth Press* and *Philadelphia, The Westminster Press, 1959.*

Die Kirche zwischen Ost und West. Vortrag, gehalten am 20. Juni 1949 im Pfarrverein des Kantons Zürich. 38 S., Stuttgart, Evang. Verlagswerk, 1949.

Christus am Kreuz, unser Heil. In: Unser Bekenntnis zu Jesus Christus; 4 Vorträge im Fraumünster. Zürich, Zwingli-Verlag, 1938, S. 31–52.

Christoph Blumhardt. In: Neue Zürcher Zeitung, 1938, Nr. 1008. Pfingstausgabe, (Juni).

22. *Die Kirche unserer Tage.* In: Schweizer Buch. Zürich, Schweizer Druck- und Verlagshaus, 1938, S. 72–77.

Wahrheit als Begegnung. Sechs Vorlesungen über das christliche Wahrheitsverständnis. IV, 155 S., Berlin, Furche-Verlag, 1938. Zürich, Zwingli-Verlag, 1941. Trans. Stockholm, Sveriges Kristliga Studentrörelses, 1938. *Trans. Philadelphia, The Westminster Press, 1943. Trans. London, Student Christian Movement Press, 1944.* Trans. Tokyo, YMCA, 1953.

Weihnachtspredigt. 13 S., Zürich, Zwingli-Verlag, 1938.

Die Mitte der Bibel. 2. Kor. 5, 17–21. Abschiedspredigt, gehalten am 21. August 1938, im Fraumünster. 12 S., Zürich, Zwingli-Verlag, 1938.

Herr, lehre uns beten: Das Unservater. In: Zwinglikalender 1938. Basel, Reinhardt.

Die reformierte Staatsauffassung. Vortrag vor der Neuen Helvetischen Gesellschaft in Zürich. 32 S., Zürich, Rascher, 1938.

Die Machtfrage. 27 S., Zürich, Zwingli-Verlag, 1938.

Schisksal und Freiheit in christlicher Sicht. In: Neue Schweizer Rundschau. N.F. 5, 1938, Heft 9.

Saat und Frucht. 10 Predigten über Gleichnisse Jesu. 128 S., Berlin, Furche-Verlag, 1938. 2. Aufl., 139 S., Zürich, Zwingli-Verlag, 1946. Trans. Tokyo, Kyo Bun Kwan, 1950. Ebendort: Volksausgabe 1959.

Det ekumeniska Problemet och Grupprörelsen. Skrifter I Teologiska och Kyrkliga Amnen. 9. 34 S., Lund, CWK Gleerups Förlag.

23. The Christian Understanding of Man. *In: The Christian Understanding of Man. (Church, Community and State. Vol. II)* London, 1938, S. 139–178.

1939

Warum? (Flugblatt, enthaltend eine religiöse Betrachtung zum Kriegsanfang). 4 S., Zürich, 1939.

Grundsätzliche Erwägungen. Bericht der theologischen Subkommission der Kommission zur Prüfung der Beziehungen zwischen Kirche und Staat, erstattet zuhanden der Gesamtkommission. In: Zürcher Kirchengesetz und christliche Kirche. Zürich, Kirchenrat des Kt.s Zürich, 1939, S. 10–33.

Das Christentum und die Mächte der Zeit. Einleitung zu einem Vorlesungszyklus an der Universität Zürich. In: Neue Schweizer Rundschau. N.F. 7, 1939, Heft 8.

Eiserne Ration. 32 S., Tornister Bibliothek Heft 1, Erlenbach, Rentsch, 1939. Trans. Genève, Kündig, 1942.

Schweizer Freiheit und Gottesherrschaft. Vortrag am Bettag 1939 an der Landesausstellung. 16 S., Im Dienste unserer Heimat, Heft 1. Zürich, Zwingli-Verlag, 1939.

Kirche und Staat. In: Zwinglikalender 1939. Basel, Reinhardt.

Bausteine geistigen Lebens. Ausschnitte aus den Werken von Prof. Dr. Emil Brunner, zusammengestellt von Ernst Hermann Müller-Schürch. 46 S., Zürich, Zwingli-Verlag, 1939.

Reflexionen über amerikanische Pfarrerausbildung. In: Jahresbericht des zürcherisch-aargauischen Stipendienvereins für Theologiestudierende. 78, 1939, Berichthaus, Zürich.

Die ethische Bedeutung des christlichen Dogmas. I. Lehre und Leben. In: Der Grundriss. 1, 1939, Nr. 9. II. Das grosse Missverständnis des Glaubens. In: Der Grundriss. 1, 1939, Nr. 10. III. Ich glaube an Gott, den Schöpfer. 2. Teil. Die Schöpfungsordnungen und der Bolschewismus. In: Der Grundriss, 1, 1939, Nr. 12.

24. The Present-Day Task of Theology. *In: Religion in Life, a Christian Quarterly. 8, 1939. Nr. 2, S. 176–186.*

1940

25. Zur Lage und Aufgabe der Kirche in der Gegenwart. IV, 23 S., Zürich, Zwingli-Verlag, 1940. Trans. Genève, Labor, 1943. *Trans. in: The Predicament of the Church. London, Lutterworth Press, S. 82–99.*

Banalität oder Irrlehre. Zum Problem der Anthropologie und des Anknüpfungspunktes. In: Kirchenblatt für die ref. Schwiez. 96, 1940, Nr. 17.

Der konfessionelle Frieden in der Schweiz. In: Neue Zürcher Zeitung. 1940, Nr. 489, (April).

Vom Neuanfangen. Predigt. 14 S., Zürich, Zwingli-Verlag, 1940.

26. Ich glaube an den lebendigen Gott. Predigten über das altchristliche

Glaubensbekenntnis. 159 S., Zürich, Zwingli-Verlag, 1940. 2. unveränd. Auflage, 1945. *Trans. Philadelphia, The Westminster Press, 1959.*
Die Überwindung der Angst. Abendandacht. In: Der Grundriss. 2, 1940, Nr. 6.
Die ethische Bedeutung des christlichen Dogmas. V. Die Menschwerdung des Gottessohnes. In: Der Grundriss. 2, 1940, Nr. 1. VI. Die Versöhnung. In: Der Grundriss. 2, 1940, Nr. 4. VII. Die Rechtfertigung des Sünders. In: Der Grundriss. 2, 1940, Nr. 5.
Reformation und Gemeinschaft. In: Der Grundriss. 2, 1940, Nr. 10.
Unbekanntes Amerika. In: Zwinglikalender 1940. Basel, Reinhardt.
Rezension, unter dem Titel *Pestalozzi, der Christ,* von: Karl Würzburger, «Der Angefochtene, ein Buch über Heinrich Pestalozzi.» In: Neue Zürcher Zeitung, 1940, Nr. 1857 (Dezember).
Die Christusbotschaft und der Staat. In: Der Grundriss. 2, 1940, Nr. 20.
Festen Boden unter den Füssen. Radioansprache. In: Volksfreund. 1940, Nr. 42, (Mai).
Die Bedeutung des theologischen Wörterbuches zum Neuen Testament für die Theologie. In: Theologisches Wörterbuch z. N.T., Band IV, Liefg. 13. Stuttgart, Kohlhammer, August 1940 (letzte Umschlagseite).
Der Kampf des Christen in der Gegenwart. 27 S., Zürich, Zwingli-Verlag, 1940. Trad. La Chaux-de-Fonds, Comité Central des Liens Nationaux, 1940.
Bolschewismus und Christentum. In: Neue Schweizer Rundschau. N.F. 7, 1940, Heft 10.

1941

27. Offenbarung und Vernunft. Die Lehre von der christlichen Glaubenserkenntnis. XII, 429 S. Zürich, Zwingli-Verlag, 1941. *Trans. Philadelphia, The Westminster Press, 1946. Trans. London, Student Christian Movement Press, 1947.*
Der Zweck der Verkündigung. In: Sinn und Wesen der Verkündigung. Vorträge anlässlich der 2. Studenten-Zusammenkunft in Gwatt. Zollikon-Zürich, Evang. Verlag, 1941, S. 40–55.
Die Weihe zum heiligen Krieg. Festpredigt zur Einsegnungsfeier im Münster. In: Lasset uns halten an dem Bekenntnis der Hoffnung. Vom 126. Jahresfest der Basler Mission. Basel, Basler Missionsbuchhandlung, 1941, 7.
Heilige Ordnung. In: Neue Zürcher Zeitung. 1941, Nr. 2099 (Dezember).
Von der Mission des Bildes. In: Aktualis. 1941, Nr. 105 (Mai).
Christentum und Bildung. In: Neue Schweizer Rundschau. N.F. 8, 1941, Heft 10.
Vom Ältestnamt. Vorwort zum: «Kleinen Handbuch für Kirchenvorste-

her.» Zürich, Zwingli-Verlag, 1941, I–VII. Also in: Der Grundriss. 3, 1941, Nr. 3.

Das christliche Erbe. In: Beiträge zu: Eidg. Rechenschaft und Verpflichtung. Neue Zürcher Zeitung. 1941, Nr. 567 (April).

Der christliche Staat. In: Vom Wesen der Eidgenossenschaft. Ansprache, gehalten an der akad. Feier: 650 Jahre Eidgenossenschaft, am 21. Juni 1941 in der Aula der Universität Zürich. Zürich, Orell Füssli, 1941, S. 21–27. Also in: «Geisteserbe der Schweiz.» Hersg. von Eduard Corrodi, Erlenbach, Rentsch 1943, S. 418–415.

Die Bedeutung der systematischen Theologie für die Gemeinde. In: Der Kirchenfreund. 75, 1941, Nr. 8/9.

Vom Tod und der Todesangst. In: Zwinglikalender 1941. Basel, Reinhardt.

Die Famili als Schöpfungsordnung. In: Du. 1, 1941, Heft 4.

Im Namen Gottes des Allmächtigen, 1291–1941. In: «Im Namen Gottes des Allmächtigen, 1291–1941.» Zürich, Verlag der «Jungen Kirche,» 1941, S. 31–42. Also in: Der Grundriss. 3, 1941, Nr. 8.

Qu'est-ce qu'une église vivante? Extraits de la conférence, donnée au Synode de l'Eglise jurassienne, le 3 juin 1941 à Bienne. In: Les Cahiers protestants. 25, 1941, Nr. 4.

«Je suis l'Eternel, ton Dieu.» In: L'ordre de Dieu. La vie chrétienne à la lumière du décalogue. Genève, Messager, 1941, p. 4–11. 2e édit., Delachaux & Niestlé, 1946, p. 5–20. Deutsch in: «Der heilige Wille Gottes.» Das christliche Leben im Lichte der zehn Gebote. Zürich, Gotthelf-Verlag, 1942.

1942

Die Kirche und die Todesurteile wegen Landesverrats. In: Neue Zürcher Zeitung. 1942, Nr. 1743 (November).

Bettag 1942. In: Neue Zürcher Zeitung, 1942, Nr. 1484 (September).

Zur Todesstrafe. In: Zwei Stimmen aus der Kirche. Referate, gehalten an der Kirchensynode am 28. Okt. 1942. Zürich, Zwingli-Verlag, S. 19–26. Also in: Zofingue. Feuille centrale de la Société suisse de Zofingue. Neuchâtel, 92, 1952, Nr. 4.

Gehört Politik auf die Kanzel? In: Der Grundriss. 4, 1942, Nr. 1.

28. *Das helle Herz.* Weihnachtspredigt 1942. 15 S., Zürich, Zwingli-Verlag, 1942. *Trans in: Best Sermons, 1947–48 Edition. Edited by G. Paul Butler. New York and London, Harper & Brothers, 1947.*

Die Kirche spricht zur Welt. In: Der Grundriss. 4, 1942, Nr. 5.

Grundlagen christlicher Wirtschaftsordnung. In: Schweiz. Arbeitgeber-Zeitung. 37, 1942, Nr. 14, 15, 16 (April). SA. Zürich, 1942, 31 S. Auszug: Arbeit, Lohn und Eigentum. In: Der Grundriss. 4, 1942, Nr. 6.

Arbeit, Lohn und Eigentum. In: Grundriss. 4, 1942, Nr. 6.

Zur Frage der kirchlichen Verantwortung. Zur Diskussion über die Todesstrafe. In: Kirchenblatt für die ref. Schweiz. 98, 1942, Nr. 24.

Wir Christen und unser Staat. In: Zwinglikalender 1942. Basel, Reinhardt, 1942.

Die Menschenrechte nach reformierter Lehre. Festrede des Rektors, gehalten an der 109. Stiftungsfeier der Universität Zürich, am 29. April 1942. In: Jahresbericht 1941/42. Zürich, Orell Füssli, 1942, S. 3–22. Auch erschienen als: Das Menschenbild und die Menschenrechte. In: Universitas, 2, 1947, Heft 3. Trans. in: Var Lösen, 33, 1942, Nr. 8.

Zwei Predigten von der Gerechtigkeit. 30 S., Zürich, Zwingli-Verlag, 1942.

Drei Predigten vom ewigen Leben. 43 S., Zürich, Zwingli-Verlag, 1942.

Préface. In: Franz J. Leenhardt, «Le protestantisme tel que Rome le voit.» Genève, Labor, 1942. Trans. Zürich, Zwingli-Verlag, 1943.

1943

Glaube und Forschung. Festrede des Rektors, gehalten an der 110. Stiftungsfeier der Univrsität Zürich, am 29. April 1943. In: Jahresbericht 1942/43. Zürich, Orell Füssli, 1943, S. 3–20. Trans. par Georges Méautis, Zürich, Orell Füssli, 1943.

Die Grundlagen nationaler Erziehung. Referat vor der Neuen Helvetischen Gesellschaft in Aarau, 12. April 1942. In: Jahrbuch «Die Schweiz» 1943, S. 9–21. Brugg, Effingerhof, 1943. SA. 13 S. Brugg, Effingerhof, 1943.

29. Gerechtigkeit. Eine Lehre von den Grundgesetzen der Gesellschaftsordnung. IV, VIII, 336 S., Zürich, Zwingli-Verlag, 1943. *Trans. London and Redhill, Lutterworth Press, 1945. Trans. New York and London, Harper & Brothers, 1945.* Trans. Stockholm, Svenska Kyrkans Diakonistyrelses Bokförlag, 1945. Trans. Amsterdam, Uitgeverij W. Ten Have N. V., 1948. Trans. Oslo, Forlaget Land og Kirke, 1952. Trans. Tokyo, San-itsu Shoten, 1952. Trans. Seoul, The Christian Literature Society of Korea, 1954.

Der gerechte Zins. Kap. 18 aus «Gerechtigkeit,» 1. Fassung, Zürich, Zwingli-Verlag, 1943. In: Der Grundriss. 5, 1943, Nr. 9.

Gewissenloser Journalismus. In: Neue Zürcher Zeitung. 1943, Nr. 1465 (September).

50 Jahre Libertas. Jubiläumsansprache. In: Die Junge Schweiz. 19, 1943, Nr. 3.

Friede auf Erden. In: Neue Zürcher Zeitung. 1943, Nr. 2096 (Dezember).

Die gistigen Ursachen der Ehekrise. Vortrag am 1. Okt. 1943, gehalten am Kongress Pro Familia im Kongresshaus Zürich. In: Kongressbericht «Pro Familia.» Zürich, Zentralsekretariat Pro Juventute, 1943, S. 6–16. SA. Beilage zu: Kirchenbote für den Kanton Zürich, Februar 1944.

Sprachverwirrung und Sprachenwunder. In: Grundriss, 5, 1943. Nr. 5/6.

Zur christologischen Begründung des Staates. In: Kirchenblatt für die ref. Schweiz. 99, 1943, Nr. 1–3.

Da dürfen wir nicht schweigen. (Ansprache, gehalten an der Sympathiekundgebung der Studentenschaft der Zürcher Hochschulen für den Kampf der norwegischen Akademiker.) In: Neue Zürcher Zeitung. 1943, Nr. 1932 (Dezember).

1944

Zwischen Scylla und Charybdis. (Betrifft Frage nach der Grundlage einer Lehre von den gerechten sozialen Ordnungen.) In: Kirchenblatt für die ref. Schweiz. 100, 1944, Nr. 23/24.

Friede auf Erden. Luk. 2, 14, Weihnachtspredigt 1943. In: Der Grundriss. 6, 1944, Nr. 1/2.

Falscher und wahrer Biblizismus. In: Kirchenblatt für die ref. Schweiz. 100, 1944, Nr. 9.

Wissenschaft und Glaube. Vortrag anlässlich der Generalversammlung des Technischen Vereins Winterthur. In: «Neues Winterthurer Tagblatt» 1944, 23–29. Dez. 1944, SA. 16 S., 1944.

Zum christlichen Verständnis des Staates. In: Neue Zürcher Zeitung. 1944, Nr. 1000 (Juni).

Geist und Form in der Demokratie. In: Neue Zürcher Zeitung. 1944, Nr. 1116 (Juli).

Ist Christus zerteilt? In: Zwinglikalender 1944. Basel, Reinhardt.

Die politische Verantwortung des Christen. In: Der Grundriss. 6, 1944, Nr. 3/4. SA., 22 S., Kirchliche Zeitfragen, Heft 11. Zürich, Zwingli-Verlag, 1944.

Die Lehre vom heiligen Geist. Referat, gehalten an der 84. Versammlung des Schweiz. Ref. Pfarrvereins, 25.–27. Sept. 1944 in Luzern. In: Verhandlungen des Schweizerischen Reformierten Pfarrvereins. Luzern, Buchdruckerei C. J. Bucher, AG., 1944, S. 26–53. SA. 32 S. Kirchliche Zeitfragen, Heft 15. Zürich, Zwingli-Verlag, 1945.

Der Kapitalismus als Problem der Kirche. In: Der Grundriss. 6, 1944, Nr. 9 und 11. SA. 23 S. Kirchliche Zeitfragen, Heft 14. Zürich, Zwingli-Verlag, 1945.

Kants Schrift vom ewigen Frieden. In: Festschrift Max Huber «Vom Krieg und vom Frieden.» Zürich, Berichthaus, 1944, S. 29–39.

Die Freiheit der christlichen Gemeinde im heutigen Staat. Vortrag, gehalten am Evang. Seminar Unterstrass. In: Kirche und Schule. Zürich, Zwingli-Verlag, 1944, S. 5–27.

Theologie. In: Schriften der Mlle Marie Gretler-Stiftung der Universität Zürich, Heft 1, Wissenschaft und Glaube. Erlenbach-Zürich, Rentsch, 1944, S. 9–28.

Verwirrung in Staatsbegriff. In: Neue Zürcher Zeitung. 1944, Nr. 875 (Mai).

Schwarz ist weiss. In: Neue Zürcher Zeitung. 1944, Nr. 2057 (November).

Responsabilités et tâches de l'Eglise. Conférence, donnée le 30 Octobre 1944 aux pasteurs de l'Eglise nationale vaudoise à Lausanne. 31 S., Lausanne, Le semeur Vaudois, 1944.

1945

30. *Was hat Amerika uns, was haben wir Amerika zu geben?* Vortrag vor der Swiss American Society for cultural Relations. IV, 19 S., Zürich, Schulthess & Co., 1945. *Trans. USA-Switzerland, No. 1 and 2, May, July, 1946.*

Zum Zeugnis für Dr. Gerstenmaier. In: Neue Zürcher Zeitung. 1945, Nr. 1124 (Juli).

Max Huber zum siebzigsten Geburtstag. In: Neue Schweizer Rundschau. N.F. 12, 1945, Heft 9.

Die geistigen Voraussetzungen eines Neuaufbaus. In: Neue Schweizer Rundschau. N.F. 13, 1945, Heft 3.

Erklärungen zum Fall Gerstenmaier. In: Kirchenblatt für die ref. Schwiez. 101, 1945, Nr. 19.

Friedenshoffnung, Friedensaufgabe, Friedensillusion. In: Zwinglikalender, 1945. Basel, Reinhardt.

Glaube und Ethik. Vortrag, gehalten in der Kunstgesellschaft Thun. 30 S., Thun, Krebser & Co., 1945.

Theologie und Gemeinde. Referat, gehalten an der Jahresversammlung des Schweiz. Evangelisch-kirchlichen Vereins in Frauenfeld, Herbst 1944. In: Der Kirchenfreund. 79, 1945, Nr. 1–3.

Ein Wort der Zürcher Kirche zur Ehefrage. Im Auftrag der Zürcher Kirchensynode, herausgegeben vom Kirchenrat des Kantons Zürich. 16 S., Zürich, Zwingli-Verlag, 1945.

Technik und Religion. Vortrag, gehalten vor der Generalversammlung des SIA am 22. Sept. 1945 in Zürich. In: Schweiz. Bauzeitung. 126, 1945, Nr. 14.

Liebesbund oder Ehe. In: Ins Leben hinaus. Schriftenreihe der Jungbürgerinnen. Bd. 5. Bern, Paul Haupt, 1945, S. 7–9.

Nachkriegsaufgabe der weltweiten Kirche. In: Reformierte Schweiz. 2, 1945, Heft 7.

Das Äegernis der Nichteinheit der Kirche. In: Der Grundriss. 7, 1945, Nr. 1/2.

31. *The War as a Problem of the Christian Church. In: Christendom. An Ecumenical Review. New York City, The American Committee for the World Council of Churches, 1945, 10, 1945, Nr. 4, 472–478.*

Christianisme et démocratie. In: La vie protestante. 8, 1945, Nr. 20.

1946

Der Alkoholismus und unsere Verantwortlichkeit. In: Neue Zürcher Zeitung. 1946, Nr. 732 (April). Exzerpt unter dem Titel: Soll ich meines Bruders Hüter sein? In: Kirchenbote für den Kanton Zürich, 42, 1956, Nr. 10.

Wie wir Schweizer heute Martin Luther sehen. Die am 400. Todestage des deutschen Reformators unter dem Titel «Martin Luther» gehaltene Ansprache über den Landessender Beromünster. In: Reformierte Schweiz. 3, 1946, Heft 4.

Das Brot des Abendmahlcs und das tägliche Brot. In: Zwinglikalender 1946. Basel, Reinhardt.

32. *Zum wirtschaftlich-sozialen Problem.* In: Neue Zürcher Zeitung. 1946, Nr. 354 (März). Die christliche Lehre von Gott. *Dogmatik Band I.* XII, 391 S., Zürich, Zwingli-Verlag, 1946. *Trans. London, Lutterworth Press, 1949. Trans. Philadelphia, The Westminster Press, 1950.*

1947

33. Deutschlands Not. In: Neue Zürcher Zeitung, 1947, Nr. 1005 (Mai). *Trans. in: Christianity and Crisis. A Bi-Weekly Journal of Christian Opinion. 7, 1947, 14. Trans. in: Motive. 8, 1947, 29.*

Gerechtigkeit. In: Neue Zürcher Zeitung, 1947, Nr. 2353 (November).

Bach, der Spielmann Gottes. Predigt, gehalten am Internat. Bach-Fest 1946 in Schaffhausen. In: Musik und Gottesdienst. Zeitschrift für evangelische Kirchenmusik. 1, 1946, Nr. 6.

Zur kirchlichen Lage in Deutschland. In: Kirchenblatt für die ref. Schweiz. 103, 1947, Nr. 11.

Göttliche und menschliche Weisheit. In: Der Kirchenfreund. 18, 1947, Nr. 9. In: Evangelisch-soziale Warte. 1947, Nr. 26.

John R. Mott, ein Pionier des Völkerfriedens. In: Kirchenbote für den Kanton Zürich. 33, 1947, Nr. 2.

Friede auf Erden. In: Schweizerische Allgemeine Volks-Zeitung. 63, 1947, Nr. 52.

Bettag 1947. In: Neue Zürcher Zeitung. 1947, Nr. 1831 (September).

34. One Holy Catholic Church. *In: Theology Today. Princeton, N.J., John A. Mackay, 1947, S. 318–331.*

35. The Christian Message to Postwar Youth. *In: Preparatory Documents. World's Committee of YMCA's Genf. 3, 1947.*

1948

Ich glaube an eine heilige allgemeine apostolische Kirche. In: Auf dem Grunde der Apostel und Propheten. Festgabe für Landesbischof D.

Theophil Wurm zum 80. Geburtstag am 7. Dezember 1948. Stuttgart. Quell-Verlag der Evang. Gesellschaft. 1948, S. 119–131.

Wie soll man das verstehen? Offener Brief an Karl Barth. In: Kirchenblatt für die ref. Schweiz. 104, 1948, Nr. 12. Also in: Christliche Gemeinde im Wechsel der Staatsordnungen. Zollikon-Zürich, Evang. Verlag. 1948, 59–66.

Zeitliche Ordnung und Ewigkeitshoffnung. 20 S., Schriftenreihe. Lebendige Wissenschaft, Heft 5. Stuttgart, Kreuz-Verlag, 1948.

36. Kommunismus, Kapitalismus und Christentum. 35 S., Kirchliche Zeitfragen, Heft 23. Zürich, Zwingli-Verlag, 1948. Also in: Christ und Welt, 1, 1948, Nr. 15 (Exzerpt). Trans. London, Lutterworth Press, 1949.

Zwischen Kommunismus und Kapitalismus. In: Evangelische Welt. Nachrichtendienst der Evangelischen Kirche von Westfalen. 1948, Nr. 18. Trans. 40, Stockholm, Svenska Kyrkans Diakonistyrelses Bokförlag, 1949.

Das Wort ward Fleisch. In: Leben und Glauben. Evangelisches Wochenblatt. 23, 1948, Nr. 52.

Wo ist nun dein Gott? In: Zwinglikalender 1948. Basel, Reinhardt.

37. Last Chance. Eleven questions on issues determining our destiny. *Edited by Clara Urquhart. Boston USA., The Beacon Press, 1948.* S. 66, 81, 88/90, 101, 109/110, 120, 131, 141, 149, 159.

38. The Foundations of Personalism. In: *Manhood. YMCA National Magazine. 2, 1948, No. 10.*

39. Roots and Fruit. In: *Manhood. YMCA National Magazine. 3, 1948, No. 1.*

40. Open Letters.–I. Answer to the question: Can you prove God to me? In: *World Communique. 7, 1948, Nr. 2.*–II. The Mystery of Life. In: *World Communique. 7, 1948, Nr. 3.* Also in: Ceylon Men v. Januar 1949.–III. The Christian Idea of God. In: *World Communique. 7, 1948, Nr. 3.* Also in: Ceylon Men v. Februar 1949.–IV. How can we believe in the Myths of Christianity? In: *World Communique. 7, 1948, Nr. 4.* Also in: Ceylon Men v. April 1949.–V. Is Religion really «idealistic» as the Marxists declare? In: *World Communique. 7, 1948, Nr. 4.* Also in: Ceylon Men v. Mai 1949. Also in: Manhood. 3, 1948, Nr. 7.*–VI. Why say, Men are born Sinners? In: *World Communique. 7, 1948, Nr. 5.*–VII. Real Freedom. In: *World Communique. 7, 1948, Nr. 5.* Also in: Ceylon Men v. Juli 1949.–VIII. Must I believe in Jesus Christ? In: *World Communique. 7, 1948, Nr. 6.*–IX. Is there a personal Relationship to Jesus Christ? In: *World Communique. 7, 1948, Nr. 6.*

41. Christianity and Civilisation. First Part: Foundations. *Gifford Lectures delivered at the University of St. Andrews, 1947. VII, 167, London, Nisbet & Co., Ltd.*

1949

42. An Open Letter. (Betrifft die Frage nach dem Leiden der Völker in Asien.) In: *World Communique. From the Far East.* 8, 1949, Nr. 2.

43. Two Answers to one Question by Professor Emil Brunner of Zürich and Mark Sunder-Rao of Madras. In: *World Communique. Focus on Asia.* 8, 1949, Nr. 3. (Betrifft Zusammenarbeit von Christen und Andersgläubigen.)

44. An open Letter. Democracy and Christianity. In: *World Communique. Pan-America.* 8, 1949, Nr. 4.

Professor G. Schrenk. Zum 70. Geburtstag. In: Neue Zürcher Zeitung. 1949, Nr. 284 (Februar).

Was nachher? (Betrachtung über das ewige Leben.) In: Kirchenbote für den Kanton Zürich. 41, 1949, Nr. 4.

45. Menschheit, Technik—wohin? In: Neue Schweizer Rundschau. N.F. 16, 1949, Nr. 9. Trad. In: Teknish Tidskrift. 1, 1948, 1. *Trans. In: The Christian Newsletter edit. by Kathleen Bliss. Suppl. to 302, 1948. 7–16.* Trans. In: Les Cahiers Protestants. 33°, 1949, Nr. 2.

Die oekumenische Aufgabe in den reformierten Kirchen der Schweiz. Vortrag, gehalten an der kirchlichen Tagung in Zürich-Wipkingen am 14. März 1949 von Prof. Dr. Karl Barth. Mit den einleitenden Diskussionsvoten von Prof. Emil Brunner und Gymnasiallehrer Dr. Erich Studer. Zollikon-Zürich, Evang. Verlag, 1949, S. 48–56.

Das Einmalige und die Geschichte. In: Hortulus Amicorum, Fritz Ernst zum sechzigsten Geburtstag. Zürich, Fretz & Wasmuth, 1949, 45–49.

Die Unordnung der Welt und der Heilsplan Gottes. In: Zwinglikalender 1949. Basel, Reinhardt.

46. The Church between East and West. An address delivered to the Assembly of the Congregational Union of England and Wales, May 1949. In: *The Congregational Quarterly.* 27, 1949, Nr. 3.

Die Kirche zwischen Ost und West. Vortrag, gehalten am 20. Juni 1949 im Pfarrverein des Kantons Zürich. 38 S., Stuttgart, Evang. Verlagswerk, 1949.

47. Toward a missionary Theology. Eighth article on «How my mind has changed in the last decade.» In: *The Christian Century.* 46, 1949, Nr. 27. Trans. in: Christianity and culture (japanisch). No. 40, Oct. 1949.

Verheißung und Erfüllung. In: Der Kirchenfreund. 83, 1949, Nr. 8.

Was bedeutet das Werk auf der Mainau vom Standort der Gemeinde aus? In: Die Glocke. 3, 1949, Heft 7.

Das christliche Zeugnis für die Ordnung der Gesellschaft und des nationalen Lebens. Vortrag, gehalten in Amsterdam anläßlich der Weltkirchenkonferenz. In: Amsterdamer Dokumente. 1. Beiheft zu «Evangelische Welt.» Bethel, 1948, S. 234–243.

Japanische Reiseeindrücke. In: I. Neue Zürcher Zeitung. 1948, Nr. 2232
(Oktober). II. Neue Zürcher Zeitung. 1948, Nr. 2394 (November). III.
Neue Zürcher Zeitung. 1948, Nr. 2514 (Dezember). Reiseeindrücke
aus Korea. In: Neue Zürcher Zeitung. 1948, Nr. 2586 (Dezember).
48. Christianity in the World Today. Four Lectures. 110 S., Texte japanisch. 1. Spiritual Foundations of Democracy. 2. Christianity and
the Crisis of Culture. 3. Christianity and the Middle Road. 4. The
Task of the Church Today. Tokyo, YMCA, 1949.
49. Christianity and Civilisation. *Second Part:* Specific Problems. *Gifford
Lectures,* delivered at the University of St. Andrews. 1948. IX, 143,
London, Nisbet & Co., Ltd.

1950

50. Die christliche Lehre von Schöpfung und Erlösung. *Dogmatik, Band
II.* VIII, 455 S., Zürich, Zwingli-Verlag, 1950. *Trans. London, Lutter-
worth Press, 1952. Trans. Philadelphia, The Westminster Press, 1953.*
Der Gott, der Wunder tut. In: Zwinglikalender 1950. Basel, Reinhardt.
Morgenandacht (über Eph. 4, 1–6), gehalten in der Wasserkirche vor-
gängig den Verhandlungen der Kirchensynode vom 9. Mai 1950. In:
Protokoll der Kirchensynode des Kantons Zürich. 17. Amtsdauer. VI.
Die Verhandlungen der ausserordentlichen Versammlung vom 9. Mai
1950. S. 61–64.
Der Apostel Paulus. In: Schweizer Monatshefte. 30, 1950, Heft 7. Also
in: Universitas. 6, 1951, Heft 1. Also in: Paulus-Hellas-Oikumene.
(Ein Oekumenisches Symposium.) Athen, Christlicher Studentenbund
Griechenlands, 1951, S. 3–9. Also in: Christ und Welt. 3, 1950, Nr.
41 (Excerpt).
51. Impressions of a Trip through Asia. In: *Christianity and Crisis. A Bi-
Weekly Journal of Christian Opinion. 10, 1950, No. 12.* Trans. in:
Evangelisches Missionsmagazin. 95, 1951, Heft 2.
52. The Gospel and Modern India. Speech at the Convocation of Serampore College, held on Saturday, Jan. 21, 1950. In: *Serampore College
Magazine and the Students' Chronicle. 9, 1950, No. 2.*
53. A Message to the Plenary. In: *Forward Together in Faith.* Report of
the Plenary Meeting of the World's Committee of the Young Men's
Christian Association at Nyborg Strand, Denmark, 1950. Genf, World's
Committee of Young Men's Christian Association, 1950, S. 84–88. Unter dem Titel: The YMCA—Success or Failure? also in: Work Book
of the 5th Asian Y. M. C. A. Leaders' Conference, 16th–25th April,
1959, at Gotemba, Japan. Unter dem Titel: The Uniqueness of the
Y. M. C. A., auch in: Ceylon Men, April/May, 1959.

1951

54. Geistige Hindernisse und Brücken zwischen Amerika und Europa.
Vortrag, gehalten an der Generalversammlung der Swiss-American So-
ciety for Cultural Relations am 17. Nov. 1951 in Bern. In: Neue
Schweizer Rundschau. N.F. 19, 1951, Heft 8. SA. 14 S. *Trans. by Mary
Hottinger. Zürich, Swiss-American Society for Cultural Relations, 1952.*
Auch in: Revista da UCBEU, 1952, 1, No. 1. (União Cultural Brasil-
Estados Unidos.)
Kirche und Fernsehen. In: Schweizer Radiozeitung. 28, 1951, Nr. 32.
Also in: Der Ruf. 95, 1953, Nr. 2.

55. The Christian Understanding of Time. In: *Scottish Journal of Theology. 4, 1951, Nr. 1.*

56. Critic or Apologist of Civilization? In: *Religion in Life. A Christian
Quarterly. 20, Summer Number 1951, No. 3.*
Von der Bibel, dem Worte Gottes. In: Kirchenbote für den Kanton Zü-
rich. 37, 1951, Nr. 9.
Vom Sinn der Arbeit. In: Völker an der Arbeit. Zürich, Max S. Metz
Verlag AG. I., 1951, S. 11–15. Trans. Lausanne, Editions Metz, I.,
1952, S. 11–15.

57. Das Missverständnis der Kirche. 154 S., Zürich, Zwingli-Verlag, 1951.
Deutsche Lizenzausgabe, Stuttgart, Evangelisches Verlagswerk GmbH,
1951. Trans. Oslo, Land og Kirke, 1951. *Trans. London, Lutterworth
Press* and *Philadelphia, The Westminster Press, 1952.* Trans. Stockholm,
Svenska Kyrkans Diakonistyrelses Bokvörlag, 1952. Trans. Tokyo,
Taishindo, 1955. Trans. Neuchâtel, Editions H. Messeiller, 1956.

58. The Scandal of Christianity. Als: *The Andrew C. Zenos Lectures*
gehalten im McCormick Theological Seminary, Chicago, vom 21.–25.
Oktober 1946 und als: *The Robertson Lectures* im Trinity College,
Glasgow, im März 1948. 116 S., *Philadelphia, The Westminster Press*
and *London, SCM Press Ltd. 1951.* Trans. Tokyo, Nihon Kirisuto-
Kyodan, 1955. Deutscher Originaltext: Zürich, Zwingli-Verlag, 1957.
Kagawa. In: Zwinglikalender 1951. Basel, Reinhardt.

59. A Great Time for Preaching. In: *The Christian Century. Undenominational. 68, 1951, Nr. 28.*
Protestantismus und Tiefenpsychologie. In: Universitas. 6, 1951, Heft 1.

60. Der neue Barth. Bemerkungen zu Karl Barths Lehre vom Menschen.
In: Zeitschrift für Theologie und Kirche, 48, 1951, Heft 1. *Trans. in:
Scottish Journal of Theology. 4, 1951, Nr. 2.*

1952

Persönlichkeit und Person. In: Festschrift zu Ehren von Alt Rektor Dr.
Hans Fischer, veröffentlicht anlässlich des 50 jährigen Bestehens des

Gymnasiums Biel. Biel, Graphische Anstalt Schüler AG., 1952, S. 7–10.
Cela va de soi ... In: Donnez-nous des Messieurs! Agence de la Croix-Bleue, 1952, S. 8–10.
61. The Church in the New Social Order. An Address Delivered to the National Congress of the Free Church Federal Council, Cardiff, on 26th March 1952. 29 S., *London, SCM Press Ltd., 1952.*
Vom Kommunismus. In: Zwinglikalender 1952. Basel, Reinhardt.
62. The Year in Europe. In: *World Communique. World Review Number. 62, 1952, No. 1.* Trans. in: Das Hilfswerk, 1952, Nr. 61.
Pfingsten. In: Neue Zürcher Zeitung. 1952, Nr. 1201 (Juni).
Die Alternative zum Nihilismis der Gegenwart. In: Reformatio. 1, 1952, Nr. 1.

1953

Warum wir nach Japan gehen. In: Kirchenbote für den Kanton Zürich. 39, 1953, Nr. 9.
Was ist Kirche? In: Zwinglikalender 1953. Basel, Reinhardt.
Von der Angst. Vortrag, gehalten am 24. Aug. 1953 auf der zweiten CVJM-Europa-Konferenz in Kassel. In: Pastoral-Blätter. 93, 1953, Heft 11.
63. Fraumünsterpredigten. 156 S., Zürich, Zwingli-Verlag, 1953. *Trans. The Lutterworth Press of London* and *The Westminster Press of Philadelphia. 1955.* (Engl. Title: The Great Invitation.) Trans. Tokyo. Shinkyo Shuppansha, 1955. Trans. Hong Kong, The Council on Christian Literature for Overseas Chinese, 1958.
64. Das Ewige als Zukunft und Gegenwart. 240 S., Zürich, Zwingli-Verlag, 1953. *Trans. London, The Lutterworth Press* and *Philadelphia, The Westminster Press, 1954.* (Engl. Title: Eternal Hope.) Trans. Tokyo, Shinkyo Shuppansha, 1957.
65. Why I returned to Japan. Emil Brunner, interviewed by James Scherer. In: *The Japan Christian Quarterly. 20, 1954, No. 1.*

1954

66. The Church as a Gift and a Task. Lecture delivered on April 1, 1954, at the Kyodan-related Missionary Conference at Yumoto. In: *The Japan Christian Quarterly. 20, 1954, No. 3.*
Christus ist die Antwort. In: Zwinglikalender 1954. Basel, Reinhardt.
67. The Christian University and its Importance for Japan. 15 S. (englisch/japanisch), Food for all People. No. 1. Mitaka-Tokyo, Institute of Educational Research and Service, International Christian University, 1954.
68. Preface to «God's Grace and Man's Condition» by David Bryn-

Jones. Tokyo, Charles E. Tuttle Company (published for ICU, Tokyo), 1954.

69. Christ, the Hope of the World. In: *World Christian Education. Third Quarterly, 1954.*

1955

70. Justice and Freedom in Society. Stenographic Record of the Extension Lecture Series, given at Seiko Gakuin, Shinjuku, Tokyo. October, 1954–February, 1955. 369 S., Texte englisch und japanisch. Tokyo, Institute of Educational Research and Service, International Christian University, 1955.

71. Japanese Christianity. In: *The Christian Century.* Undenominational. 72, 1955, Nr. 21.

72. The Mystery of I Am. Sermon on John 14, 6. In: *The Pulpit. A Journal of Contemporary Preaching. 26, 1955, No. 5.*

73. Ecclesia and Evangelism. A Message to the General Assembly of the United Church of Christ in Japan, October 27, 1954. In: *The Japan Christian Quarterly, 21, 1955, No. 2.*

Japan heute. In: Schweizer Monatshefte. 14, 1955, Heft 12.

74. The Hope for Japan. Dr. Brunner's Farewell Address. In: The ICU News, Special issue on Dr. Brunner. Tokyo, 1955, Nr. 4. Deutsch: Meine Hoffnung für Japan. Abschiedsansprache an der Internationalen Christlichen Universität in Tokyo am 12. Juni 1955. In: Evangelisches Missionsmagazin. 100, 1956, Heft 1.

75. Christianity and Culture. First Takeshi Saito Lecture, delivered on 19 Jan. 1955 at Tokyo Joshi Daigaku. 7 S., Tokyo, The Academic Society of Tokyo Women's Christian College, 1955.

76. A Spiritual Autobiography. Fourth Lecture given at the Spring Conference of Kyodan-related Missionaries at Yumoto on April 1. In: The Japan Christian Quarterly. 21, 1955, No. 3. Trans. in: Jap. edit. of: Faith, Hope and Love. Tokyo, Shinkyo Shuppansha, 1957.

1956

Japan in der Entscheidung. Interview von Pfr. Dr. P. Vogelsanger mit Emil Brunner. In: Reformatio, 5, 1956, Nr. 1.

Erfahrungen im Fernen Osten. In: Gott füllt leere Hände. Geistliche Woche für Südwestdeutschland der Evang. Akademie Mannheim vom 15. April–22. April 1956. Mannheim, Evang. Akademie, 1956.

Schöpfung und Technik. Predigt zum Jubiläum der Eidg. Techn. Hochschule im Grossmünster zu Zürich am 31. Okt. 1955. In: Reformatio. 5, 1956, Nr. 3. Also in: Schweiz. Bauzeitung. 73, 1955, Nr. 52. SA. 7 S.

Christlicher Existenzialismus. Vortrag, gehalten vor der Studentenschaft der Univeristät Zürich. 23 S., Kirchliche Zeitfragen, Heft 39, Zürich,

Zwingli-Verlag, 1956. Also in: Neue Zürcher Zeitung 1956, Nr. 841, 842 u. 843 (März).

Die Mukyokai-Bewegung in Japan. In: Zwinglikalender 1956. Basel, Reinhardt.

Ostern. In: Neue Zürcher Zeitung, 1956, Nr. 920 (April).

Peter Winteler zum 70. Geburtstag. In: Der Fürsorger. Mitteilungsblatt des Verbandes Schweiz. Fürsorger für Alkoholgefährdete. 24, 1956, Heft 1.

77. Faith, Hope and Love. 79 S., *Philadelphia, The Westminster Press, 1956. London, Lutterworth Press, 1957.* Trans. Tokyo, Shinkyo Shuppansha, 1957.

78. Some Remarks on Reinhold Niebuhr's Work as a Christian Thinker. In: Niebuhr, Reinhold, His Religious, Social and Political Thought; edited by Charles W. Kegley and Robert W. Bretall. *(The Library of Living Theology. Vol. II.) New York, The Macmillan Company, 1956,* S. 27–33.

Die Ekklesia des Neuen Testamentes und die CVJM. 3 S., Bern, Merkblätter für CVJM-Arbeit. Bundeszentrale der CVJM der deutschsprachigen Schweiz, 1956.

Predigten im Fraumünster Zürich. Je 7 S., Nr. 1–Nr. 11. Zürich, Evang. Buchhandlung, 1956.

1957

79. Das Ärgernis des Christentums. 110 S., Deutscher Text: Zürich, Zwingli-Verlag, 1957. Englischer Text: The Scandal of Christianity. *Philadelphia, The Westminster Press, und London, SCM Press, 1951.* Trad. Neuenburg, Editions H. Messeiller, 1959.

Auf der Suche nach einem internationalen Ethos. In: Reformatio. 6, 1957, Nr. 7 u. Nr. 8.

Freiheit als Verantwortlichkeit. Vortrag, gehalten in der Universität Zürich auf Einladung der Kulturwissenschaftl. Abteilung des Schweiz. Instituts für Auslandsforschung. In: Schweizer Monatshefte, 37, 1957, Heft 5. Auch in: Theologia Oecumenica in honor of William Enkichi Kan. Tokyo, Rikkyo University, 1958, S. 15–25.

80. The Significance of Existential Philosophy. Trans. in: Jap. Edit. of: Faith, Hope and Love. Tokyo, Shinkyo Shuppansha, 1957.

Volk, Schweizervolk, höre des Herrn Wort! Eidgenöss. Dank-, Buss- und Bettag. 4 S., Berlingen, Schweiz. Traktat-Missionsgesellschaft, 1957.

Das Nichts oder Gott. In: Reformatio. Sonderheft: Die Bedrohung des Menschen heute. Vorträge des Schweiz. evang. Akademikertages in Zürich. 6, 1957, Heft 11/12. Auch in: Universitas unter dem Titel: Die Bedrohung des Menschen und der lebendige Gott. 13, 1958, Heft 7. Trans. in: Les Cahiers Protestants, 42, Janv.–Mars 1958.

81. Christianity in the Age of Crisis. Four Lectures at YWCA, Tokyo. 111 S., Texte japanisch. 1. What is the Meaning of Life? 2. On Human Happiness. 3. The Christian Idea of Love and the Modern World. 4. The Time of Crisis and the Practice of Faith. Tokyo, YWCA, 1957.
Predigten im Fraumünster Zürich. Je 7 S., Nr. 12–Nr. 23. Zürich, Evang. Buchhandlung, 1957.

1958

Warum allein Christus? In: Zwinglikalender 1958. Basel, Reinhardt.
Pazifismus als Kriegsursache. In: Neue Zürcher Zeitung, 1958, Nr. 1050 (April). Also in: Neue Bünder Zeitung, 82, 1958 (Mai).
82. Moon Shot: Its Meaning to 25 Scholars. In: *Christianity Today.* 3, 1958, Nr. 1.
83. A Message to American Christians. Explaining the Significance of the International Christian University in Japan. In: *The Watchman-Examiner. A National Baptist Paper.* 40, 1958, Nr. 23.
75 Jahre Schweiz. Ostasien-Mission. In: Ostasien. Mitteilungen der Schweiz. Ostasien-Mission. 75, Nr. 6.
Gott und sein Rebell. Eine Studienausgabe von «Der Mensch im Widerspruch» (s. o. 1937), bearbeitet und herausgegeben von Ursula Berger-Gebhardt in der Reihe «rowohlts deutsche enzyklopädie,» mit freundl. Genehmigung des Zwingli-Verlages Zürich. 157 S., Hamburg, Rowohlt, 1958. Trans. Tokyo, Shinkyo Shuppansha, 1956.
Beitrag zu: Ergebnis einer höchst aktuellen Rundfrage. In: Das Schweizerische Rote Kreuz. 67, 1958, Nr. 2.
Predigten im Fraumünster Zürich. Je 7 S., Nr. 24–Nr. 36. Zürich, Evang. Buchhandlung, 1958.

1959

Die Antwort eines Schweizer Theologen auf die Frage: Was geht uns Amerika an? In: Kontakt. Taschenzeitschrift der Jungen. 2, 1959, Heft 10.
84. Thoughts for Japan and for ICU (Internat. Christ. University.) In: Kokusai Kirisutokyo Daigaku Shimbun. 1959, No. 28.
Die christliche Nicht-Kirche-Bewegung in Japan. Gottlob Schrenk, dem Mann der Mission, zum 80. Geburtstag. In: Evang. Theologie. 19, 1959, Heft 4.
85. A Unique Christian Mission: The Mukyokai («*Non-Church*») Movement in Japan. In: *Religion and Culture. Essays in Honor of Paul Tillich.* New York, Harper & Brothers. 1959, S. 287–290.
Auf dem Wege zur Erneuerung der Kirche. In: Der Schweizerspiegel. 34, 1959, Nr. 11.
86. The Message from abroad for Japan Calvin Translation Society. In:

Fukuin to Sekai (Gospel and World). Special Number: John Calvin (japanisch). Tokyo, Shinkyo Shuppansha, 1959, Nr. 8.

87. A Tribute to John Mackay. In: *Theology Today.* A Thesaurus of Tributes. 16, 1959, Nr. 3.

Beitrag zur Umfrage: Wir und die farbigen Völker. In: Die Weltwoche. 27, 1959, Nr. 1355 (Oktober).

Christ und Friede. Predigt, gehalten am 8. Nov. 1959 im Fraumünster Zürich. In: Reformatio. Sonderheft: Christ und Weltfriede. Vorträge der 2. Schweiz. evang. Akademikertagung in Zürich, 7.–9. November 1959. 8, 1959, Heft 11/12. Also in: Predigten im Fraumünster, Zürich, Evang. Buchhandlung, 1959, Nr. 45.

Ein Wort an die Christen in Japan. In: Fukuin to Sekai (Gospel and World). Special Number: Emil Brunner (japanisch). Tokyo, Shinkyo Shuppansha, 1959, Nr. 12.

Beitrag zur Umfrage: Welches war mein nachhaltigstes Weihnachtserlebnis? In: Reformierte Schweiz. 16, 1959, Nr. 12.

Predigten im Fraumünster Zürich. Je 7 S., Nr. 37–Nr. 46. Zürich, Evang. Buchhandlung, 1959.

1960

88. Im Frühjahr 1960 ist erschienen: Die christliche Lehre von der Kirche, vom Glauben und von der Vollendung. *Dogmatik, Band III,* 503, Zürich, Zwingli-Verlag, 1960.

89. *Die christliche Lehre von der Kirche, vom Glauben und von der Vollendung.* Dogmatik, Band III, 503 S., Zürich, Zwingli-Verlag, 1960. *Trans. London, Lutterworth Press, 1962. Trans. Philadelphia, The Westminster Press, 1960.*

Christlicher Glaube und Philosophie der Existenz. In: Philosophie und christliche Existenz. Festschrift für Heinrich Barth zum 70. Geburtstag. Basel und Stuttgart, Verlag Helbling und Lichtenhahn, 1960, 119–130.

Beitrag zur Umfrage: Wie war Ihre erste Reaktion auf das Weltuntergangs-Geschwätz? In: Sie und Er. 36, 1960. Nr. 29 (Juli).

90. *The Cleveland Report on Red China.* In: Christianity Today. 4, 1960, Nr. 15.

91. *Beitrag zur Umfrage: Do you see any hopeful basis of Protestant-Roman Catholic church unity?* 25 Scholars' View. In: Christianity Today. 5, 1960, Nr. 1.

1961

Zur Erinnerung an Max Huber. In: Zwinglikalender 1961. Basel, Reinhardt.

92. *Emil Brunner on His Faith and Work.* A Television Interview with

Vernon Sproxton. In: The Listener, and B.B.C. Television Review. 65, 1961, Nr. 1664 (February).

Rezension, unter dem Titel: Eine protestantische Heilige, von Amy Carmichael von Dohnavur, eine Mutter für indische Tempelkinder. Nach dem Englishchen des Bischof Frank Houghton. Autorisierte deutsche Bearbeitung von Fritz Enderlin. In: Neue Zürcher Zeitung, 1961, Nr. 2296 (Juni).

93. *Und wenn der Kommunismus siegte . . . ?* In: Neue Zürcher Zeitung, 1961, Nr. 1991 (Mai). Auch in: Kirche und Mann, 1961, Nr. 8 (August). SA. 7 S., Zürich, Neue Zürcher Zeitung, 1961. Dasselbe: Bern, Schriftenreihe des Schweiz. Ostinstituts, 1961, Heft 6. Trans. in: Swiss Review of World Affairs. 11, 1961, Nr. 4 (July). *Trans. in: Christian Economics. 13, 1961, Nr. 16 (September).*

Zwanzig Jahre später. In: Kirchenbote für den Kanton Zürich. 47, 1961, Nr. 7.

94. *Karl Barth's Alternatives for Liberal Theology: A Comment.* In: The Hibbert Journal. 59, 1961, July.

1962

Welt und Person. In: Zwinglikalender 1962, Basel, Reinhardt.

Ergänzung zu 1934 sh. in de Bibliographie S. 355 1 15.

95. Natur und Gnade. Zum Gespräch mit . . . The Centenary Press, 1946, S. 15–64. Dasselbe London, University Microfilms Limited, 1959, (Full size single copies).

MAIN PUBLICATIONS OF EMIL BRUNNER
IN ENGLISH

God and Man. Four Essays on the Nature of Personality, trans. by David Cairns (London: Student Christian Movement Press, 1936).

Our Faith. Trans. by John Rilling (New York: Charles Scribner's Sons, 1936).

Philosophy of Religion. In the International Library of Christian Knowledge, edited by William Adams Brown (New York: Charles Scribner's Sons, 1937).

The Predicament of the Church Today (London: Lutterworth Press, 1940).

The Divine-Human Encounter. Trans. by Amandus W. Loos (Philadelphia: Westminster Press, 1943) for The Presbyterian Board of Christian Education (also Toronto: Ambassador Books, Ltd., 1943 and London: Student Christian Movement Press, 1944).

Justice and the Social Order. Trans. by Mary Hottinger (New York: Harper & Brothers, 1945).

Revelation and Reason. The Christian Doctrine of Faith and Knowledge, Trans. by Olive Wyon (Philadelphia: The Westminster Press, 1946).

The Mediator. A Study of the Central Doctrine of the Christian Faith. Trans. by Olive Wyon (Philadelphia: The Westminster Press, 1947).

The Divine Imperative. A Study in Christian Ethics. Trans. by Olive Wyon (Philadelphia: The Westminster Press, 1947).

Man in Revolt. A Christian Anthropology. Trans. by Olive Wyon (Philadelphia: The Westminster Press, 1947).

Christianity and Civilization (London: John Nisbet and Company, Part I, 1947, Part II, 1948).

Christianity and Civilization (New York: Charles Scribner's Sons, 1948).

The Christian Doctrine of God. Dogmatics, Vol. I. (London: Lutterworth Press, 1949).

The Christian Doctrine of God. Dogmatics, Vol. I. Trans. by Olive Wyon (Philadelphia: The Westminster Press, 1950).

The Christian Doctrine of Creation and Redemption. Dogmatics, Vol. II. Trans. by Olive Wyon (Philadelphia: The Westminster Press, 1952).

The Misunderstanding of the Church. Trans. by Harold Knight (Philadelphia: The Westminster Press, 1953).

The Christian Doctrine of Creation and Redemption. Dogmatics, Vol. II. (London: Lutterworth Press, 1954).

Eternal Hope. Trans. by Harold Knight (Philadelphia: The Westminster Press, 1954).

The Great Invitation. Zurich Sermons of Emil Brunner. Trans. by Harold Knight (London: Lutterworth Press, 1955).

The Great Invitation. Trans. by Harold Knight (Philadelphia: The Westminster Press, 1955).

The Letter to the Romans. Trans. by H. A. Kennedy (London: Lutterworth Press, 1959, also, Philadelphia: The Westminster Press, 1959).

I Believe in the Living God. Sermons on the Apostles' Creed. Trans. and edited by John Holden (Philadelphia: The Westminster Press, 1960).

The Christian Doctrine of the Church, Faith, and the Consummation. Dogmatics, Vol. III (Zürich: Zwingli Verlag, 1960). Trans. by David Cairns (London: Lutterworth Press, 1962) (Philadelphia: The Westminster Press, 1961).

SUBJECT INDEX

NAME INDEX

Abélard, Peter, 201
Alexander the Great, 197
Amsdorf, Nikolaus von, 42
Anselm, St., 169, 201
Aquinas, St. Thomas, 56
Ariga, Tetsutaro, 344
Aristotle, 113, 256
Arnold, Gottfried, 215
Augustine, St., 113, 212, 235, 266, 308, 336

von Balthasar, Hans Ur, 208
Barnabas, St., 239
Barth, Heinrich, 5-6, 336
Barth, Karl, 6, 8, 9, 11, 12, 33, 34, 36, 55, 84, 85, 87, 99, 113, 157, 236, 257, 296, 317, 318, 326, 328, 331, 332, 340
Basil, St., 216
Berger, Ursula, 328
Bergson, Henri, 279
Blumhardt, Christoph, 4, 6, 8, 227, 230, 346
Brent, C. H., 32
Bring, Ragnar, 255
Brown, W. A., 8
Brunner, Andreas, 281
Buber, Martin, 10, 146, 190, 249, 271, 278, 341
Buchman, Frank, 10
Bultmann, Rudolf, 33, 34, 35, 36, 37, 92, 93-94, 95, 99, 166,

196, 233, 326, 328, 329, 331, 345

Caesar Augustus, 197
Cairns, David, reply to, 331-333
Calvin, John, 37, 169, 191, 198, 202, 241, 242, 255, 306
Cassirer, E., 164, 165, 344
Constantine, 240, 242
Cullmann, Oscar, 17, 196, 232, 236, 342
Cyprian, 240

Darwin, Charles, 78
Dodd, C. H., 232, 345
Dowey, Edward A., Jr., reply to, 342-344
Dulles, John Foster, 280

Ebner, Ferdinand, 11, 146, 190, 249, 278, 341

Flacius Illyricus, Matthias, 42
Florovsky, Georges, reply to, 344-345
Freud, Sigmund, 78

Geismar, Ed., 260
Gerstermaier, Eugen, xiv
Gilson, Etienne, 162
Gogarten, Friedrich, 34, 190, 249, 326
Gregory of Nyasa, St., 219, 222
Grisebach, August, 146, 249, 256

393